DISNEY SQUARE ENIX

KINGDOM HEARTS
CHAIN OF MEMORIES

1

Adapted by
Shiro Amano

HAMBURG // LONDON // LOS ANGELES // TOKYO

Kingdom Hearts Chain of Memories Vol. 1
Adapted by
Shiro Amano

Associate Editor - Peter Ahlstrom
Retouch and Lettering - Deida Terriquez
Production Artist - Mike Estacio
Cover Layout - James Lee

Editor - Bryce P. Coleman
Digital Imaging Manager - Chris Buford
Production Manager - Elisabeth Brizzi
Managing Editor - Vy Nguyen
Editor-in-Chief - Rob Tokar
VP of Production - Ron Klamert
Publisher - Mike Kiley
President and C.O.O. - John Parker
Chief Creative Officer and C.E.O. - Stuart Levy

A  Manga

TOKYOPOP Inc.
5900 Wilshire Blvd. Suite 2000
Los Angeles, CA 90036

E-mail: info@TOKYOPOP.com
Come visit us online at www.TOKYOPOP.com

ISBN: 1-59816-637-9

First TOKYOPOP printing: October 2006
10 9 8 7 6 5 4 3 2 1
Printed in the USA

KINGDOM HEARTS
CHAIN OF MEMORIES

Disney SQUARE ENIX

KINGDOM HEARTS CHAIN OF MEMORIES

Sora

A boy chosen by the Keyblade—the key for saving the world. In search of his missing friend Riku, Sora continues his journey to return to his Destiny Islands home.

Goofy

Together with Sora and Donald, he is searching for the missing King Mickey. His trademark phrases are "A-hyuck" and "Gawrsh."

Donald Duck

Sora's comrade in the journey. He's a master magician, but once he gets bent out of shape...

CHARACTER & STORY

Sora, the main character of this story, lives peacefully on the Destiny Islands together with his friends Riku and Kairi. One night, his island home is besieged by a mysterious storm and Sora and his friends are separated and whisked away to faraway worlds. Sora searches for Riku and Kairi in an unfamiliar place known as Traverse Town, but leads toward finding his friends are scarce. There he meets Donald and Goofy who are searching for their missing King, and Sora joins them, and together they search for their lost friends.

After a long journey that takes them across numerous worlds, Sora and friends find Kairi at last, and they also find Riku and the King on the other side of the door to darkness.

But strange things are happening on the other side of the door. Numerous Heartless are trying to get to the outside worlds through the door. To save all worlds, Sora must use his Keyblade to close the door to darkness, even though Riku and the King are on the other side. Sora locks the door, believing the King's parting words—that there will always be a door to the light—and that he will reunite with them no matter what.

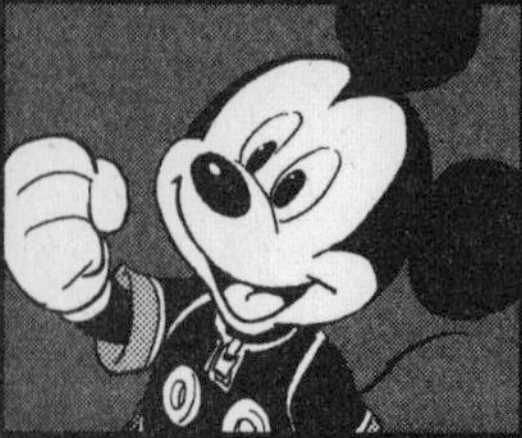

King [Mickey]

King of Disney Castle. He is missing together with Riku.

Naminé

A mysterious girl who is quietly drawing pictures alone in one of the castle rooms.

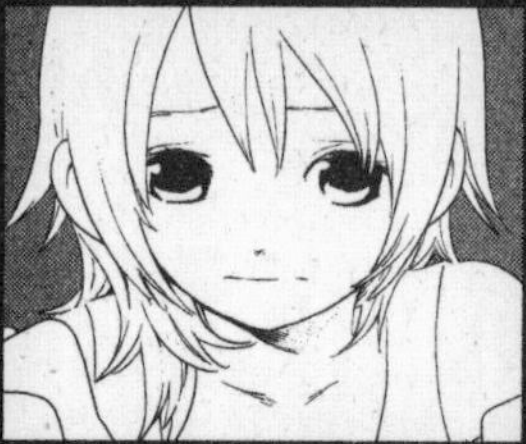

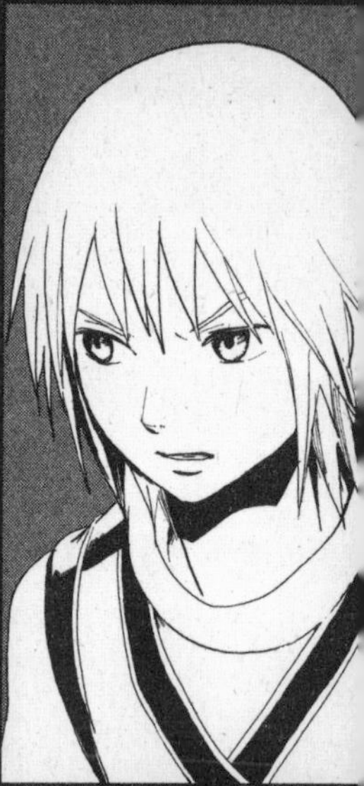

Riku

Sora's best friend. He closes the door from the inside together with the King, and gets left behind in the world of darkness.

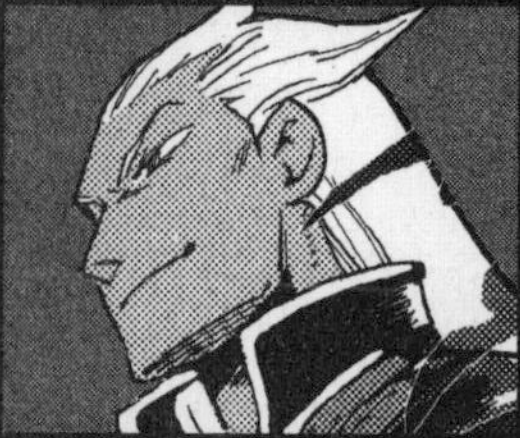

Ansem

The "Seeker of Darkness" who hid in Riku's heart to control him.

Kairi

Sora's childhood friend. She's waiting on the island for Sora to return.

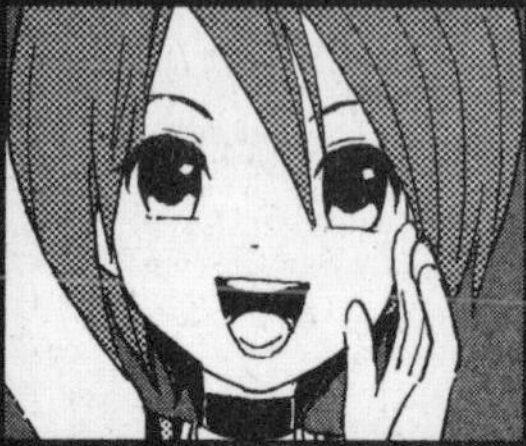

Organization XIII Members

The members of this mysterious organization dress in black robes and search for secrets of the heart...

Underground Members

Zexion

[No. 6 in the Organization]

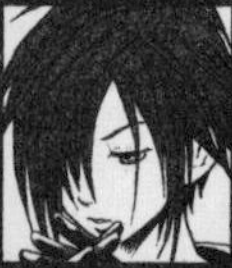

Leader of the Underground Members. Meticulous by nature, the word is that he's a surprisingly domestic type!

Lexaeus

[No. 5 in the Organization]

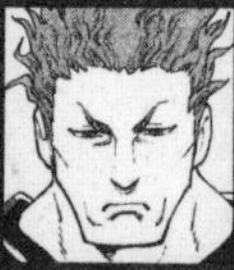

Administers the underground together with Zexion and Vexen. Avid puzzler.

Vexen

[No. 4 in the Organization]

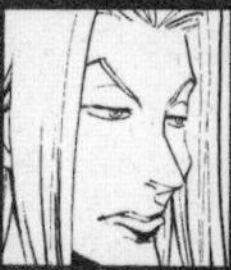

Oldest member of Castle Oblivion. But not necessarily respected by the younger members...

Aboveground Members

Larxene

[No. 12 in the Organization]

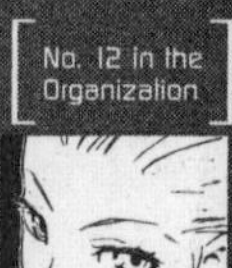

Cold-blooded, temperamental and vicious. Once she flies off the handle, there's no stopping her.

Marluxia

[No. 11 in the Organization]

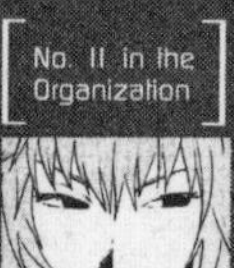

Lord of Castle Oblivion who loves flowers. It seems he's plotting something...

Axel

[No. 8 in the Organization]

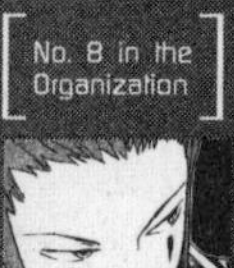

Mysterious individual who appears before Sora from time to time and leaves little bits of advice.

CONTENTS

One heart fulfills all hearts.
All hearts lead to the same heart.
"Kingdom Hearts."
A place where the mighty heart lives.
And where darkness is endlessly deep...

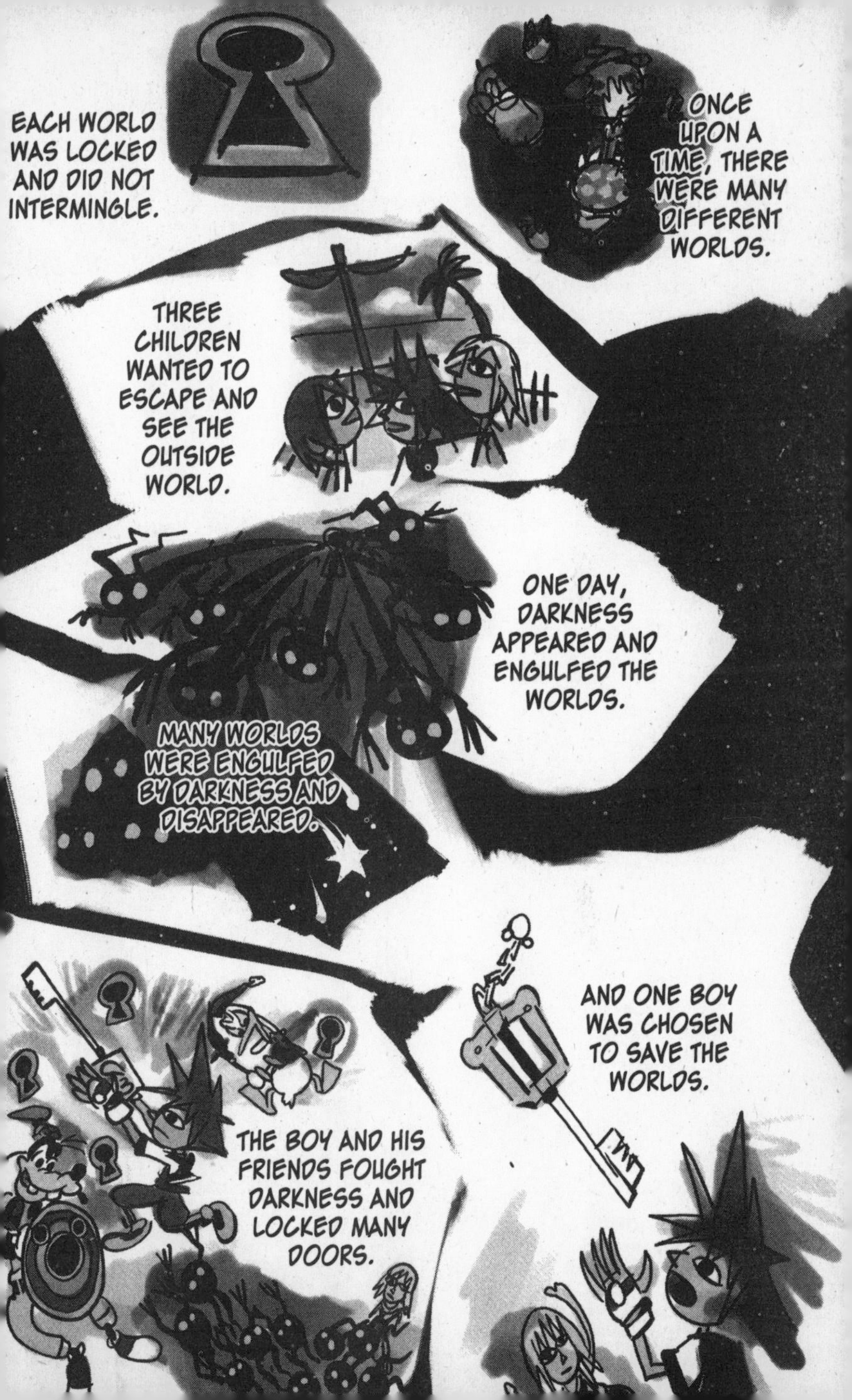
ONCE UPON A TIME, THERE WERE MANY DIFFERENT WORLDS.
EACH WORLD WAS LOCKED AND DID NOT INTERMINGLE.
THREE CHILDREN WANTED TO ESCAPE AND SEE THE OUTSIDE WORLD.
ONE DAY, DARKNESS APPEARED AND ENGULFED THE WORLDS.
MANY WORLDS WERE ENGULFED BY DARKNESS AND DISAPPEARED.
AND ONE BOY WAS CHOSEN TO SAVE THE WORLDS.
THE BOY AND HIS FRIENDS FOUGHT DARKNESS AND LOCKED MANY DOORS.

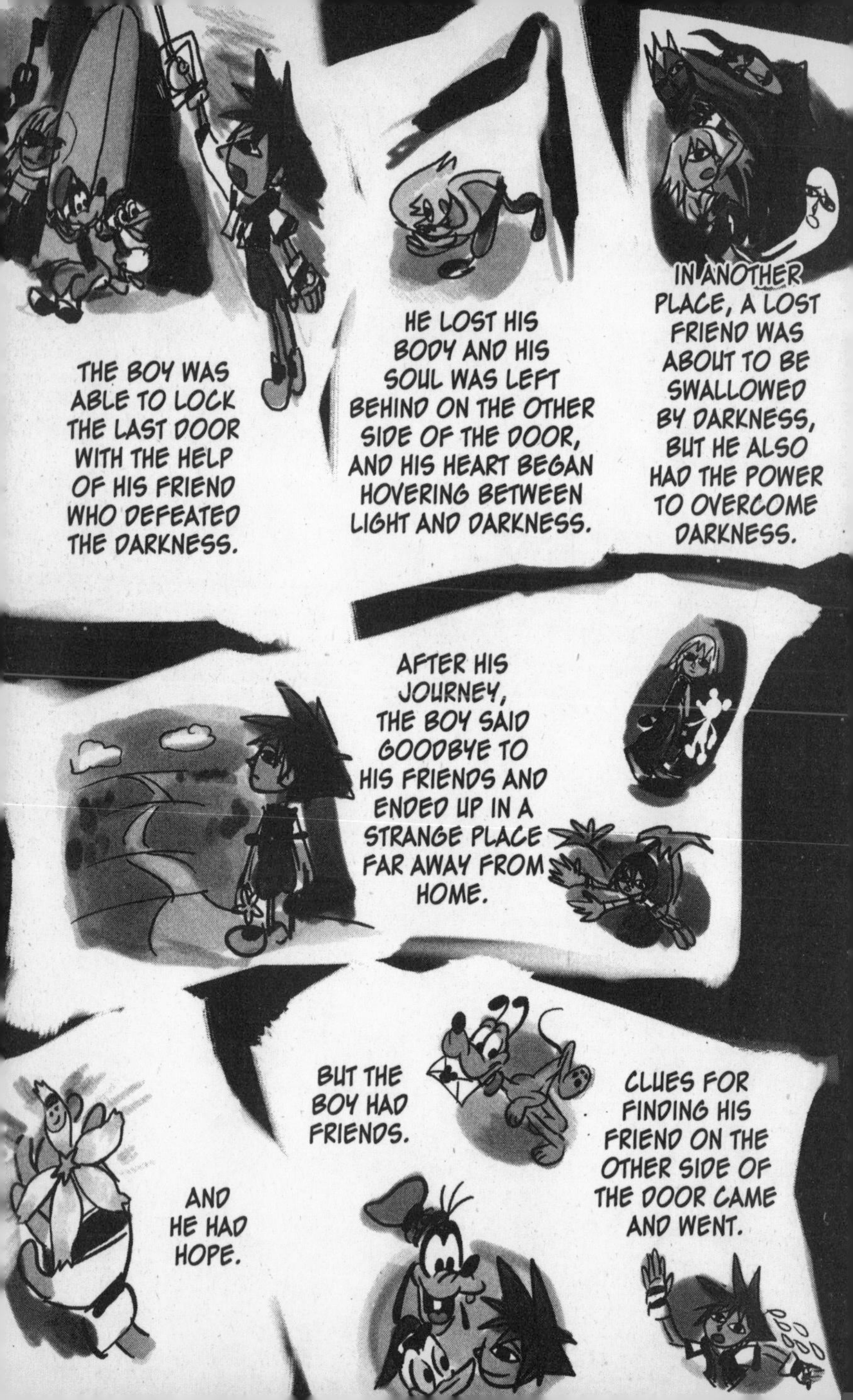
IN ANOTHER PLACE, A LOST FRIEND WAS ABOUT TO BE SWALLOWED BY DARKNESS, BUT HE ALSO HAD THE POWER TO OVERCOME DARKNESS.
HE LOST HIS BODY AND HIS SOUL WAS LEFT BEHIND ON THE OTHER SIDE OF THE DOOR, AND HIS HEART BEGAN HOVERING BETWEEN LIGHT AND DARKNESS.
THE BOY WAS ABLE TO LOCK THE LAST DOOR WITH THE HELP OF HIS FRIEND WHO DEFEATED THE DARKNESS.
AFTER HIS JOURNEY, THE BOY SAID GOODBYE TO HIS FRIENDS AND ENDED UP IN A STRANGE PLACE FAR AWAY FROM HOME.
CLUES FOR FINDING HIS FRIEND ON THE OTHER SIDE OF THE DOOR CAME AND WENT.
BUT THE BOY HAD FRIENDS.
AND HE HAD HOPE.

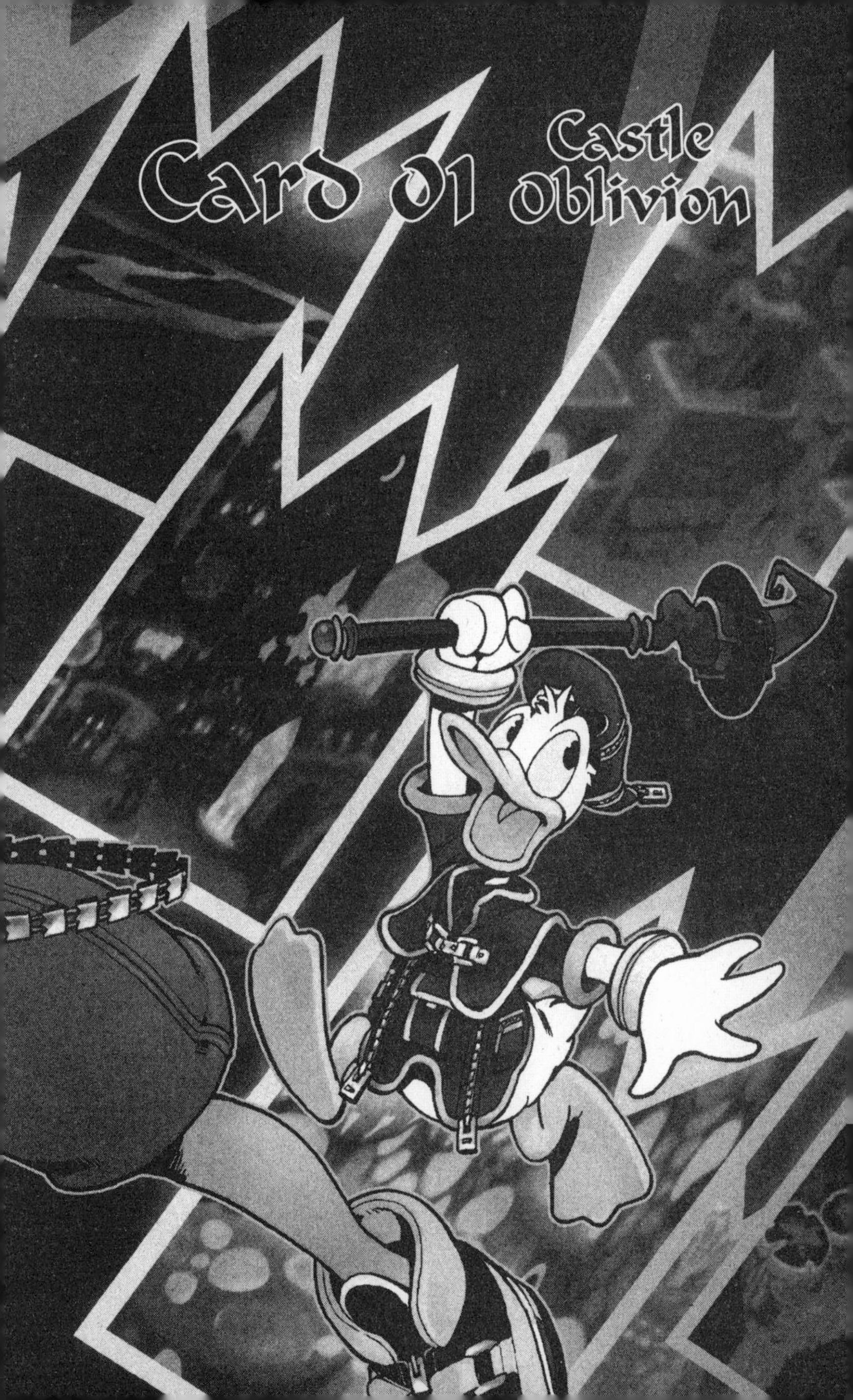
Card 01
Castle Oblivion

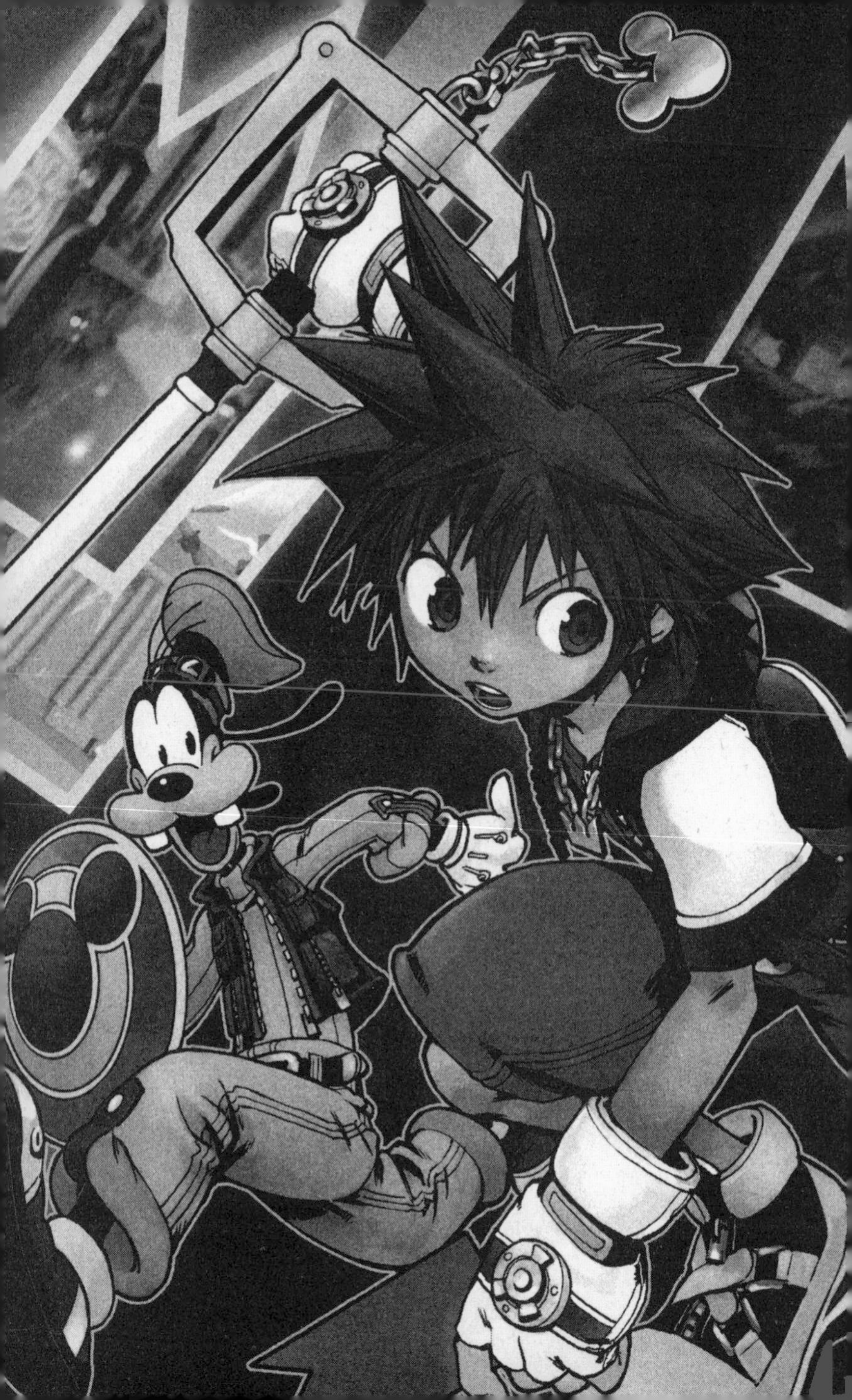

SNRKT
ZZZZZZ
CAN'T SLEEP?

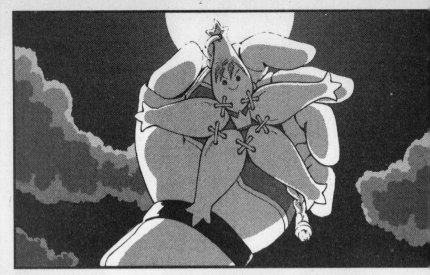

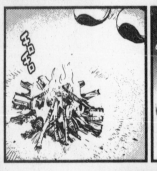

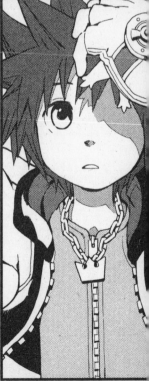

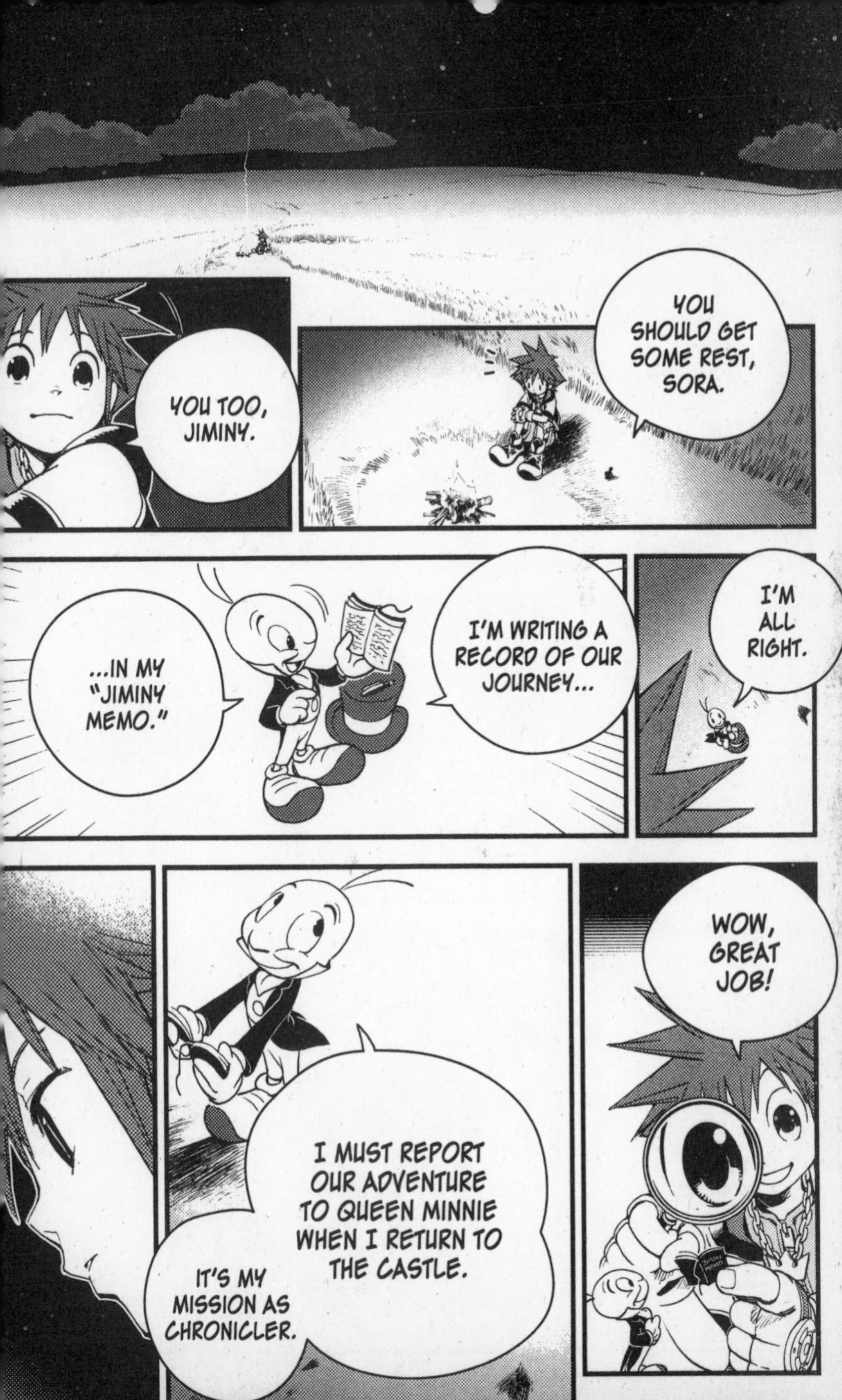
YOU SHOULD GET SOME REST, SORA.
YOU TOO, JIMINY.
I'M ALL RIGHT.
I'M WRITING A RECORD OF OUR JOURNEY...
...IN MY "JIMINY MEMO."
WOW, GREAT JOB!
I MUST REPORT OUR ADVENTURE TO QUEEN MINNIE WHEN I RETURN TO THE CASTLE.
IT'S MY MISSION AS CHRONICLER.

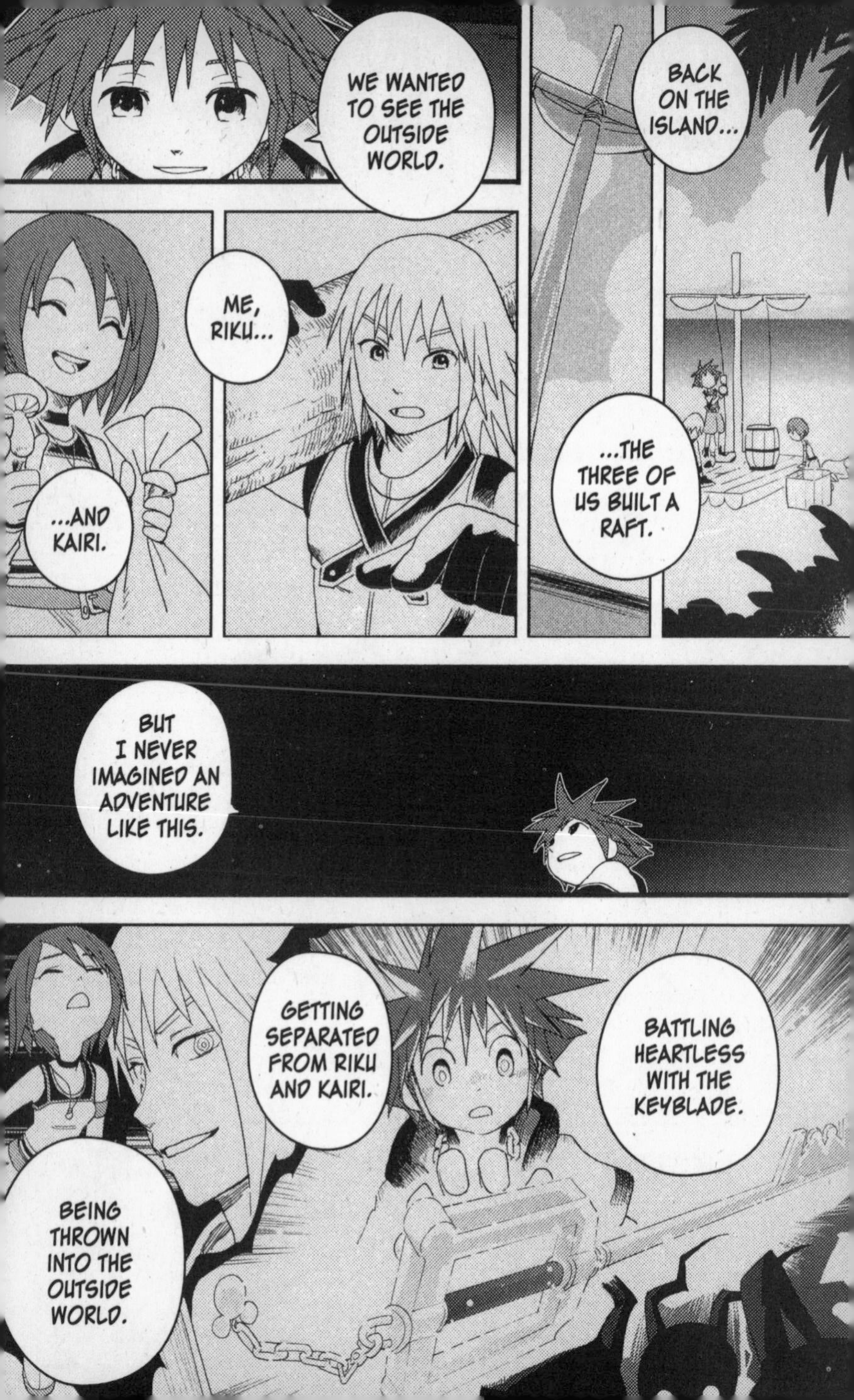
BACK ON THE ISLAND...
...THE THREE OF US BUILT A RAFT.
WE WANTED TO SEE THE OUTSIDE WORLD.
ME, RIKU...
...AND KAIRI.
BUT I NEVER IMAGINED AN ADVENTURE LIKE THIS.
BATTLING HEARTLESS WITH THE KEYBLADE.
GETTING SEPARATED FROM RIKU AND KAIRI.
BEING THROWN INTO THE OUTSIDE WORLD.

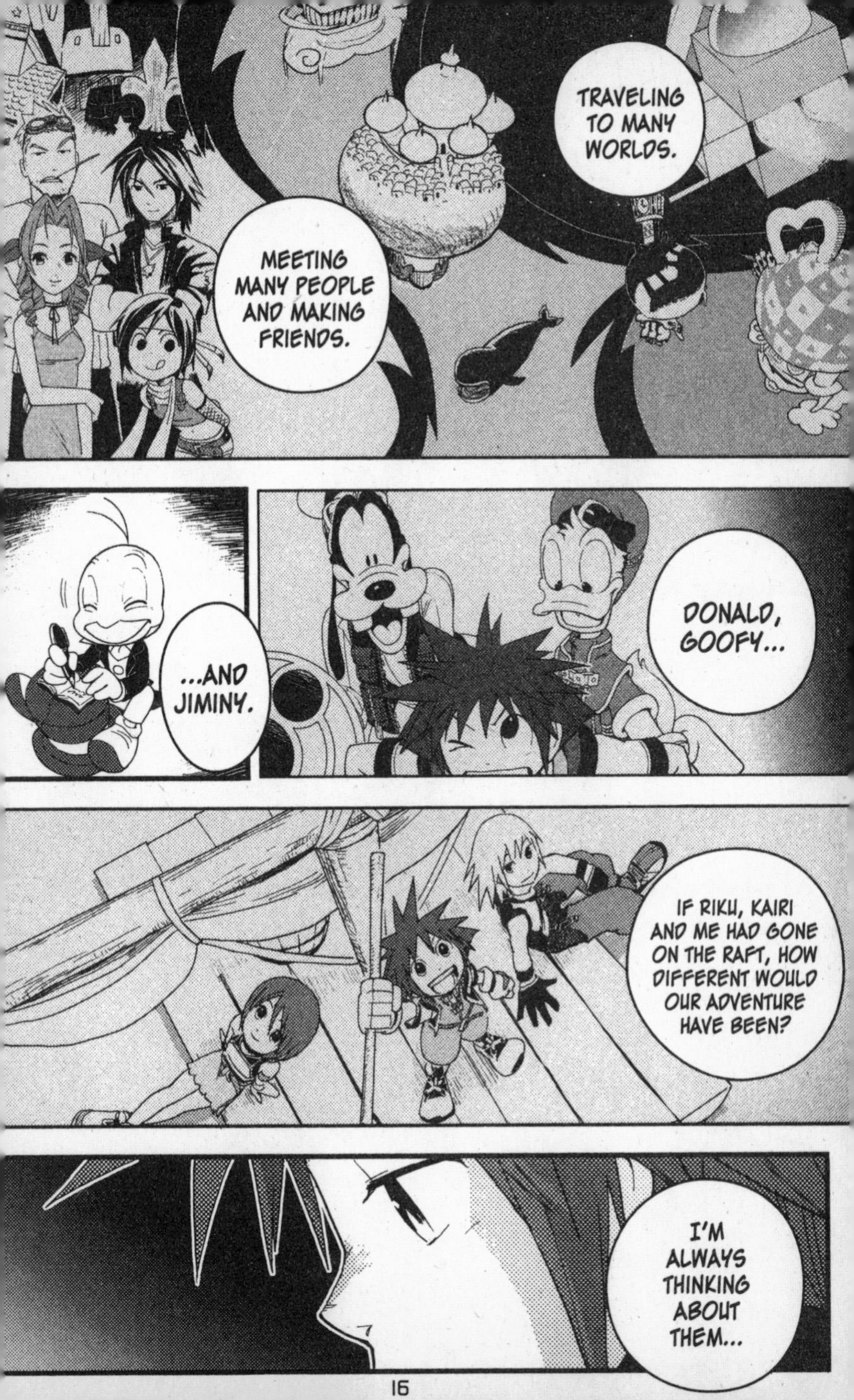
TRAVELING TO MANY WORLDS.
MEETING MANY PEOPLE AND MAKING FRIENDS.
DONALD, GOOFY...
...AND JIMINY.
IF RIKU, KAIRI AND ME HAD GONE ON THE RAFT, HOW DIFFERENT WOULD OUR ADVENTURE HAVE BEEN?
I'M ALWAYS THINKING ABOUT THEM...

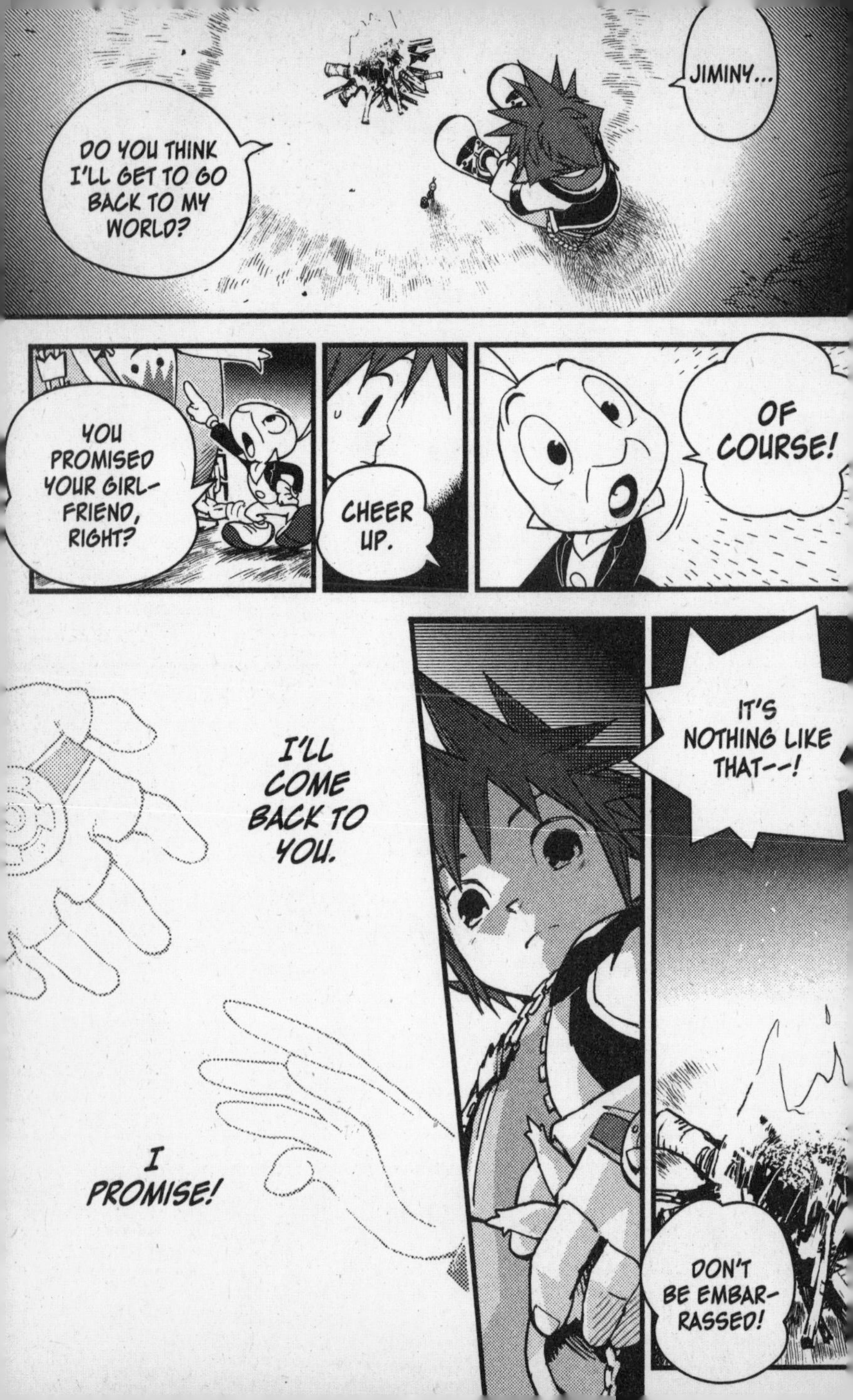
JIMINY...
DO YOU THINK I'LL GET TO GO BACK TO MY WORLD?
OF COURSE!
CHEER UP.
YOU PROMISED YOUR GIRL-FRIEND, RIGHT?
IT'S NOTHING LIKE THAT--!
DON'T BE EMBAR-RASSED!
I'LL COME BACK TO YOU.
I PROMISE!

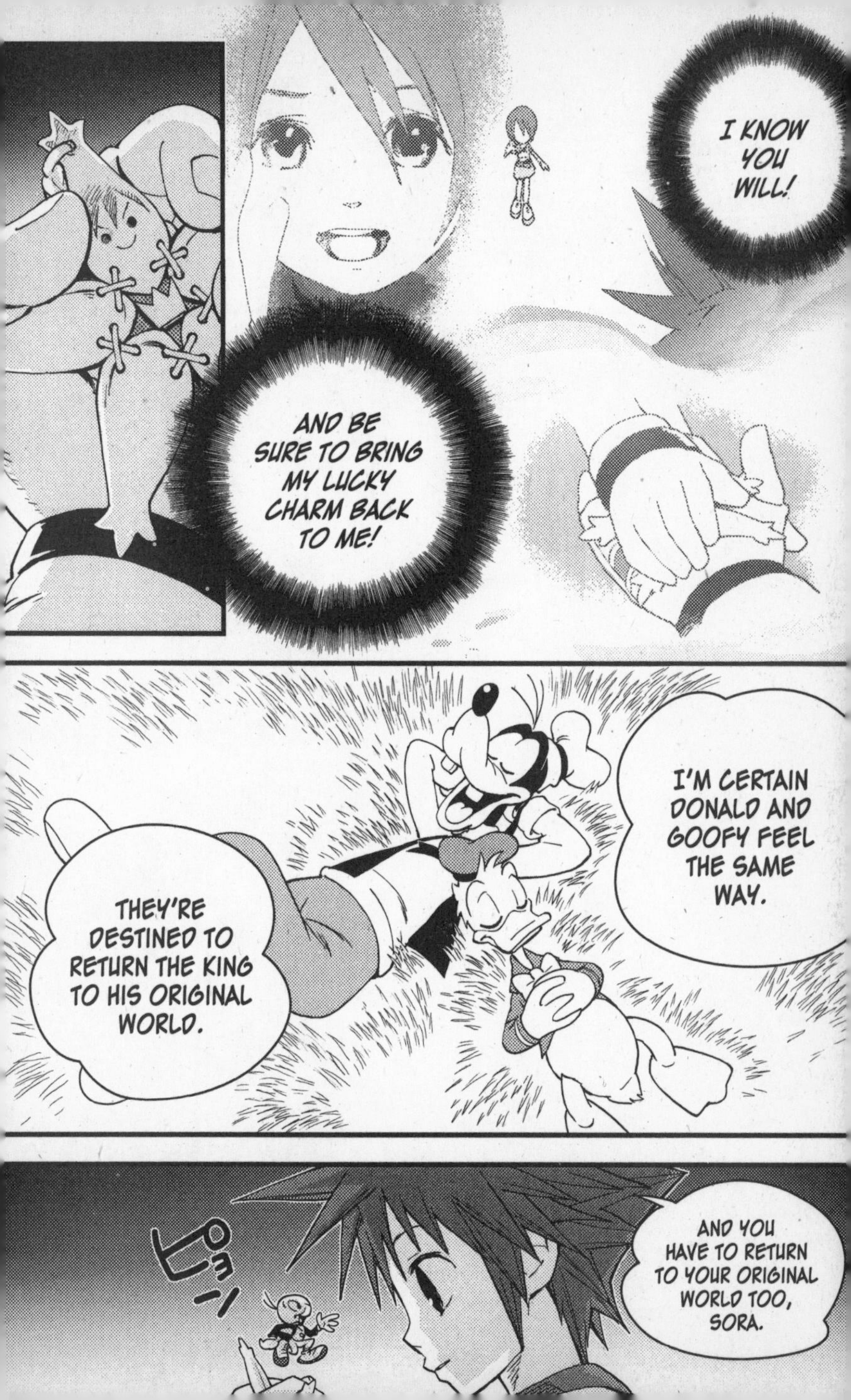
I KNOW YOU WILL!
AND BE SURE TO BRING MY LUCKY CHARM BACK TO ME!
I'M CERTAIN DONALD AND GOOFY FEEL THE SAME WAY.
THEY'RE DESTINED TO RETURN THE KING TO HIS ORIGINAL WORLD.
AND YOU HAVE TO RETURN TO YOUR ORIGINAL WORLD TOO, SORA.
ピョン

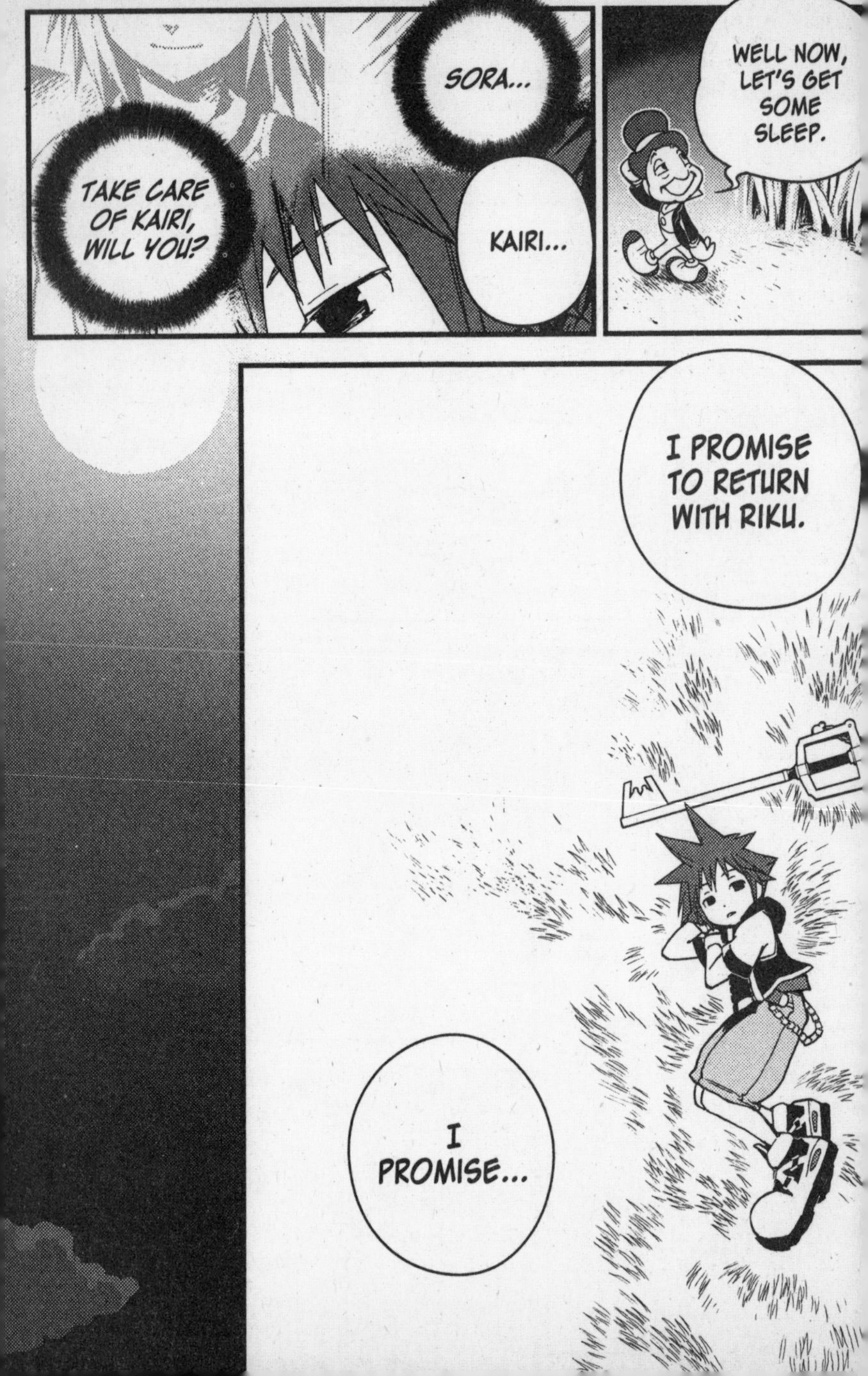
WELL NOW, LET'S GET SOME SLEEP.
SORA...
TAKE CARE OF KAIRI, WILL YOU?
KAIRI...
I PROMISE TO RETURN WITH RIKU.
I PROMISE...

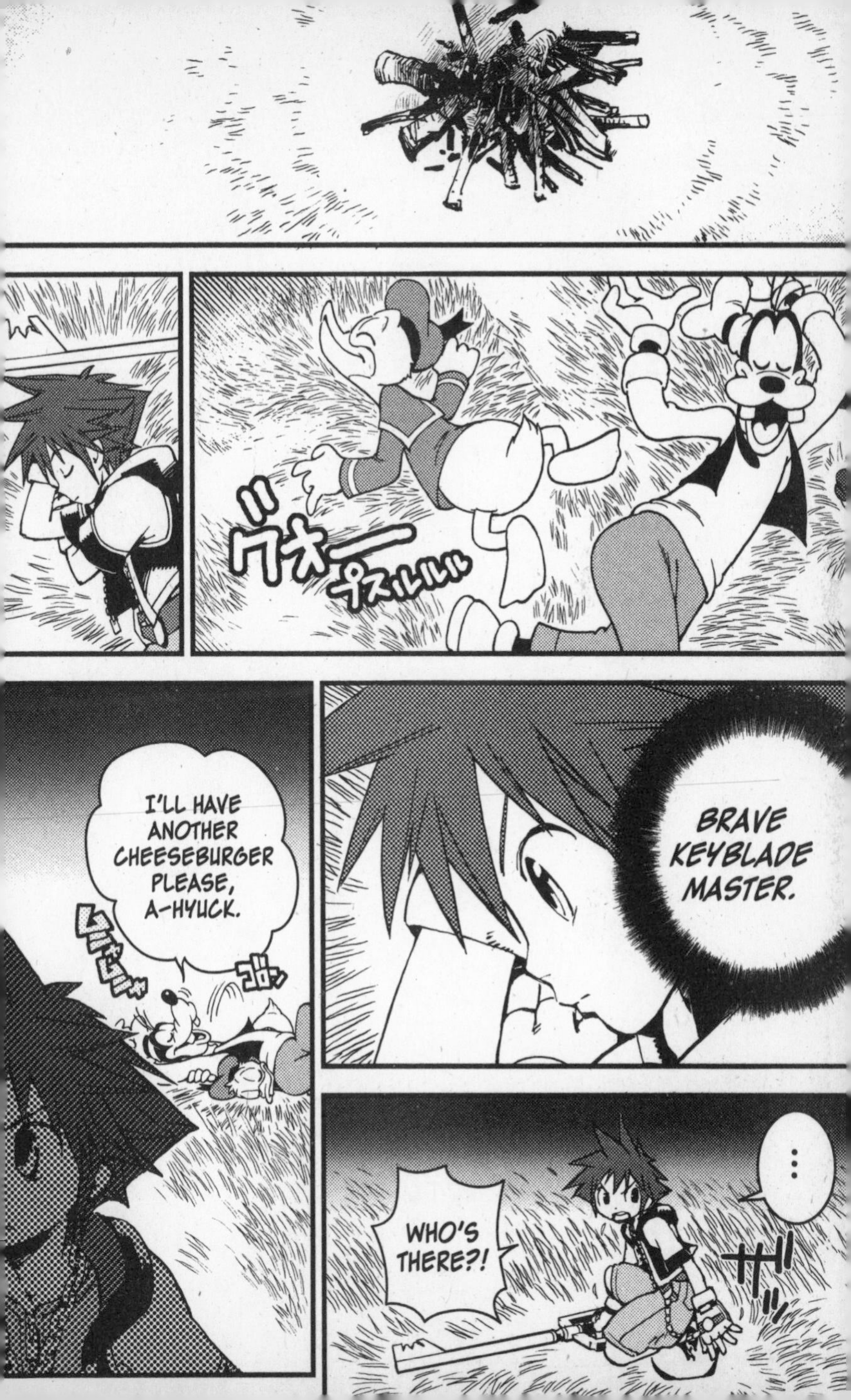

BRAVE KEYBLADE MASTER.
...
WHO'S THERE?!
I'LL HAVE ANOTHER CHEESEBURGER PLEASE, A-HYUCK.

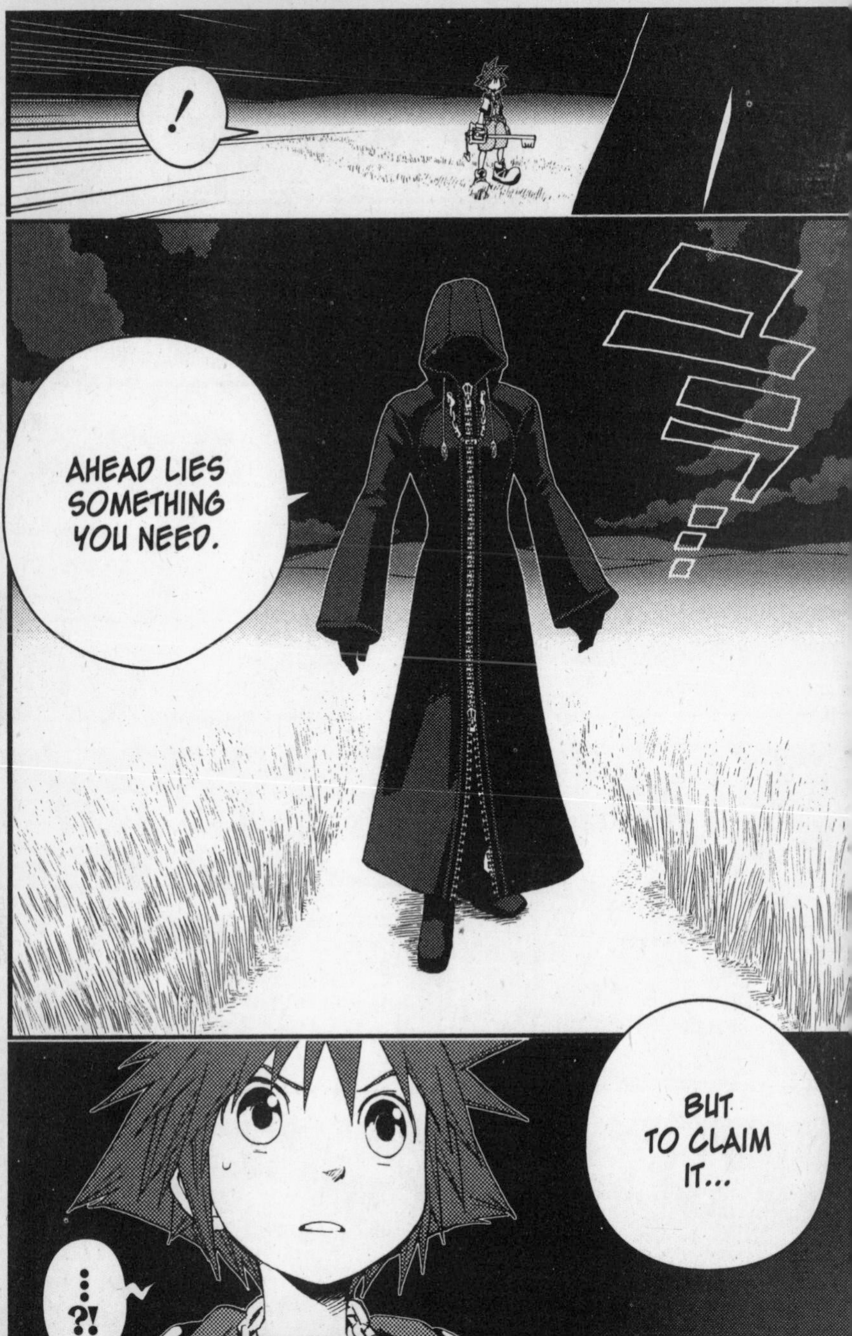
!
AHEAD LIES SOMETHING YOU NEED.
BUT TO CLAIM IT...
...?!

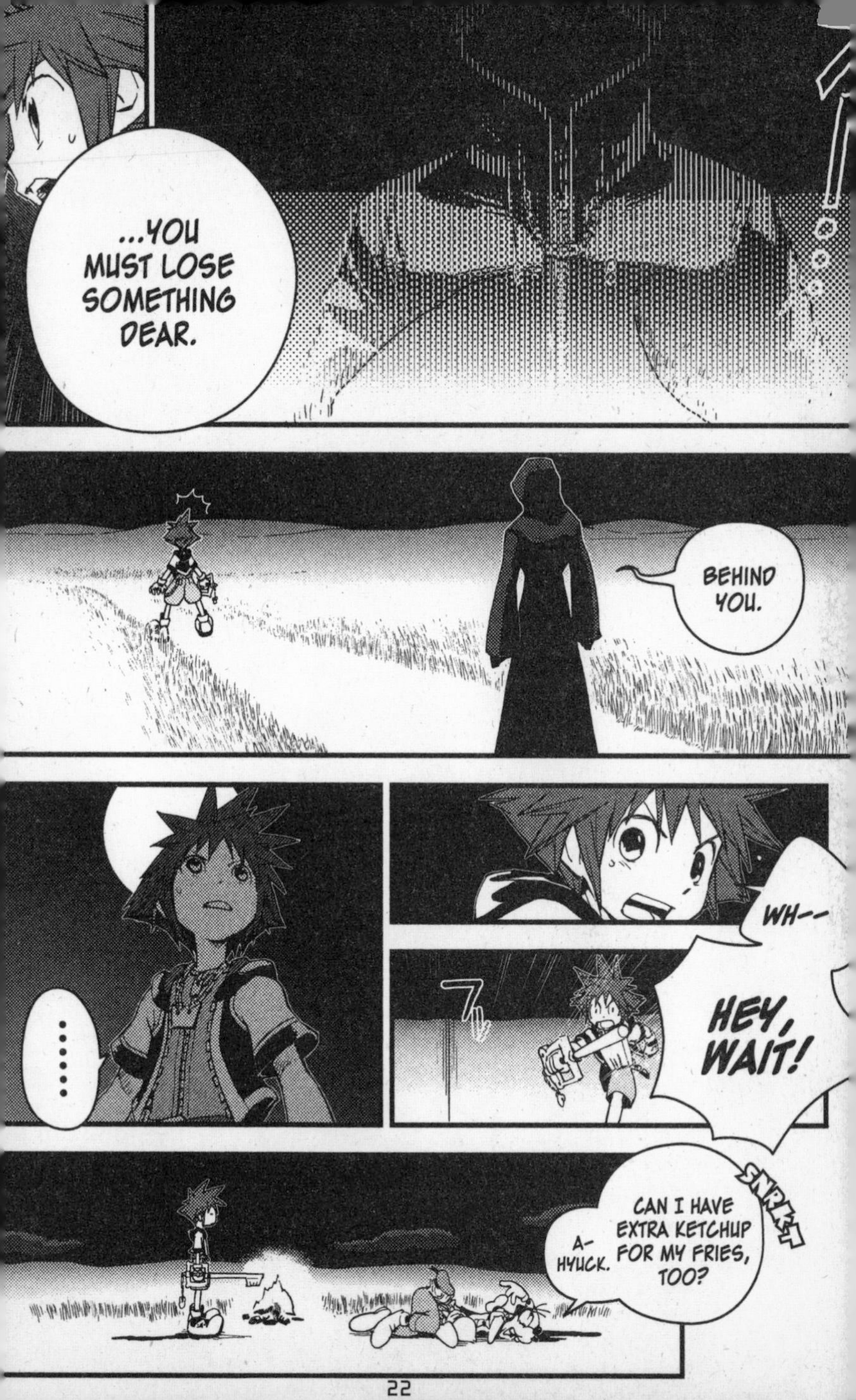
...YOU MUST LOSE SOMETHING DEAR.
BEHIND YOU.
WH--
HEY, WAIT!
......
SNRKT
CAN I HAVE EXTRA KETCHUP FOR MY FRIES, TOO?
A-HYUCK.

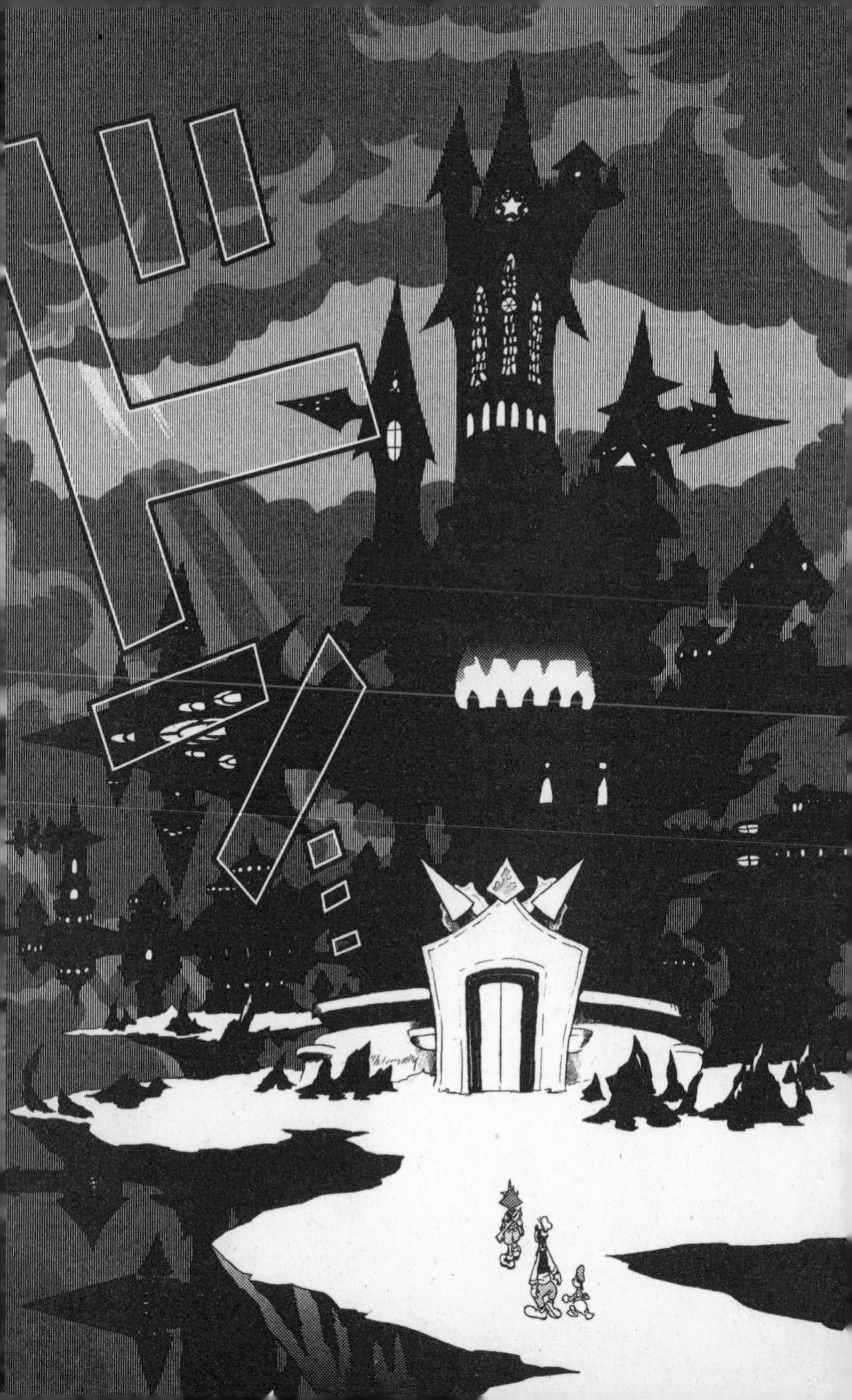
ドン

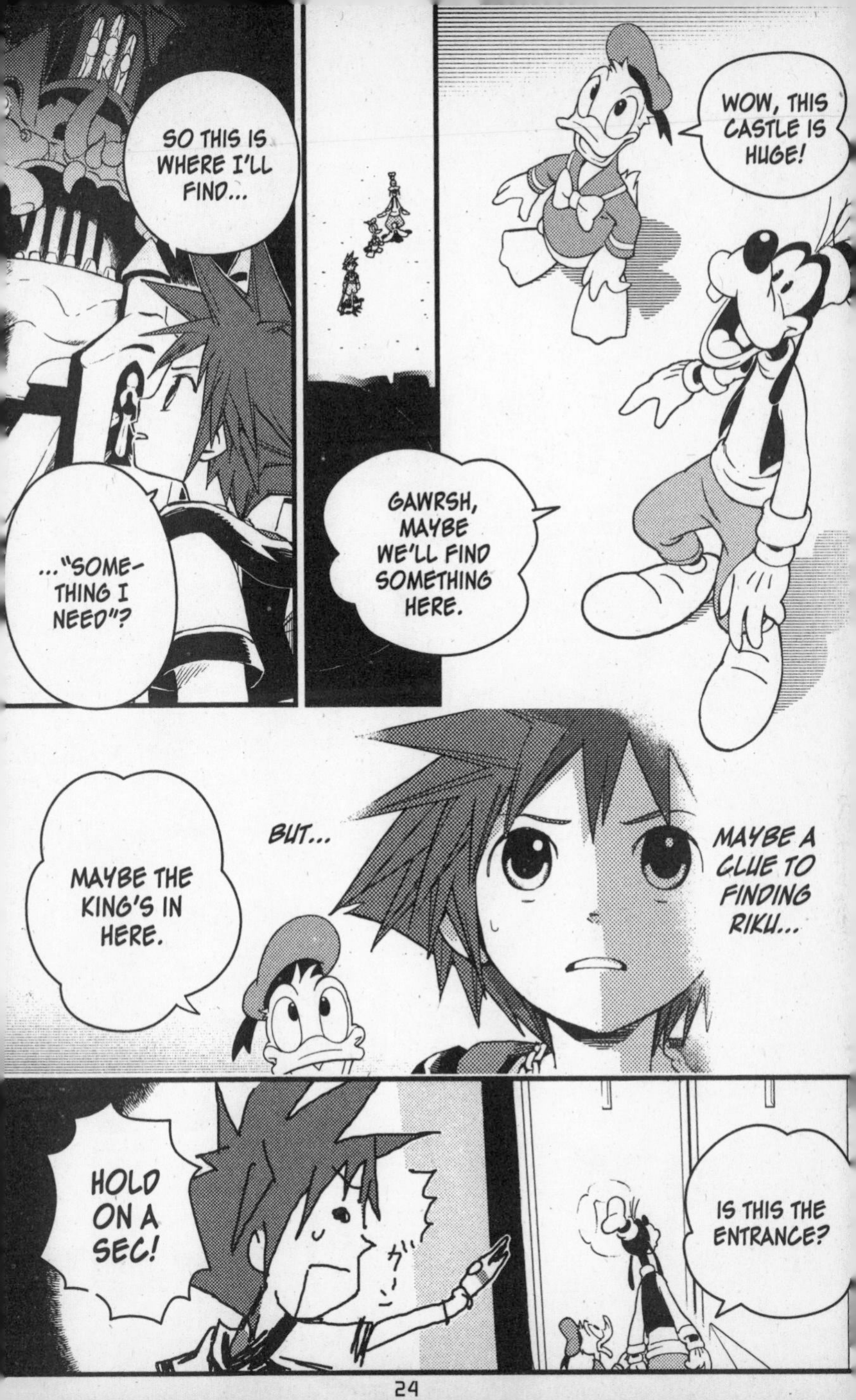
WOW, THIS CASTLE IS HUGE!
GAWRSH, MAYBE WE'LL FIND SOMETHING HERE.
SO THIS IS WHERE I'LL FIND...
..."SOME-THING I NEED"?
MAYBE A CLUE TO FINDING RIKU...
BUT...
MAYBE THE KING'S IN HERE.
IS THIS THE ENTRANCE?
HOLD ON A SEC!

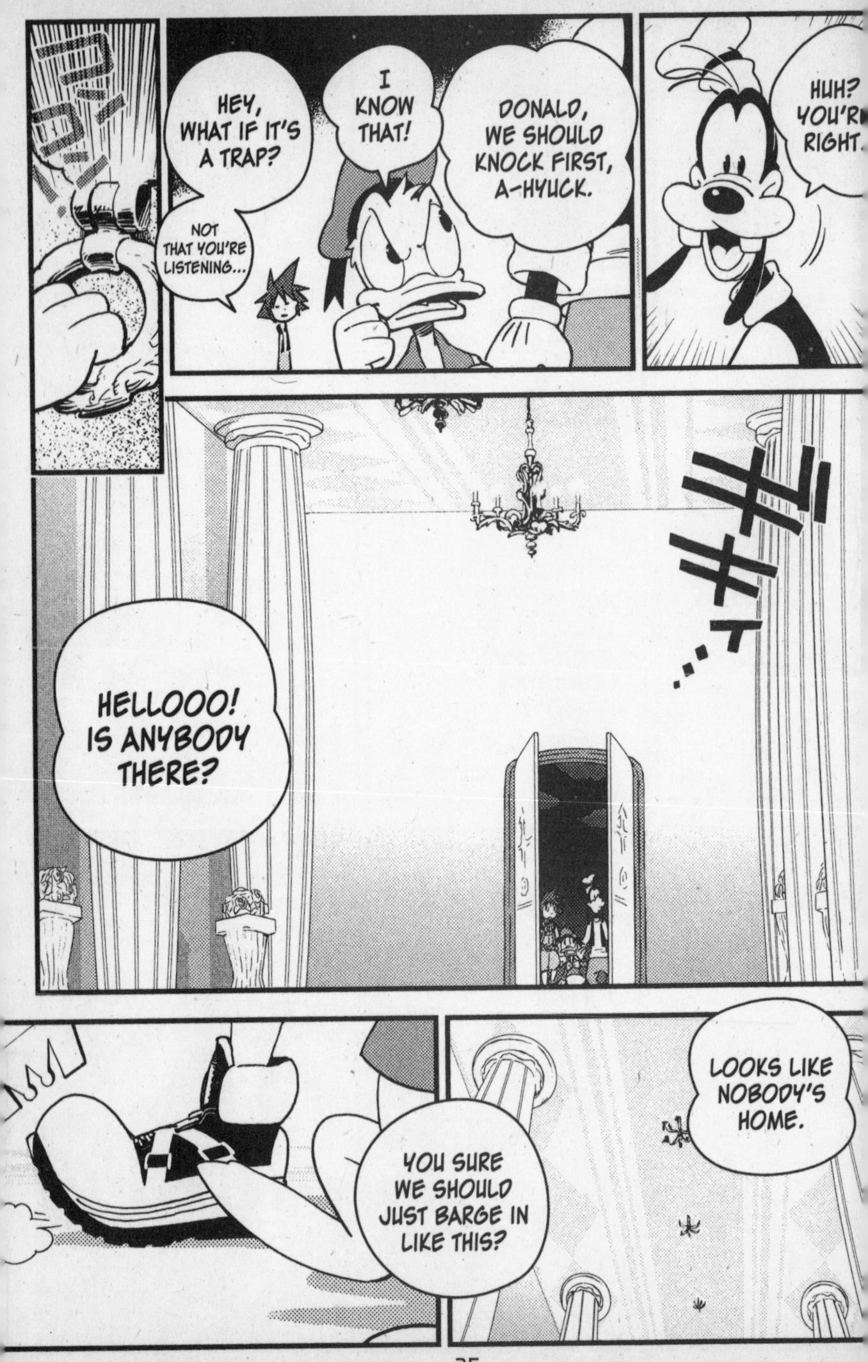
HUH? YOU'R RIGHT.
DONALD, WE SHOULD KNOCK FIRST, A-HYUCK.
I KNOW THAT!
HEY, WHAT IF IT'S A TRAP?
NOT THAT YOU'RE LISTENING...
HELLOOO! IS ANYBODY THERE?
LOOKS LIKE NOBODY'S HOME.
YOU SURE WE SHOULD JUST BARGE IN LIKE THIS?

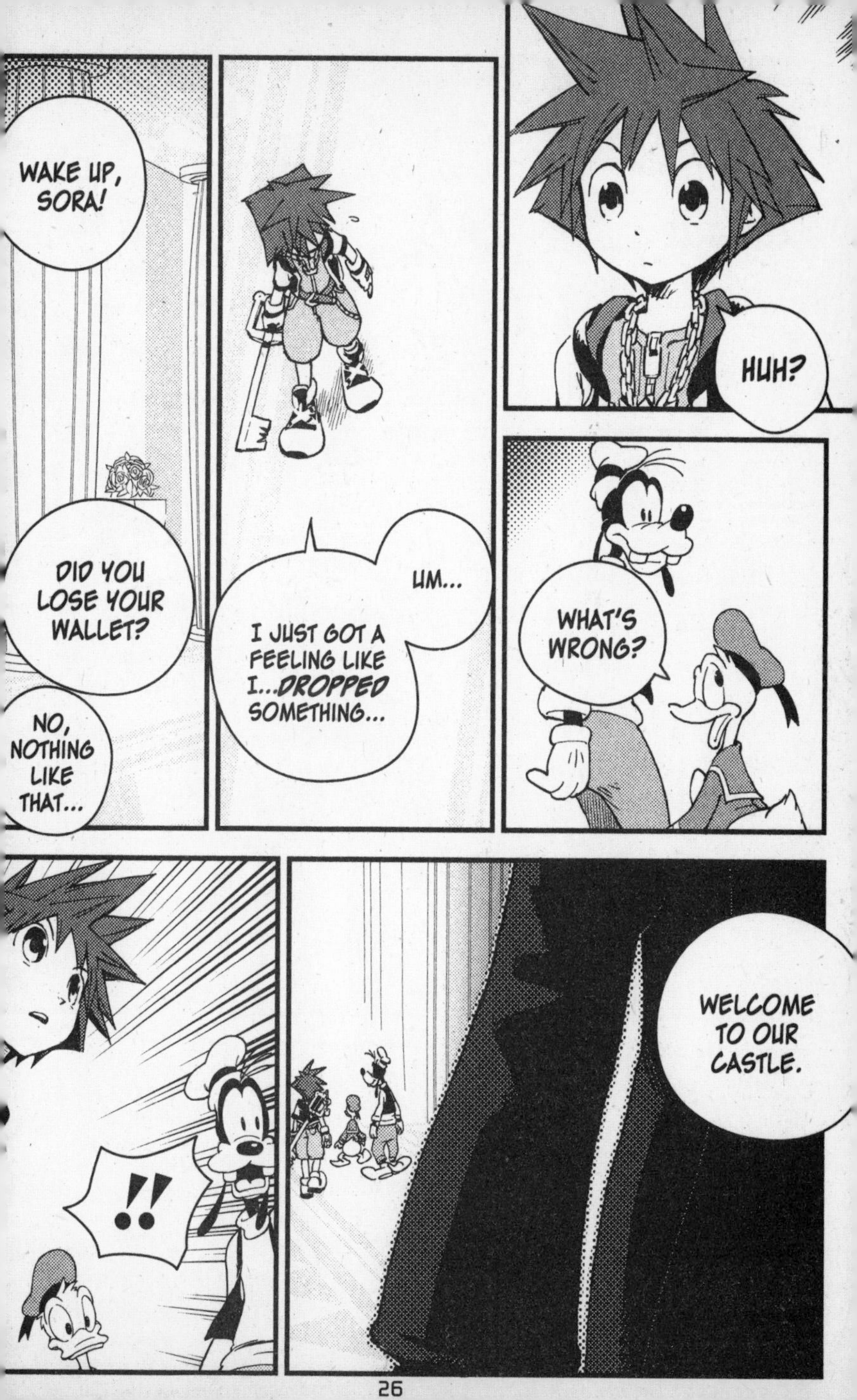
HUH?
WHAT'S WRONG?
UM...
I JUST GOT A FEELING LIKE I...*DROPPED* SOMETHING...
WAKE UP, SORA!
DID YOU LOSE YOUR WALLET?
NO, NOTHING LIKE THAT...
WELCOME TO OUR CASTLE.
!!

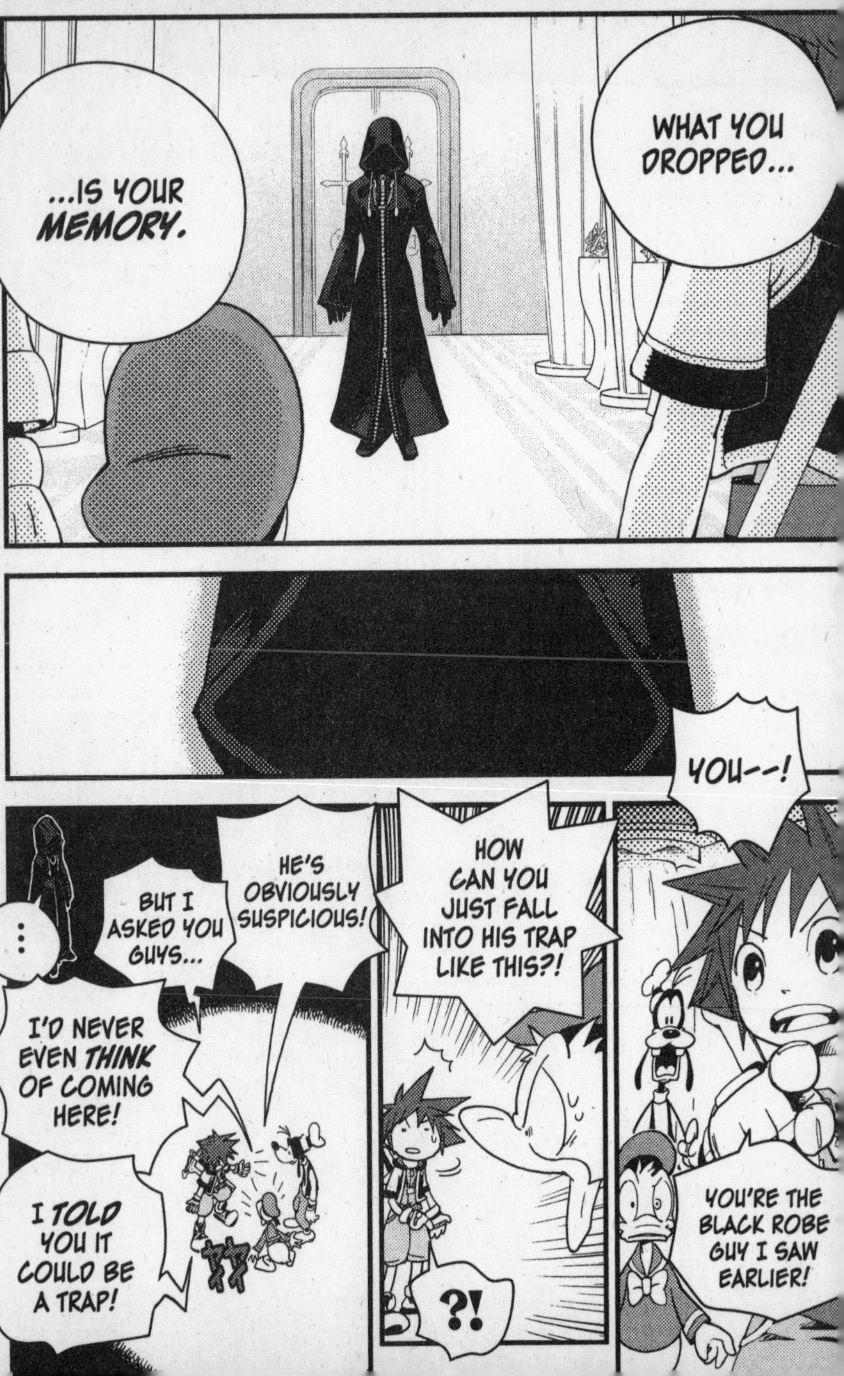
WHAT YOU DROPPED...
...IS YOUR MEMORY.
YOU--!
YOU'RE THE BLACK ROBE GUY I SAW EARLIER!
HOW CAN YOU JUST FALL INTO HIS TRAP LIKE THIS?!
?!
HE'S OBVIOUSLY SUSPICIOUS!
BUT I ASKED YOU GUYS...
...
I'D NEVER EVEN THINK OF COMING HERE!
I TOLD YOU IT COULD BE A TRAP!

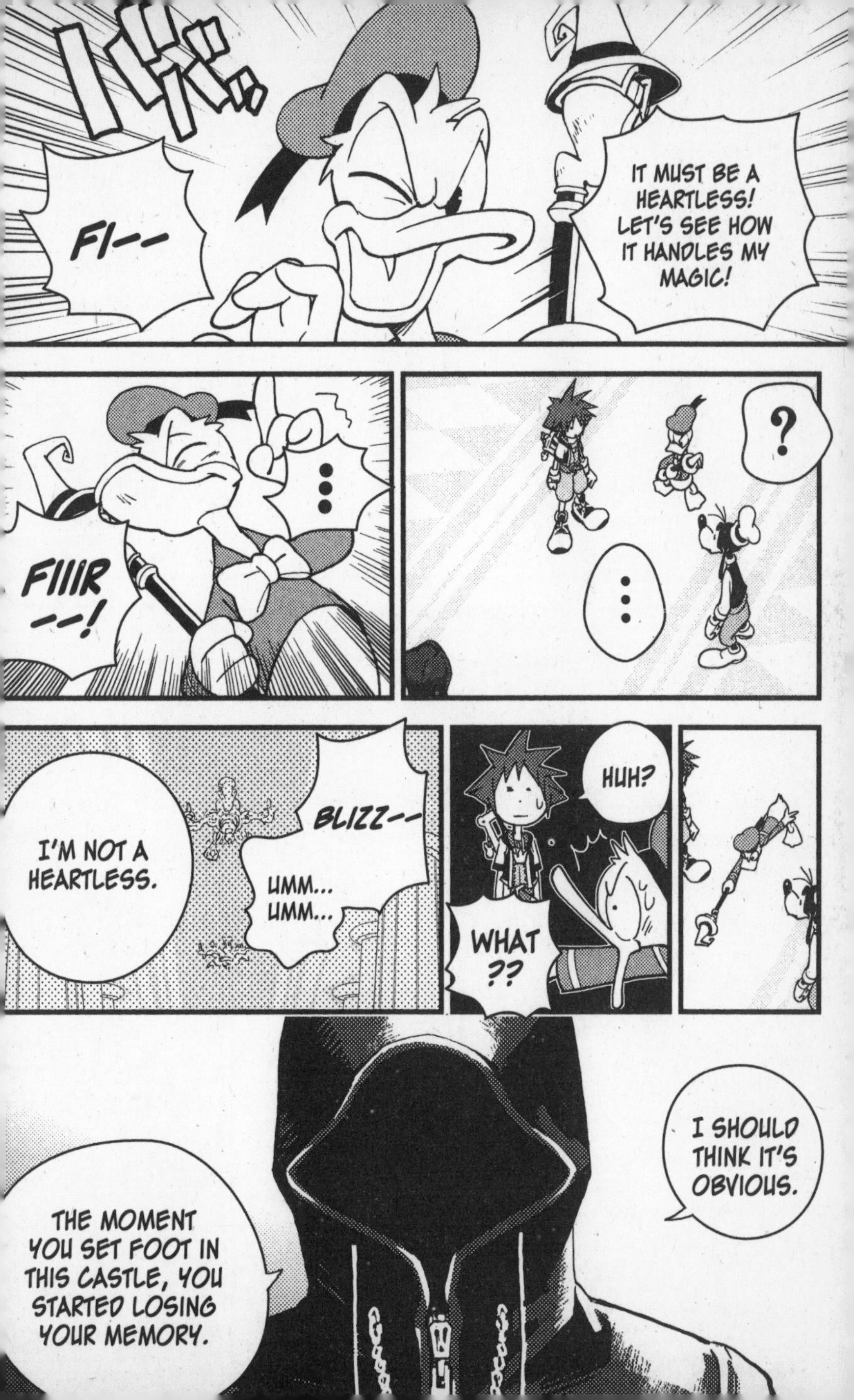
IT MUST BE A HEARTLESS! LET'S SEE HOW IT HANDLES MY MAGIC!
FI--
?
...
...
FIIIR --!
HUH?
WHAT ??
BLIZZ--
UMM... UMM...
I'M NOT A HEARTLESS.
I SHOULD THINK IT'S OBVIOUS.
THE MOMENT YOU SET FOOT IN THIS CASTLE, YOU STARTED LOSING YOUR MEMORY.

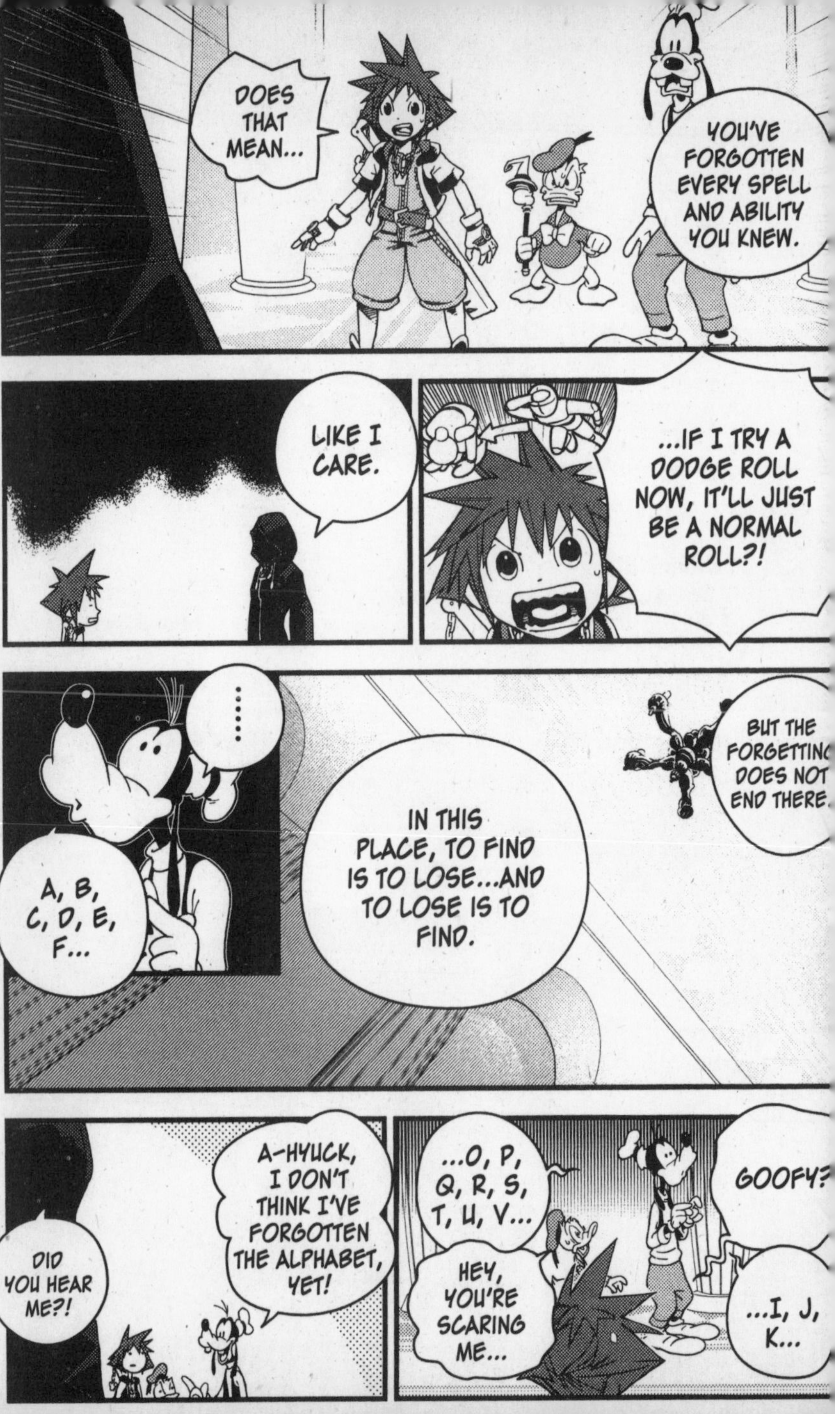
YOU'VE FORGOTTEN EVERY SPELL AND ABILITY YOU KNEW.
DOES THAT MEAN...
...IF I TRY A DODGE ROLL NOW, IT'LL JUST BE A NORMAL ROLL?!
LIKE I CARE.
BUT THE FORGETTING DOES NOT END THERE.
IN THIS PLACE, TO FIND IS TO LOSE...AND TO LOSE IS TO FIND.
......
A, B, C, D, E, F...
GOOFY?
...I, J, K...
HEY, YOU'RE SCARING ME...
...O, P, Q, R, S, T, U, V...
A-HYUCK, I DON'T THINK I'VE FORGOTTEN THE ALPHABET, YET!
DID YOU HEAR ME?!

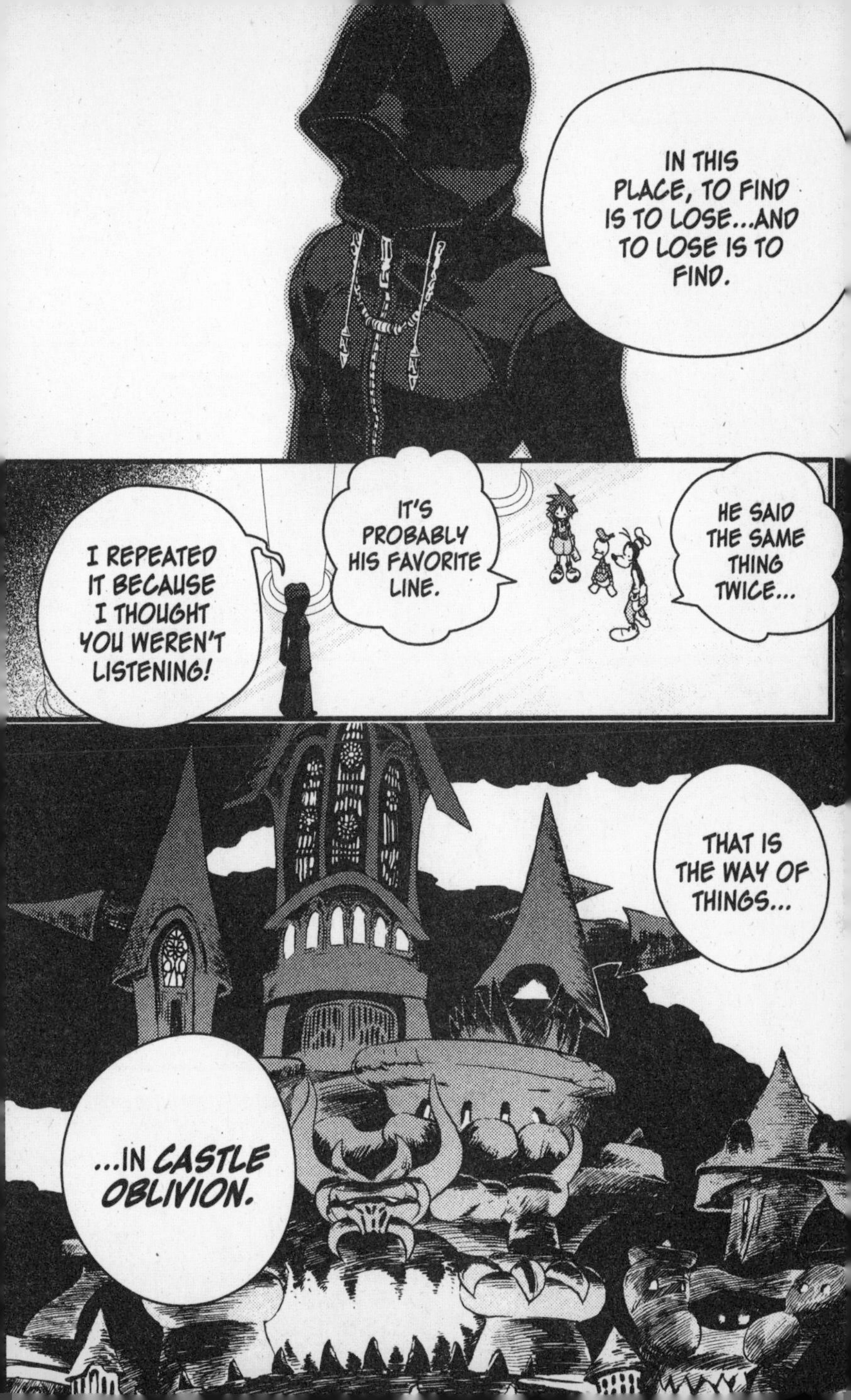
IN THIS PLACE, TO FIND IS TO LOSE...AND TO LOSE IS TO FIND.
HE SAID THE SAME THING TWICE...
IT'S PROBABLY HIS FAVORITE LINE.
I REPEATED IT BECAUSE I THOUGHT YOU WEREN'T LISTENING!
THAT IS THE WAY OF THINGS...
...IN *CASTLE OBLIVION.*

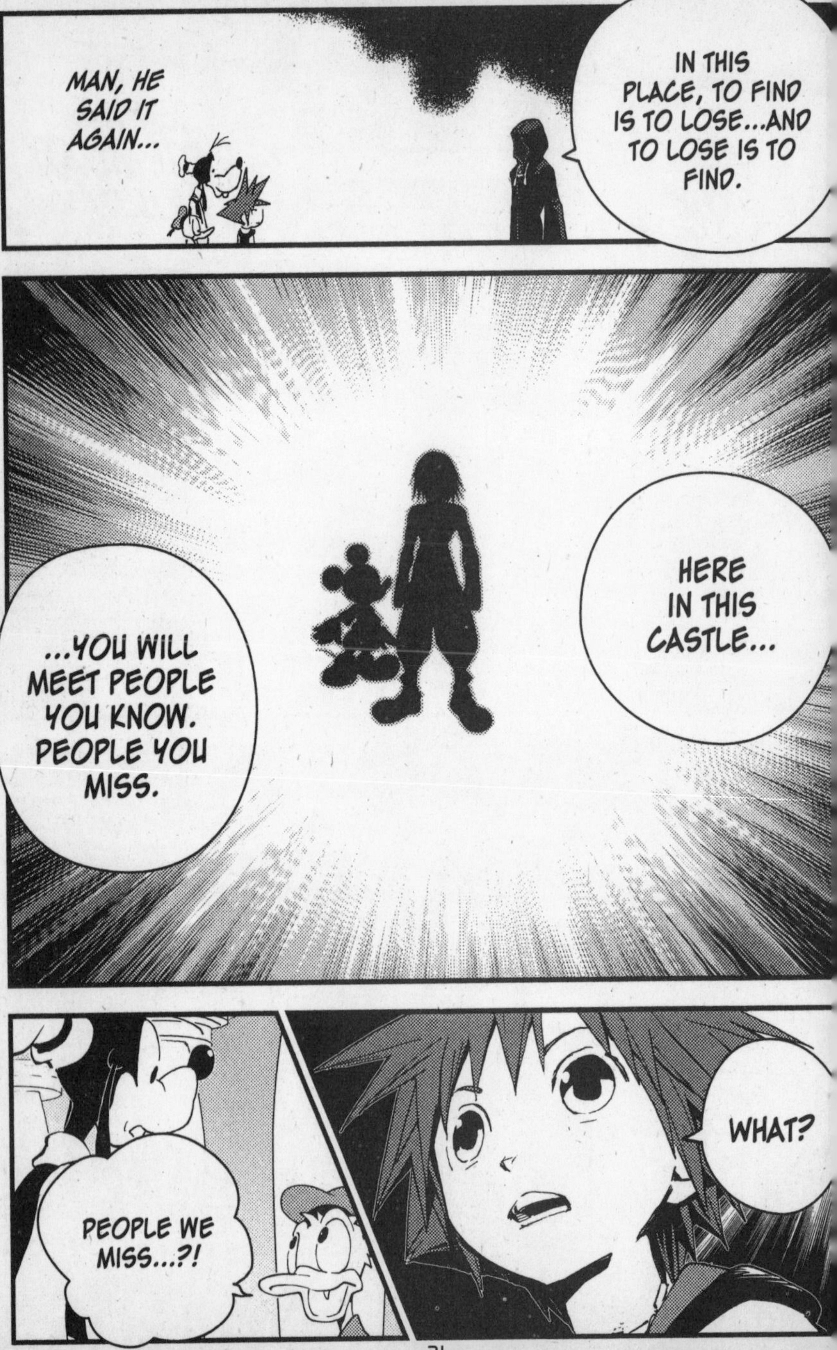
IN THIS PLACE, TO FIND IS TO LOSE...AND TO LOSE IS TO FIND.
MAN, HE SAID IT AGAIN...
HERE IN THIS CASTLE...
...YOU WILL MEET PEOPLE YOU KNOW. PEOPLE YOU MISS.
WHAT?
PEOPLE WE MISS...?!

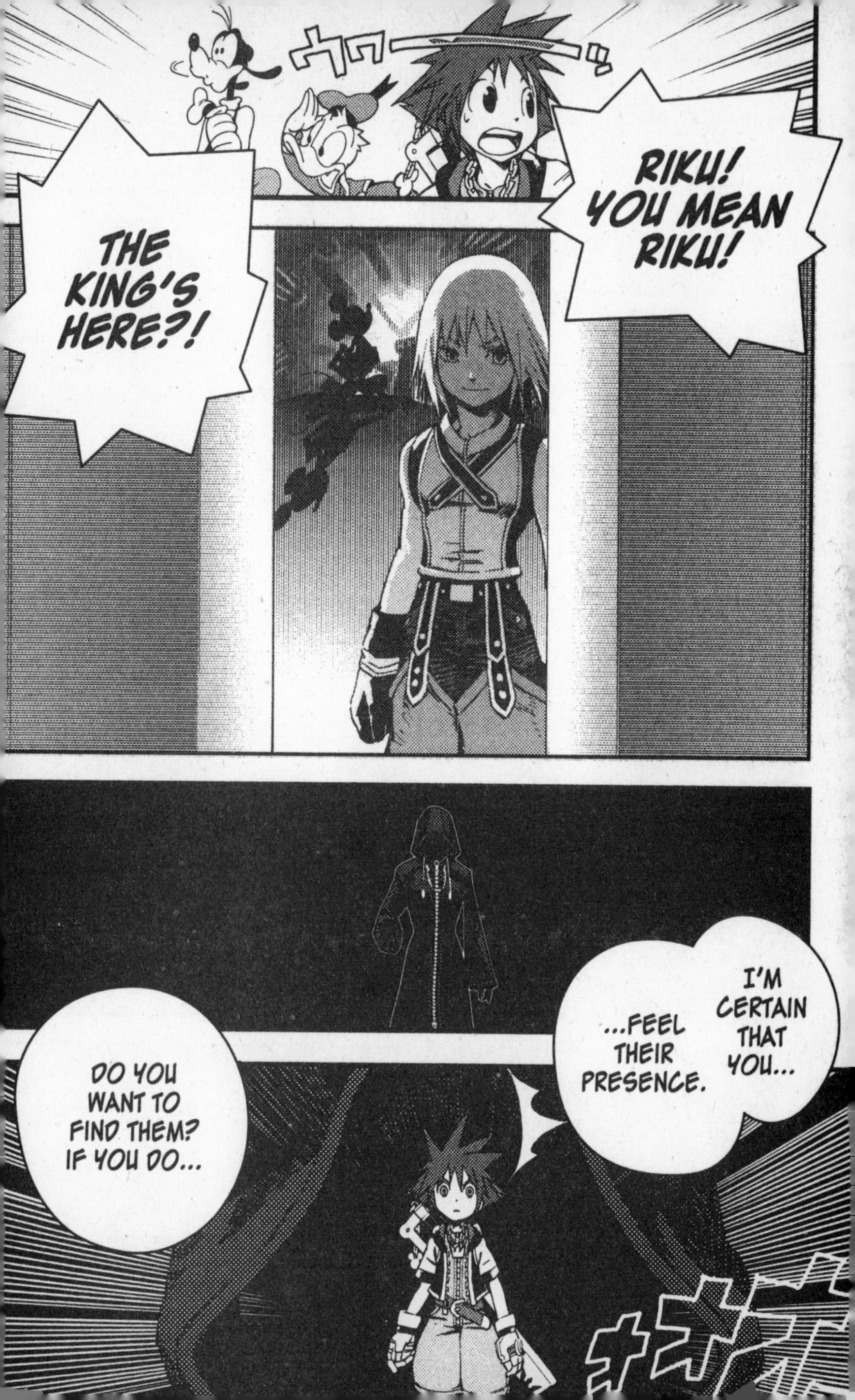
RIKU! YOU MEAN RIKU!
THE KING'S HERE?!
I'M CERTAIN THAT YOU...
...FEEL THEIR PRESENCE.
DO YOU WANT TO FIND THEM? IF YOU DO...

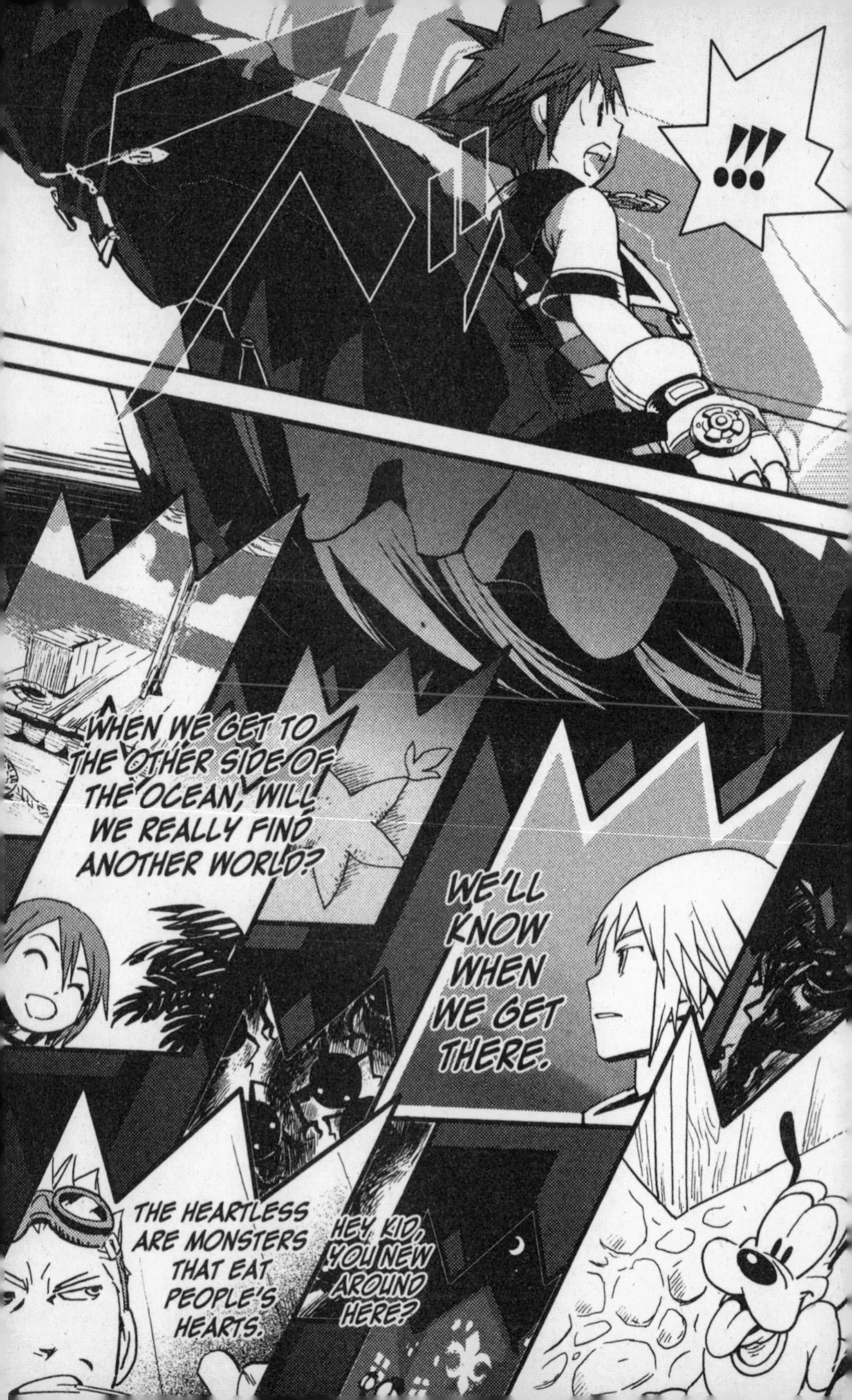
!!!...
WE'LL KNOW WHEN WE GET THERE.
WHEN WE GET TO THE OTHER SIDE OF THE OCEAN, WILL WE REALLY FIND ANOTHER WORLD?
HEY KID, YOU NEW AROUND HERE?
THE HEARTLESS ARE MONSTERS THAT EAT PEOPLE'S HEARTS.

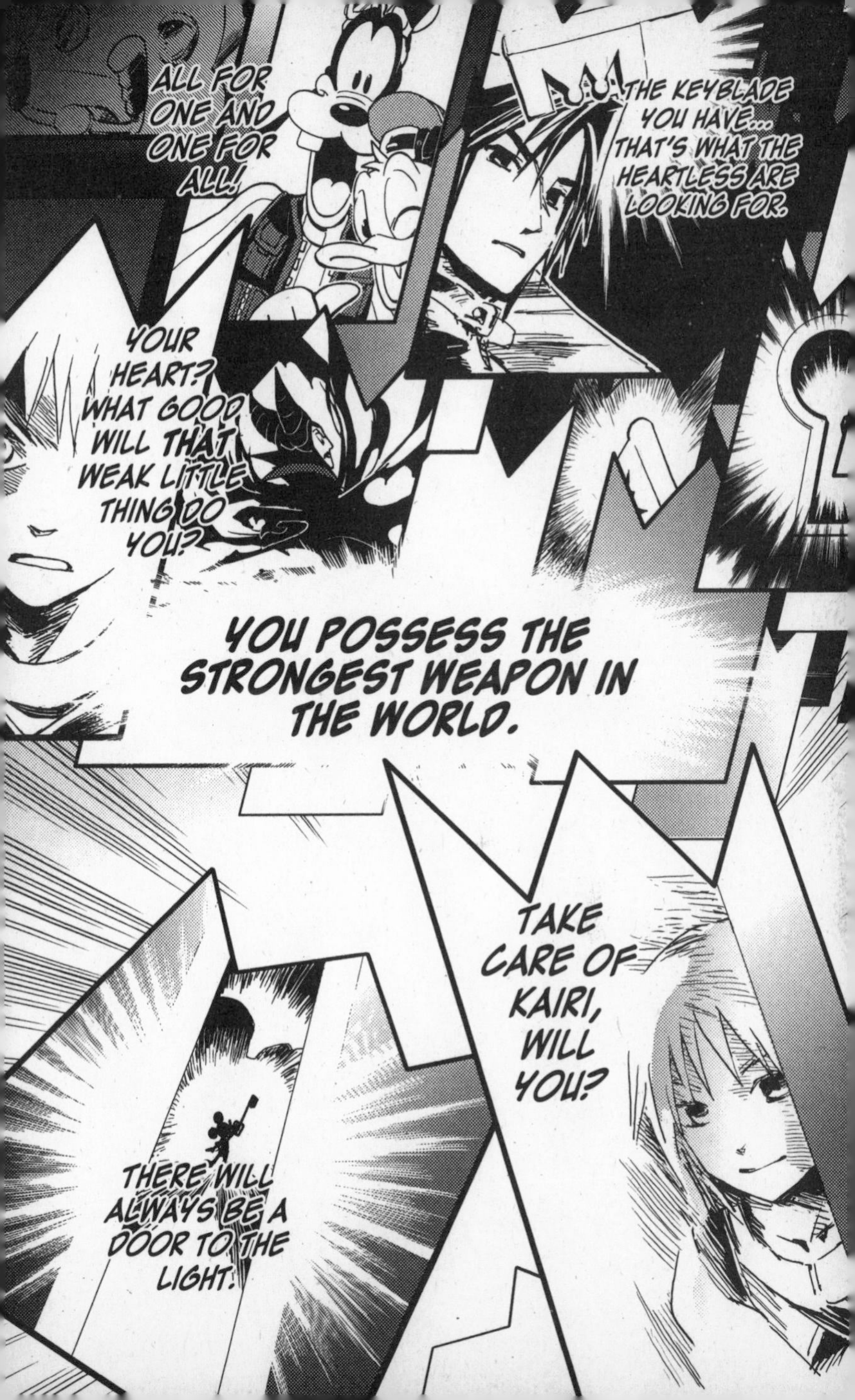
THE KEYBLADE YOU HAVE... THAT'S WHAT THE HEARTLESS ARE LOOKING FOR.
ALL FOR ONE AND ONE FOR ALL!
YOUR HEART? WHAT GOOD WILL THAT WEAK LITTLE THING DO YOU?
YOU POSSESS THE STRONGEST WEAPON IN THE WORLD.
TAKE CARE OF KAIRI, WILL YOU?
THERE WILL ALWAYS BE A DOOR TO THE LIGHT.

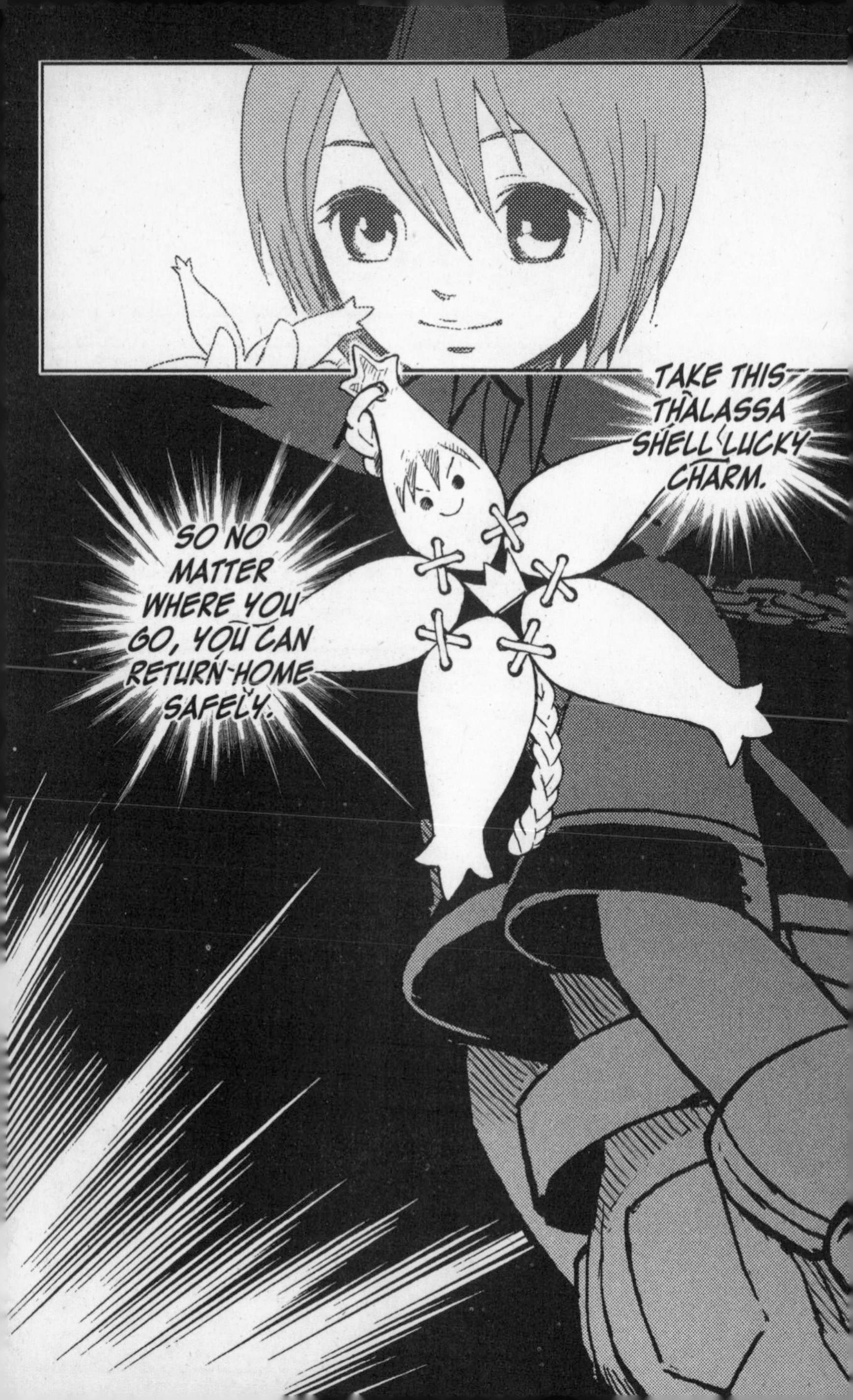
TAKE THIS THALASSA SHELL LUCKY CHARM.
SO NO MATTER WHERE YOU GO, YOU CAN RETURN HOME SAFELY.

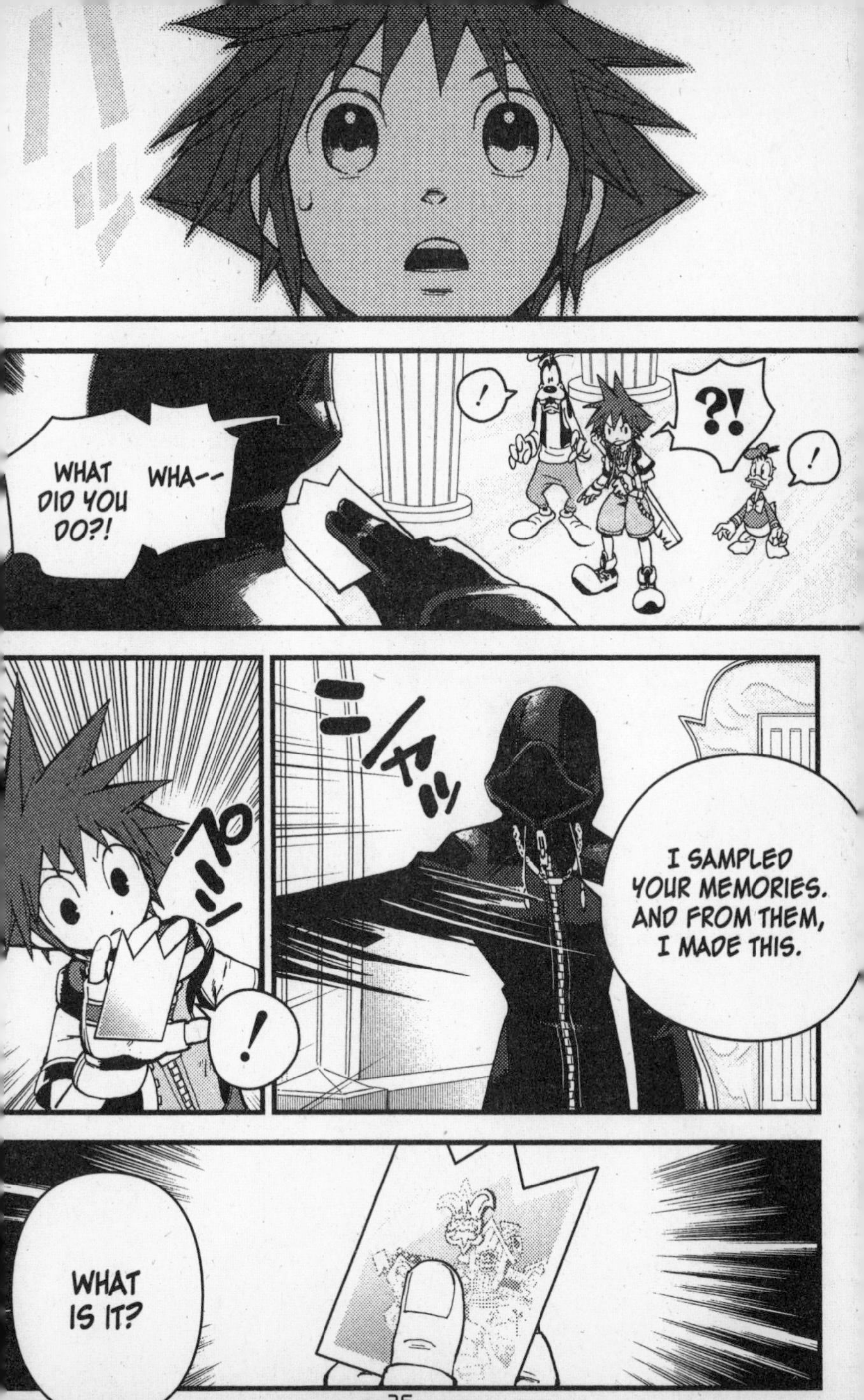
?!
!
!
WHA--
WHAT DID YOU DO?!
I SAMPLED YOUR MEMORIES. AND FROM THEM, I MADE THIS.
!
WHAT IS IT?

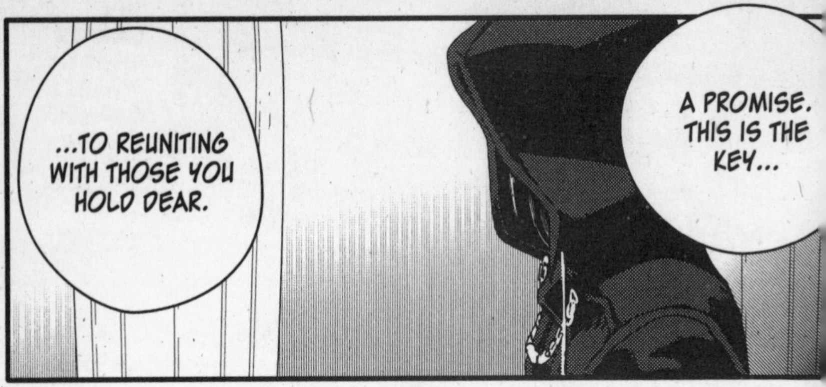
A PROMISE. THIS IS THE KEY...
...TO REUNITING WITH THOSE YOU HOLD DEAR.

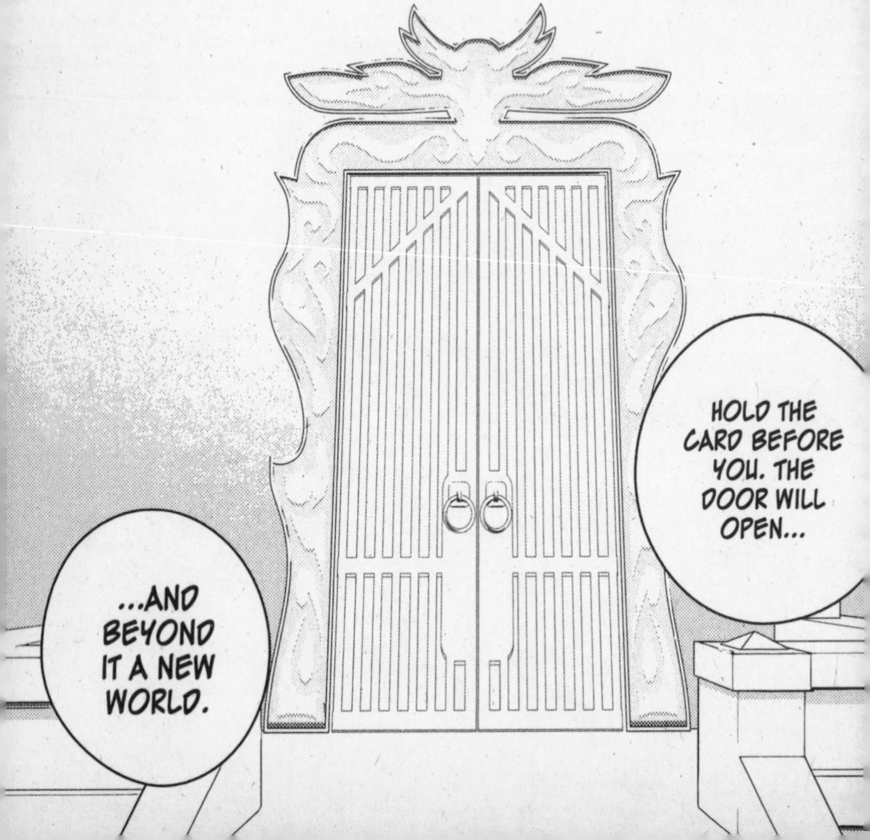
HOLD THE CARD BEFORE YOU. THE DOOR WILL OPEN...
...AND BEYOND IT A NEW WORLD.

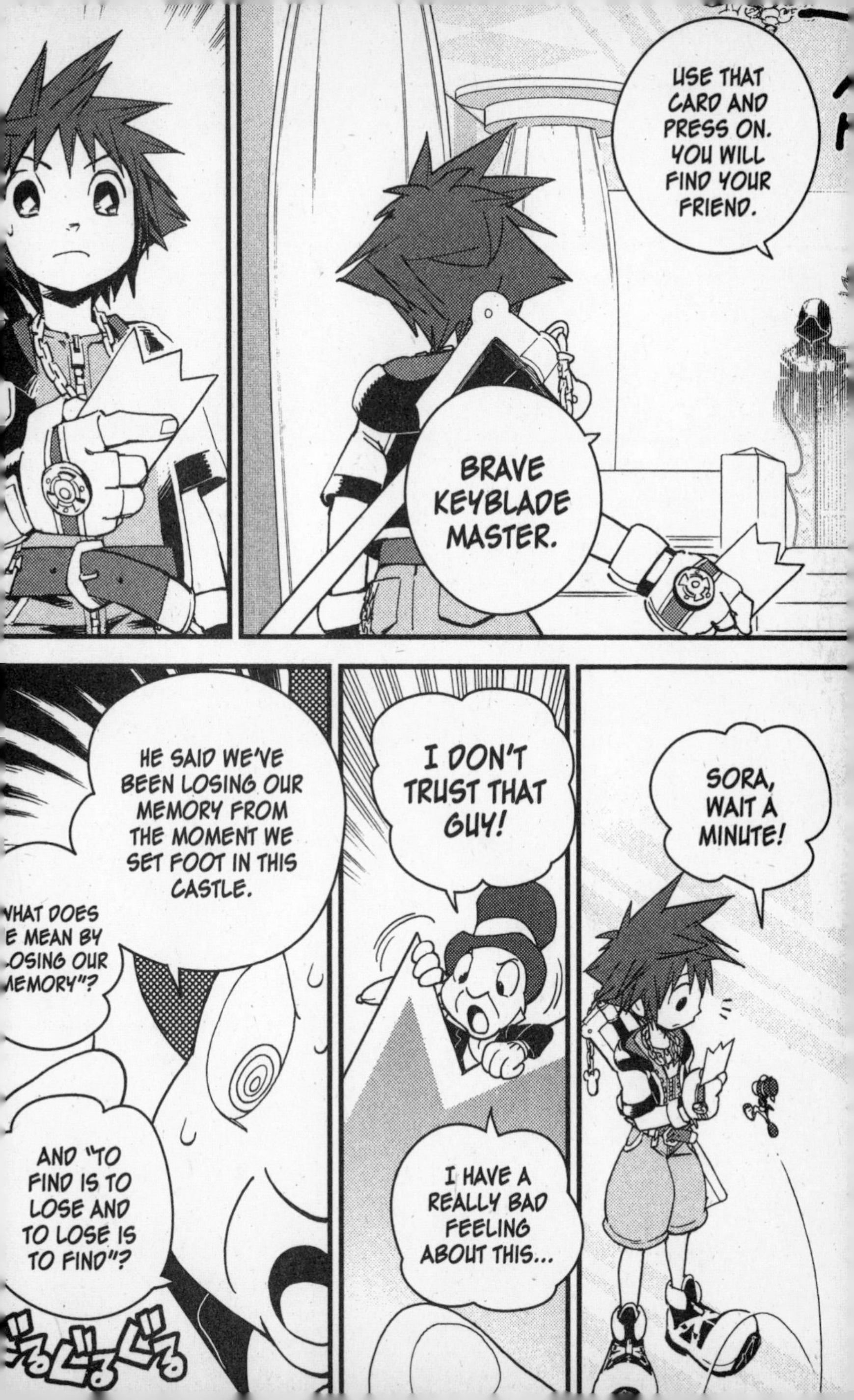
USE THAT CARD AND PRESS ON. YOU WILL FIND YOUR FRIEND.
BRAVE KEYBLADE MASTER.
SORA, WAIT A MINUTE!
I DON'T TRUST THAT GUY!
I HAVE A REALLY BAD FEELING ABOUT THIS...
HE SAID WE'VE BEEN LOSING OUR MEMORY FROM THE MOMENT WE SET FOOT IN THIS CASTLE.
VHAT DOES E MEAN BY OSING OUR IEMORY"?
AND "TO FIND IS TO LOSE AND TO LOSE IS TO FIND"?
ぐるぐるぐる

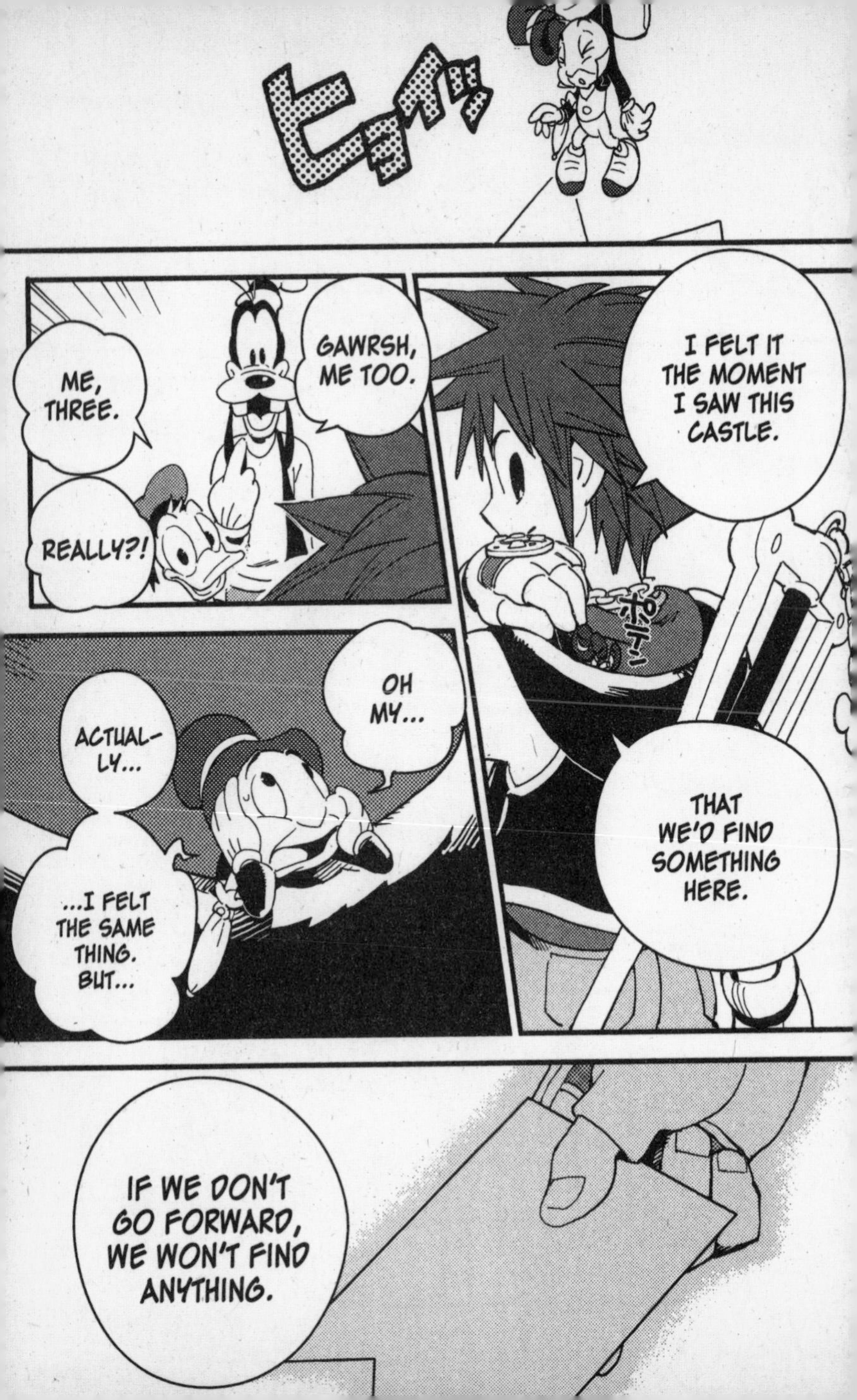
ヒョイッ
I FELT IT THE MOMENT I SAW THIS CASTLE.
THAT WE'D FIND SOMETHING HERE.
GAWRSH, ME TOO.
ME, THREE.
REALLY?!
OH MY...
ACTUAL-LY...
...I FELT THE SAME THING. BUT...
IF WE DON'T GO FORWARD, WE WON'T FIND ANYTHING.

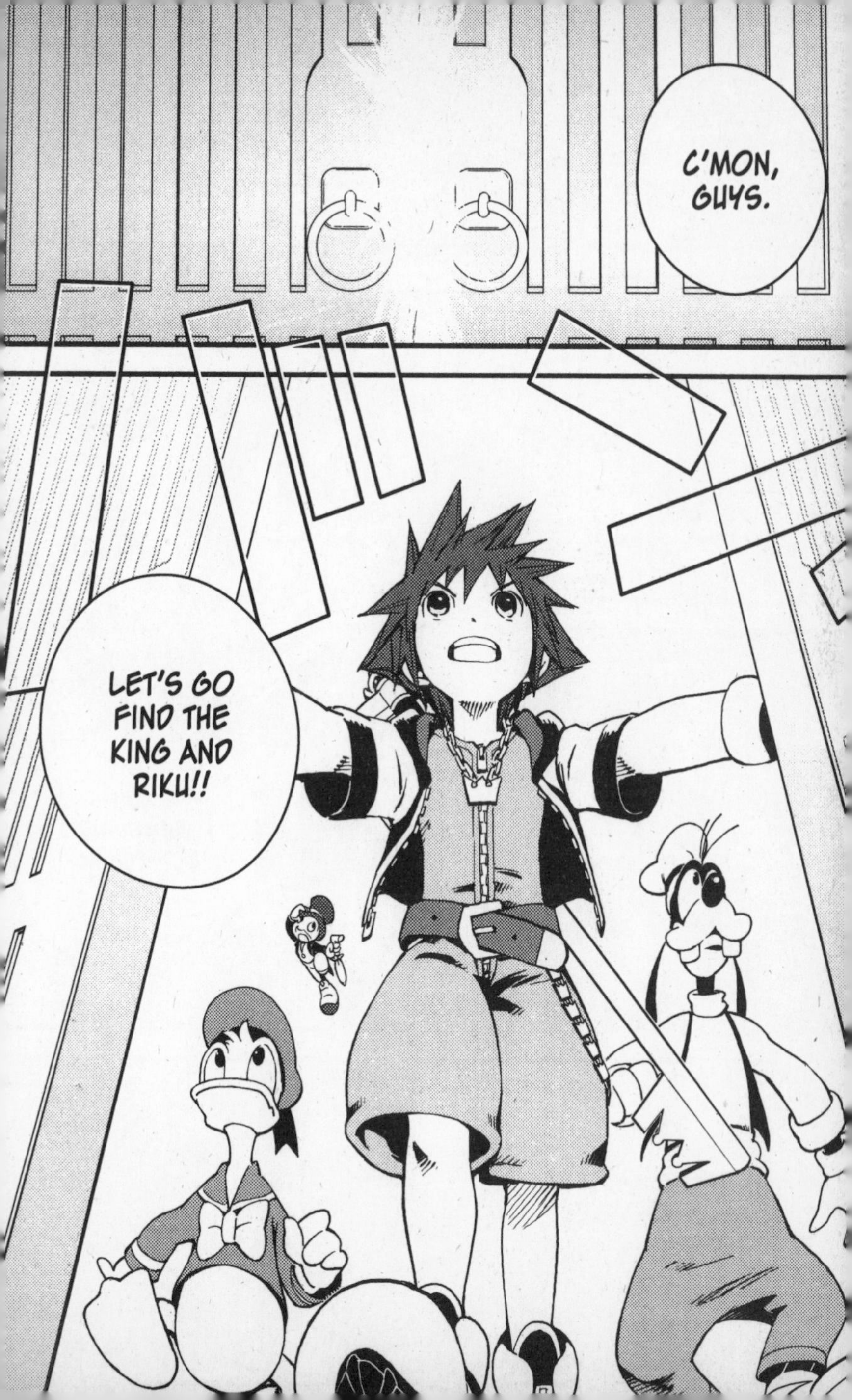
C'MON, GUYS.
LET'S GO FIND THE KING AND RIKU!!

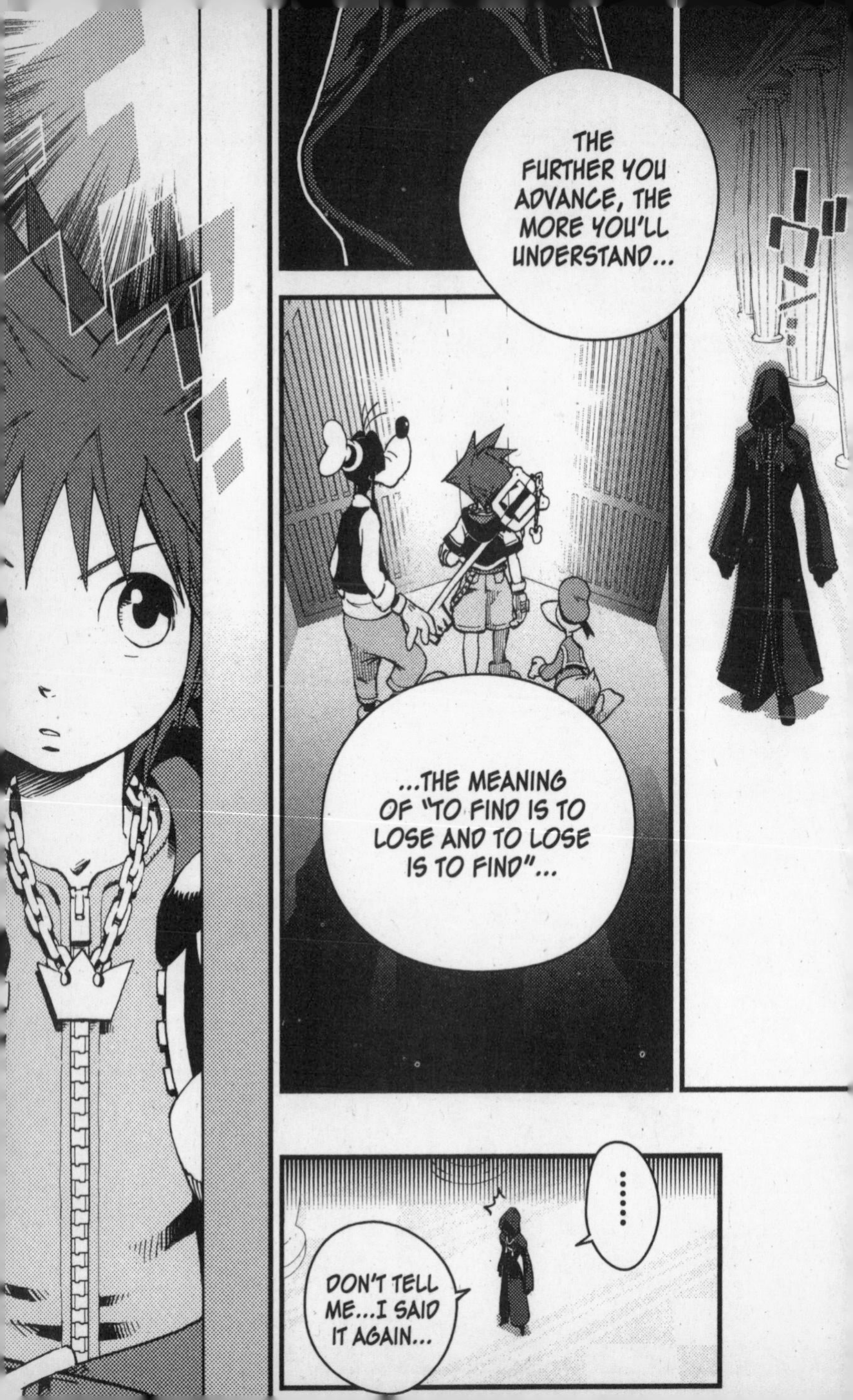
THE FURTHER YOU ADVANCE, THE MORE YOU'LL UNDERSTAND...
...THE MEANING OF "TO FIND IS TO LOSE AND TO LOSE IS TO FIND"...
......
DON'T TELL ME...I SAID IT AGAIN...

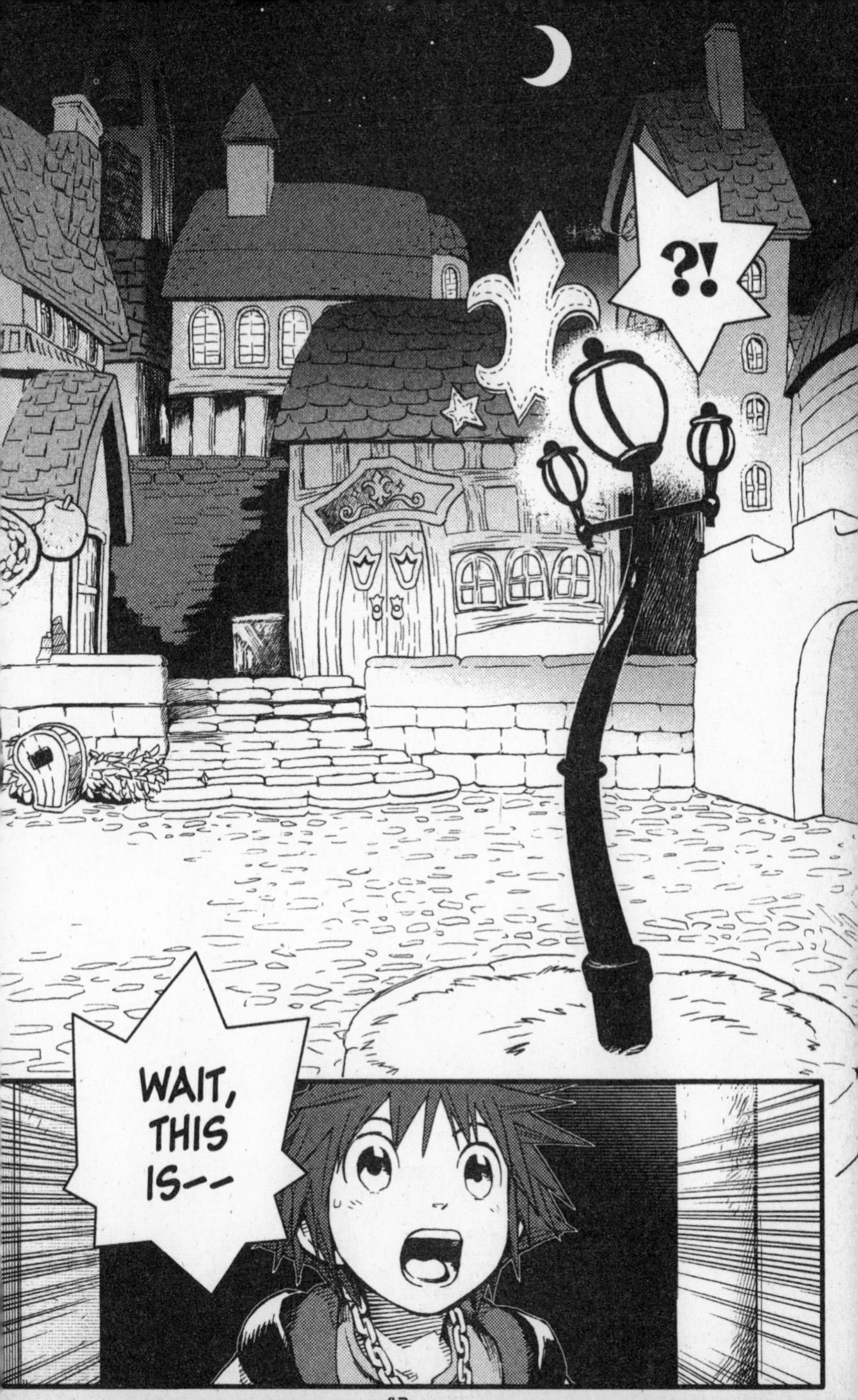
?!
WAIT, THIS IS--

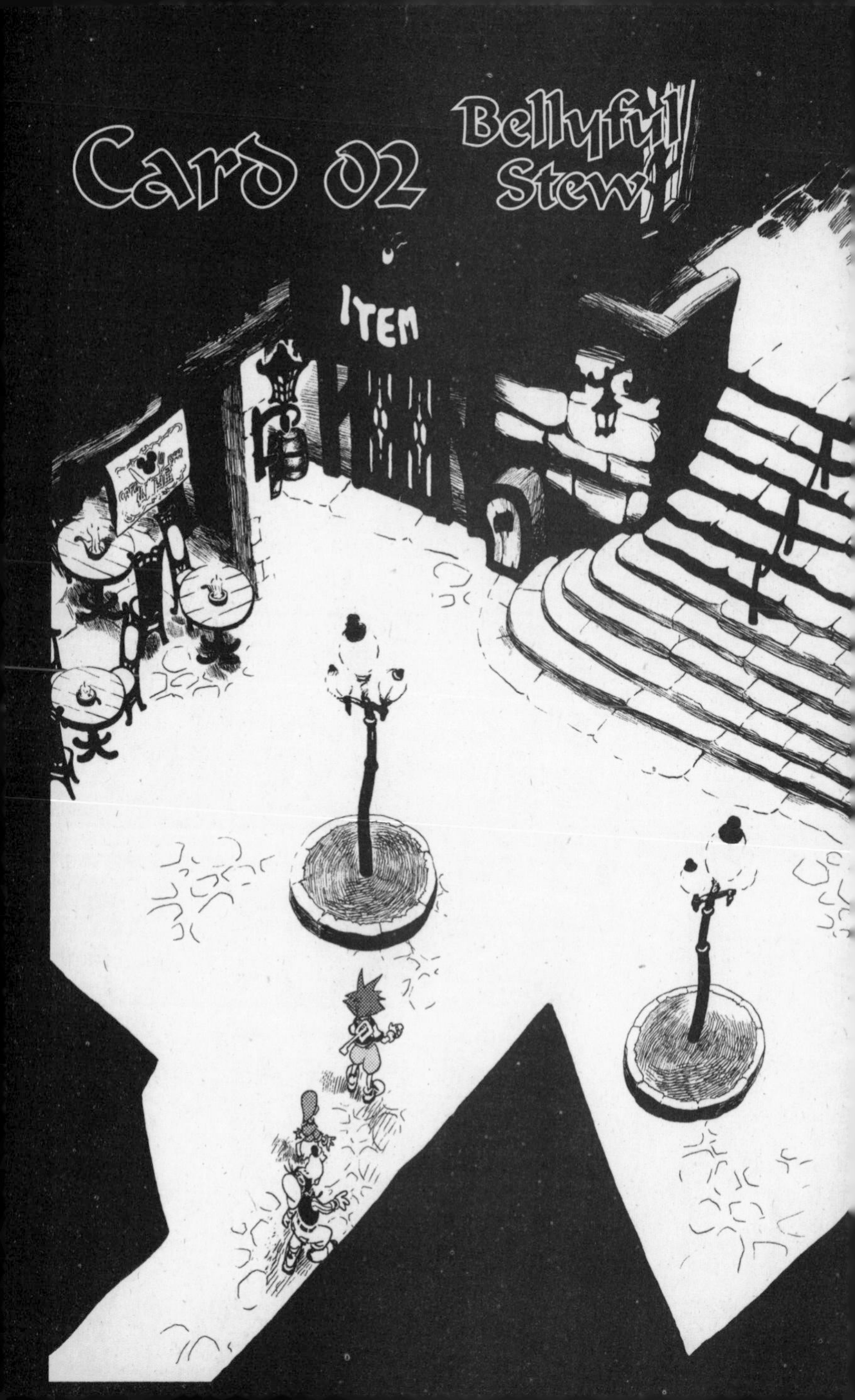
Card 02
Bellyfull Stew
ITEM

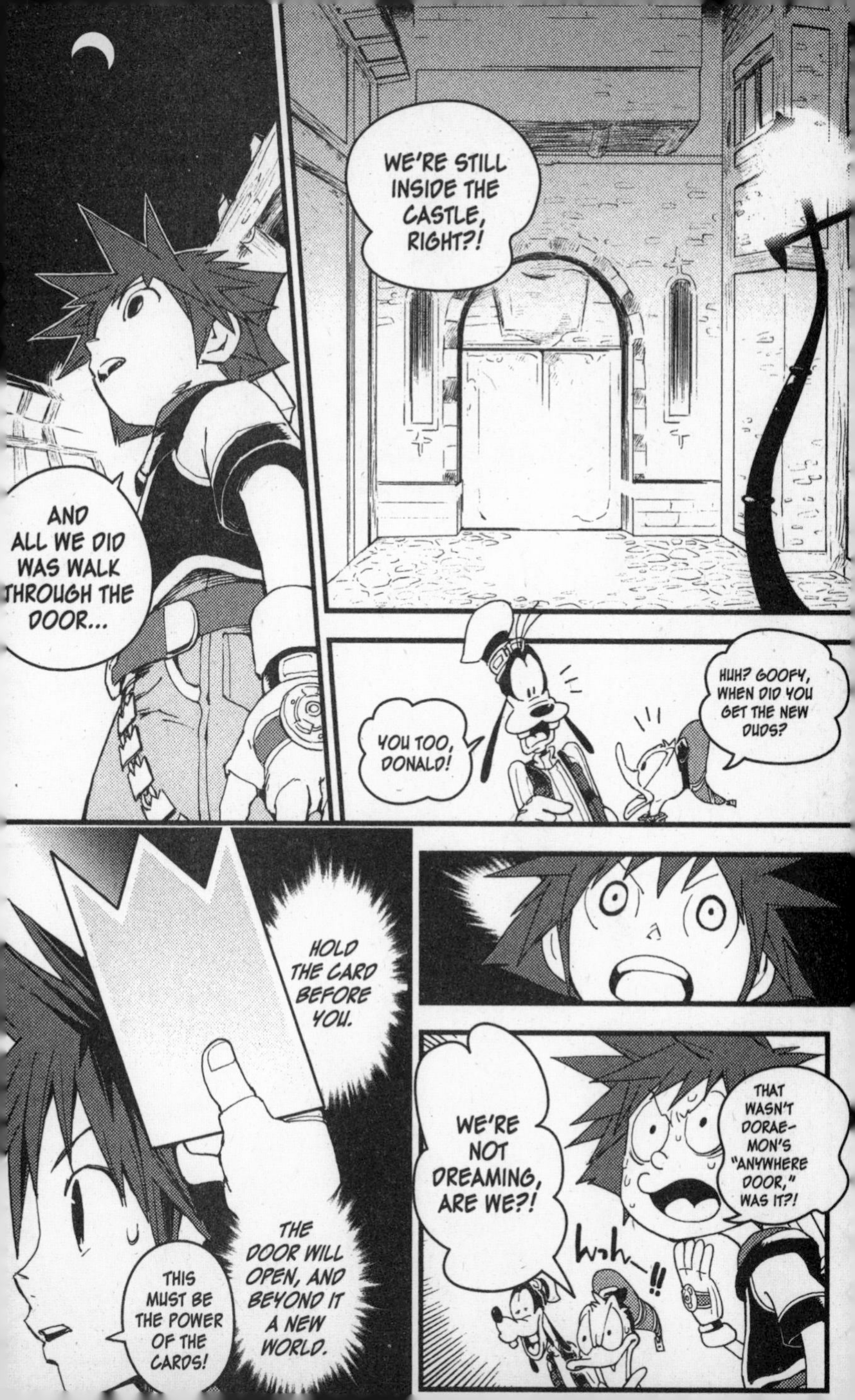
WE'RE STILL INSIDE THE CASTLE, RIGHT?!
HUH? GOOFY, WHEN DID YOU GET THE NEW DUDS?
YOU TOO, DONALD!
AND ALL WE DID WAS WALK THROUGH THE DOOR...
THAT WASN'T DORAEMON'S "ANYWHERE DOOR," WAS IT?!
WE'RE NOT DREAMING, ARE WE?!
Wah~!!
HOLD THE CARD BEFORE YOU.
THE DOOR WILL OPEN, AND BEYOND IT A NEW WORLD.
THIS MUST BE THE POWER OF THE CARDS!

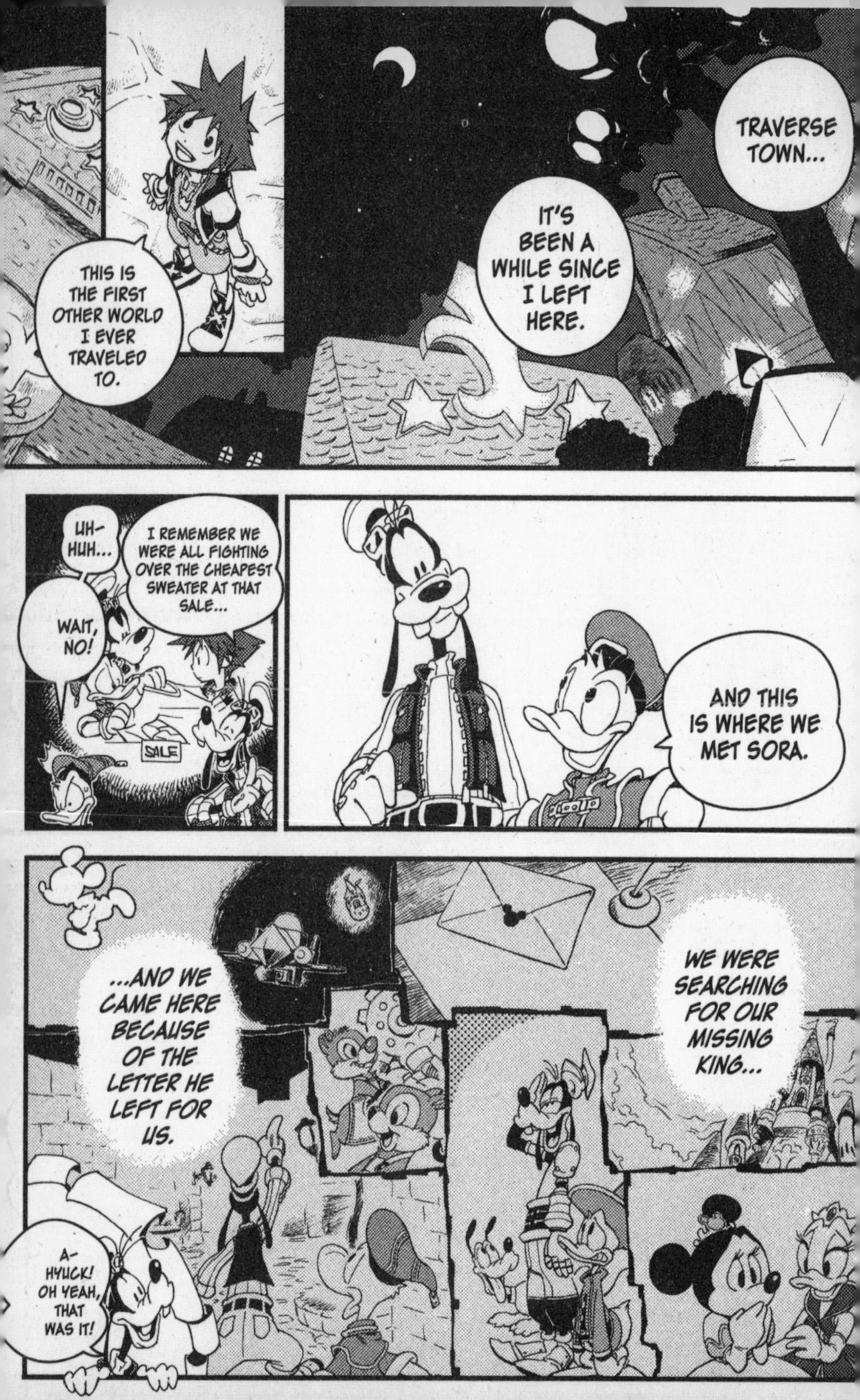
TRAVERSE TOWN...
IT'S BEEN A WHILE SINCE I LEFT HERE.
THIS IS THE FIRST OTHER WORLD I EVER TRAVELED TO.
AND THIS IS WHERE WE MET SORA.
I REMEMBER WE WERE ALL FIGHTING OVER THE CHEAPEST SWEATER AT THAT SALE...
UH-HUH...
WAIT, NO!
SALE
WE WERE SEARCHING FOR OUR MISSING KING...
...AND WE CAME HERE BECAUSE OF THE LETTER HE LEFT FOR US.
A-HYUCK! OH YEAH, THAT WAS IT!

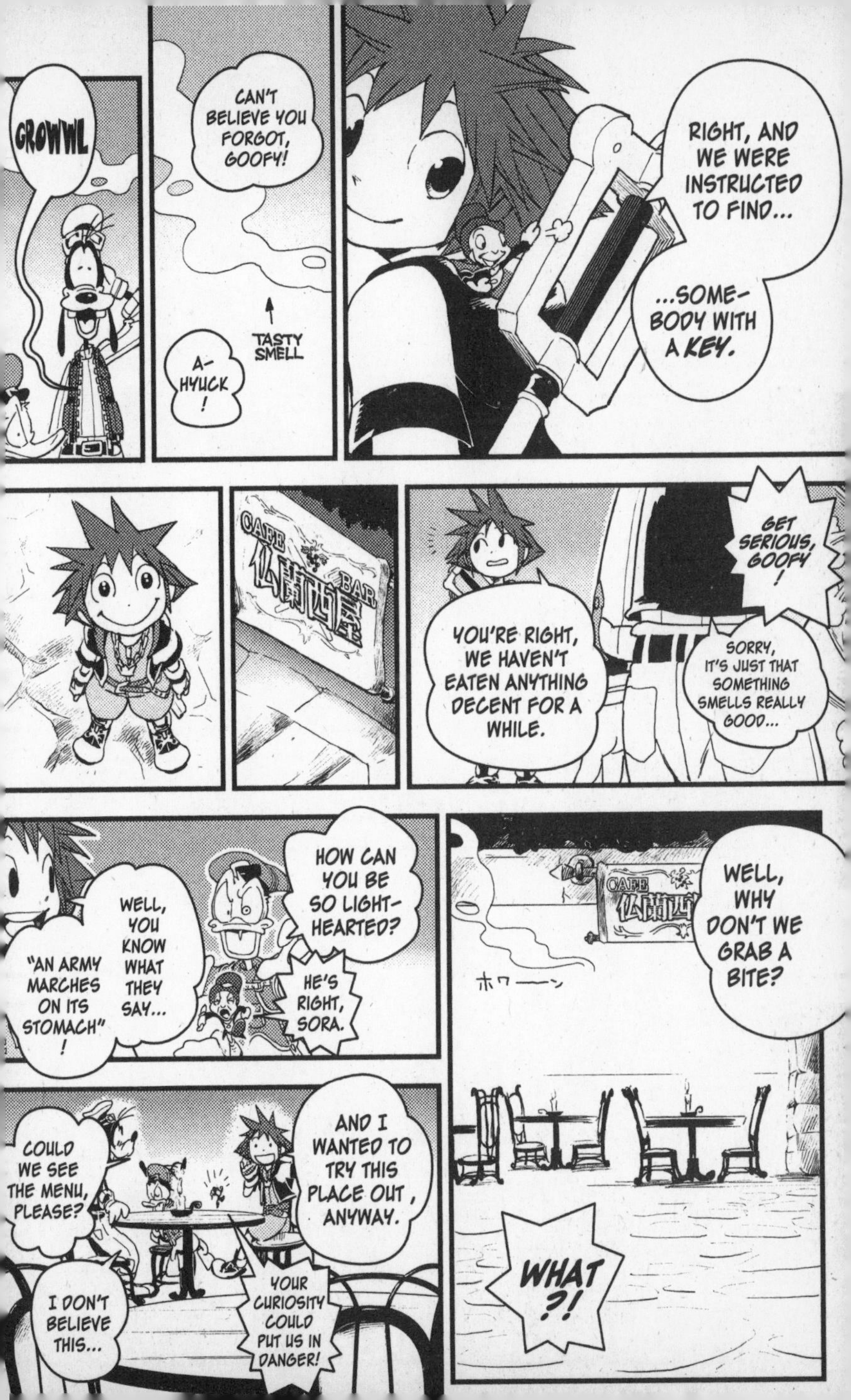
RIGHT, AND WE WERE INSTRUCTED TO FIND...
...SOME-BODY WITH A KEY.
CAN'T BELIEVE YOU FORGOT, GOOFY!
TASTY SMELL
A-HYUCK!
GROWWL
GET SERIOUS, GOOFY!
SORRY, IT'S JUST THAT SOMETHING SMELLS REALLY GOOD...
YOU'RE RIGHT, WE HAVEN'T EATEN ANYTHING DECENT FOR A WHILE.
CAFE 仏蘭西屋 BAR
WELL, WHY DON'T WE GRAB A BITE?
ホワーーン
WHAT?!
HOW CAN YOU BE SO LIGHT-HEARTED?
HE'S RIGHT, SORA.
WELL, YOU KNOW WHAT THEY SAY...
"AN ARMY MARCHES ON ITS STOMACH"!
AND I WANTED TO TRY THIS PLACE OUT, ANYWAY.
YOUR CURIOSITY COULD PUT US IN DANGER!
COULD WE SEE THE MENU, PLEASE?
I DON'T BELIEVE THIS...

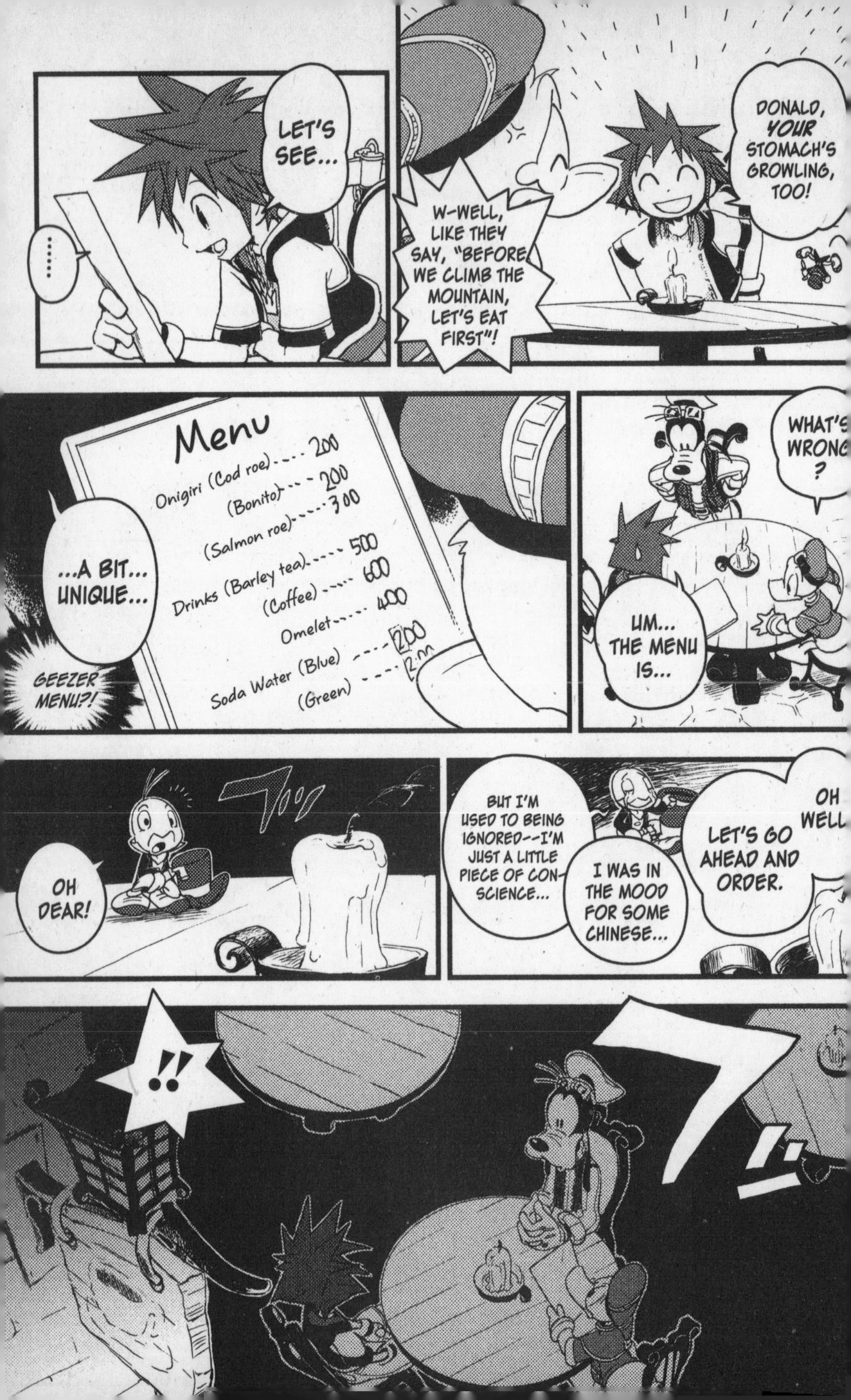
DONALD, YOUR STOMACH'S GROWLING, TOO!
W-WELL, LIKE THEY SAY, "BEFORE WE CLIMB THE MOUNTAIN, LET'S EAT FIRST"!
LET'S SEE...
......
WHAT'S WRONG?
UM... THE MENU IS...
Menu
Onigiri (Cod roe) ---- 200
(Bonito) ---- 200
(Salmon roe) ---- 300
Drinks (Barley tea) ---- 500
(Coffee) ---- 600
Omelet ---- 400
Soda Water (Blue) ---- 200
(Green)
...A BIT... UNIQUE...
GEEZER MENU?!
OH WELL
LET'S GO AHEAD AND ORDER.
I WAS IN THE MOOD FOR SOME CHINESE...
BUT I'M USED TO BEING IGNORED--I'M JUST A LITTLE PIECE OF CONSCIENCE...
OH DEAR!
!!

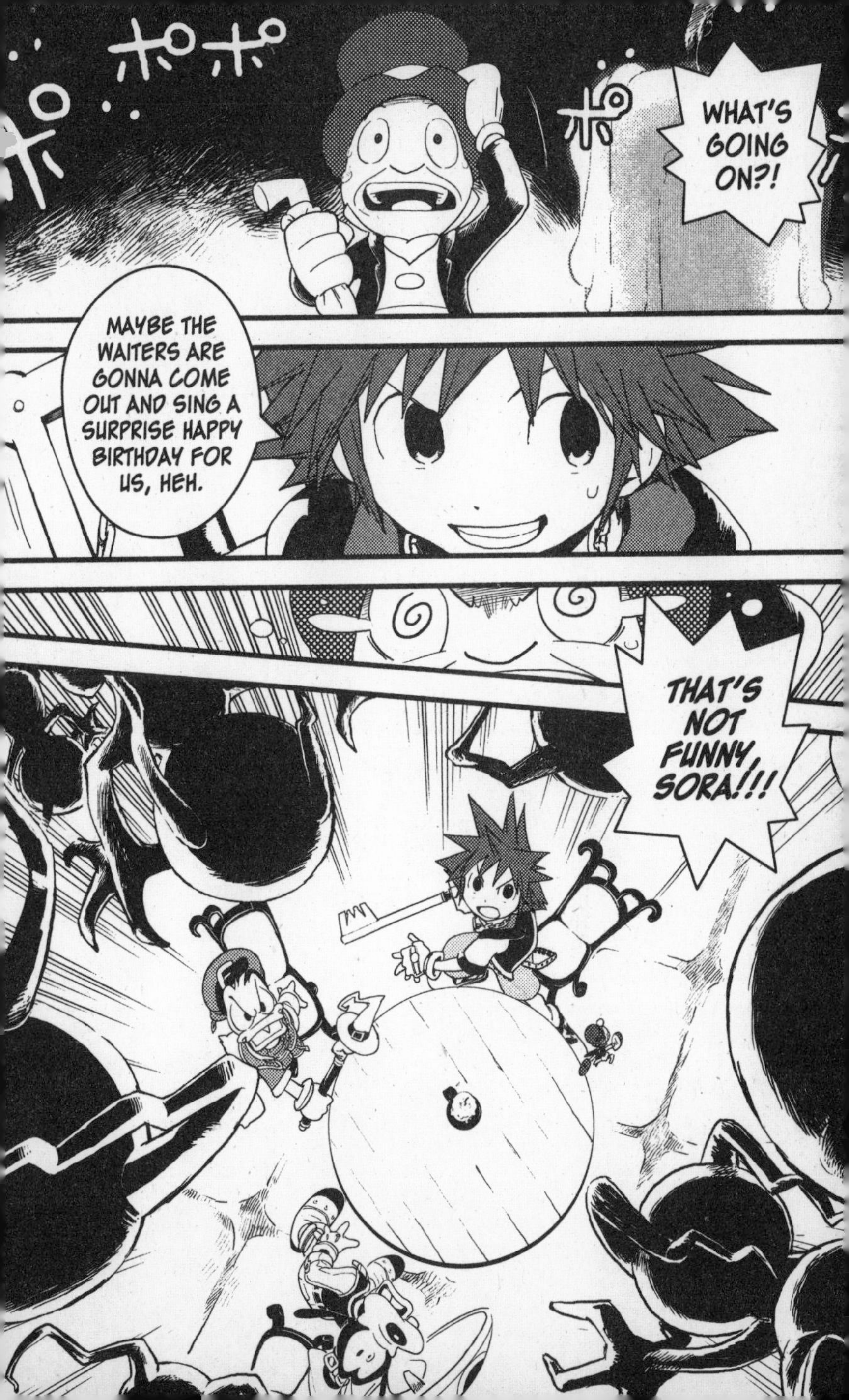
WHAT'S GOING ON?!
ポ
ポポポ
MAYBE THE WAITERS ARE GONNA COME OUT AND SING A SURPRISE HAPPY BIRTHDAY FOR US, HEH.
THAT'S NOT FUNNY, SORA!!!

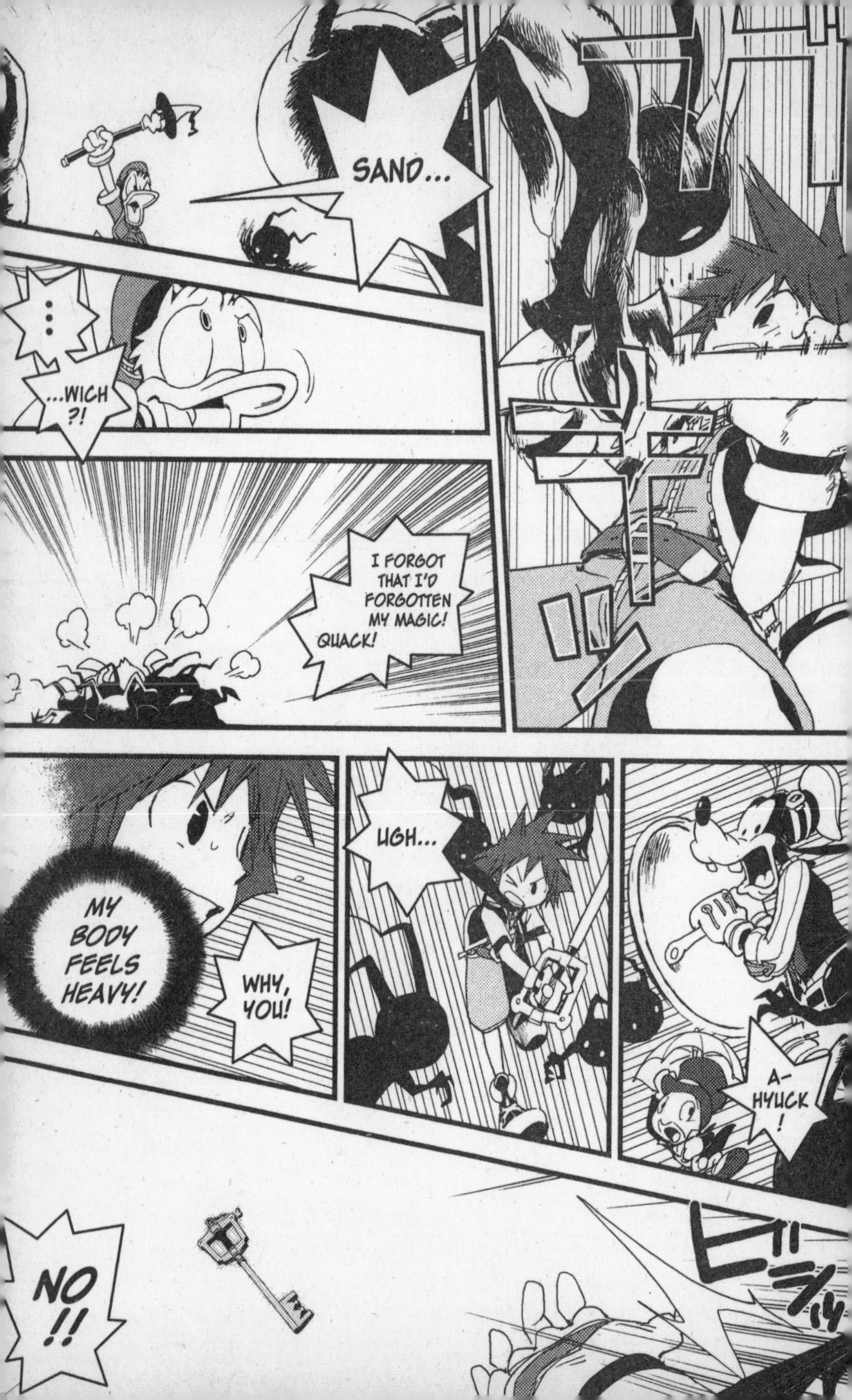
SAND...
...
...WICH ?!
I FORGOT THAT I'D FORGOTTEN MY MAGIC!
QUACK!
A-HYUCK!
UGH...
MY BODY FEELS HEAVY!
WHY, YOU!
NO!!

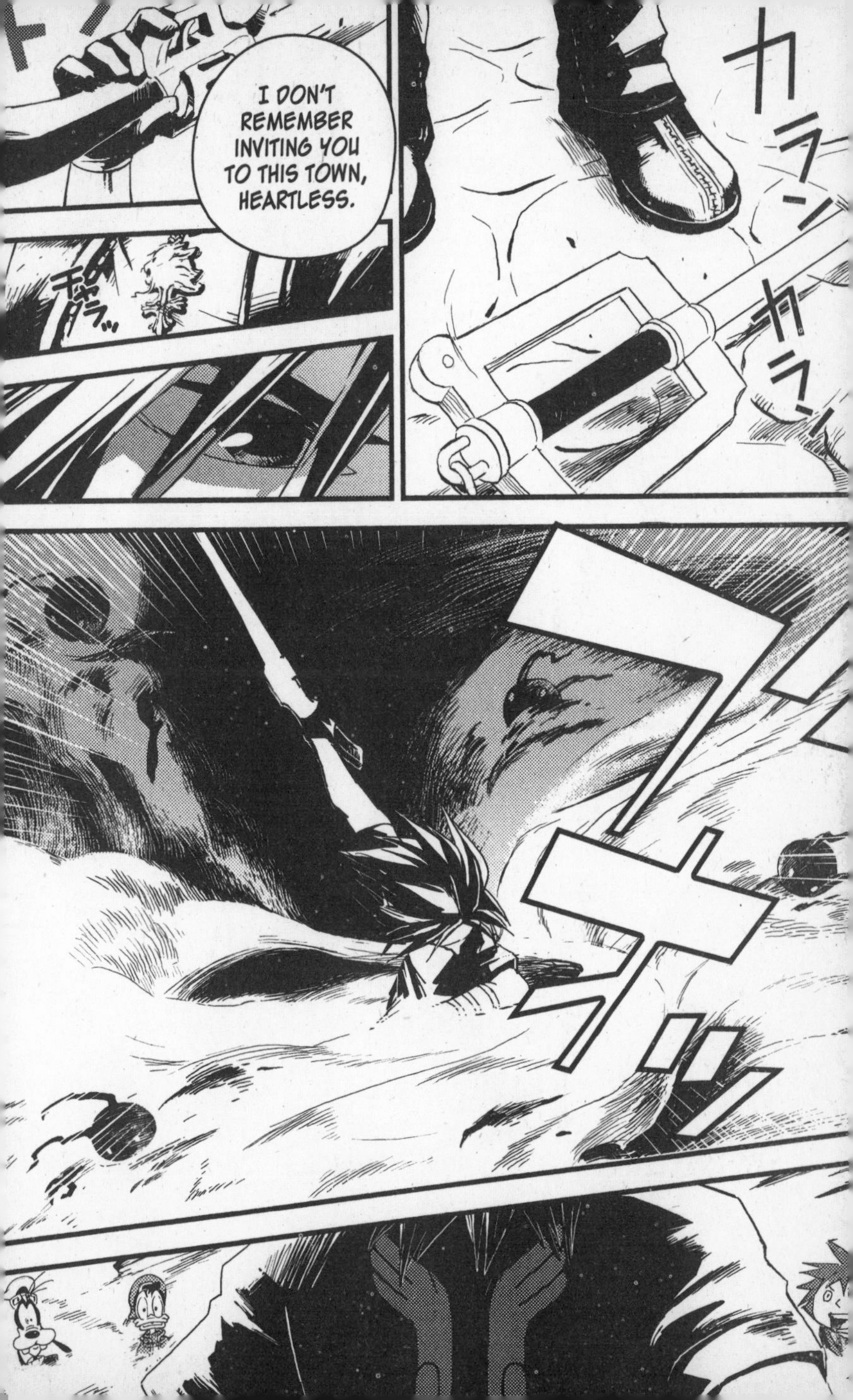
I DON'T REMEMBER INVITING YOU TO THIS TOWN, HEARTLESS.
カランカラン
チャラッ

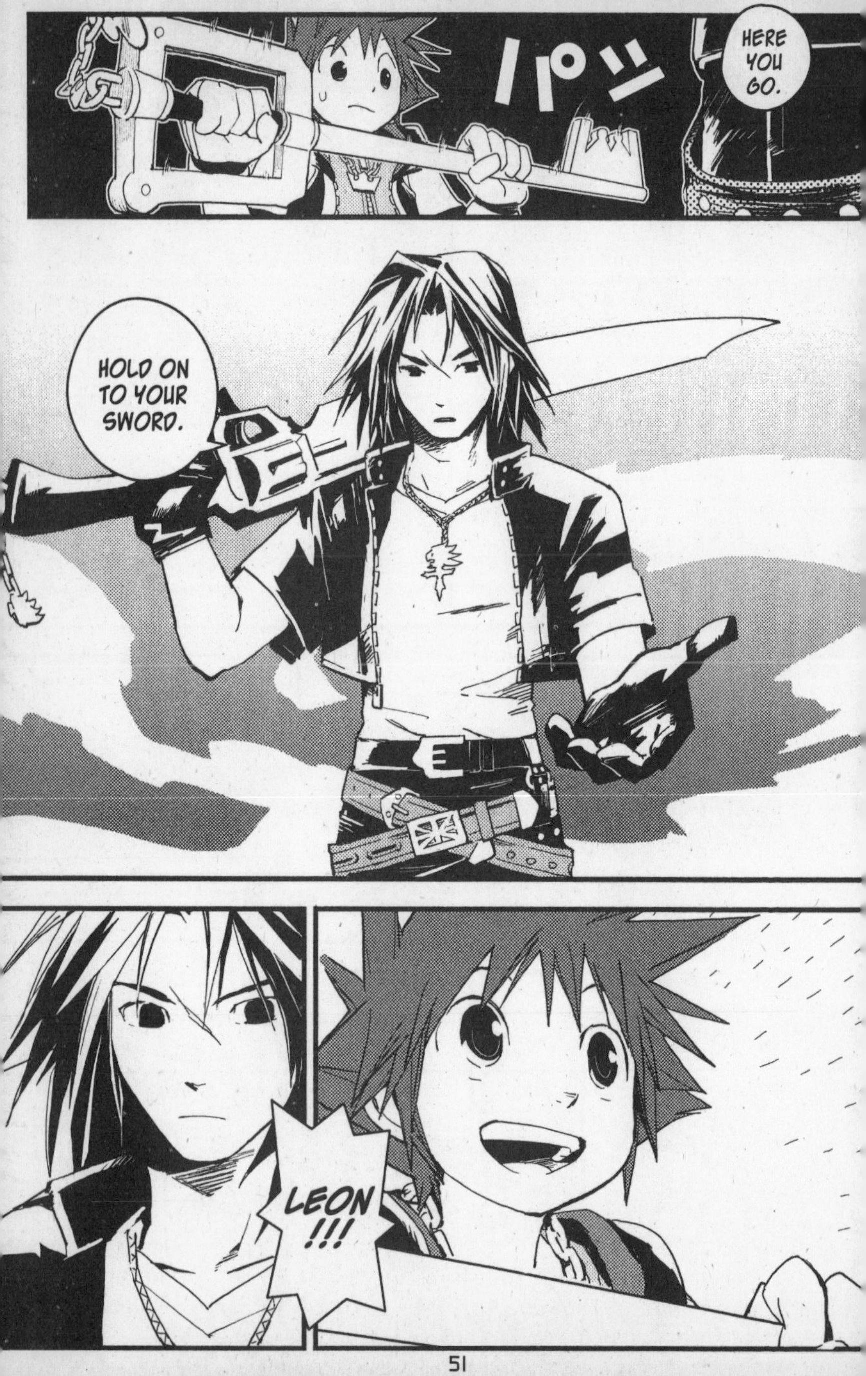
HERE YOU GO.
パッ
HOLD ON TO YOUR SWORD.
LEON !!!

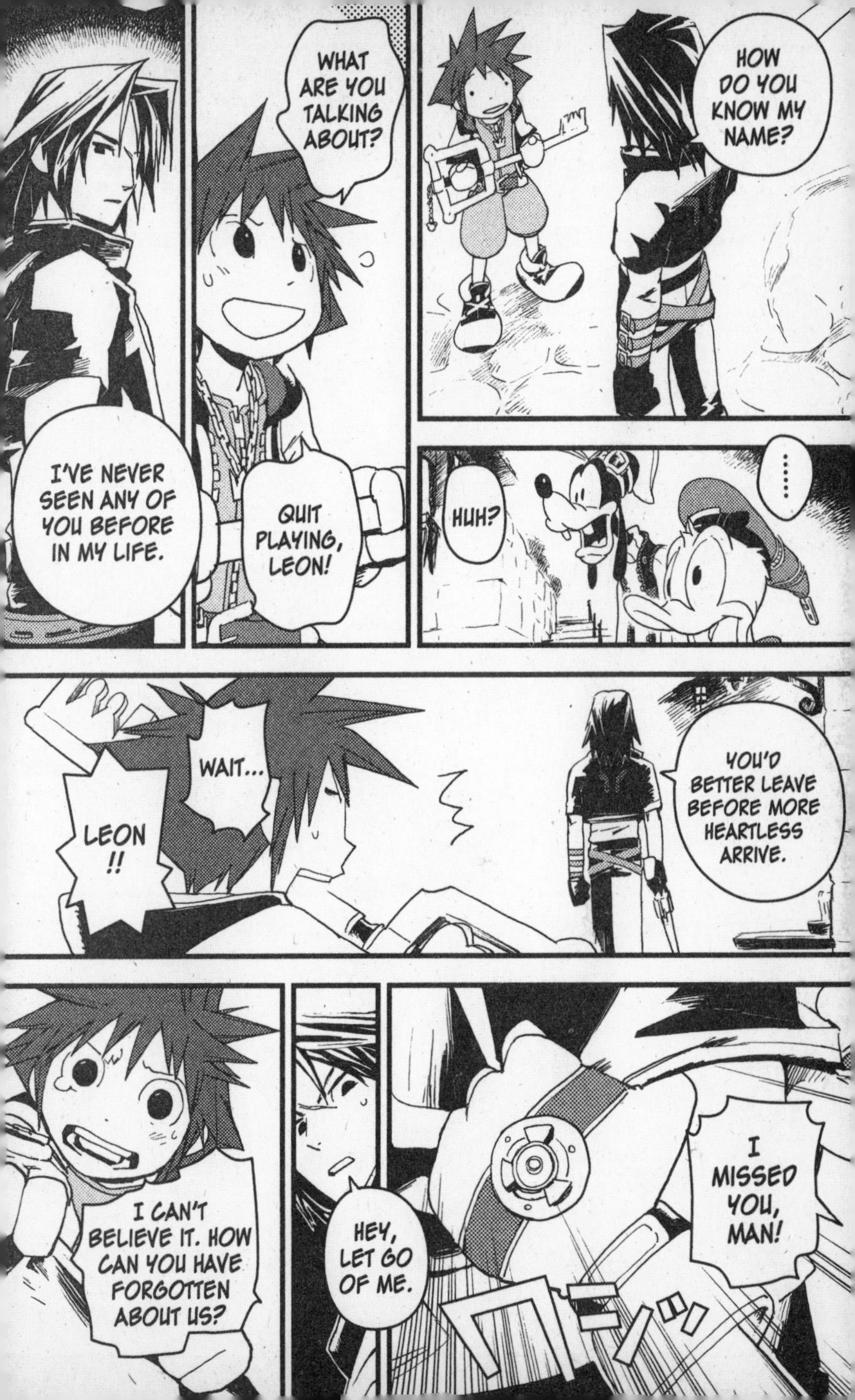
HOW DO YOU KNOW MY NAME?
......
HUH?
WHAT ARE YOU TALKING ABOUT?
QUIT PLAYING, LEON!
I'VE NEVER SEEN ANY OF YOU BEFORE IN MY LIFE.
YOU'D BETTER LEAVE BEFORE MORE HEARTLESS ARRIVE.
WAIT...
LEON !!
I MISSED YOU, MAN!
HEY, LET GO OF ME.
I CAN'T BELIEVE IT. HOW CAN YOU HAVE FORGOTTEN ABOUT US?

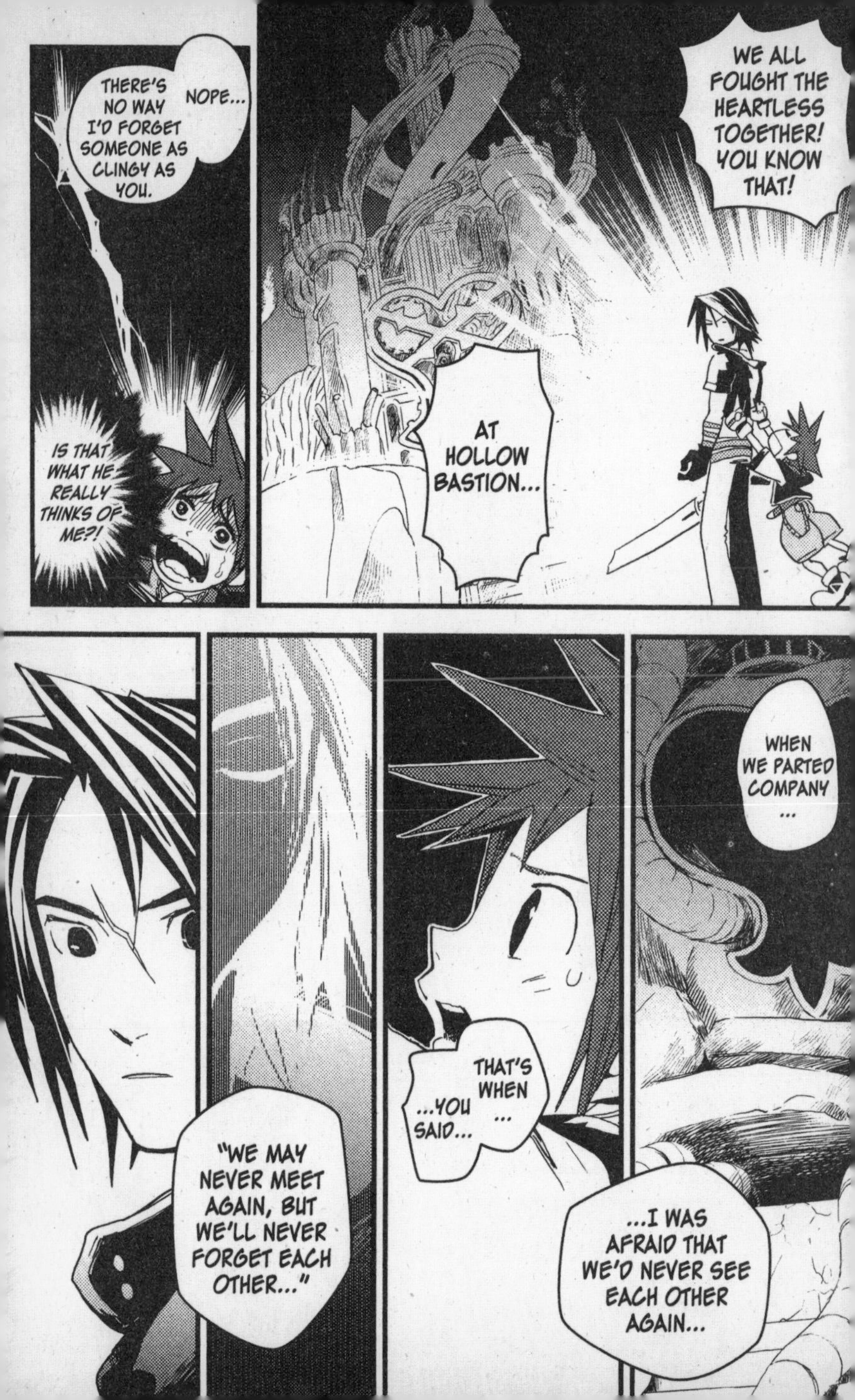
WE ALL FOUGHT THE HEARTLESS TOGETHER! YOU KNOW THAT!
AT HOLLOW BASTION...
NOPE...
THERE'S NO WAY I'D FORGET SOMEONE AS CLINGY AS YOU.
IS THAT WHAT HE REALLY THINKS OF ME?!
WHEN WE PARTED COMPANY ...
...I WAS AFRAID THAT WE'D NEVER SEE EACH OTHER AGAIN...
THAT'S WHEN ...
...YOU SAID...
"WE MAY NEVER MEET AGAIN, BUT WE'LL NEVER FORGET EACH OTHER..."

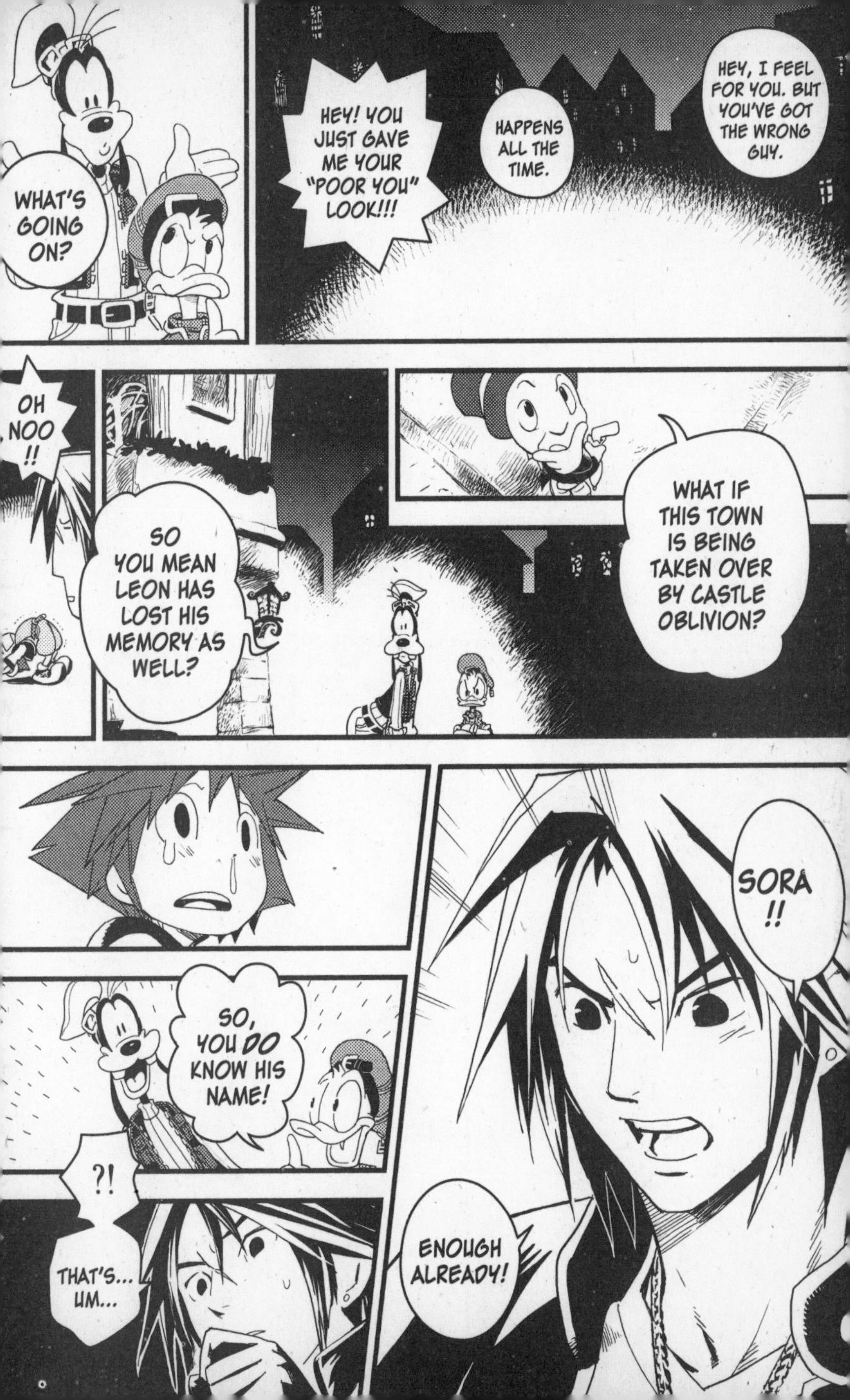
HEY, I FEEL FOR YOU. BUT YOU'VE GOT THE WRONG GUY.
HAPPENS ALL THE TIME.
HEY! YOU JUST GAVE ME YOUR "POOR YOU" LOOK!!!
WHAT'S GOING ON?
WHAT IF THIS TOWN IS BEING TAKEN OVER BY CASTLE OBLIVION?
SO YOU MEAN LEON HAS LOST HIS MEMORY AS WELL?
OH NOO !!
SORA !!
ENOUGH ALREADY!
SO, YOU DO KNOW HIS NAME!
?!
THAT'S... UM...

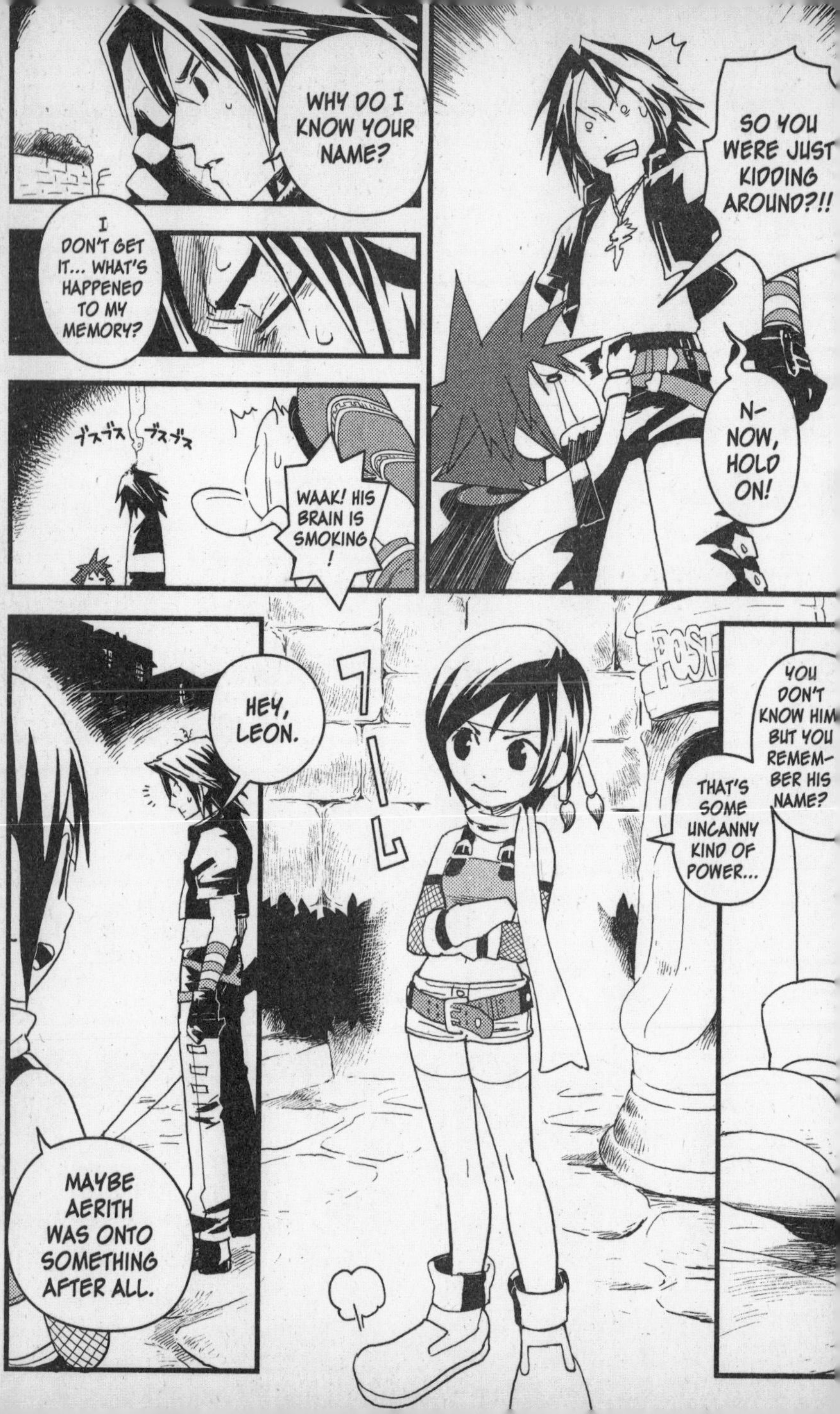
SO YOU WERE JUST KIDDING AROUND?!!
N-NOW, HOLD ON!
WHY DO I KNOW YOUR NAME?
I DON'T GET IT... WHAT'S HAPPENED TO MY MEMORY?
ブスブス ブスブス
WAAK! HIS BRAIN IS SMOKING!
YOU DON'T KNOW HIM BUT YOU REMEMBER HIS NAME?
THAT'S SOME UNCANNY KIND OF POWER...
HEY, LEON.
MAYBE AERITH WAS ONTO SOMETHING AFTER ALL.

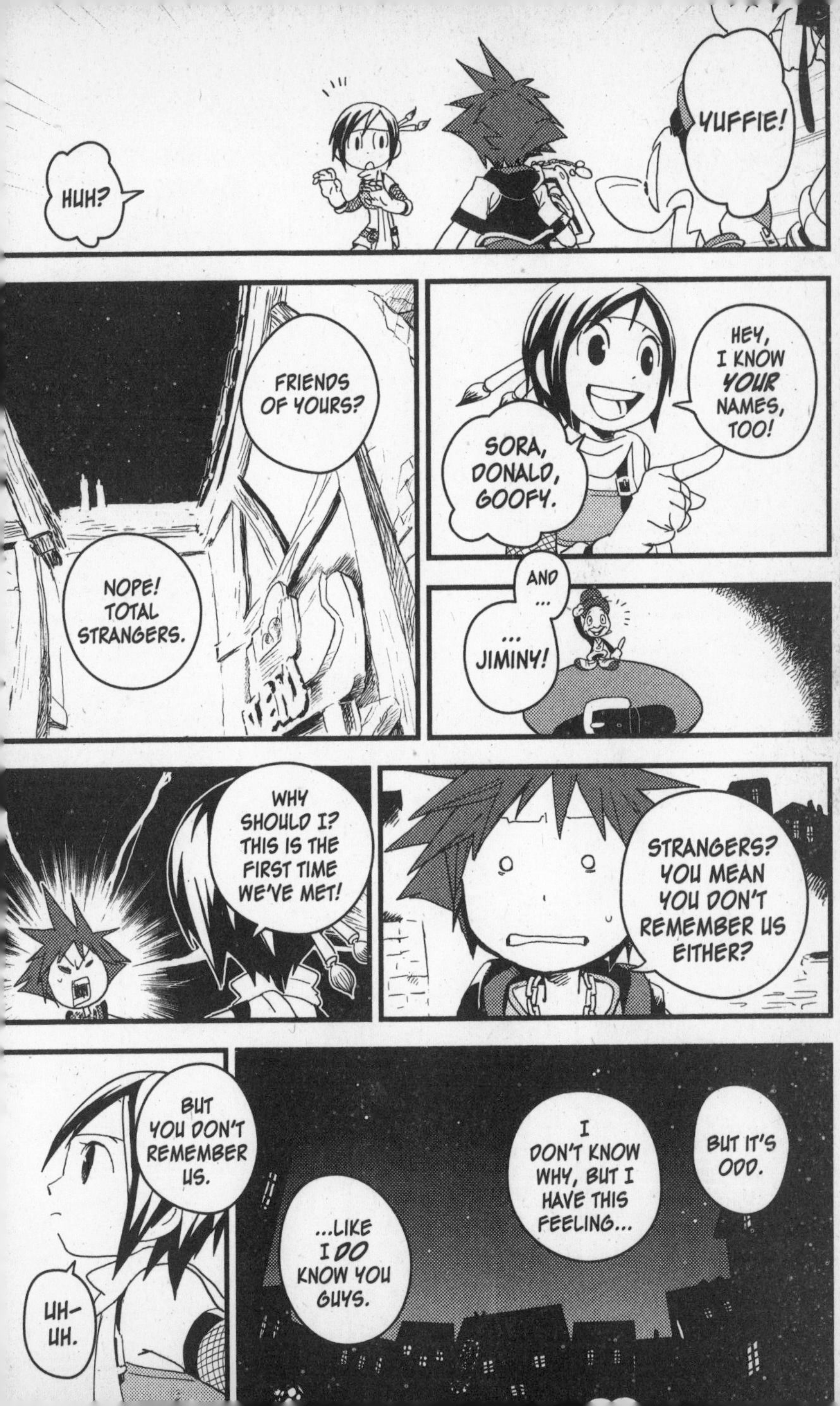
YUFFIE!
HUH?
HEY, I KNOW *YOUR* NAMES, TOO!
SORA, DONALD, GOOFY.
AND ...
... JIMINY!
FRIENDS OF YOURS?
NOPE! TOTAL STRANGERS.
STRANGERS? YOU MEAN YOU DON'T REMEMBER US EITHER?
WHY SHOULD I? THIS IS THE FIRST TIME WE'VE MET!
BUT IT'S ODD.
I DON'T KNOW WHY, BUT I HAVE THIS FEELING...
...LIKE I *DO* KNOW YOU GUYS.
BUT YOU DON'T REMEMBER US.
UH-UH.

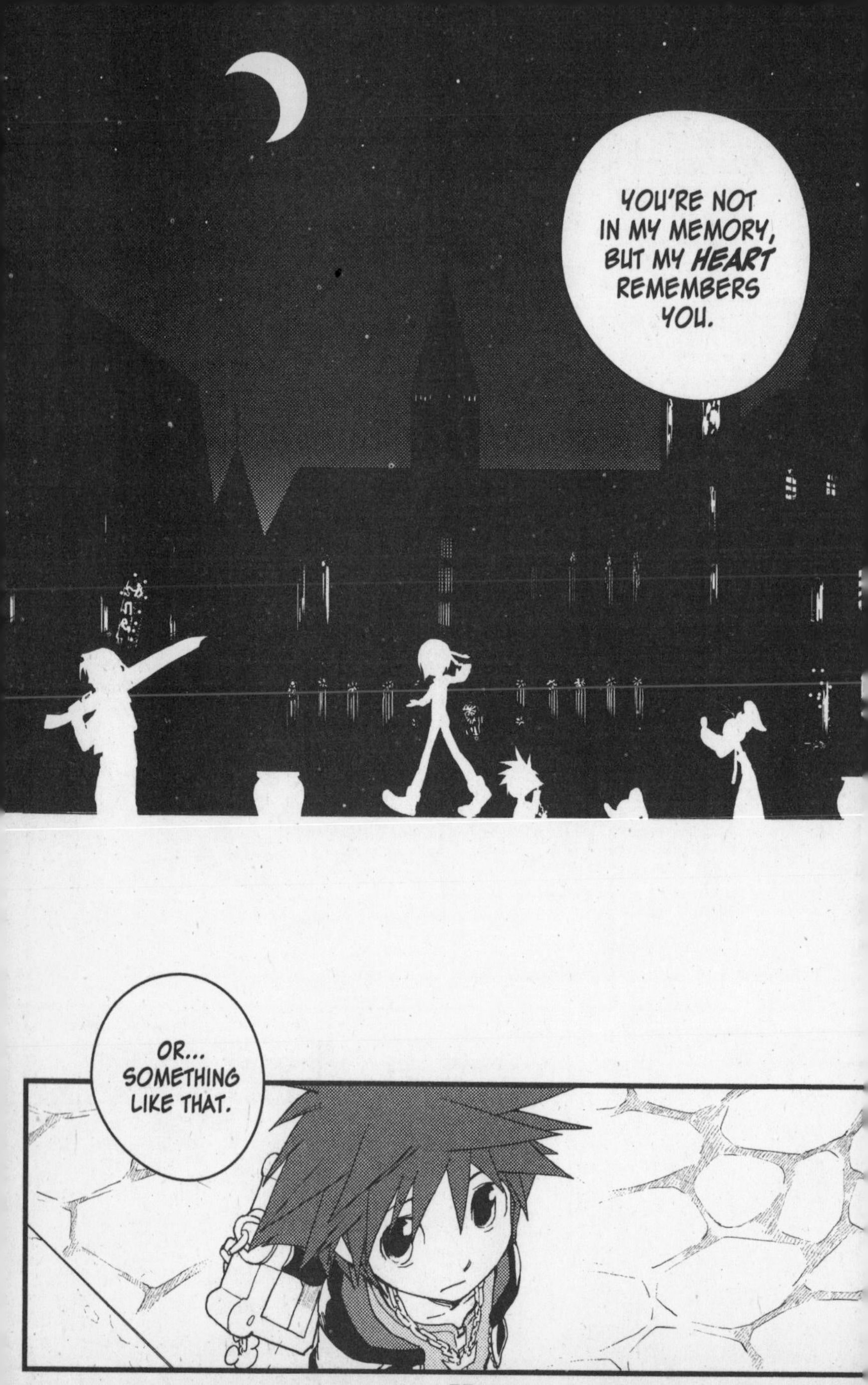
YOU'RE NOT IN MY MEMORY, BUT MY HEART REMEMBERS YOU.
OR... SOMETHING LIKE THAT.

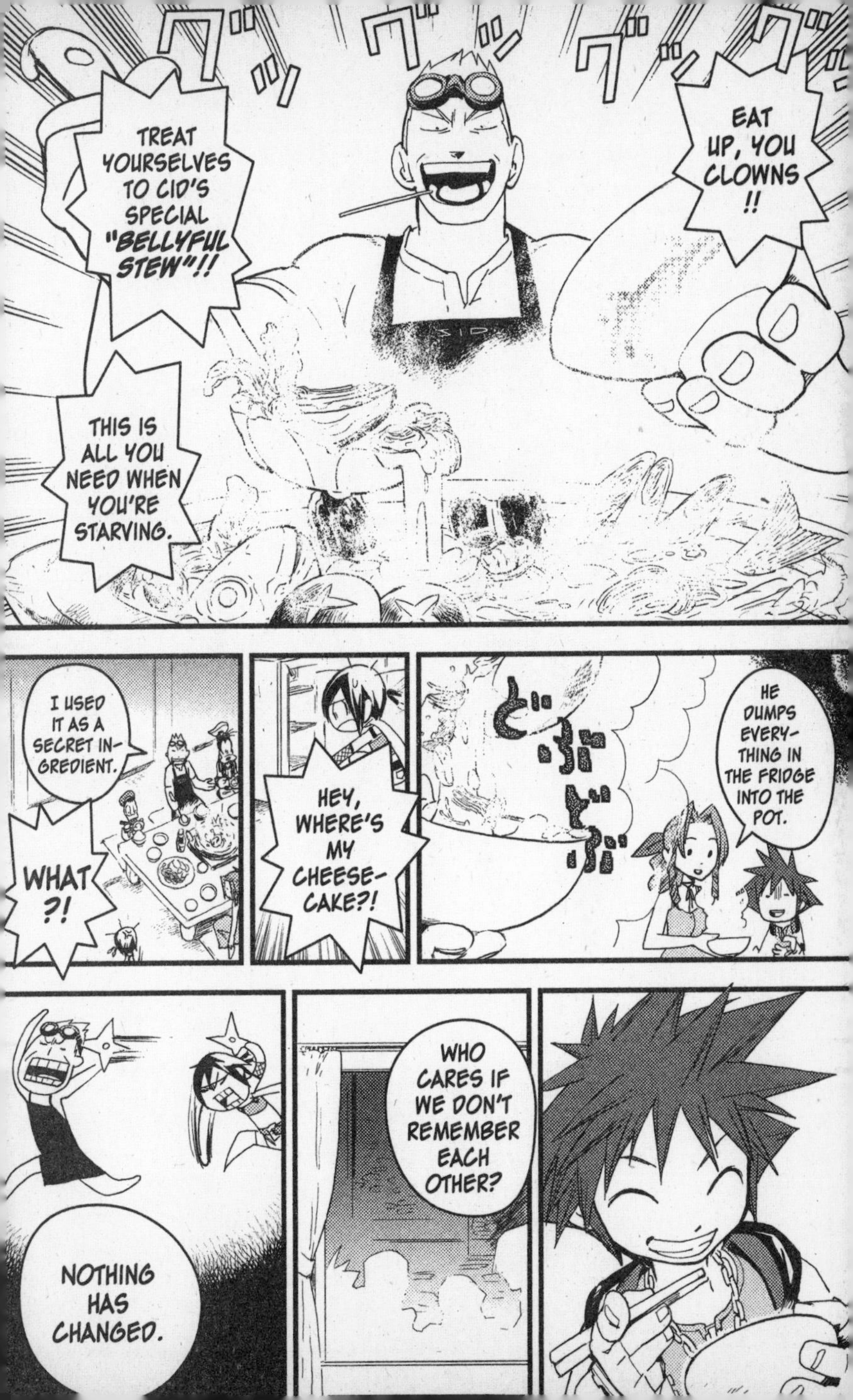
EAT UP, YOU CLOWNS!!
TREAT YOURSELVES TO CID'S SPECIAL "BELLYFUL STEW"!!
THIS IS ALL YOU NEED WHEN YOU'RE STARVING.
HE DUMPS EVERY-THING IN THE FRIDGE INTO THE POT.
HEY, WHERE'S MY CHEESE-CAKE?!
I USED IT AS A SECRET IN-GREDIENT.
WHAT?!
WHO CARES IF WE DON'T REMEMBER EACH OTHER?
NOTHING HAS CHANGED.

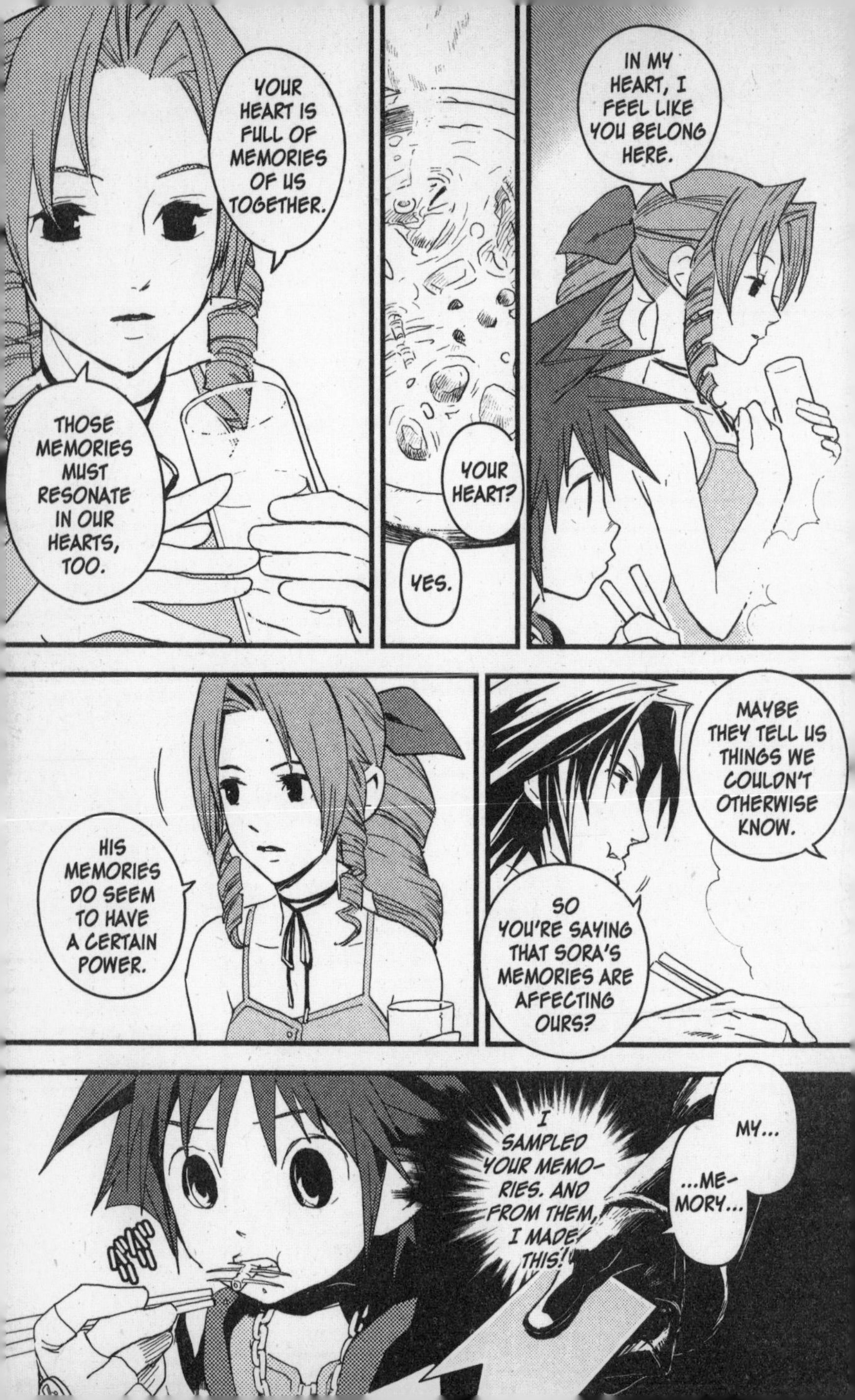
IN MY HEART, I FEEL LIKE YOU BELONG HERE.
YOUR HEART?
YES.
YOUR HEART IS FULL OF MEMORIES OF US TOGETHER.
THOSE MEMORIES MUST RESONATE IN OUR HEARTS, TOO.
MAYBE THEY TELL US THINGS WE COULDN'T OTHERWISE KNOW.
SO YOU'RE SAYING THAT SORA'S MEMORIES ARE AFFECTING OURS?
HIS MEMORIES DO SEEM TO HAVE A CERTAIN POWER.
MY...
...ME-MORY...
I SAMPLED YOUR MEMO-RIES. AND FROM THEM, I MADE THIS!

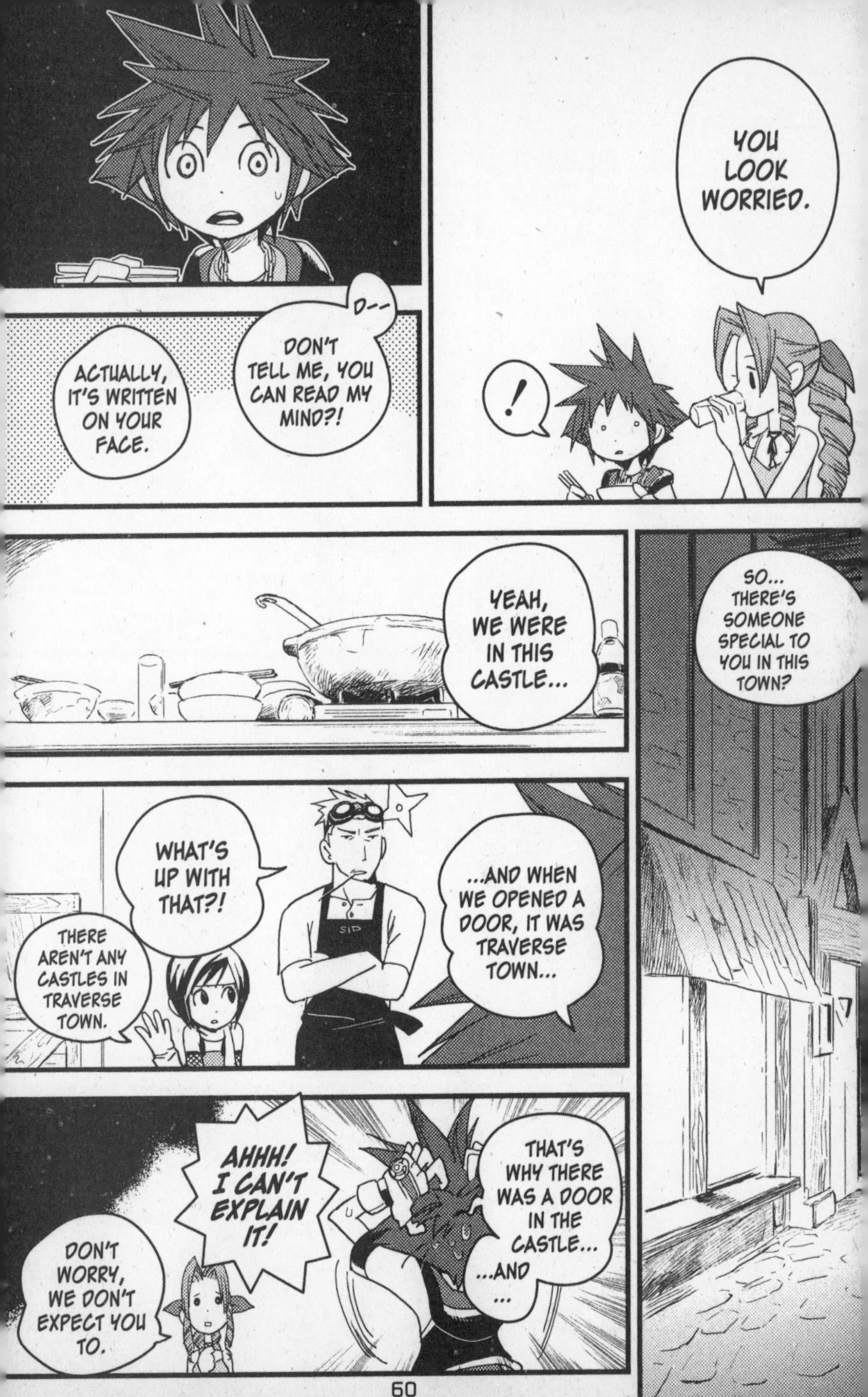
YOU LOOK WORRIED.
!
D--
DON'T TELL ME, YOU CAN READ MY MIND?!
ACTUALLY, IT'S WRITTEN ON YOUR FACE.
SO... THERE'S SOMEONE SPECIAL TO YOU IN THIS TOWN?
YEAH, WE WERE IN THIS CASTLE...
...AND WHEN WE OPENED A DOOR, IT WAS TRAVERSE TOWN...
WHAT'S UP WITH THAT?!
THERE AREN'T ANY CASTLES IN TRAVERSE TOWN.
THAT'S WHY THERE WAS A DOOR IN THE CASTLE...
...AND ...
AHHH! I CAN'T EXPLAIN IT!
DON'T WORRY, WE DON'T EXPECT YOU TO.

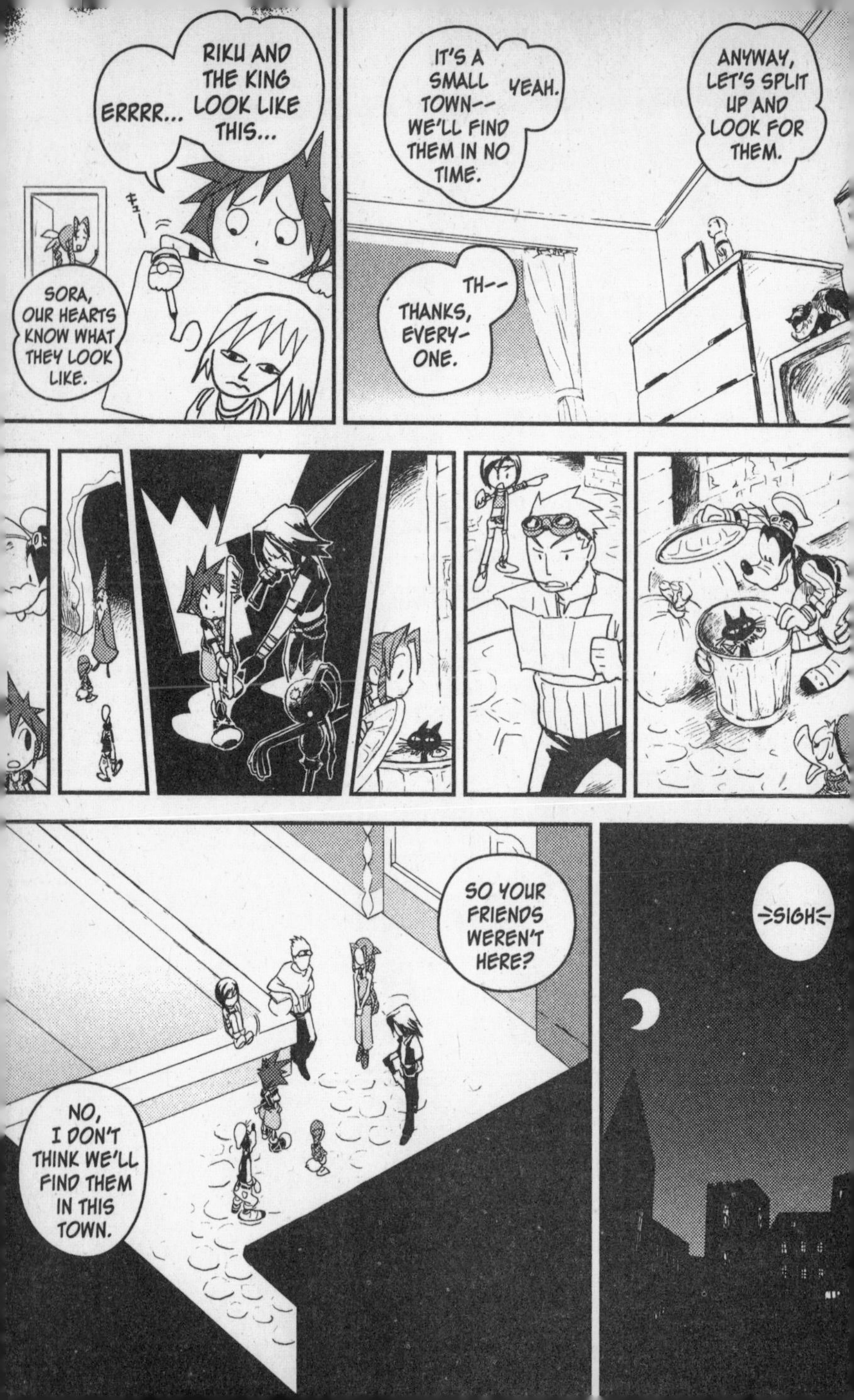
ANYWAY, LET'S SPLIT UP AND LOOK FOR THEM.
YEAH.
IT'S A SMALL TOWN--WE'LL FIND THEM IN NO TIME.
TH--THANKS, EVERYONE.
RIKU AND THE KING LOOK LIKE THIS...
ERRRR...
SORA, OUR HEARTS KNOW WHAT THEY LOOK LIKE.
SIGH
SO YOUR FRIENDS WEREN'T HERE?
NO, I DON'T THINK WE'LL FIND THEM IN THIS TOWN.

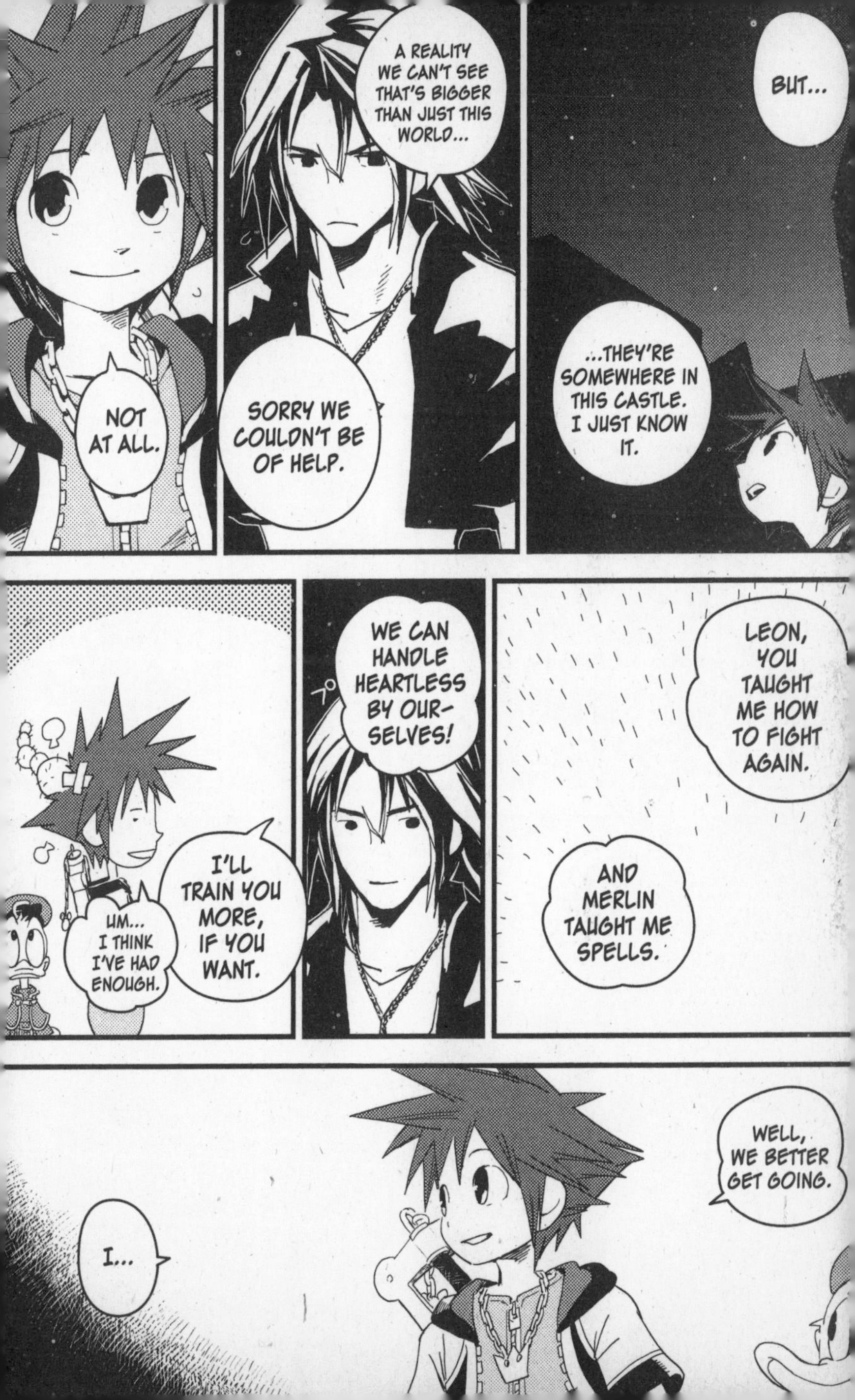
BUT...
...THEY'RE SOMEWHERE IN THIS CASTLE. I JUST KNOW IT.
A REALITY WE CAN'T SEE THAT'S BIGGER THAN JUST THIS WORLD...
SORRY WE COULDN'T BE OF HELP.
NOT AT ALL.
LEON, YOU TAUGHT ME HOW TO FIGHT AGAIN.
AND MERLIN TAUGHT ME SPELLS.
WE CAN HANDLE HEARTLESS BY OUR-SELVES!
I'LL TRAIN YOU MORE, IF YOU WANT.
UM... I THINK I'VE HAD ENOUGH.
WELL, WE BETTER GET GOING.
I...

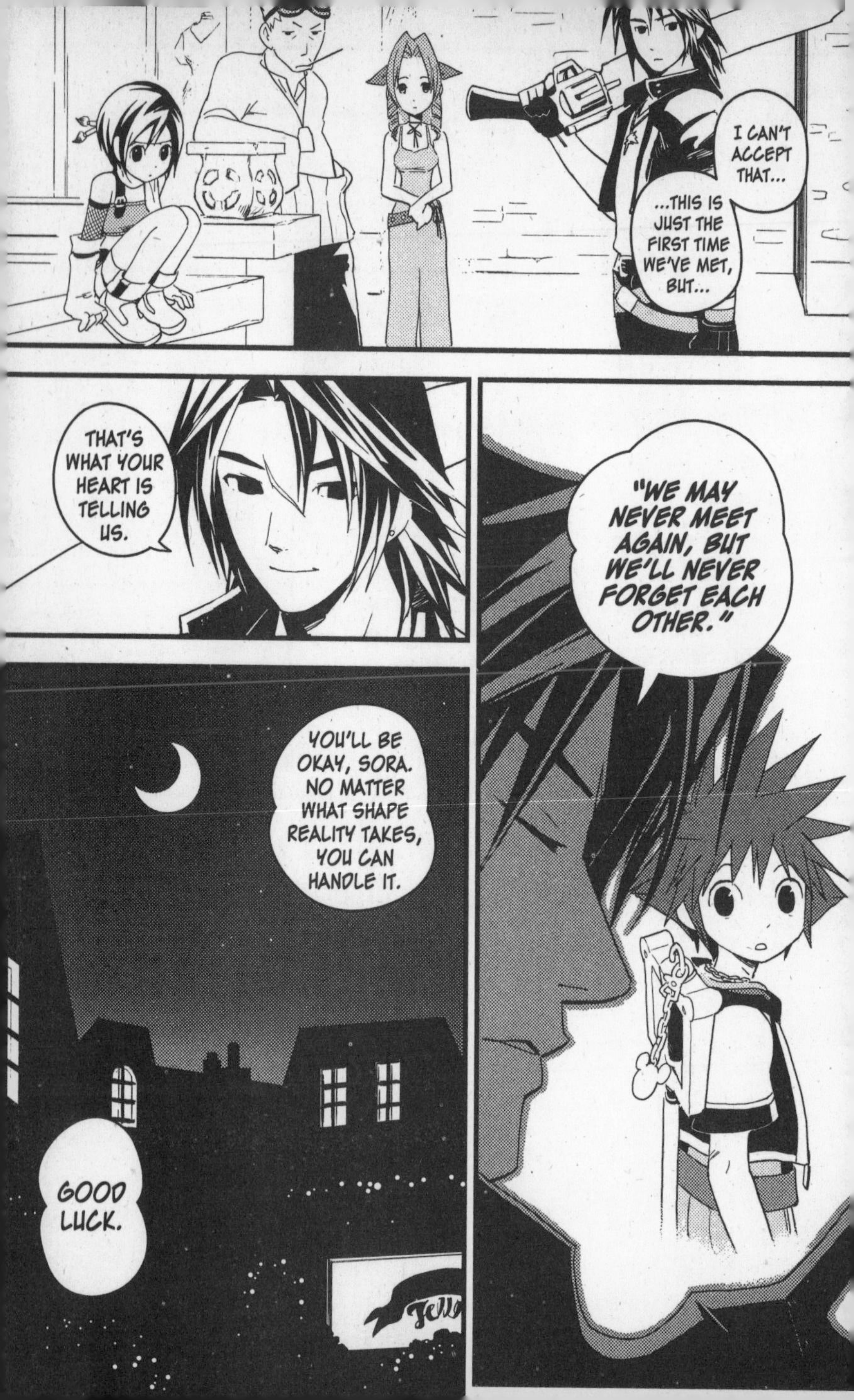
I CAN'T ACCEPT THAT...
...THIS IS JUST THE FIRST TIME WE'VE MET, BUT...
"WE MAY NEVER MEET AGAIN, BUT WE'LL NEVER FORGET EACH OTHER."
THAT'S WHAT YOUR HEART IS TELLING US.
YOU'LL BE OKAY, SORA. NO MATTER WHAT SHAPE REALITY TAKES, YOU CAN HANDLE IT.
GOOD LUCK.

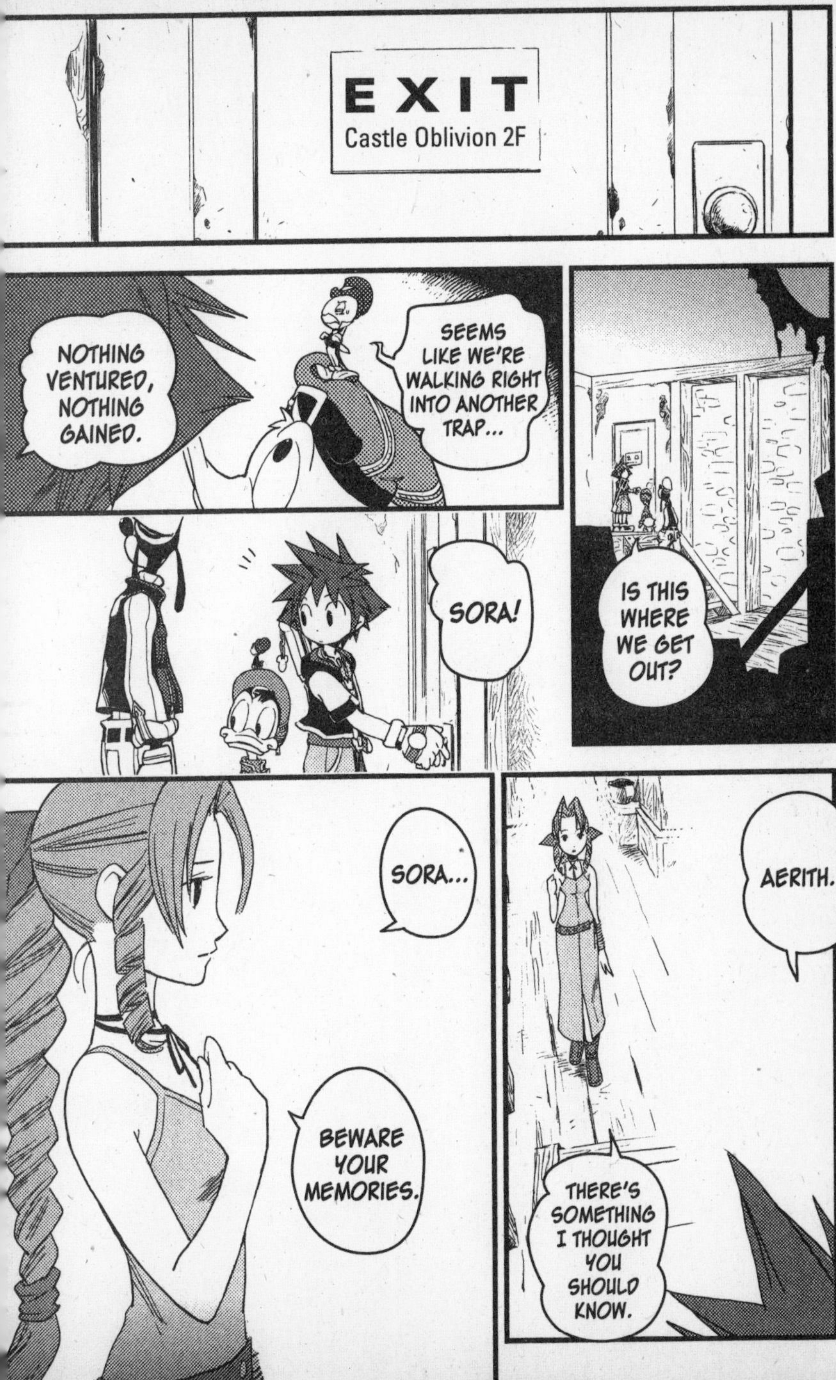
EXIT
Castle Oblivion 2F
IS THIS WHERE WE GET OUT?
SEEMS LIKE WE'RE WALKING RIGHT INTO ANOTHER TRAP...
NOTHING VENTURED, NOTHING GAINED.
SORA!
AERITH.
THERE'S SOMETHING I THOUGHT YOU SHOULD KNOW.
SORA...
BEWARE YOUR MEMORIES.

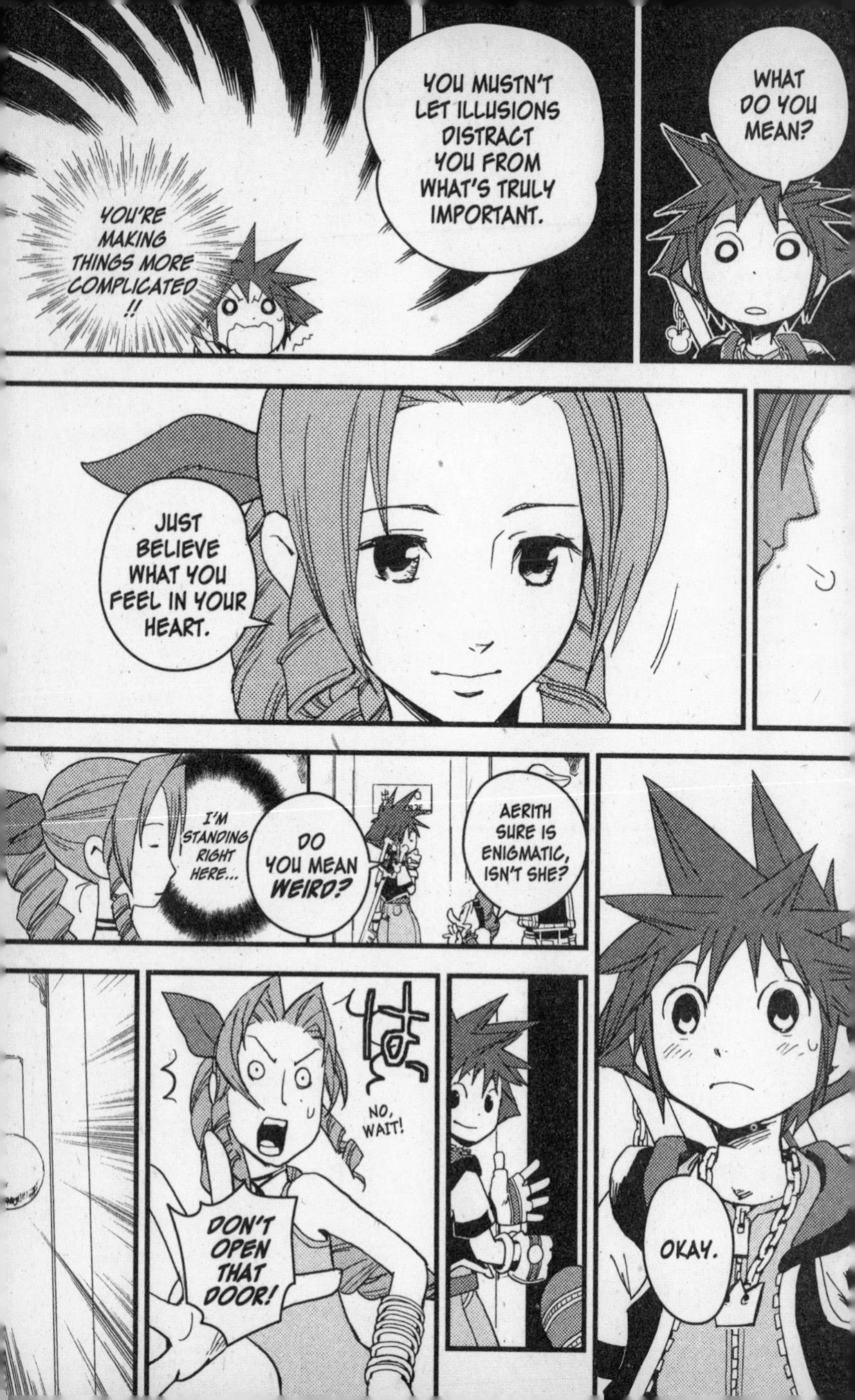
WHAT DO YOU MEAN?
YOU MUSTN'T LET ILLUSIONS DISTRACT YOU FROM WHAT'S TRULY IMPORTANT.
YOU'RE MAKING THINGS MORE COMPLICATED !!
JUST BELIEVE WHAT YOU FEEL IN YOUR HEART.
OKAY.
AERITH SURE IS ENIGMATIC, ISN'T SHE?
DO YOU MEAN WEIRD?
I'M STANDING RIGHT HERE...
はっ
NO, WAIT!
DON'T OPEN THAT DOOR!

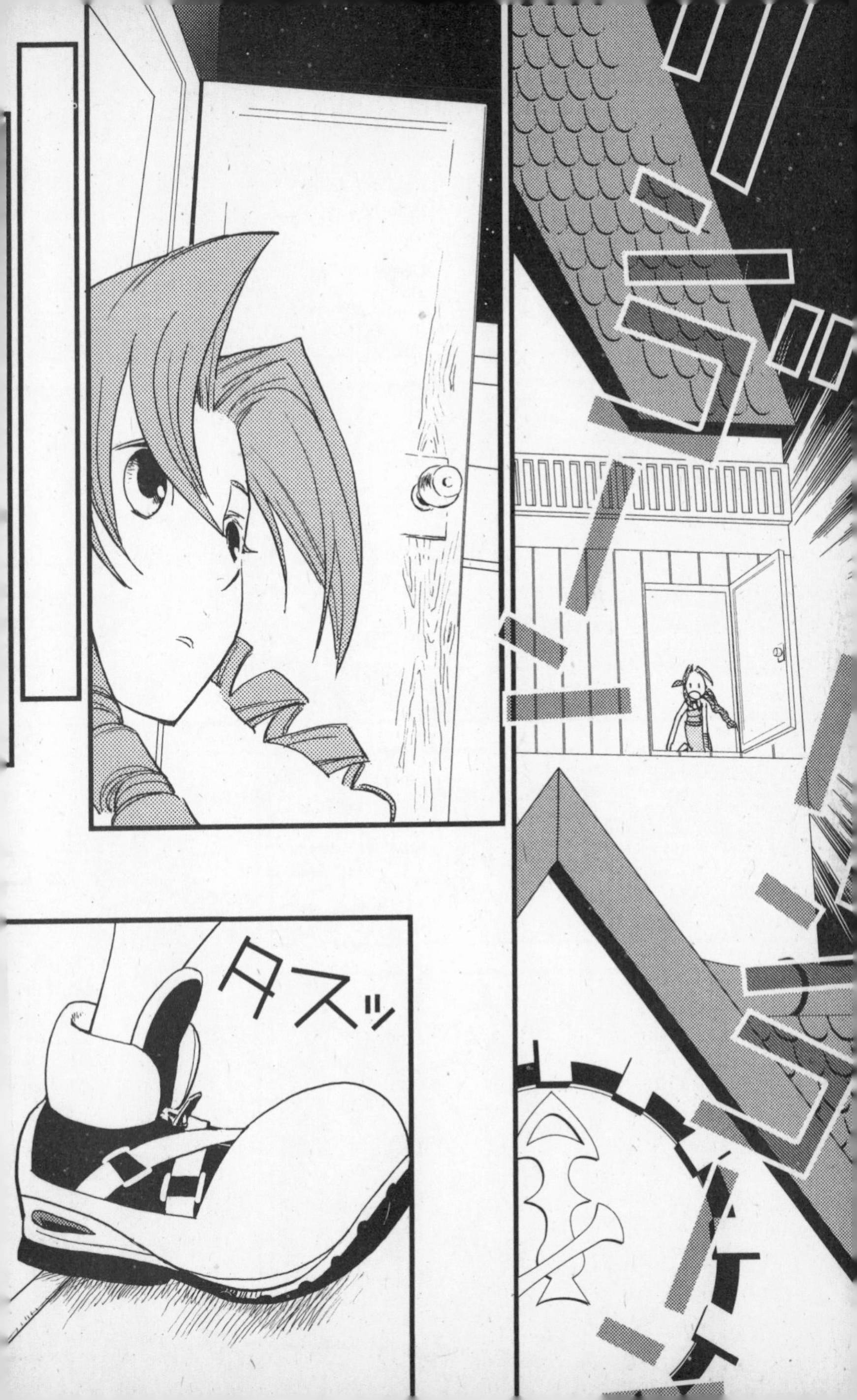
タスッ

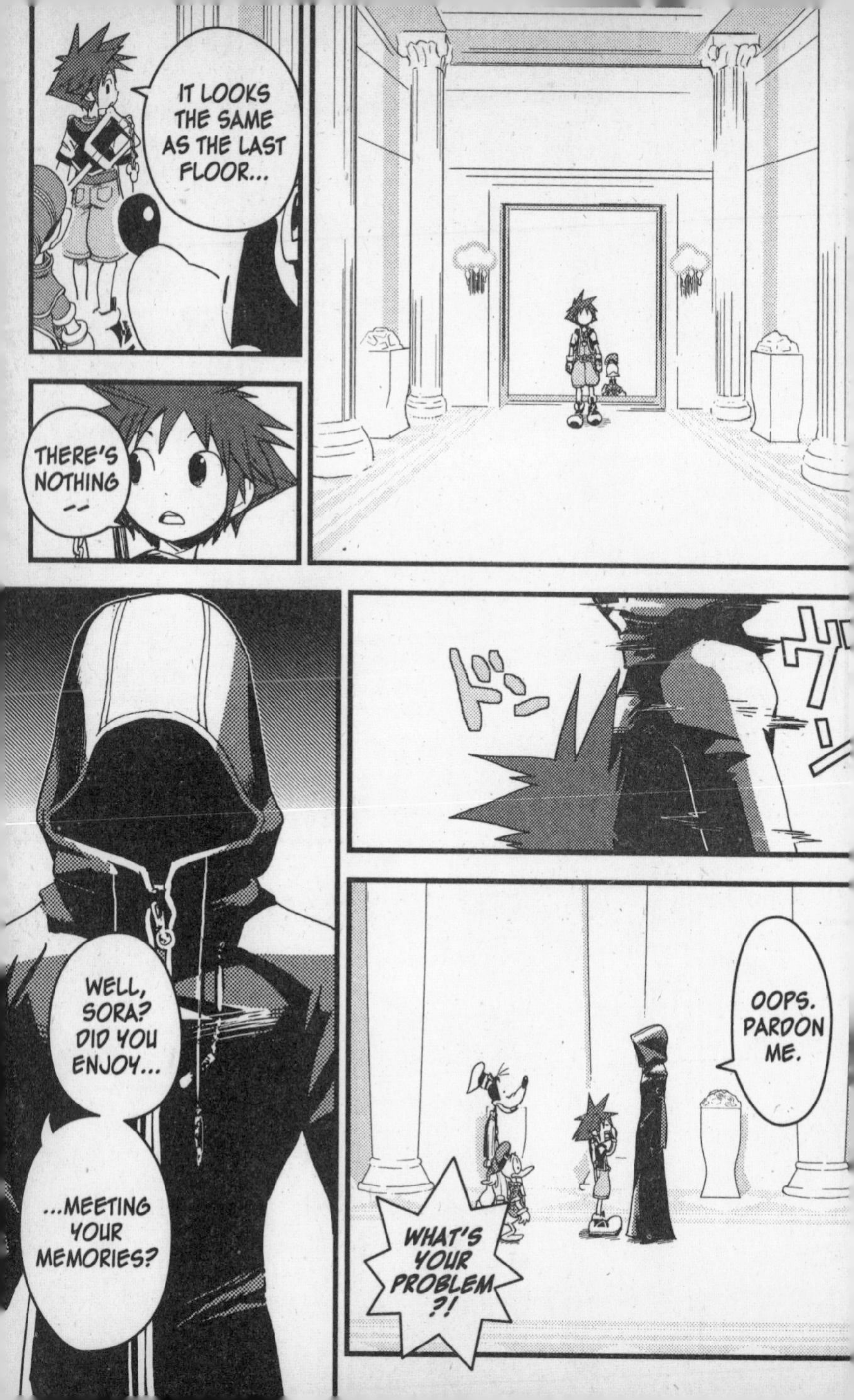
IT LOOKS THE SAME AS THE LAST FLOOR...
THERE'S NOTHING --
ドン
OOPS. PARDON ME.
WHAT'S YOUR PROBLEM?!
WELL, SORA? DID YOU ENJOY...
...MEETING YOUR MEMORIES?

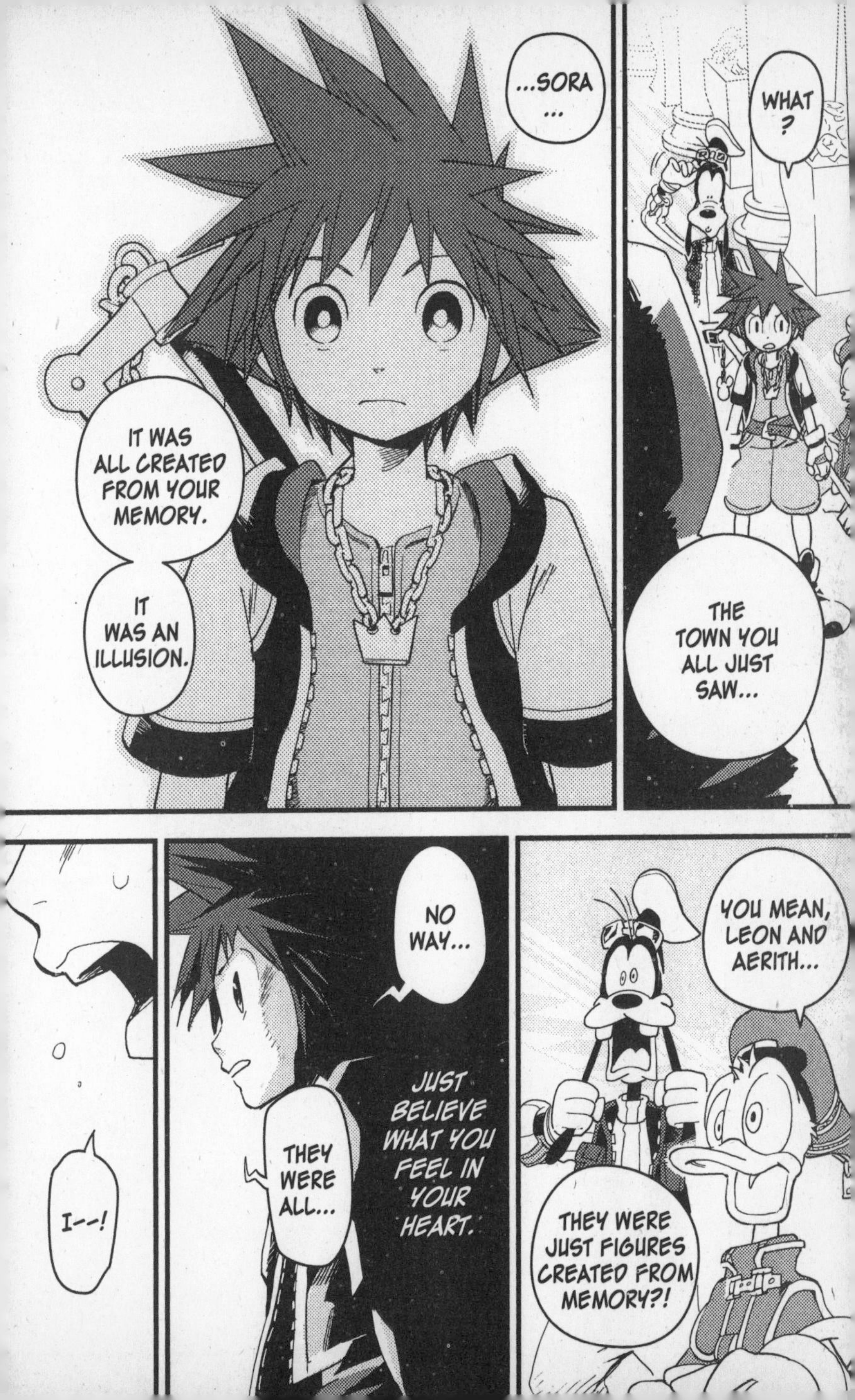
WHAT ?
THE TOWN YOU ALL JUST SAW...
...SORA ...
IT WAS ALL CREATED FROM YOUR MEMORY.
IT WAS AN ILLUSION.
YOU MEAN, LEON AND AERITH...
THEY WERE JUST FIGURES CREATED FROM MEMORY?!
NO WAY...
JUST BELIEVE WHAT YOU FEEL IN YOUR HEART.
THEY WERE ALL...
I--!

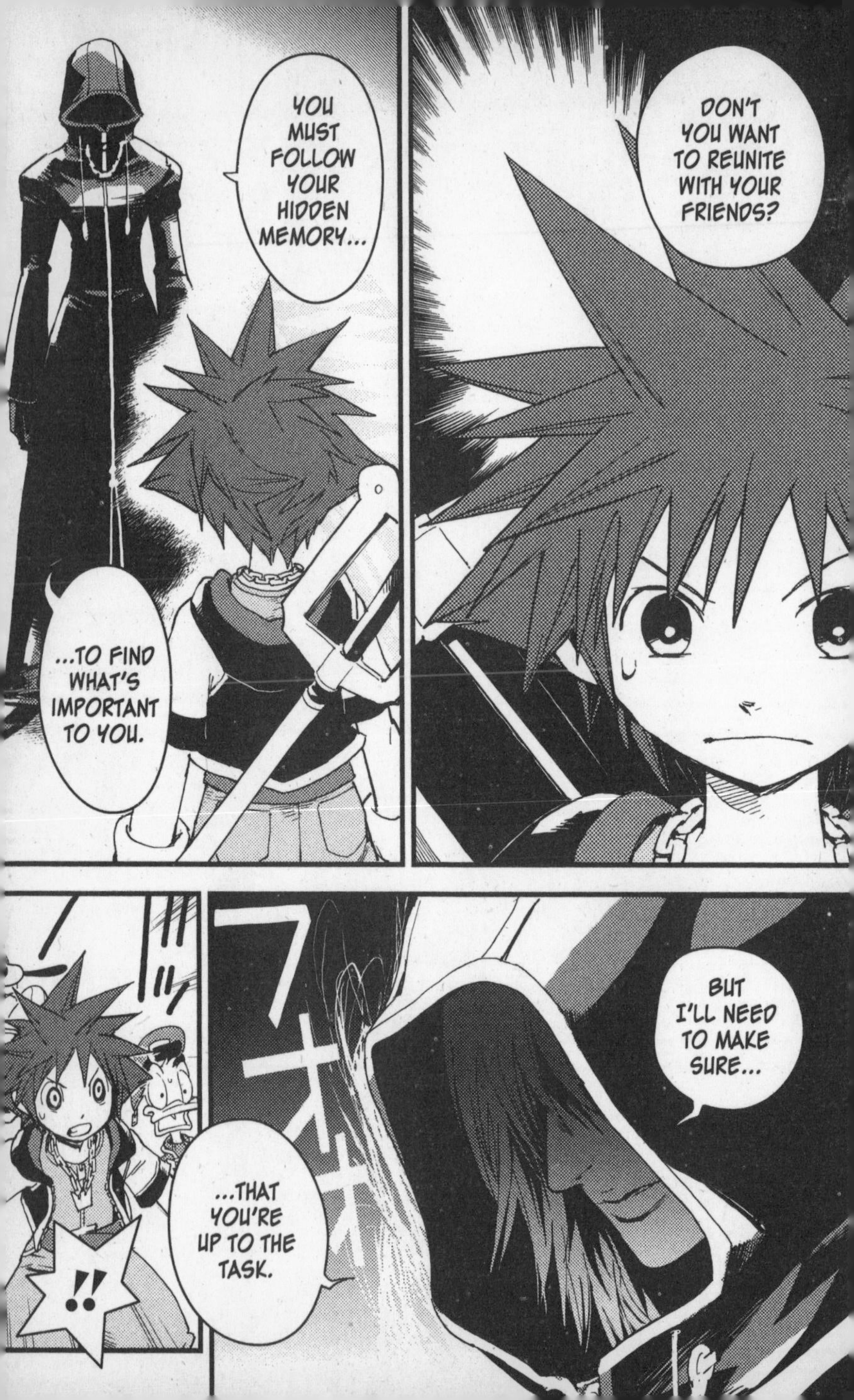
DON'T YOU WANT TO REUNITE WITH YOUR FRIENDS?
YOU MUST FOLLOW YOUR HIDDEN MEMORY...
...TO FIND WHAT'S IMPORTANT TO YOU.
BUT I'LL NEED TO MAKE SURE...
...THAT YOU'RE UP TO THE TASK.
!!

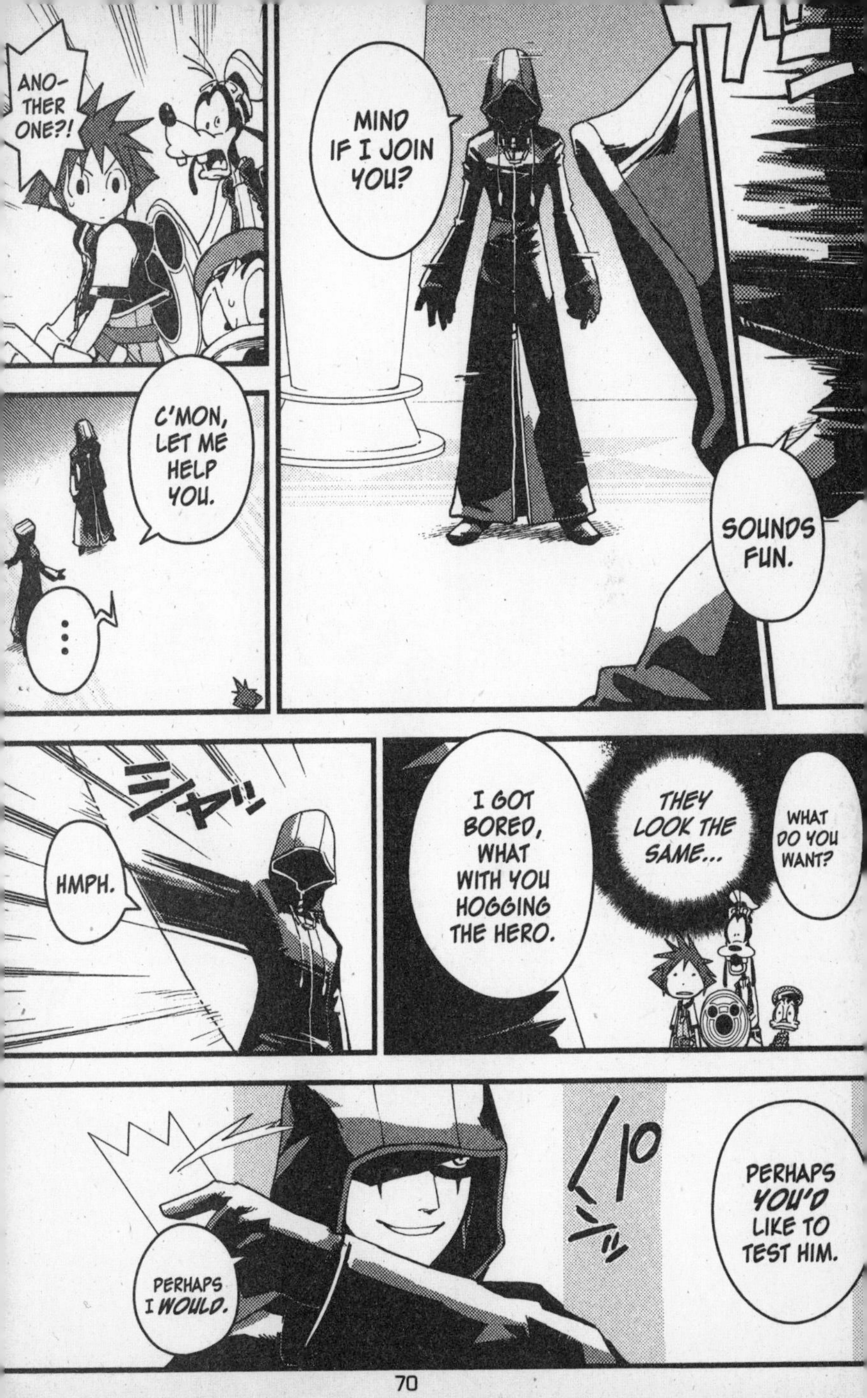
SOUNDS FUN.
MIND IF I JOIN YOU?
ANO-THER ONE?!
C'MON, LET ME HELP YOU.
...
WHAT DO YOU WANT?
THEY LOOK THE SAME...
I GOT BORED, WHAT WITH YOU HOGGING THE HERO.
HMPH.
PERHAPS YOU'D LIKE TO TEST HIM.
PERHAPS I WOULD.

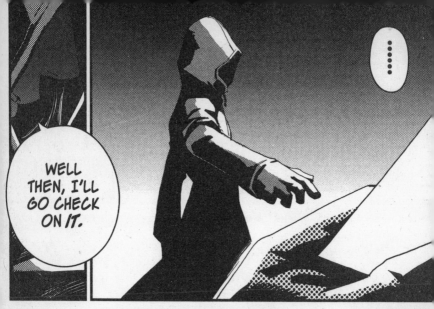

WELL THEN, I'LL GO CHECK ON *IT*.

LOOKS LIKE IT'S *MY* SHOW NOW...

...KEY-BLADE MASTER.

SEE YA...

MY NAME IS AXEL.

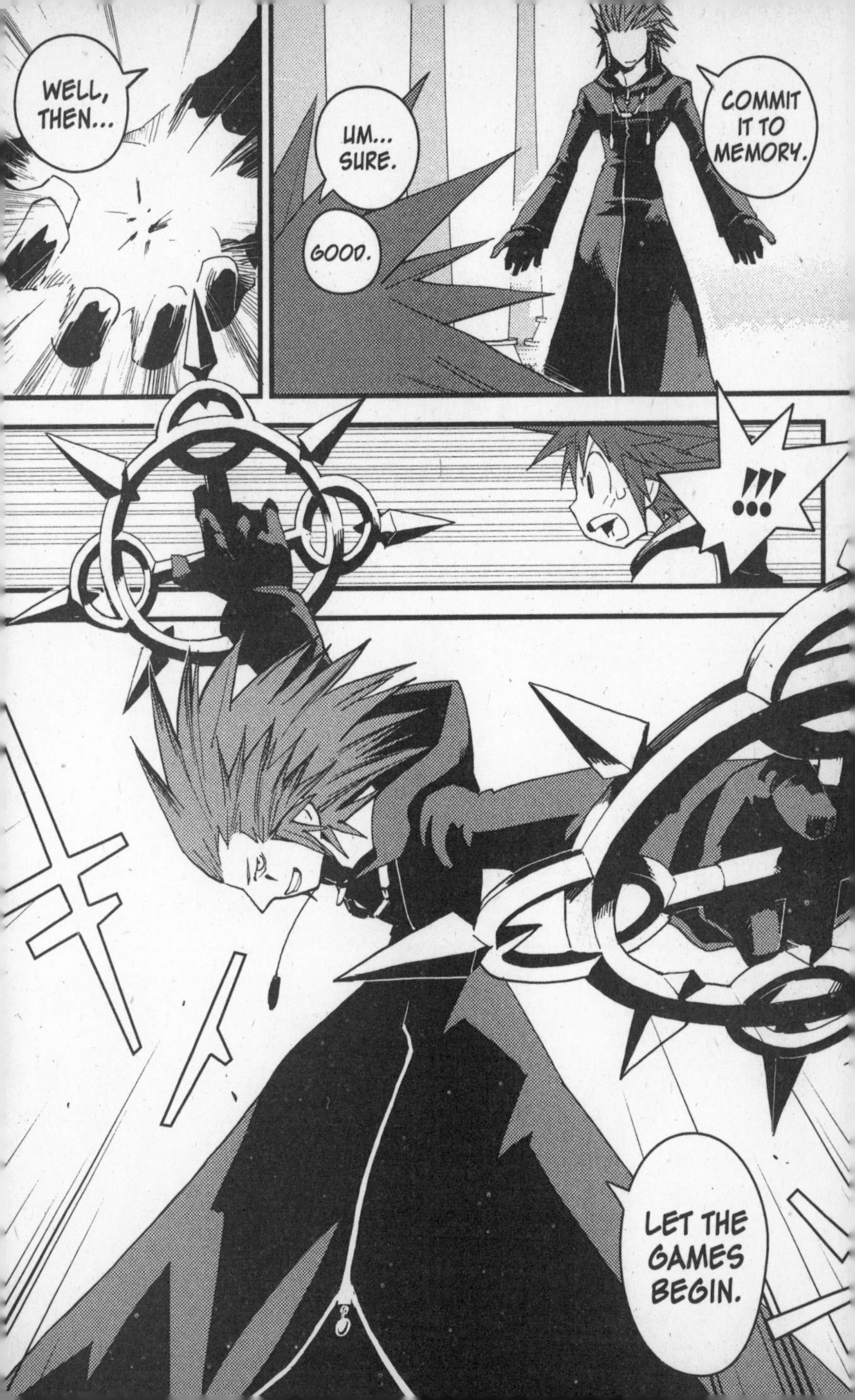
COMMIT IT TO MEMORY.
UM... SURE.
GOOD.
WELL, THEN...
!!!...
LET THE GAMES BEGIN.

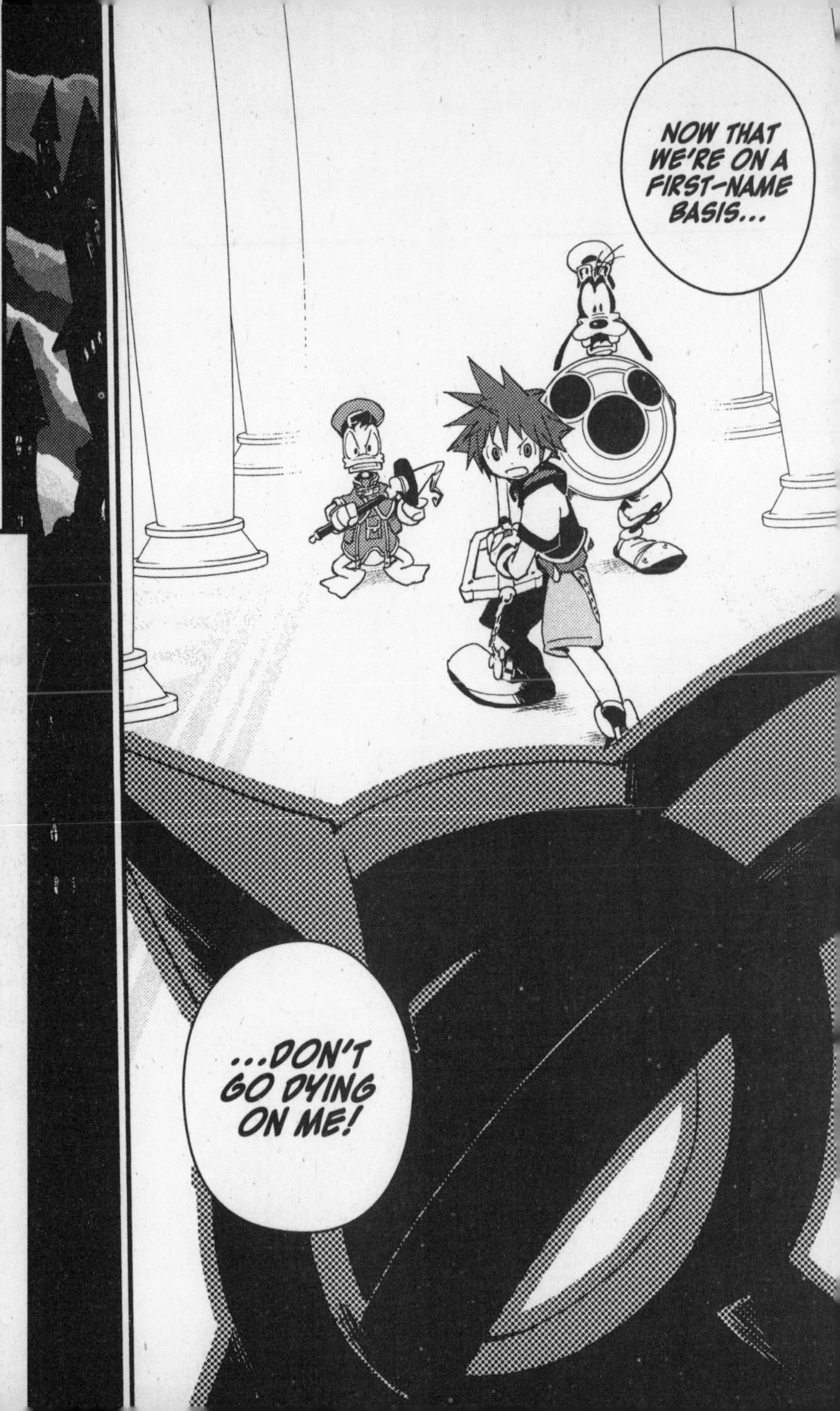
NOW THAT WE'RE ON A FIRST-NAME BASIS...
...DON'T GO DYING ON ME!

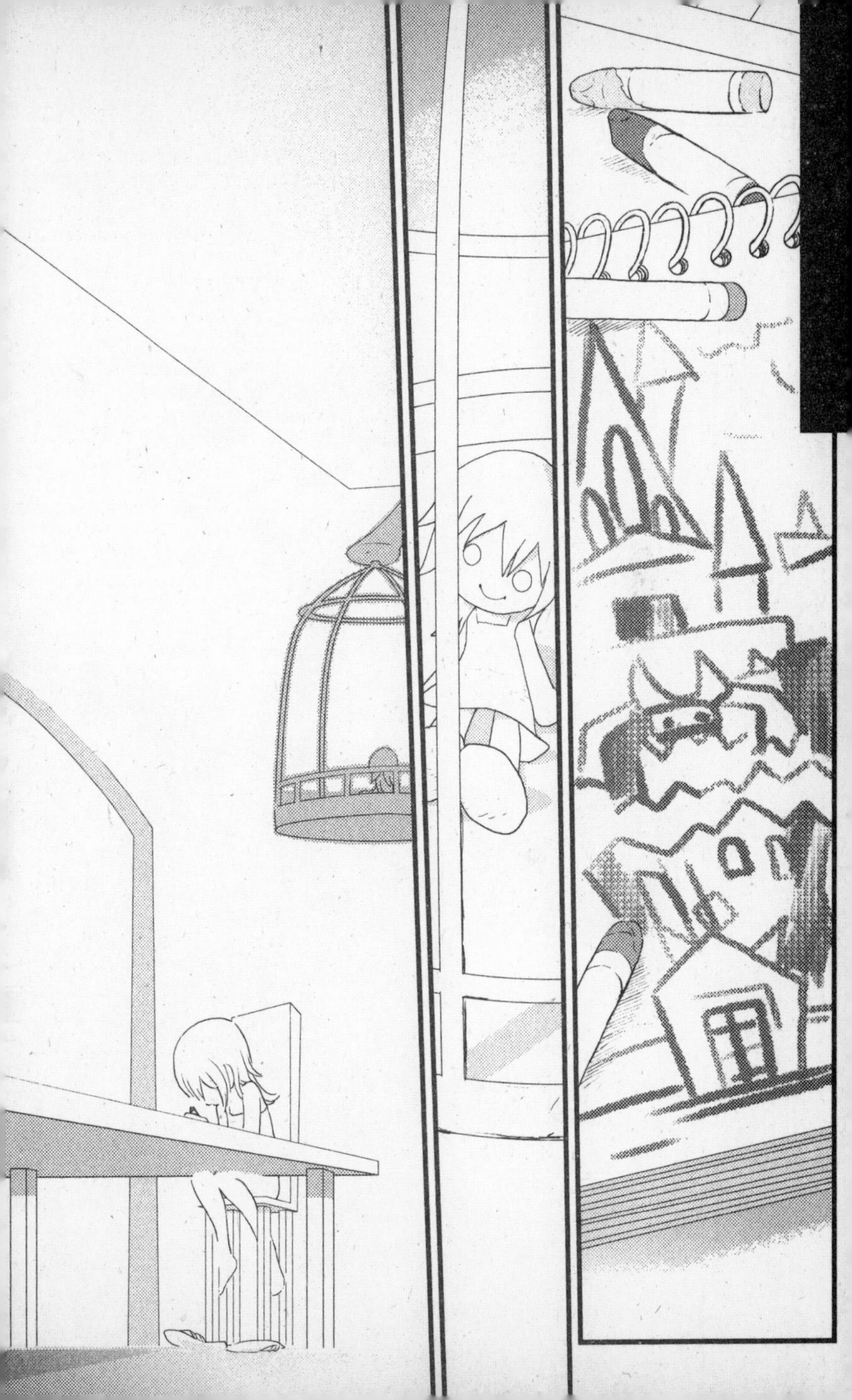

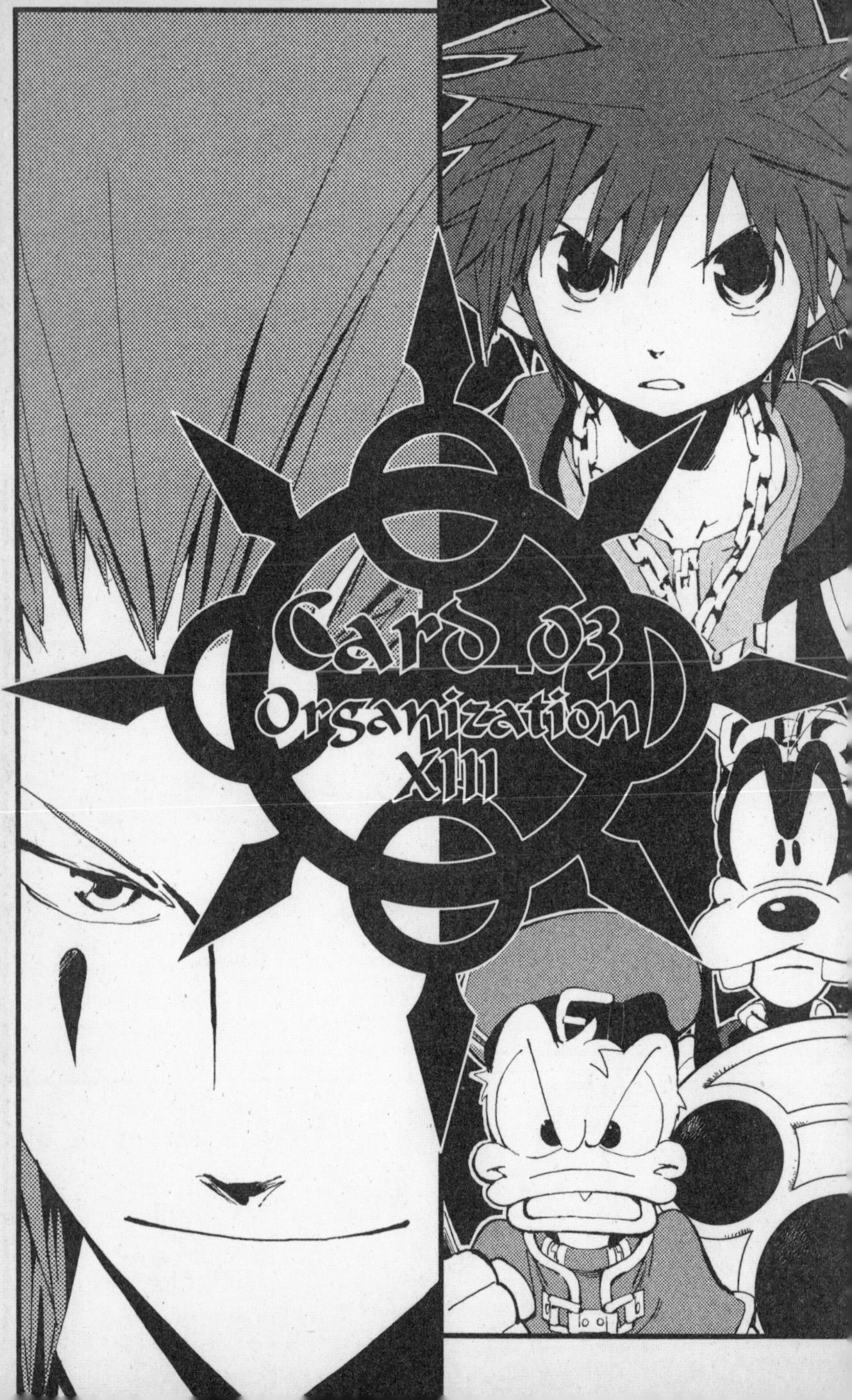
Card 03
Organization XIII

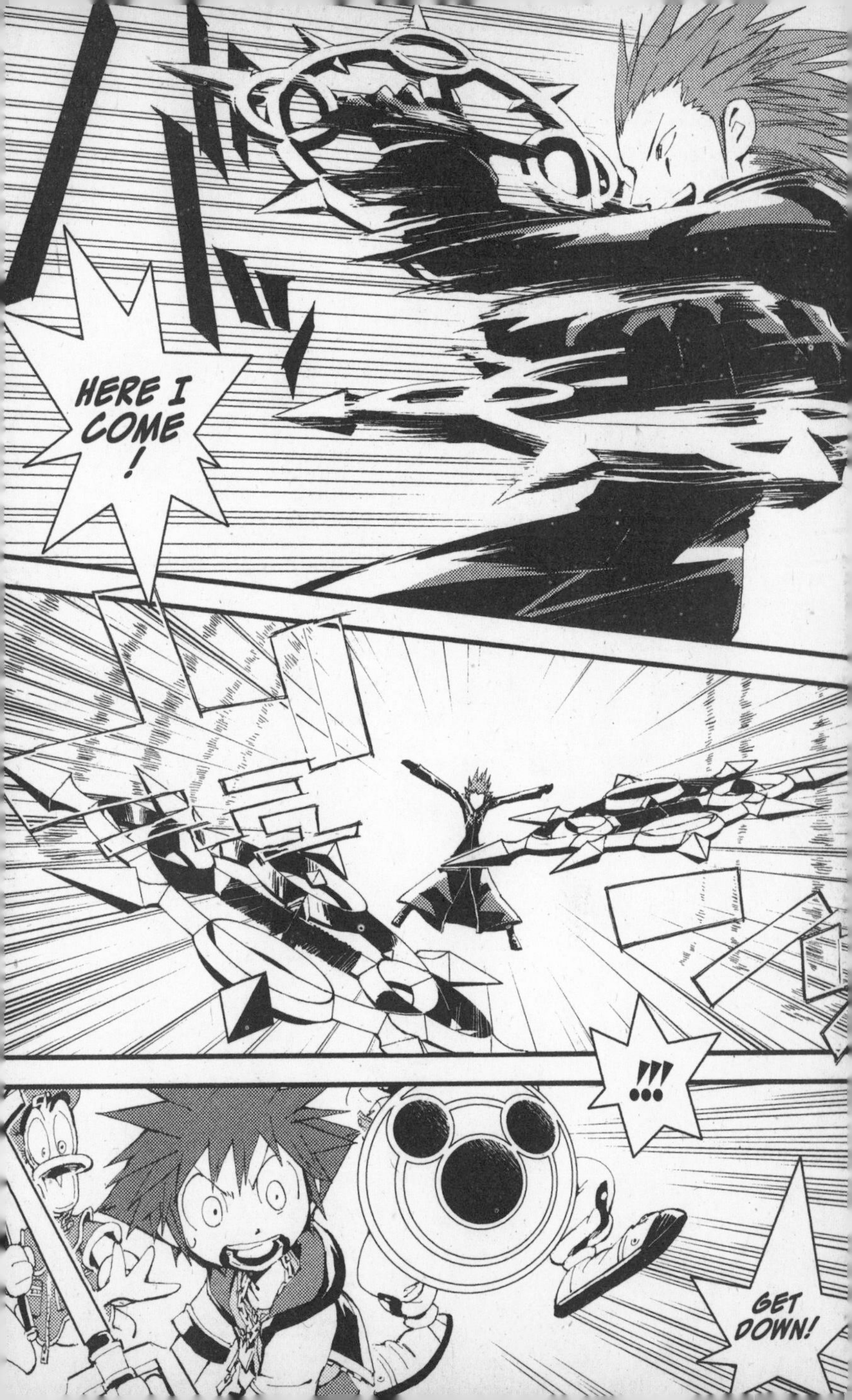
HERE I COME!
!!!
GET DOWN!

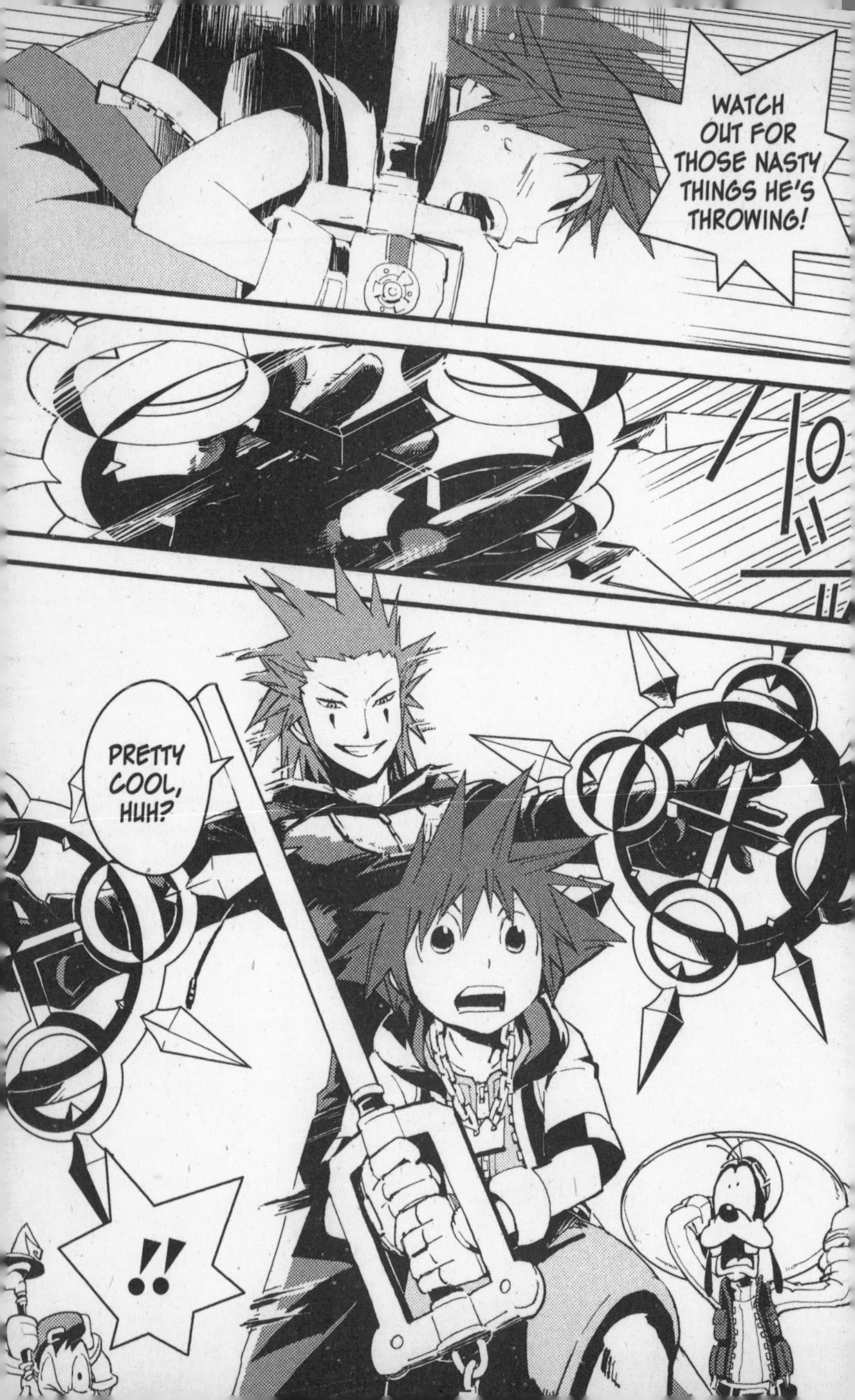
WATCH OUT FOR THOSE NASTY THINGS HE'S THROWING!
PRETTY COOL, HUH?
!!

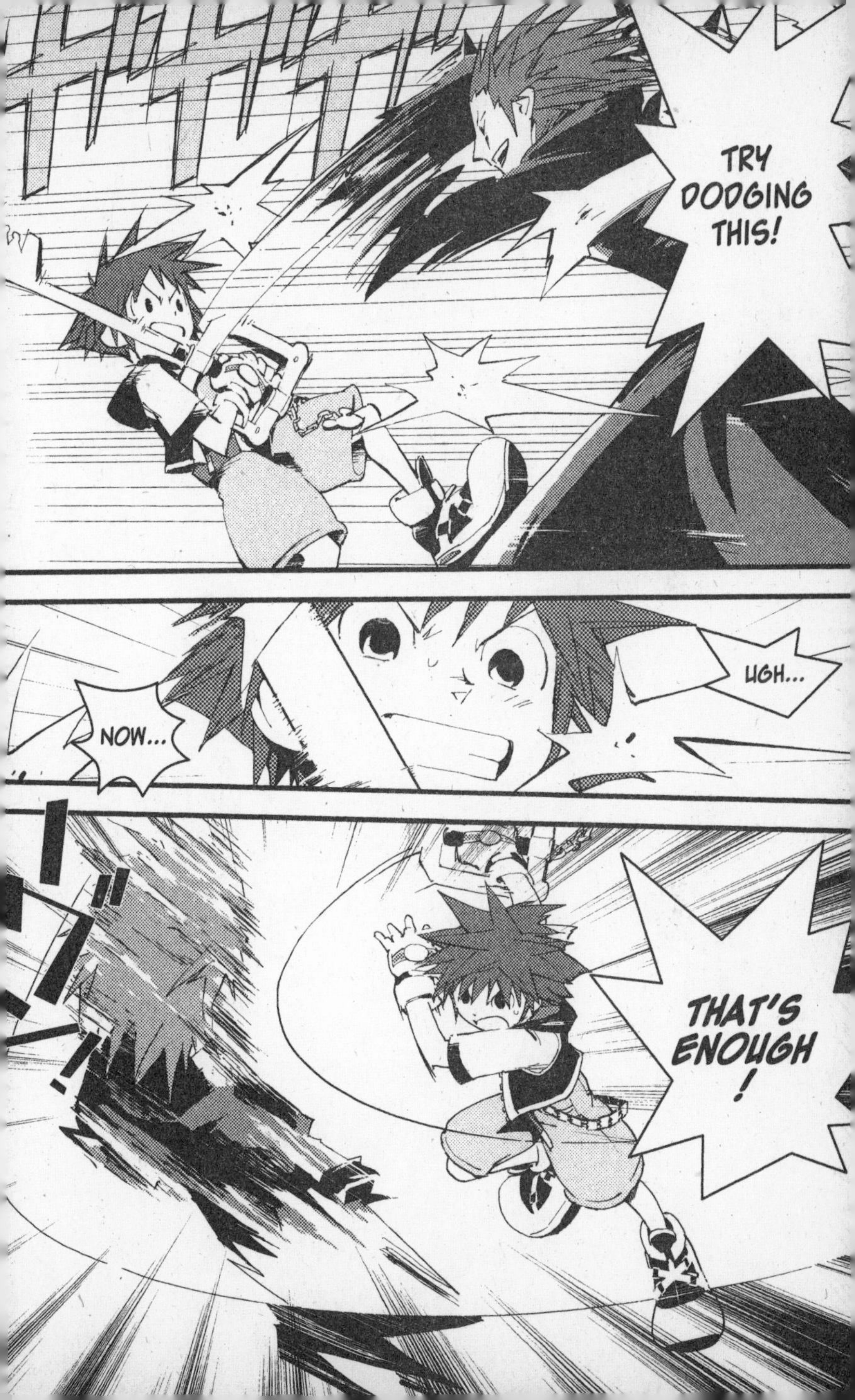
TRY DODGING THIS!
UGH...
NOW...
THAT'S ENOUGH!

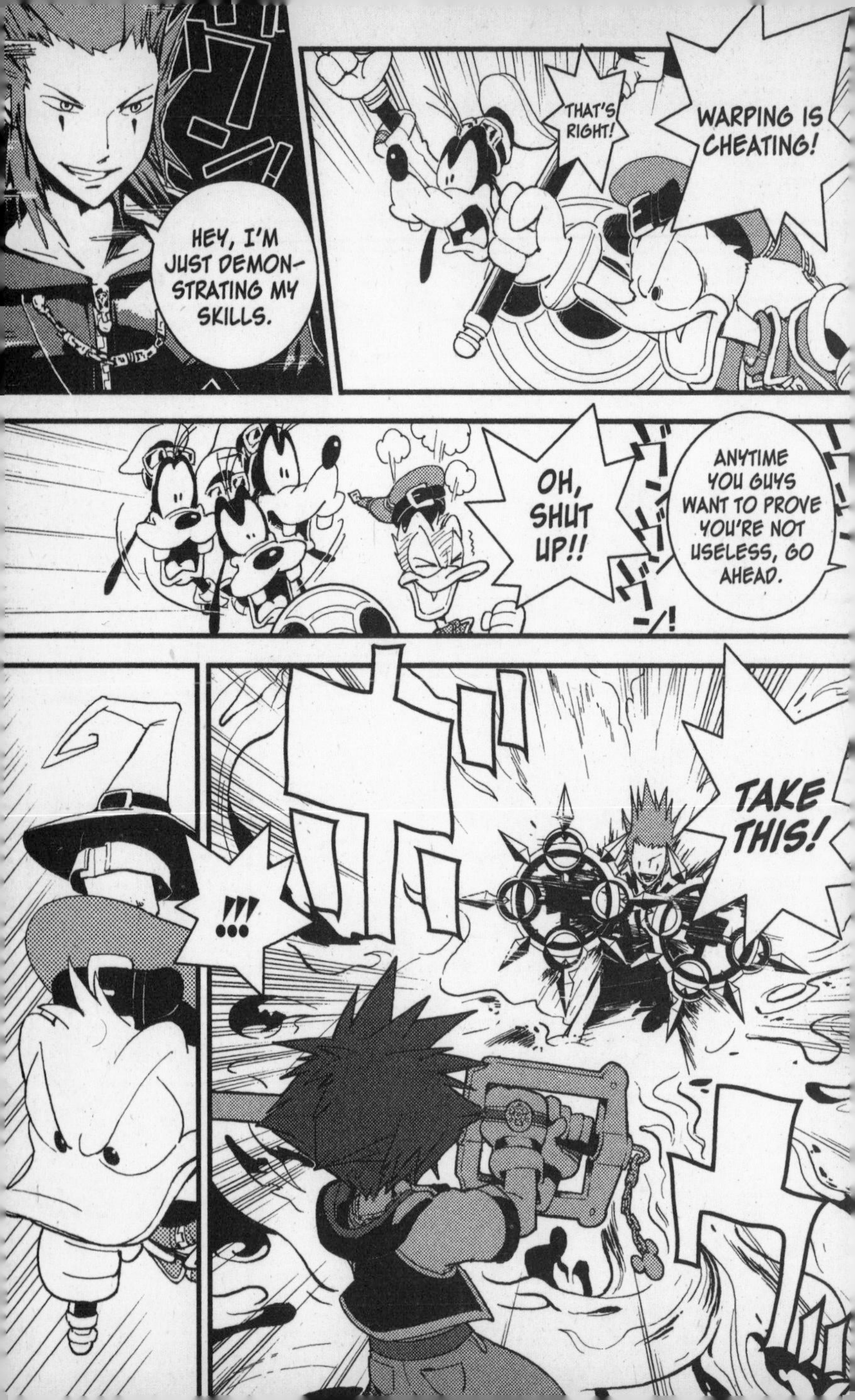
WARPING IS CHEATING!
THAT'S RIGHT!
HEY, I'M JUST DEMON-STRATING MY SKILLS.
ANYTIME YOU GUYS WANT TO PROVE YOU'RE NOT USELESS, GO AHEAD.
OH, SHUT UP!!
TAKE THIS!
!!!...

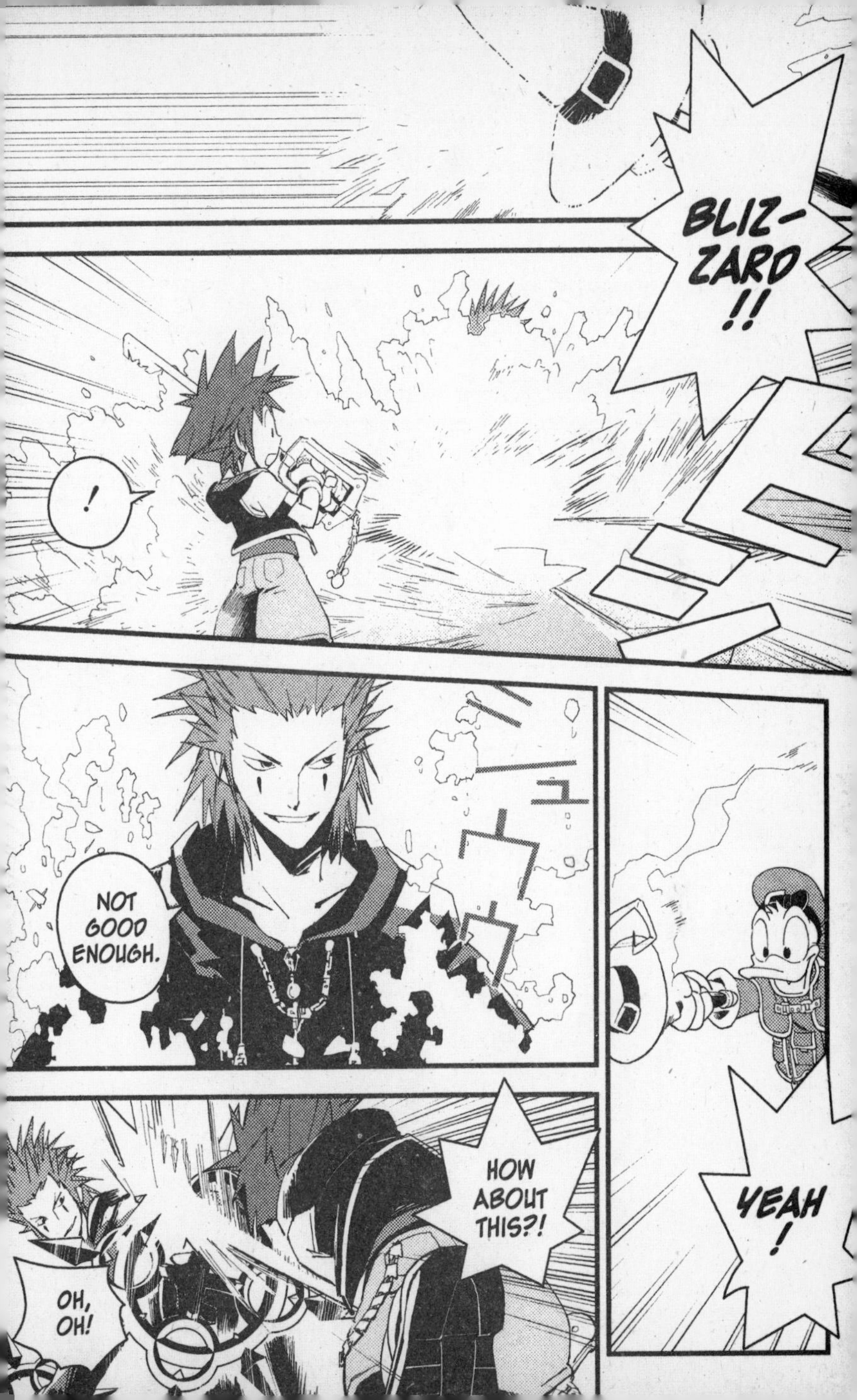
BLIZ-
ZARD
!!
!
YEAH
!
NOT
GOOD
ENOUGH.
HOW
ABOUT
THIS?!
OH,
OH!

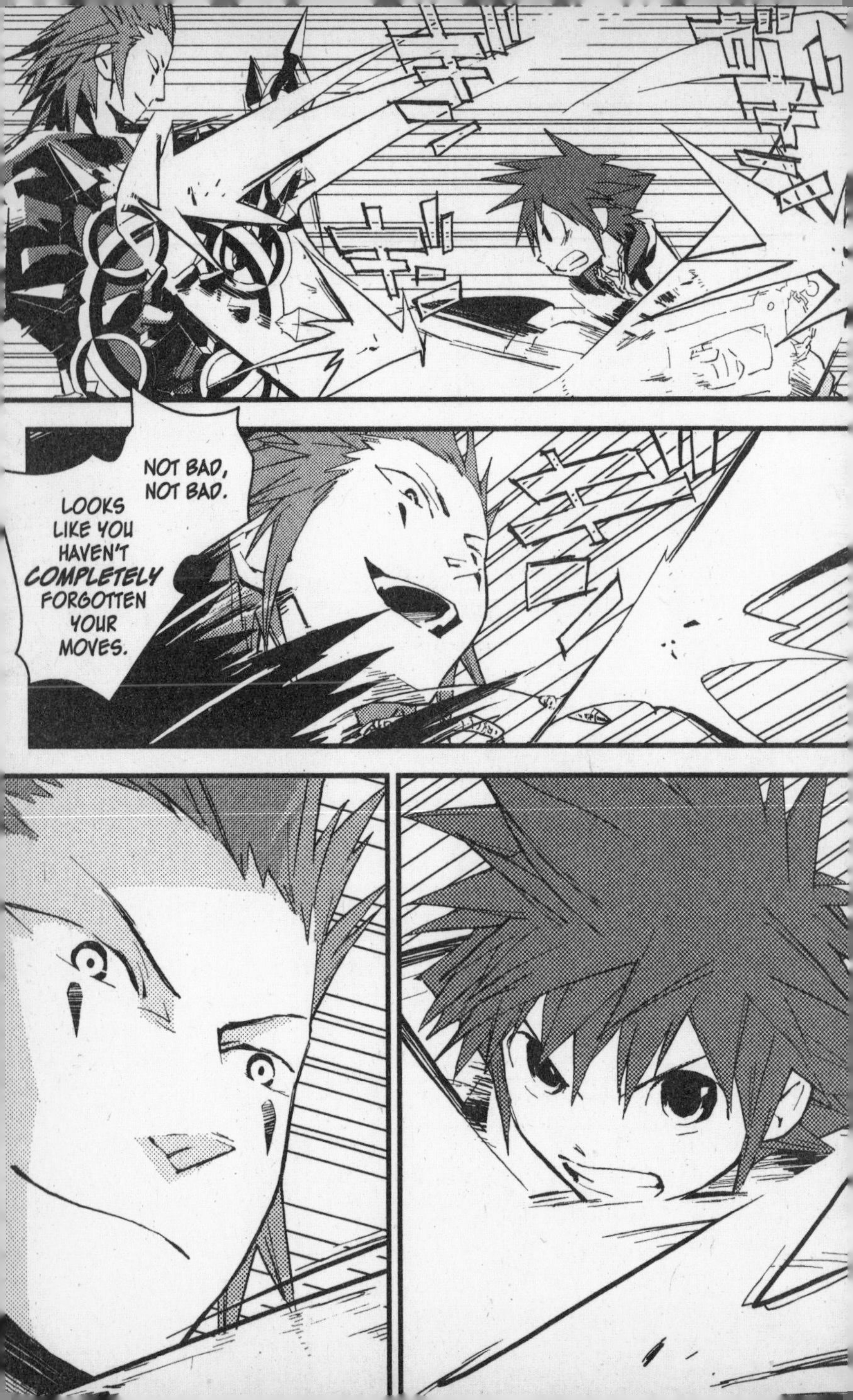
NOT BAD, NOT BAD. LOOKS LIKE YOU HAVEN'T COMPLETELY FORGOTTEN YOUR MOVES.

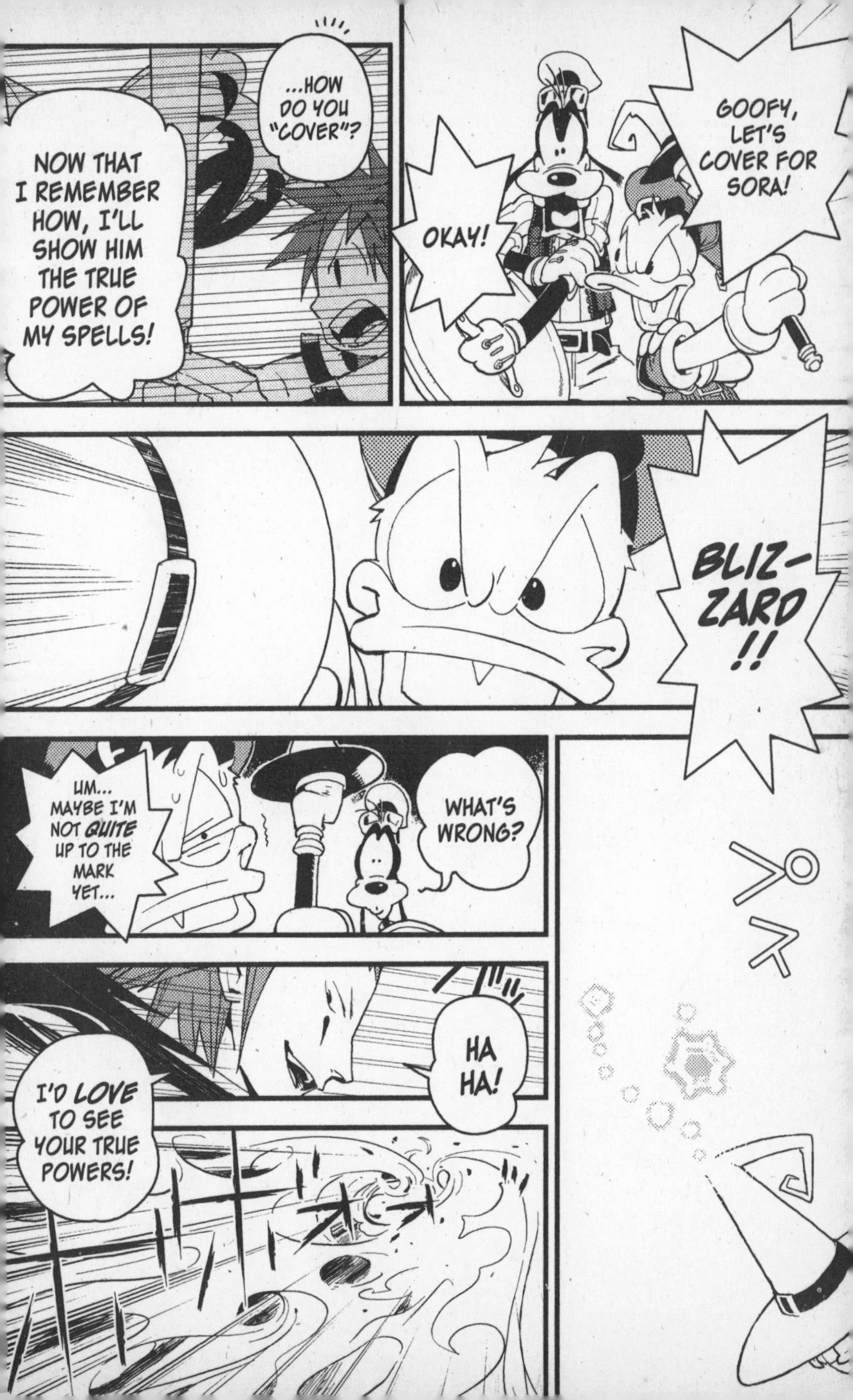
GOOFY, LET'S COVER FOR SORA!
OKAY!
...HOW DO YOU "COVER"?
NOW THAT I REMEMBER HOW, I'LL SHOW HIM THE TRUE POWER OF MY SPELLS!
BLIZ-ZARD!!
WHAT'S WRONG?
UM... MAYBE I'M NOT *QUITE* UP TO THE MARK YET...
HA HA!
I'D *LOVE* TO SEE YOUR TRUE POWERS!

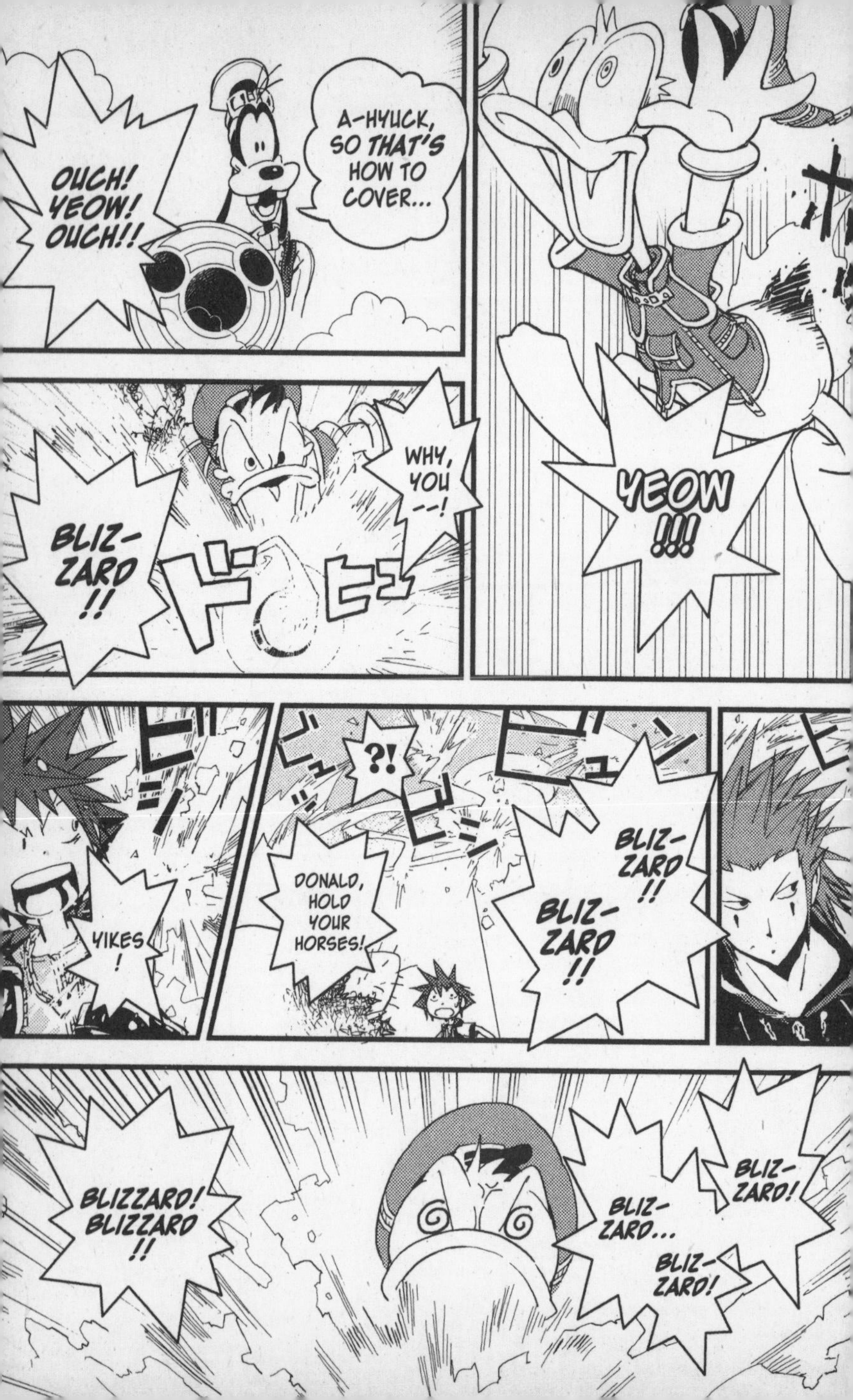
YEOW!!!
A-HYUCK, SO THAT'S HOW TO COVER...
OUCH! YEOW! OUCH!!
WHY, YOU--!
BLIZ-ZARD!!
ドヒュ
BLIZ-ZARD!!
BLIZ-ZARD!!
?!
DONALD, HOLD YOUR HORSES!
YIKES!
BLIZ-ZARD!
BLIZ-ZARD...
BLIZ-ZARD!
BLIZZARD! BLIZZARD!!

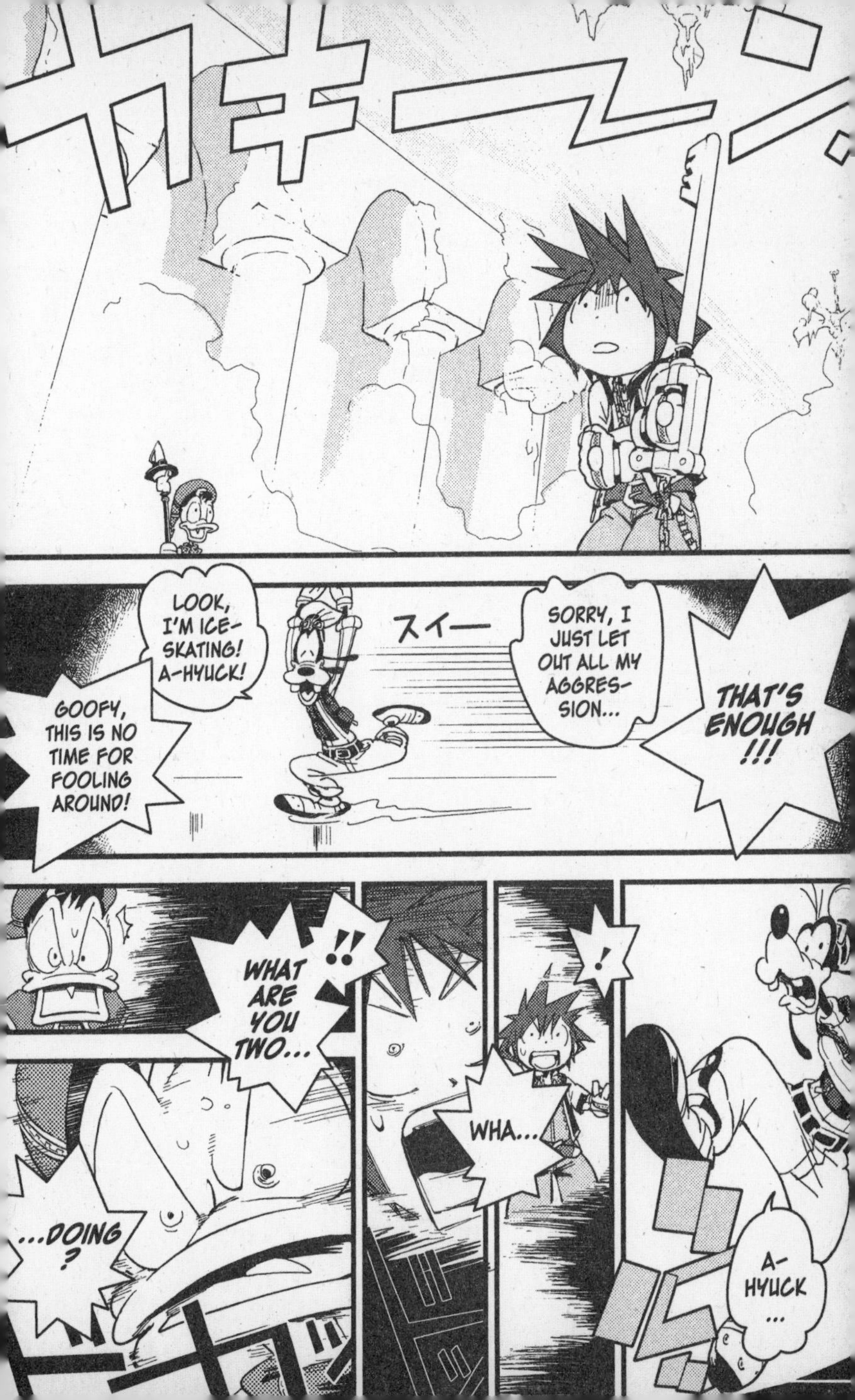
カキーン
THAT'S ENOUGH!!!
SORRY, I JUST LET OUT ALL MY AGGRES-SION...
スイー
LOOK, I'M ICE-SKATING! A-HYUCK!
GOOFY, THIS IS NO TIME FOR FOOLING AROUND!
A-HYUCK...
!
WHA...
!!
WHAT ARE YOU TWO...
...DOING?

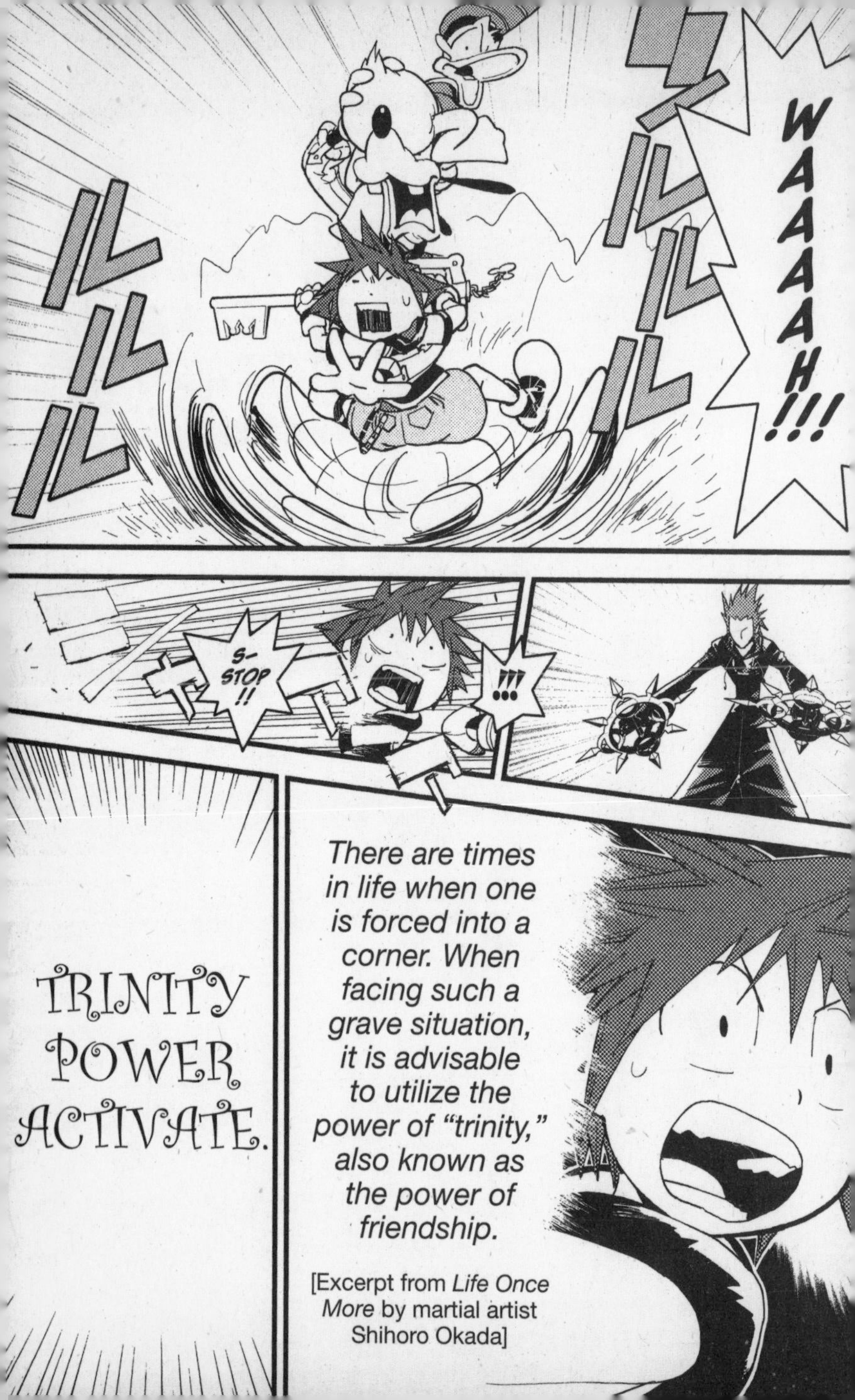
WAAAAAH!!!
!!!
S-STOP!!
There are times in life when one is forced into a corner. When facing such a grave situation, it is advisable to utilize the power of "trinity," also known as the power of friendship.
[Excerpt from *Life Once More* by martial artist Shihoro Okada]
TRINITY POWER ACTIVATE.

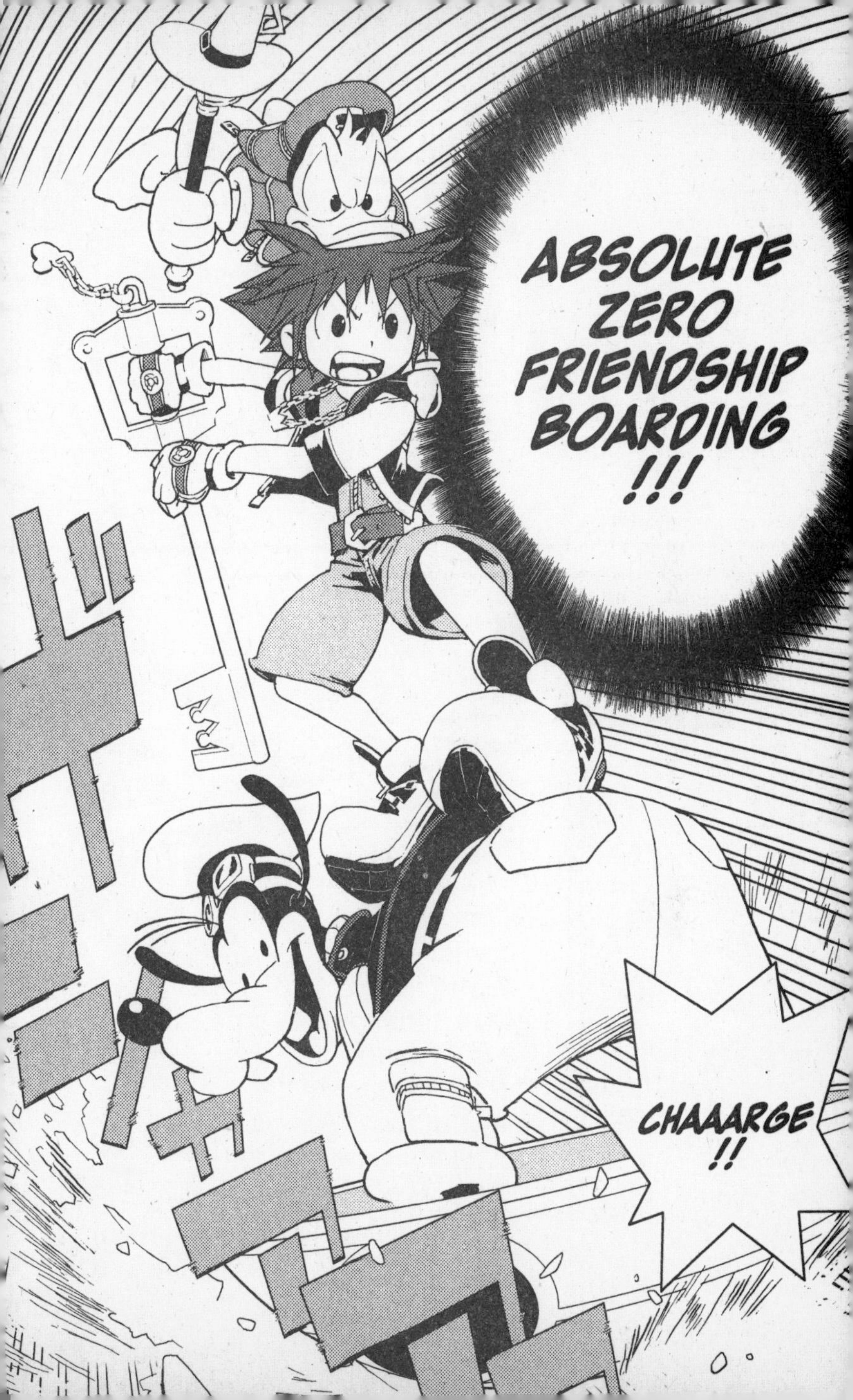
ABSOLUTE ZERO FRIENDSHIP BOARDING !!!
CHAAARGE !!

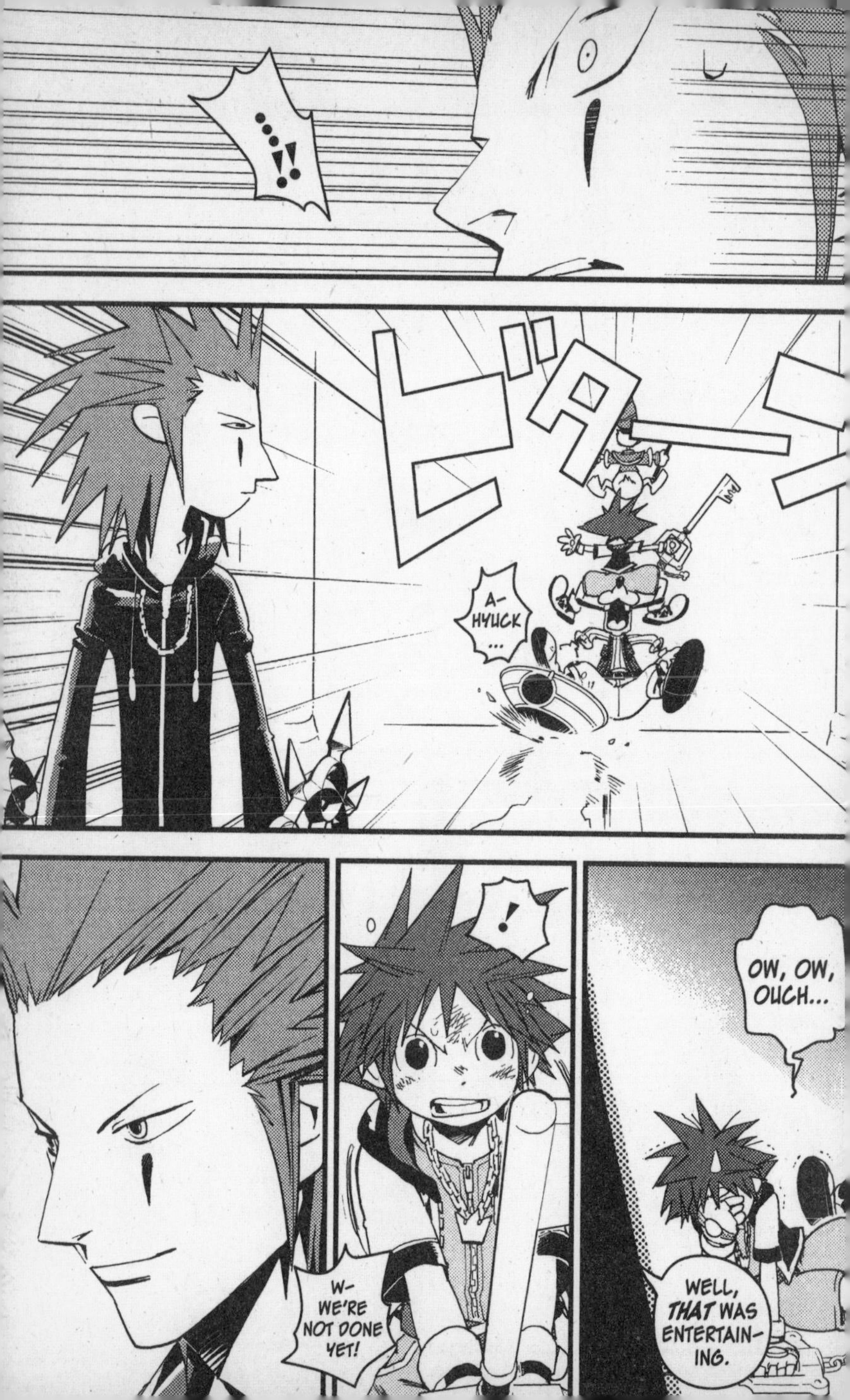
...!!
ビダー
A-HYUCK...
OW, OW, OUCH...
WELL, *THAT* WAS ENTERTAINING.
!
W-WE'RE NOT DONE YET!

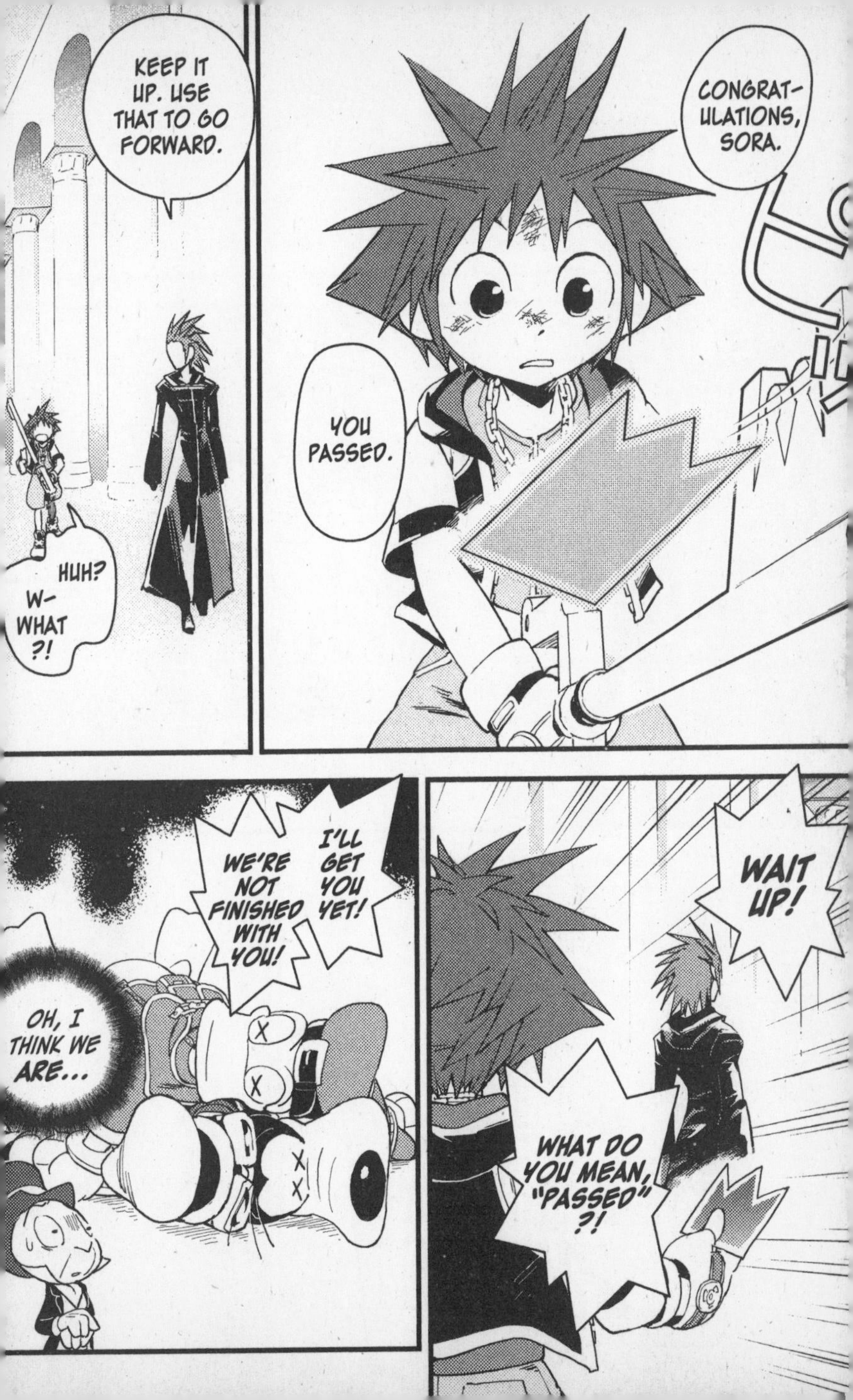
CONGRAT-ULATIONS, SORA.
YOU PASSED.
KEEP IT UP. USE THAT TO GO FORWARD.
HUH?
W-WHAT?!
WAIT UP!
WHAT DO YOU MEAN, "PASSED"?!
I'LL GET YOU YET!
WE'RE NOT FINISHED WITH YOU!
OH, I THINK WE ARE...

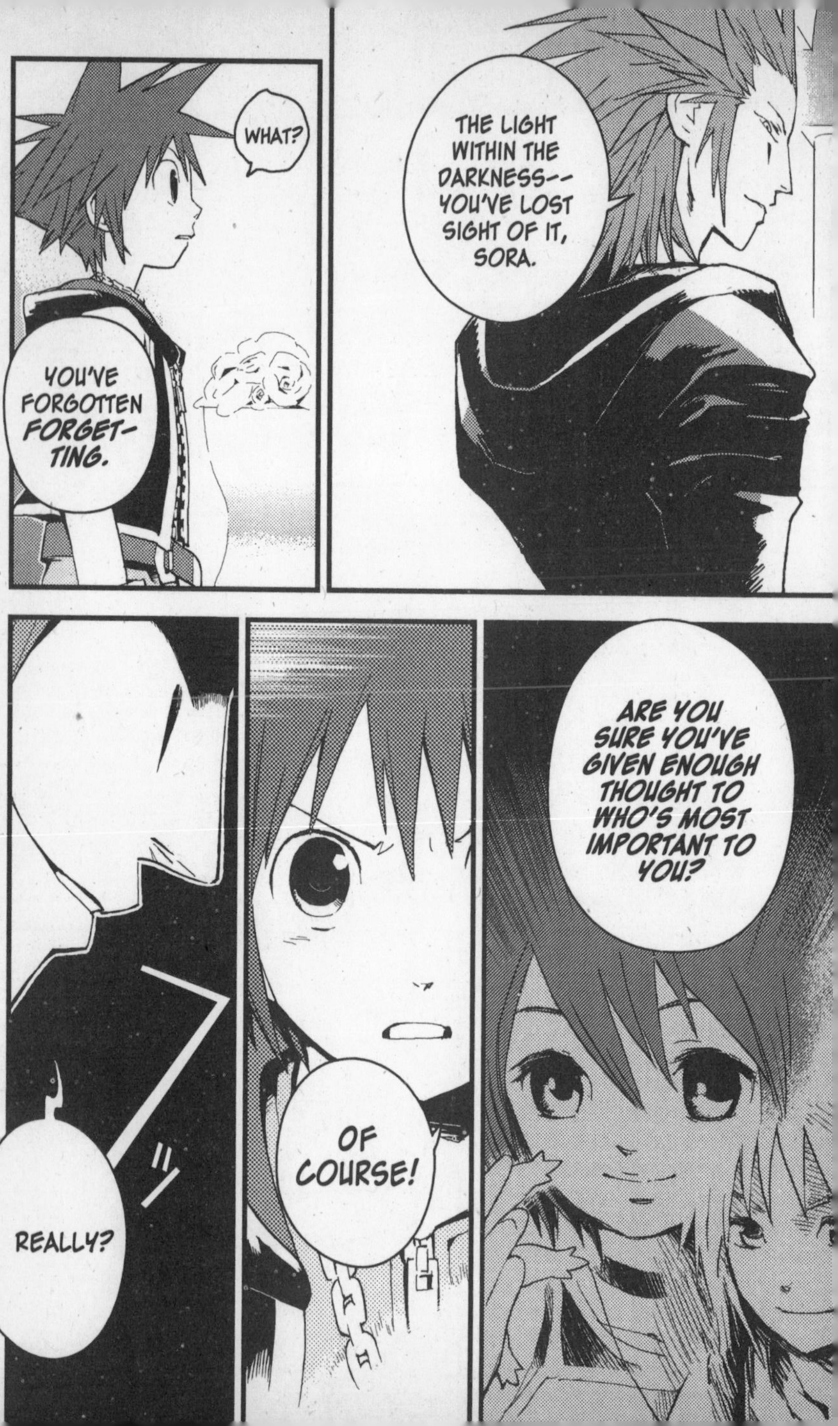
THE LIGHT WITHIN THE DARKNESS--YOU'VE LOST SIGHT OF IT, SORA.
WHAT?
YOU'VE FORGOTTEN *FORGETTING.*
ARE YOU SURE YOU'VE GIVEN ENOUGH THOUGHT TO WHO'S MOST IMPORTANT TO YOU?
OF COURSE!
REALLY?

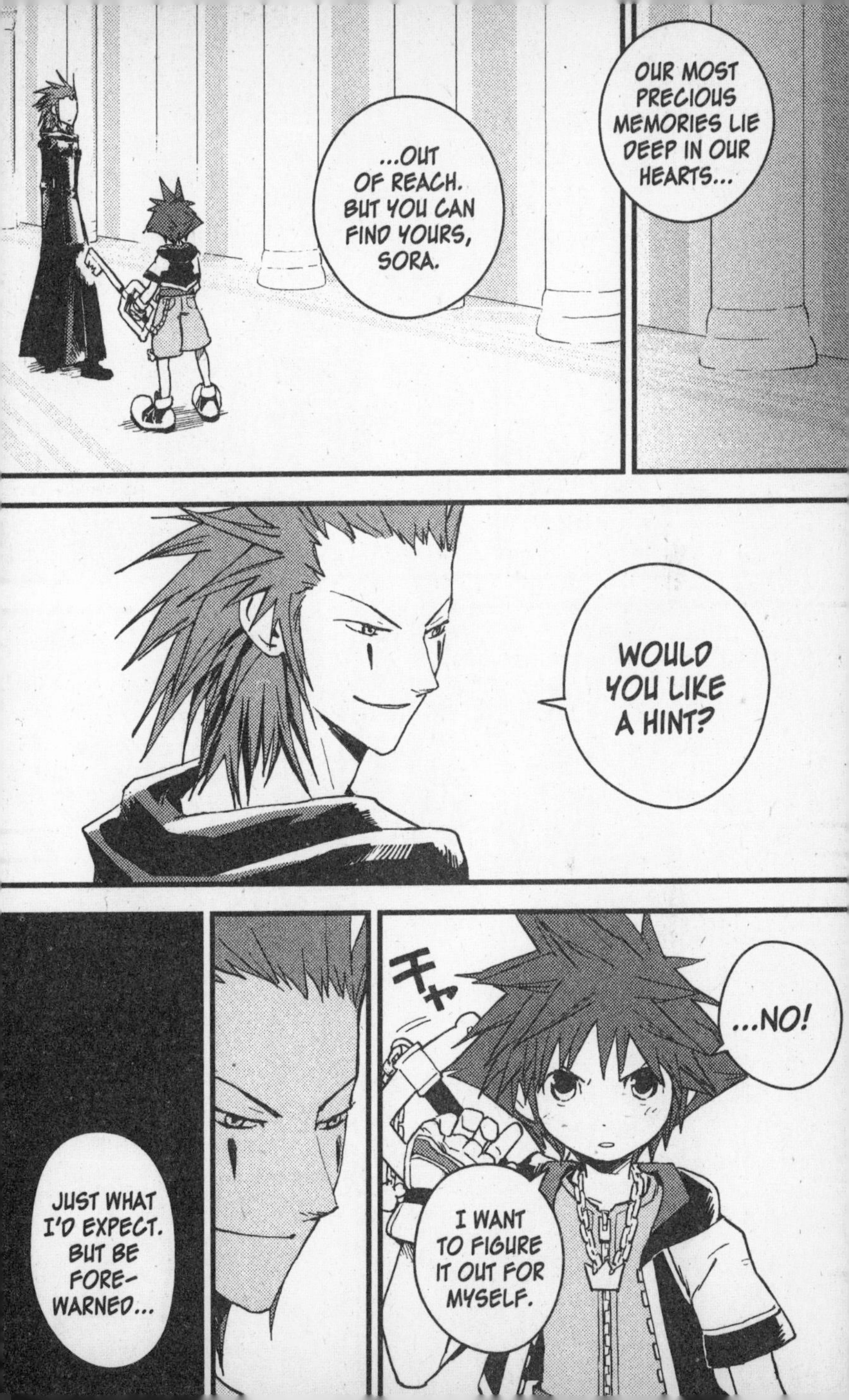
OUR MOST PRECIOUS MEMORIES LIE DEEP IN OUR HEARTS...
...OUT OF REACH. BUT YOU CAN FIND YOURS, SORA.
WOULD YOU LIKE A HINT?
...NO!
I WANT TO FIGURE IT OUT FOR MYSELF.
JUST WHAT I'D EXPECT. BUT BE FORE-WARNED...

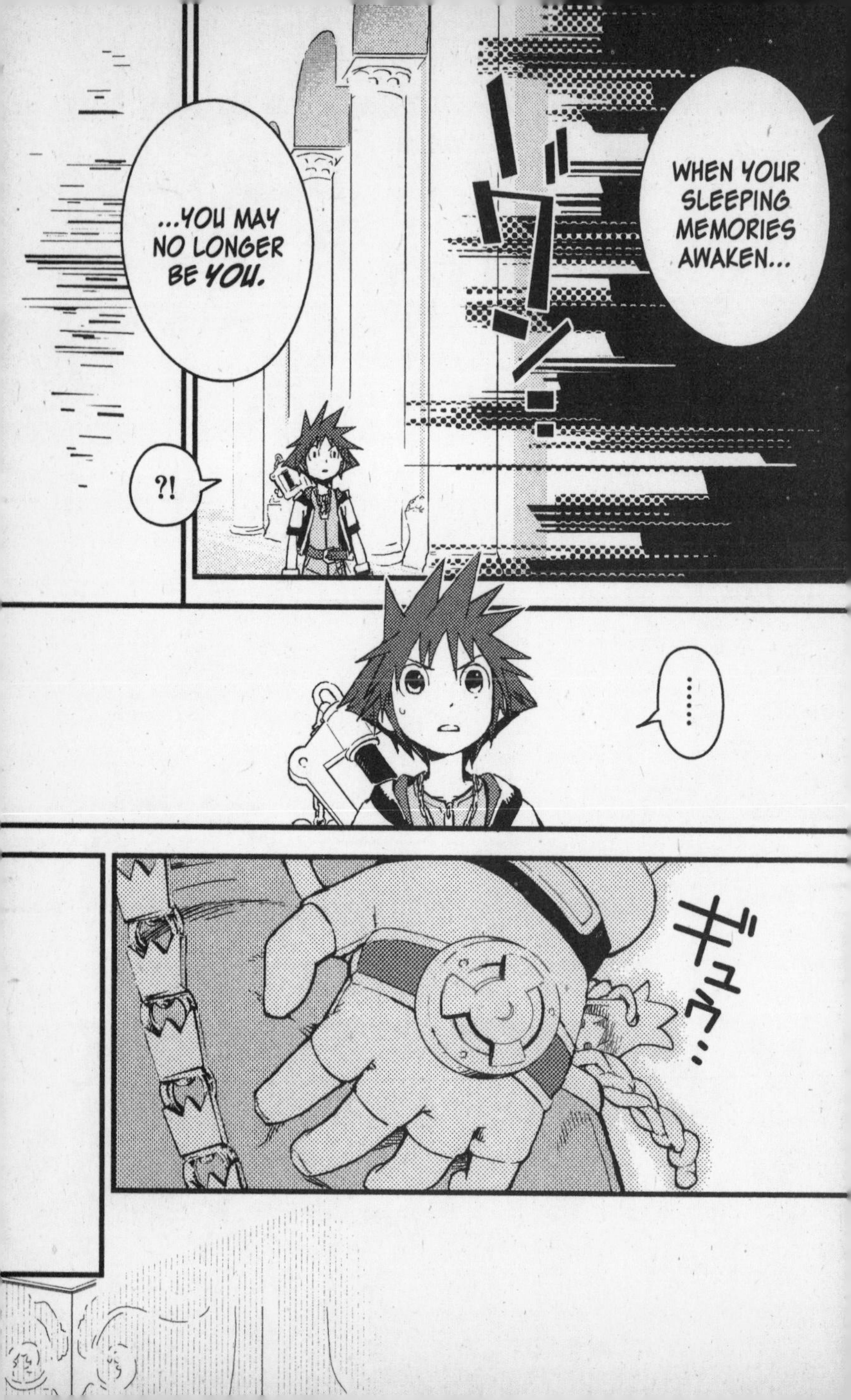
WHEN YOUR SLEEPING MEMORIES AWAKEN...
...YOU MAY NO LONGER BE YOU.
?!
......
ギュウ

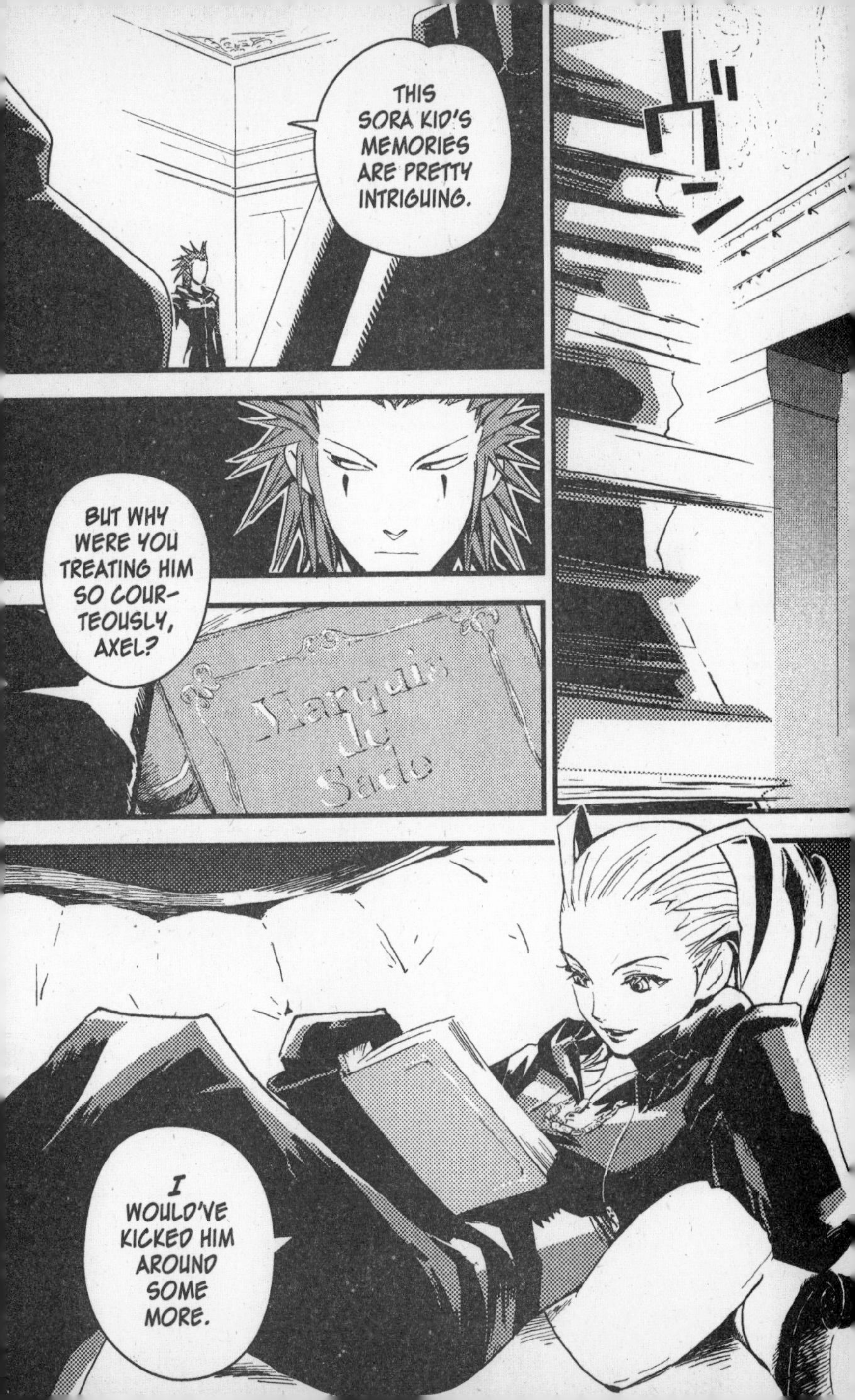
THIS SORA KID'S MEMORIES ARE PRETTY INTRIGUING.
BUT WHY WERE YOU TREATING HIM SO COUR-TEOUSLY, AXEL?
Marquis de Sade
I WOULD'VE KICKED HIM AROUND SOME MORE.

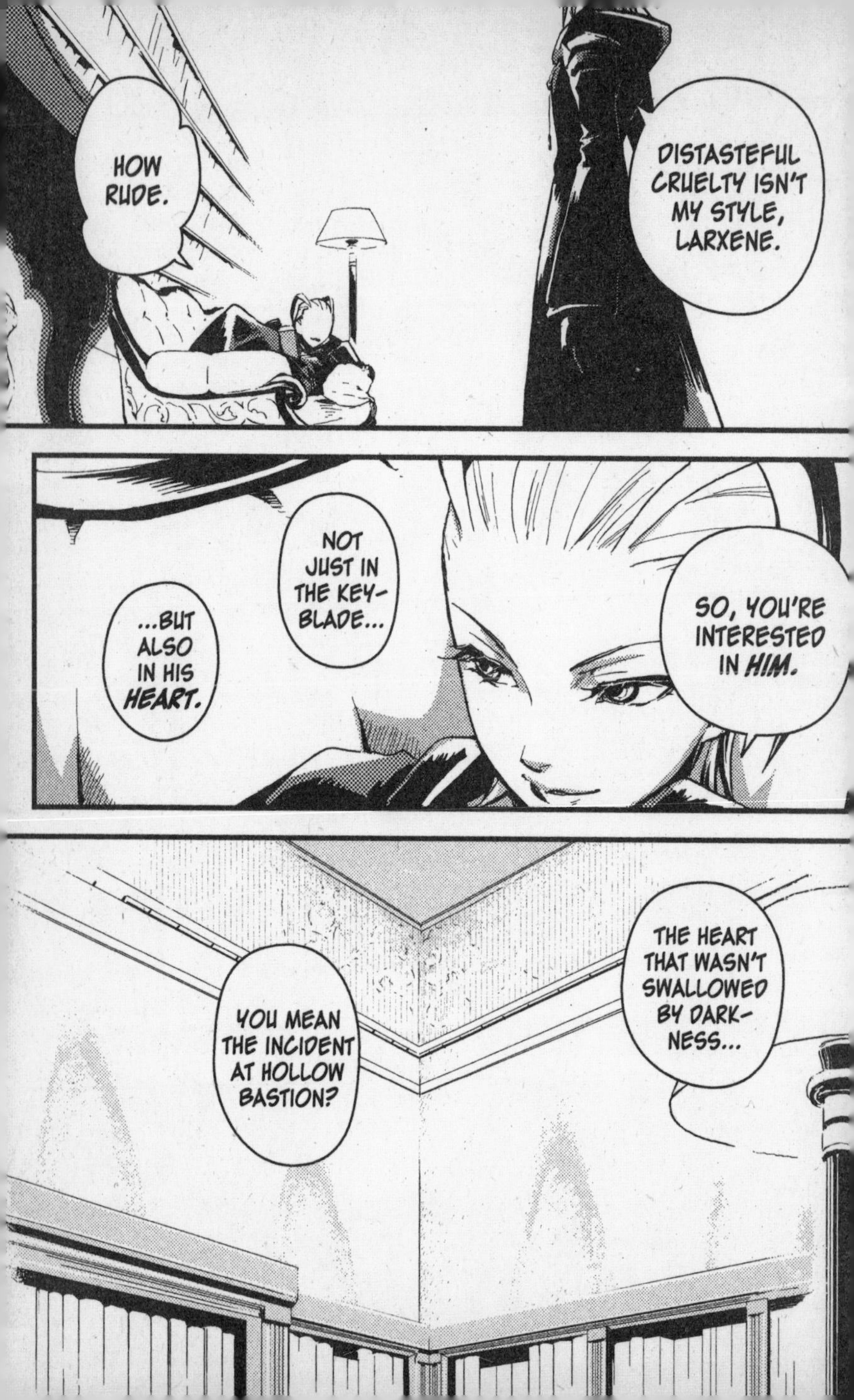
DISTASTEFUL CRUELTY ISN'T MY STYLE, LARXENE.
HOW RUDE.
SO, YOU'RE INTERESTED IN *HIM.*
NOT JUST IN THE KEY-BLADE...
...BUT ALSO IN HIS *HEART.*
THE HEART THAT WASN'T SWALLOWED BY DARK-NESS...
YOU MEAN THE INCIDENT AT HOLLOW BASTION?

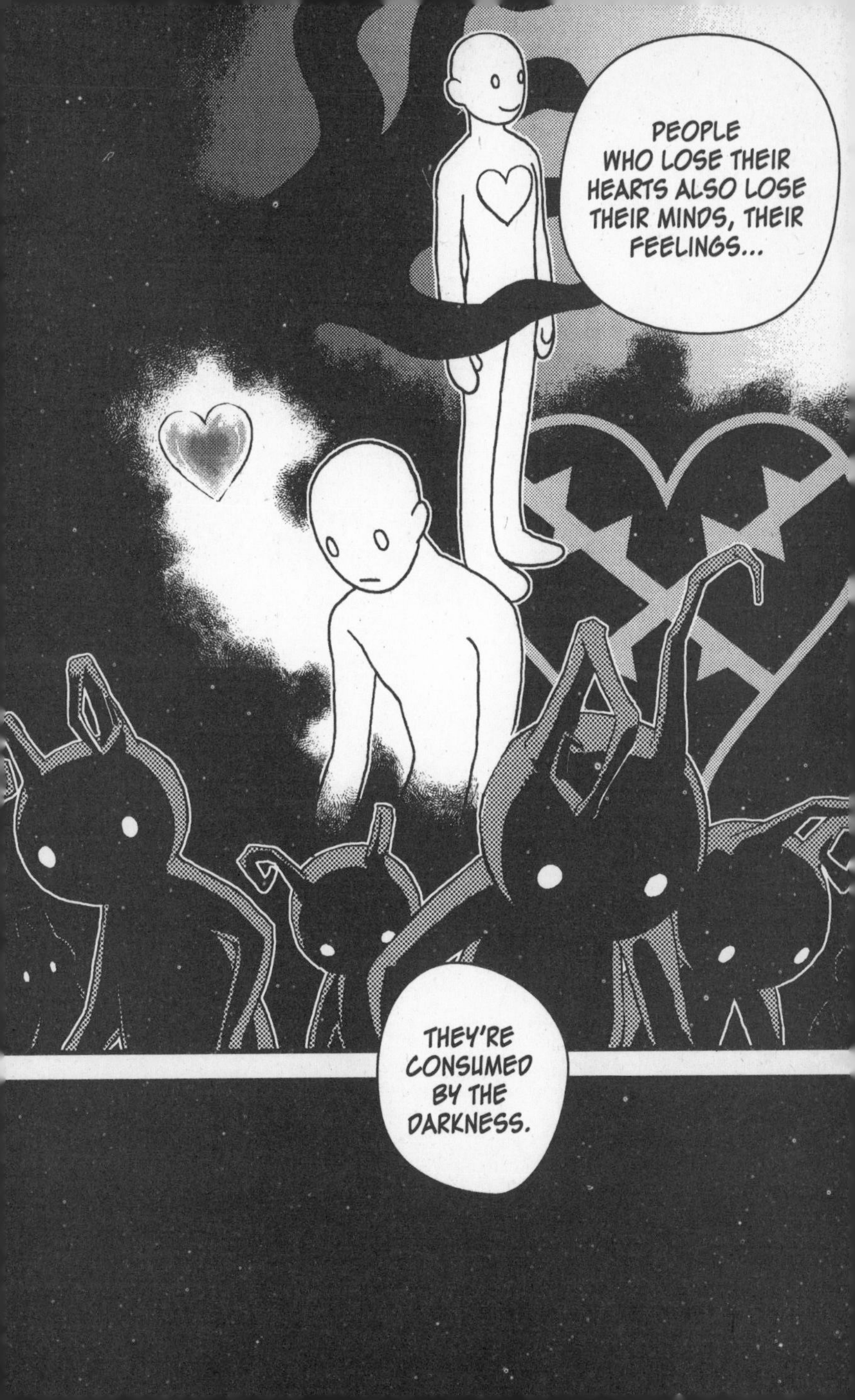
PEOPLE WHO LOSE THEIR HEARTS ALSO LOSE THEIR MINDS, THEIR FEELINGS...
THEY'RE CONSUMED BY THE DARKNESS.

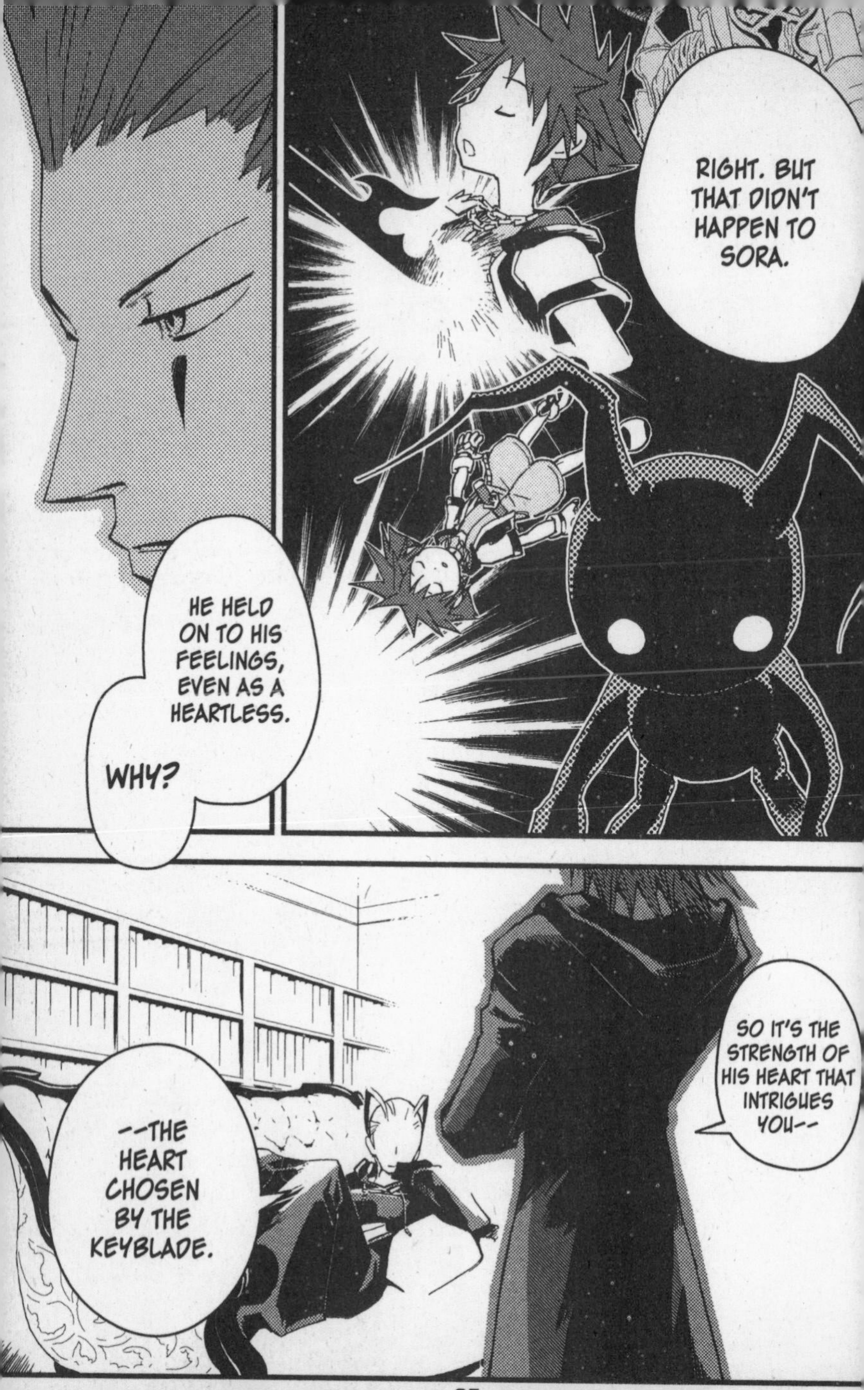
RIGHT. BUT THAT DIDN'T HAPPEN TO SORA.
HE HELD ON TO HIS FEELINGS, EVEN AS A HEARTLESS.
WHY?
SO IT'S THE STRENGTH OF HIS HEART THAT INTRIGUES YOU--
--THE HEART CHOSEN BY THE KEYBLADE.

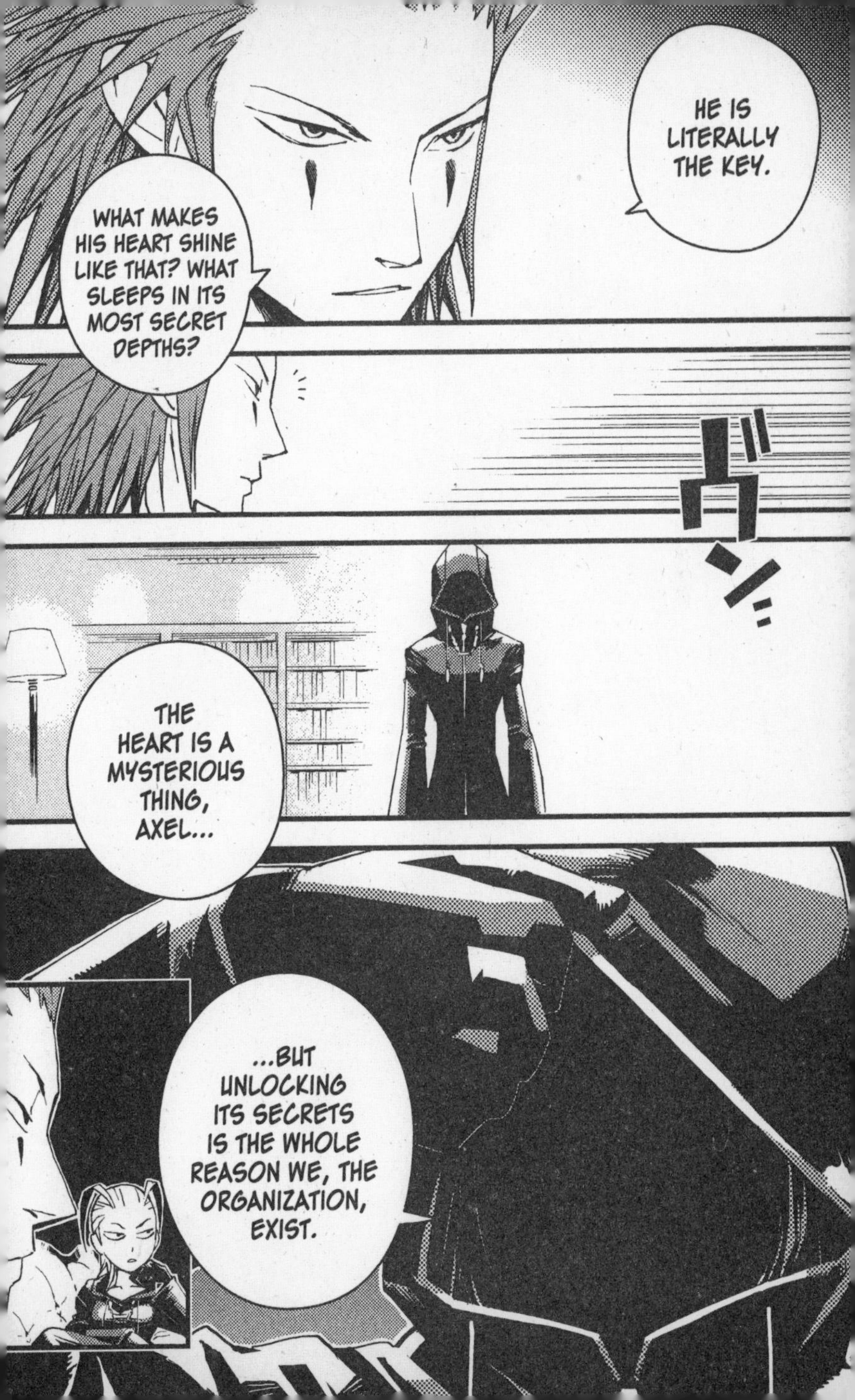
HE IS LITERALLY THE KEY.
WHAT MAKES HIS HEART SHINE LIKE THAT? WHAT SLEEPS IN ITS MOST SECRET DEPTHS?
ドン
THE HEART IS A MYSTERIOUS THING, AXEL...
...BUT UNLOCKING ITS SECRETS IS THE WHOLE REASON WE, THE ORGANIZATION, EXIST.

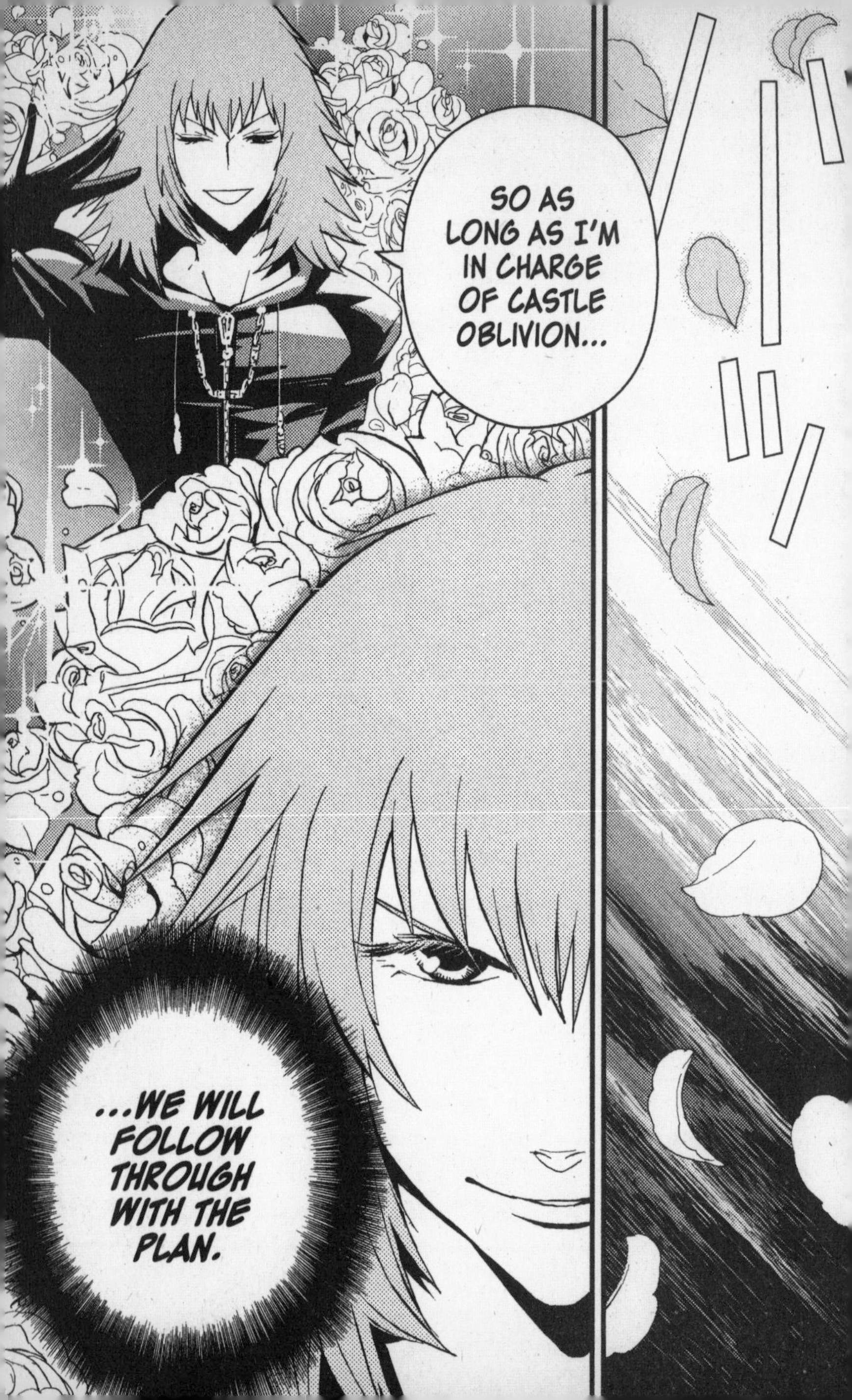
SO AS LONG AS I'M IN CHARGE OF CASTLE OBLIVION...
...WE WILL FOLLOW THROUGH WITH THE PLAN.

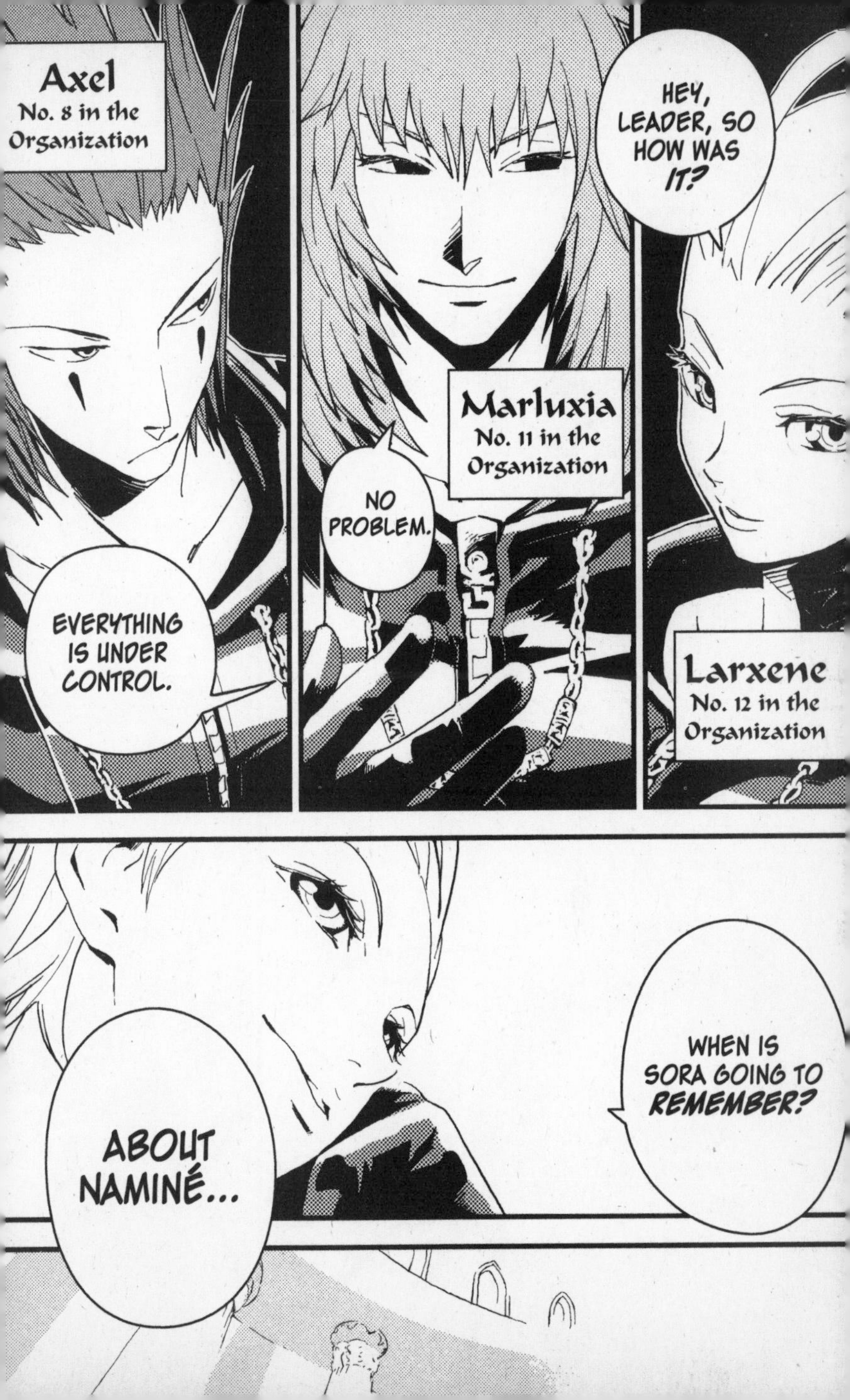
HEY, LEADER, SO HOW WAS IT?
Larxene No. 12 in the Organization
Marluxia No. 11 in the Organization
NO PROBLEM.
Axel No. 8 in the Organization
EVERYTHING IS UNDER CONTROL.
WHEN IS SORA GOING TO REMEMBER?
ABOUT NAMINÉ...

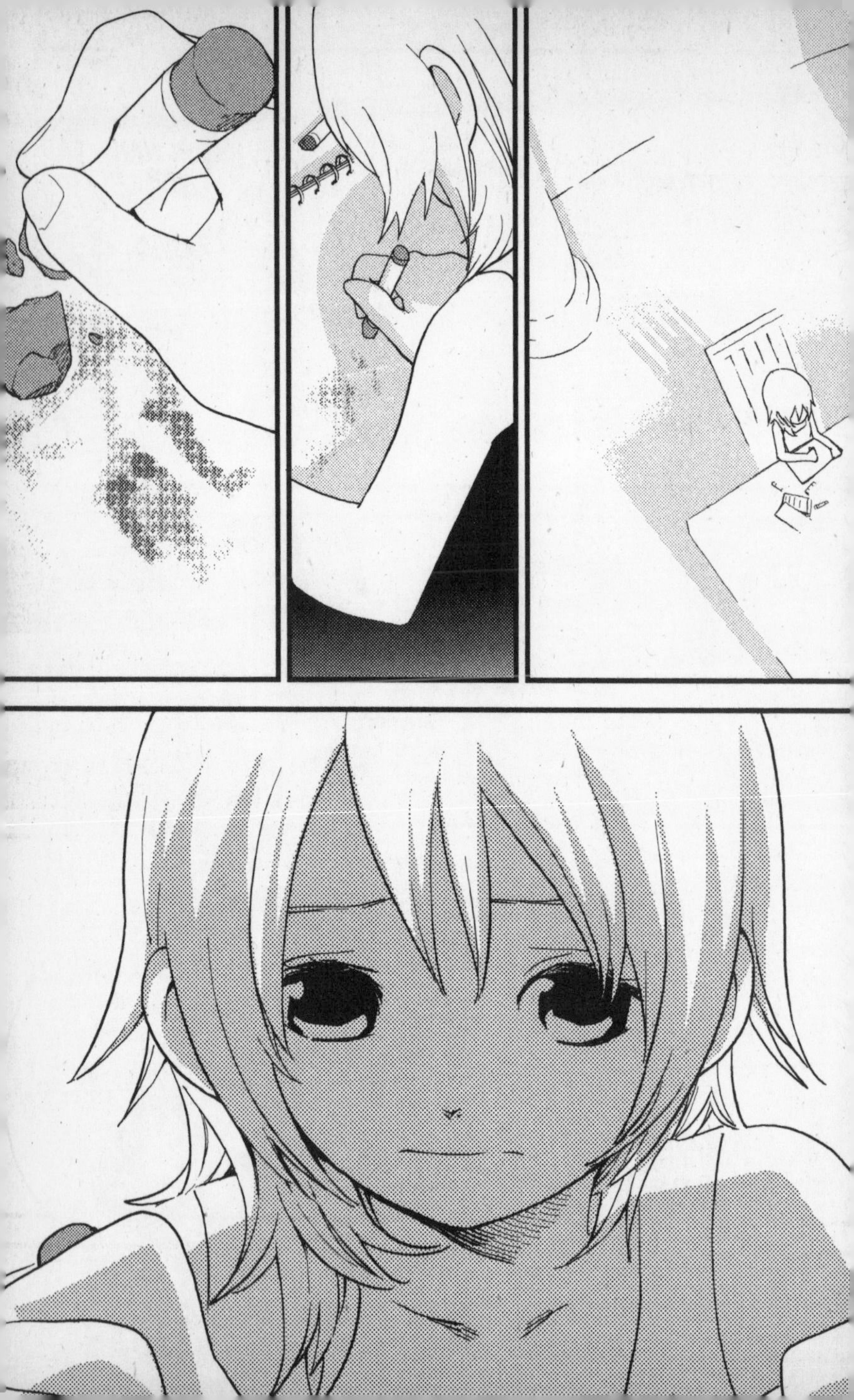

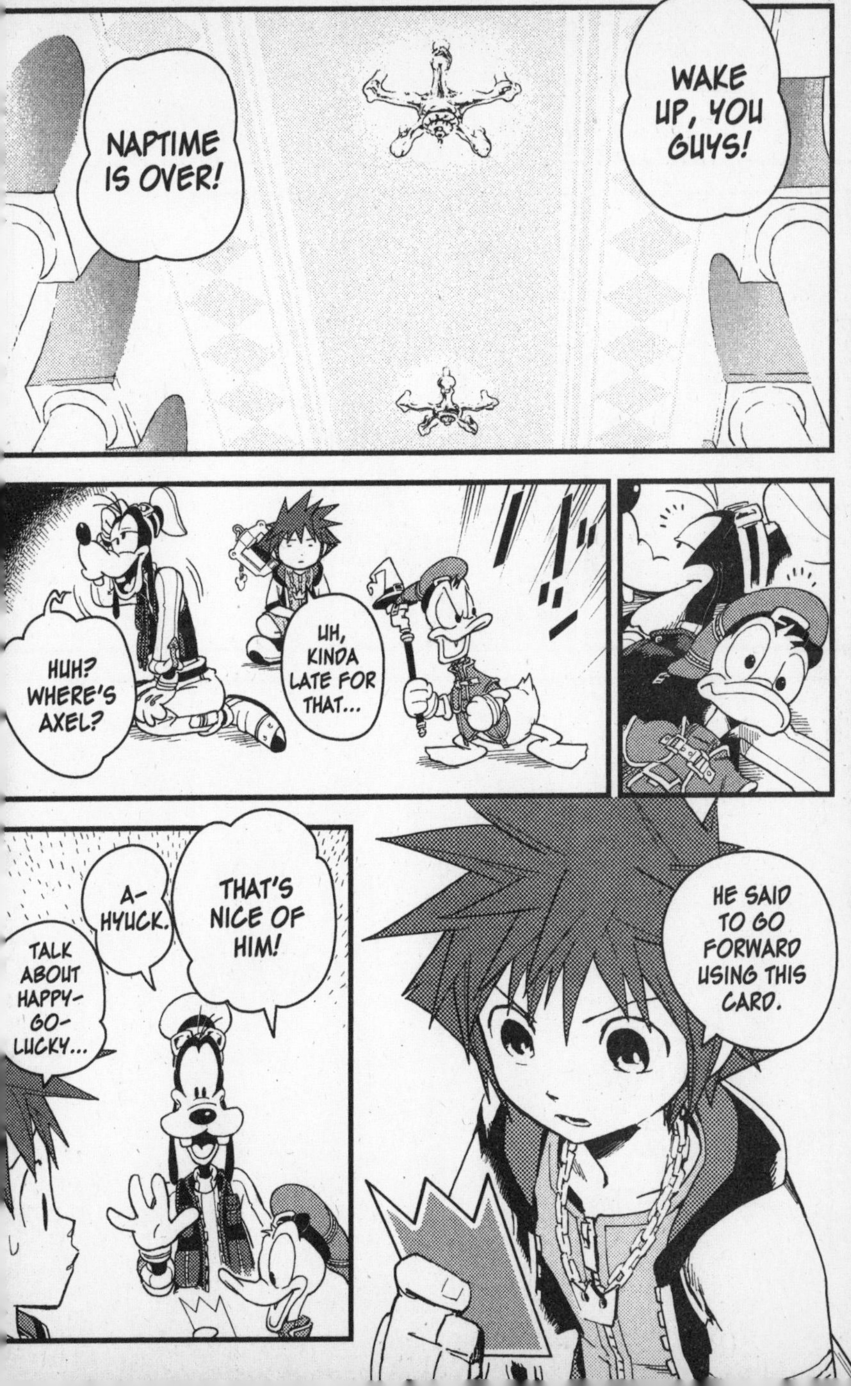
WAKE UP, YOU GUYS!
NAPTIME IS OVER!
UH, KINDA LATE FOR THAT...
HUH? WHERE'S AXEL?
HE SAID TO GO FORWARD USING THIS CARD.
THAT'S NICE OF HIM!
A-HYUCK.
TALK ABOUT HAPPY-GO-LUCKY...

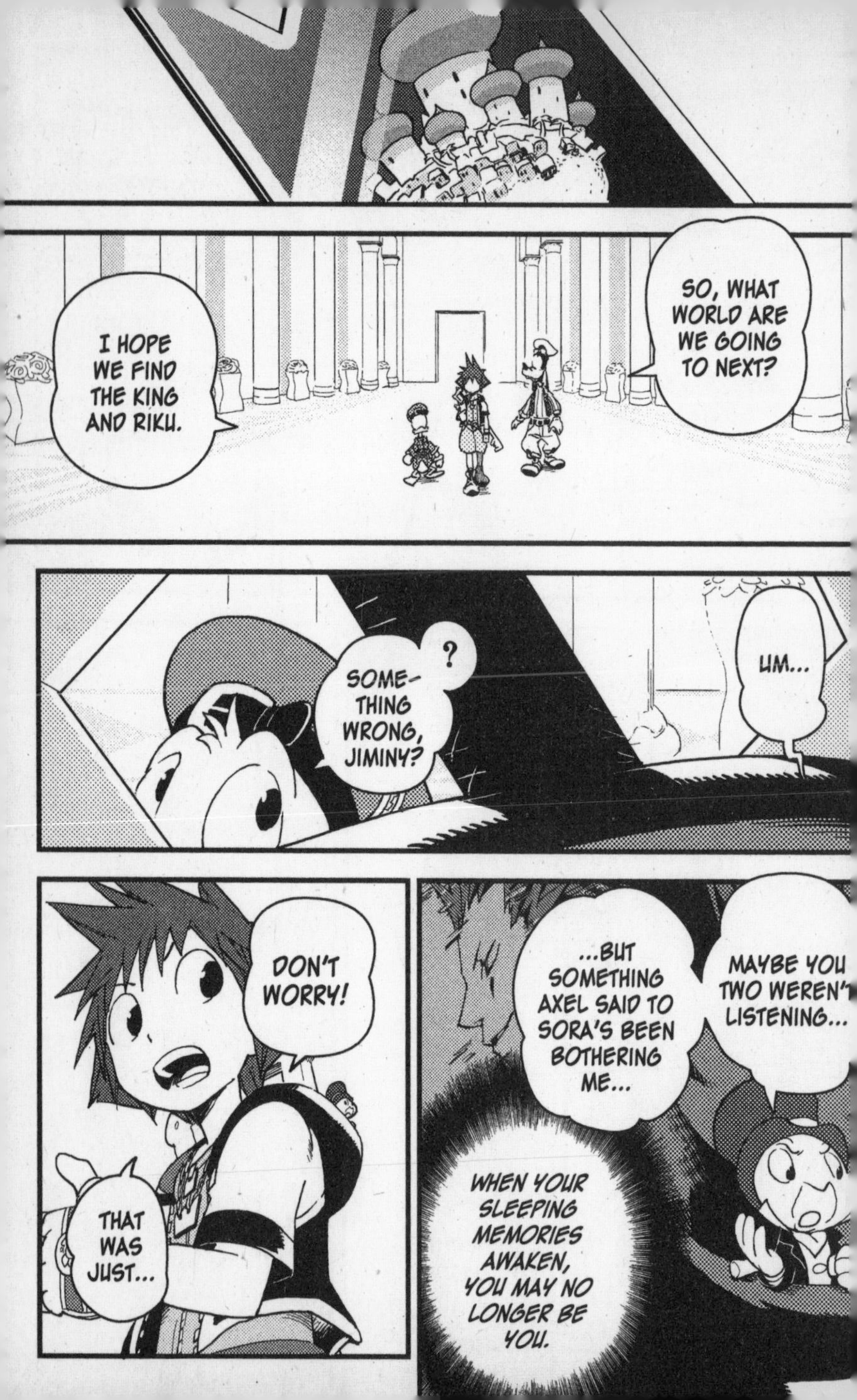
SO, WHAT WORLD ARE WE GOING TO NEXT?
I HOPE WE FIND THE KING AND RIKU.
UM...
?
SOME-THING WRONG, JIMINY?
MAYBE YOU TWO WEREN'T LISTENING...
...BUT SOMETHING AXEL SAID TO SORA'S BEEN BOTHERING ME...
WHEN YOUR SLEEPING MEMORIES AWAKEN, YOU MAY NO LONGER BE YOU.
DON'T WORRY!
THAT WAS JUST...

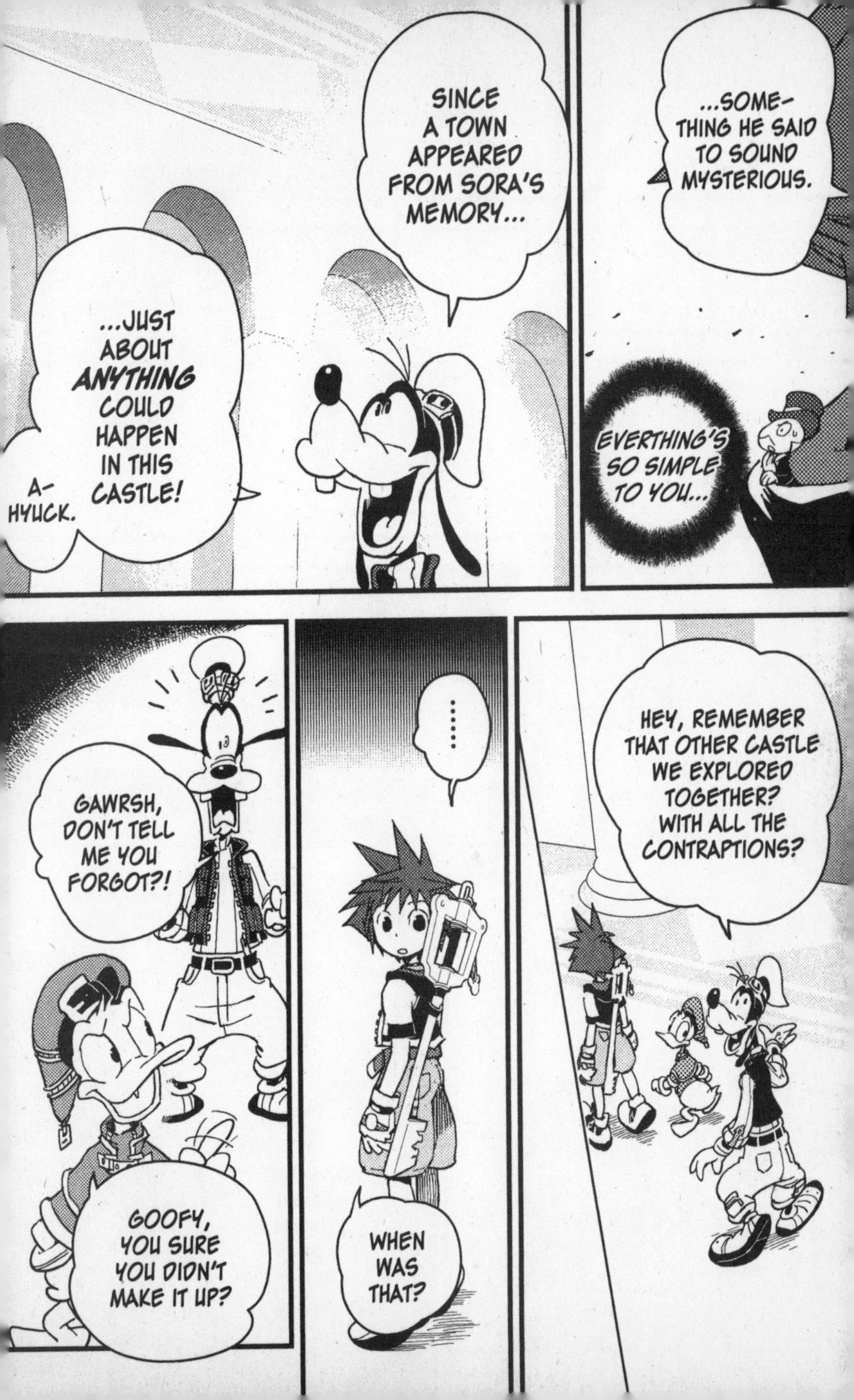
...SOME-THING HE SAID TO SOUND MYSTERIOUS.
EVERTHING'S SO SIMPLE TO YOU...
SINCE A TOWN APPEARED FROM SORA'S MEMORY...
...JUST ABOUT *ANYTHING* COULD HAPPEN IN THIS CASTLE!
A-HYUCK.
HEY, REMEMBER THAT OTHER CASTLE WE EXPLORED TOGETHER? WITH ALL THE CONTRAPTIONS?
......
WHEN WAS THAT?
GAWRSH, DON'T TELL ME YOU FORGOT?!
GOOFY, YOU SURE YOU DIDN'T MAKE IT UP?

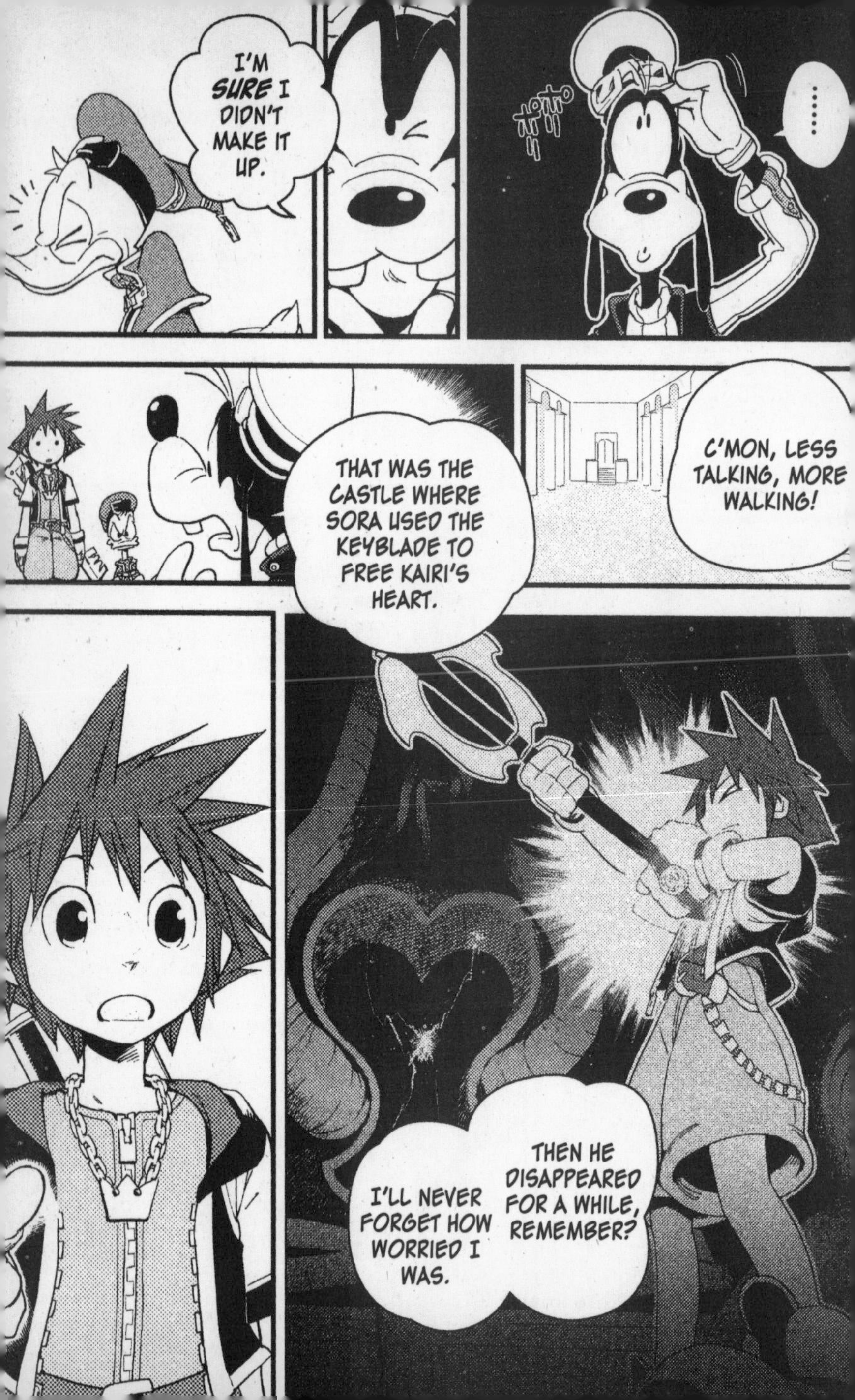
......
I'M SURE I DIDN'T MAKE IT UP.
C'MON, LESS TALKING, MORE WALKING!
THAT WAS THE CASTLE WHERE SORA USED THE KEYBLADE TO FREE KAIRI'S HEART.
THEN HE DISAPPEARED FOR A WHILE, REMEMBER?
I'LL NEVER FORGET HOW WORRIED I WAS.

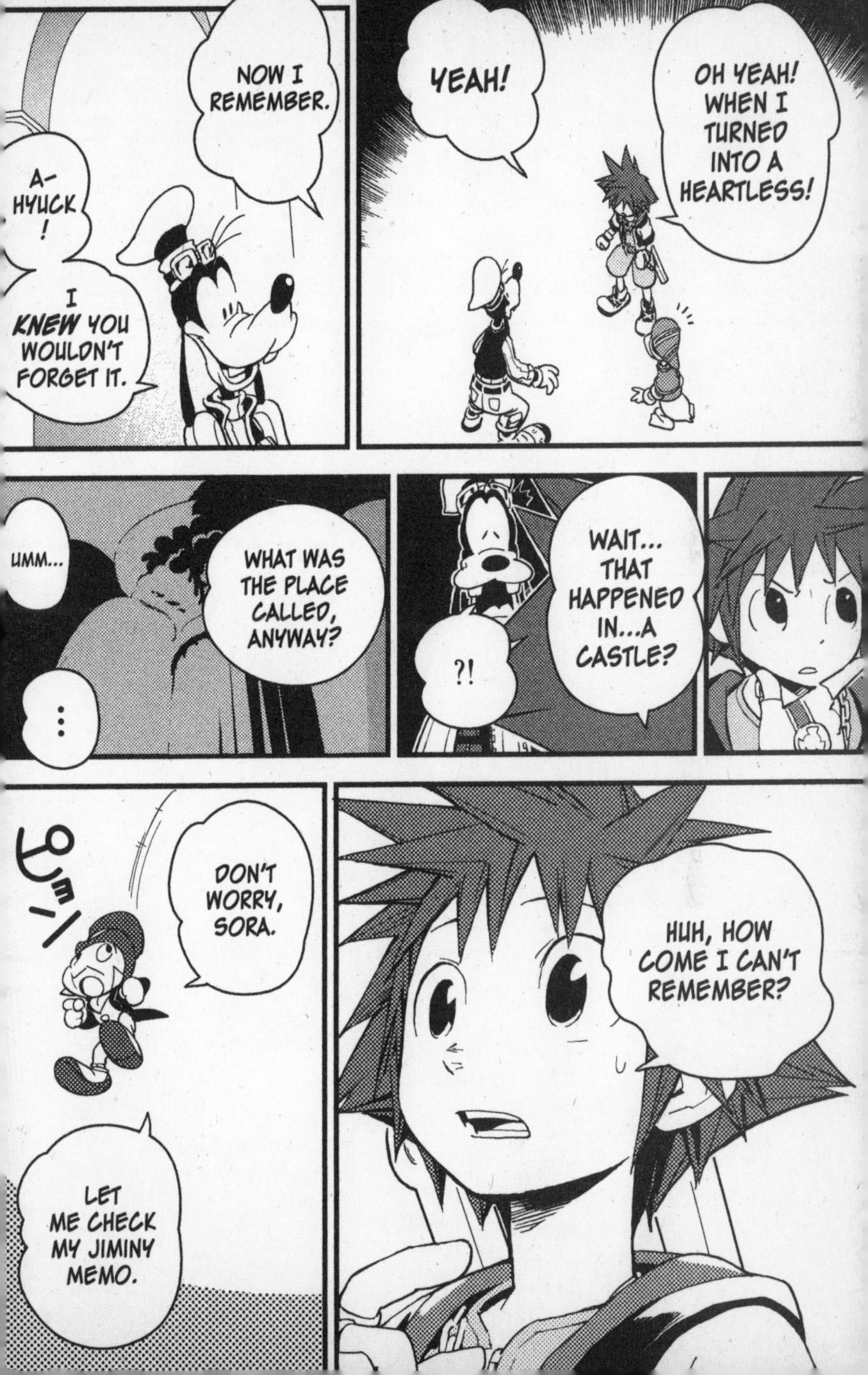
OH YEAH! WHEN I TURNED INTO A HEARTLESS!
YEAH!
NOW I REMEMBER.
A-HYUCK!
I KNEW YOU WOULDN'T FORGET IT.
WAIT... THAT HAPPENED IN...A CASTLE?
?!
WHAT WAS THE PLACE CALLED, ANYWAY?
UMM...
...
HUH, HOW COME I CAN'T REMEMBER?
DON'T WORRY, SORA.
LET ME CHECK MY JIMINY MEMO.

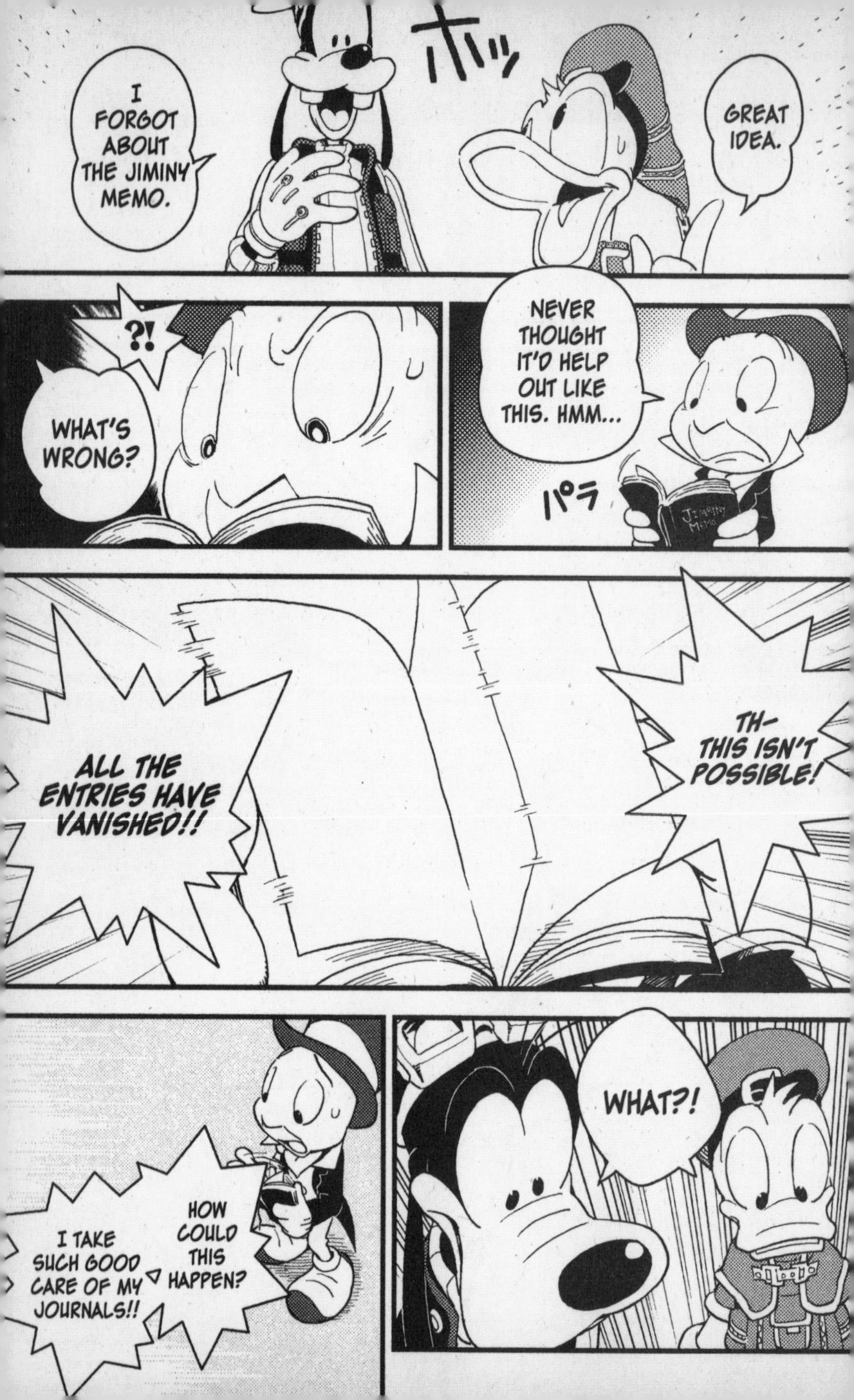
ホッ
GREAT IDEA.
I FORGOT ABOUT THE JIMINY MEMO.
NEVER THOUGHT IT'D HELP OUT LIKE THIS. HMM...
パラ
JIMINY MEMO
?!
WHAT'S WRONG?
TH- THIS ISN'T POSSIBLE!
ALL THE ENTRIES HAVE VANISHED!!
WHAT?!
HOW COULD THIS HAPPEN?
I TAKE SUCH GOOD CARE OF MY JOURNALS!!

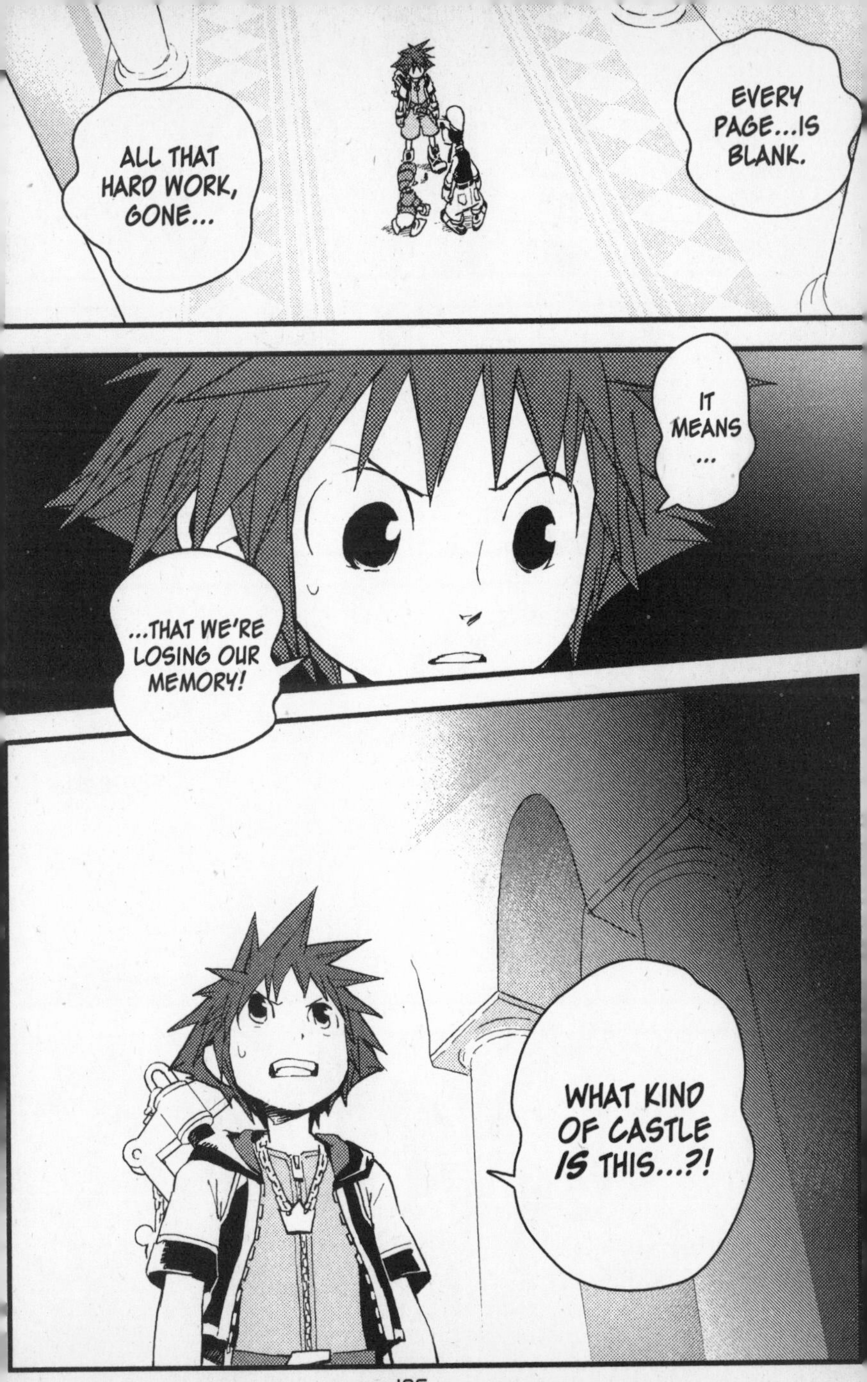
EVERY PAGE...IS BLANK.
ALL THAT HARD WORK, GONE...
IT MEANS ...
...THAT WE'RE LOSING OUR MEMORY!
WHAT KIND OF CASTLE *IS* THIS...?!

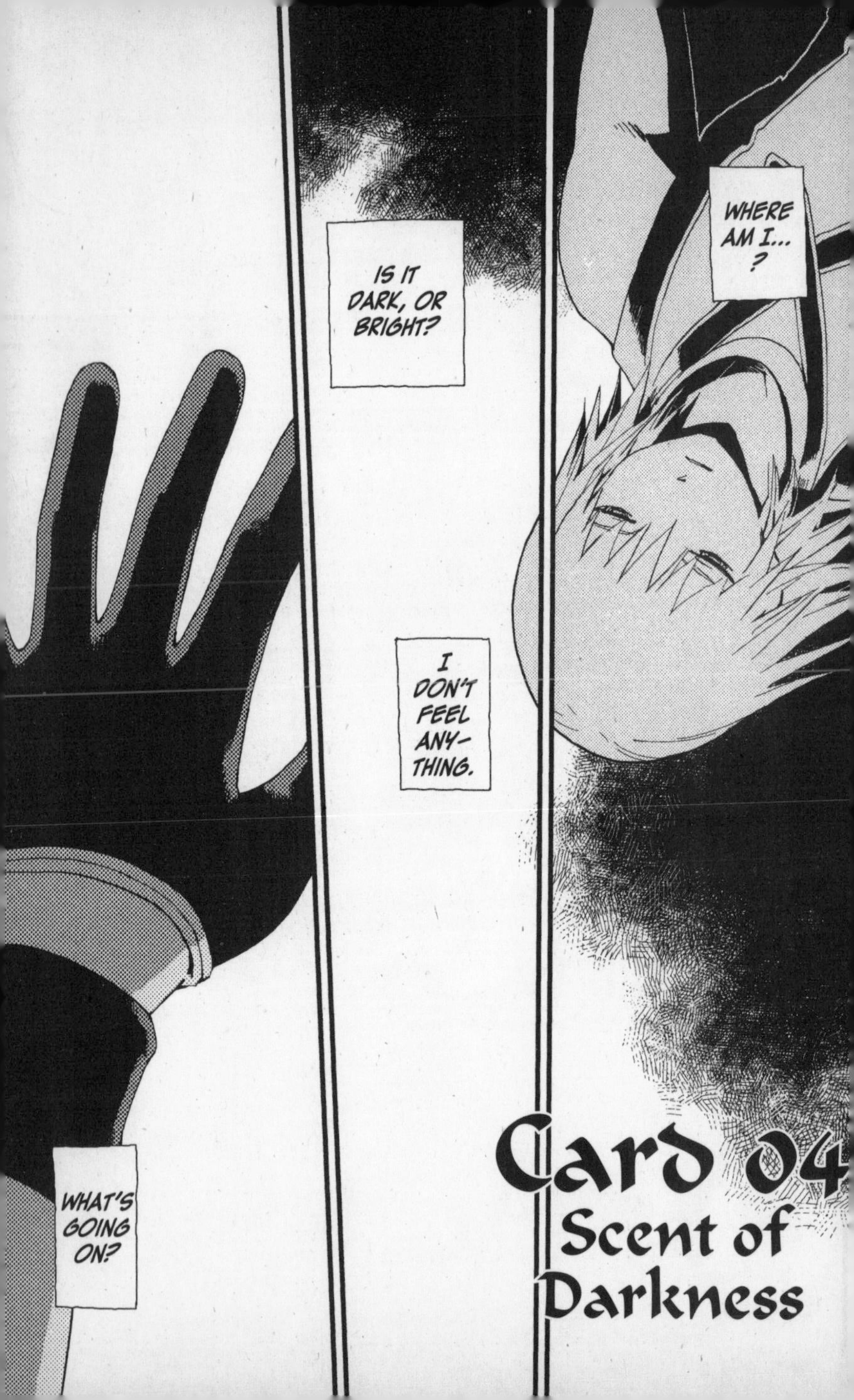
WHERE AM I... ?
Card 04
Scent of Darkness
IS IT DARK, OR BRIGHT?
I DON'T FEEL ANYTHING.
WHAT'S GOING ON?

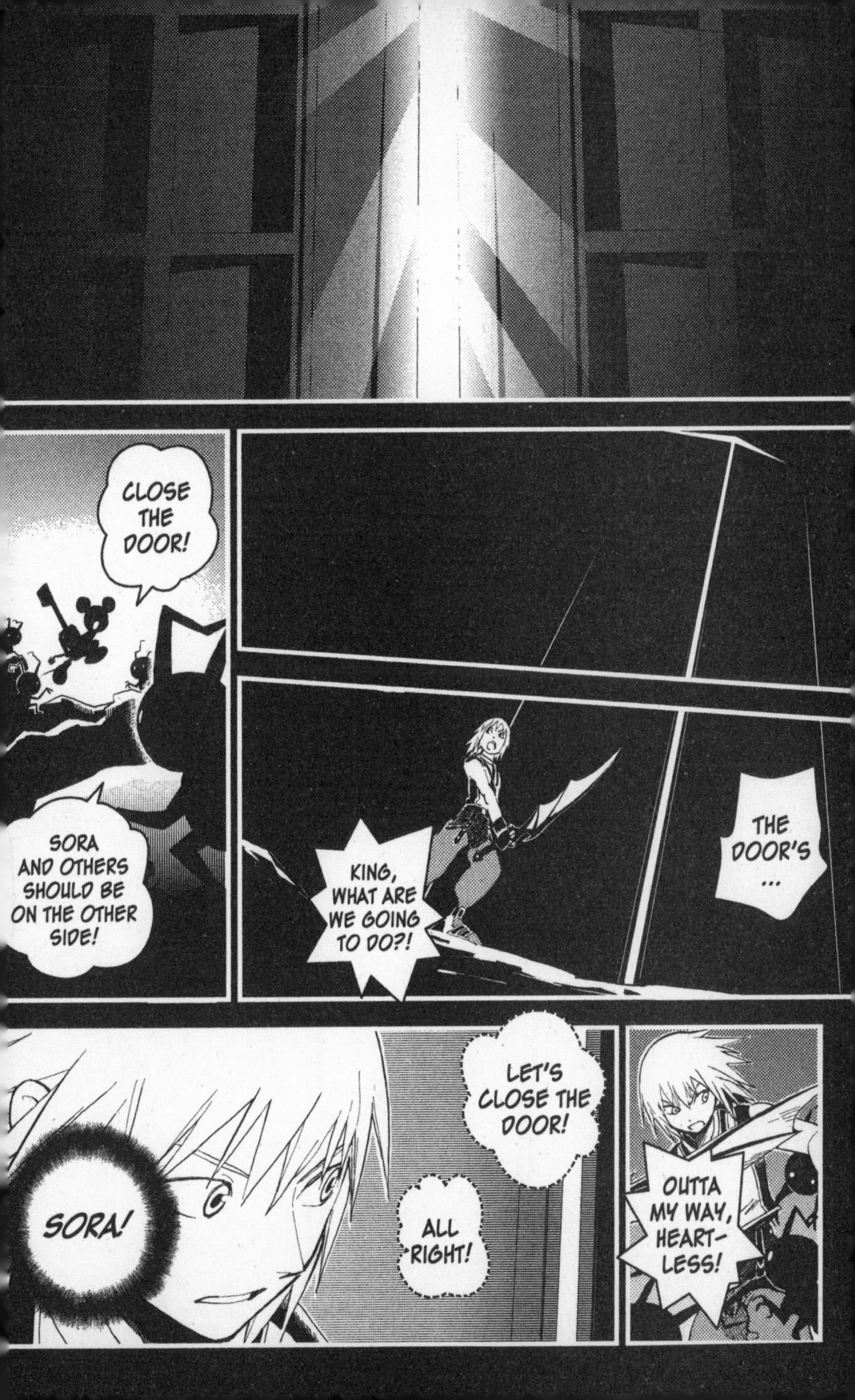
THE DOOR'S ...
KING, WHAT ARE WE GOING TO DO?!
CLOSE THE DOOR!
SORA AND OTHERS SHOULD BE ON THE OTHER SIDE!
OUTTA MY WAY, HEART- LESS!
LET'S CLOSE THE DOOR!
SORA!
ALL RIGHT!

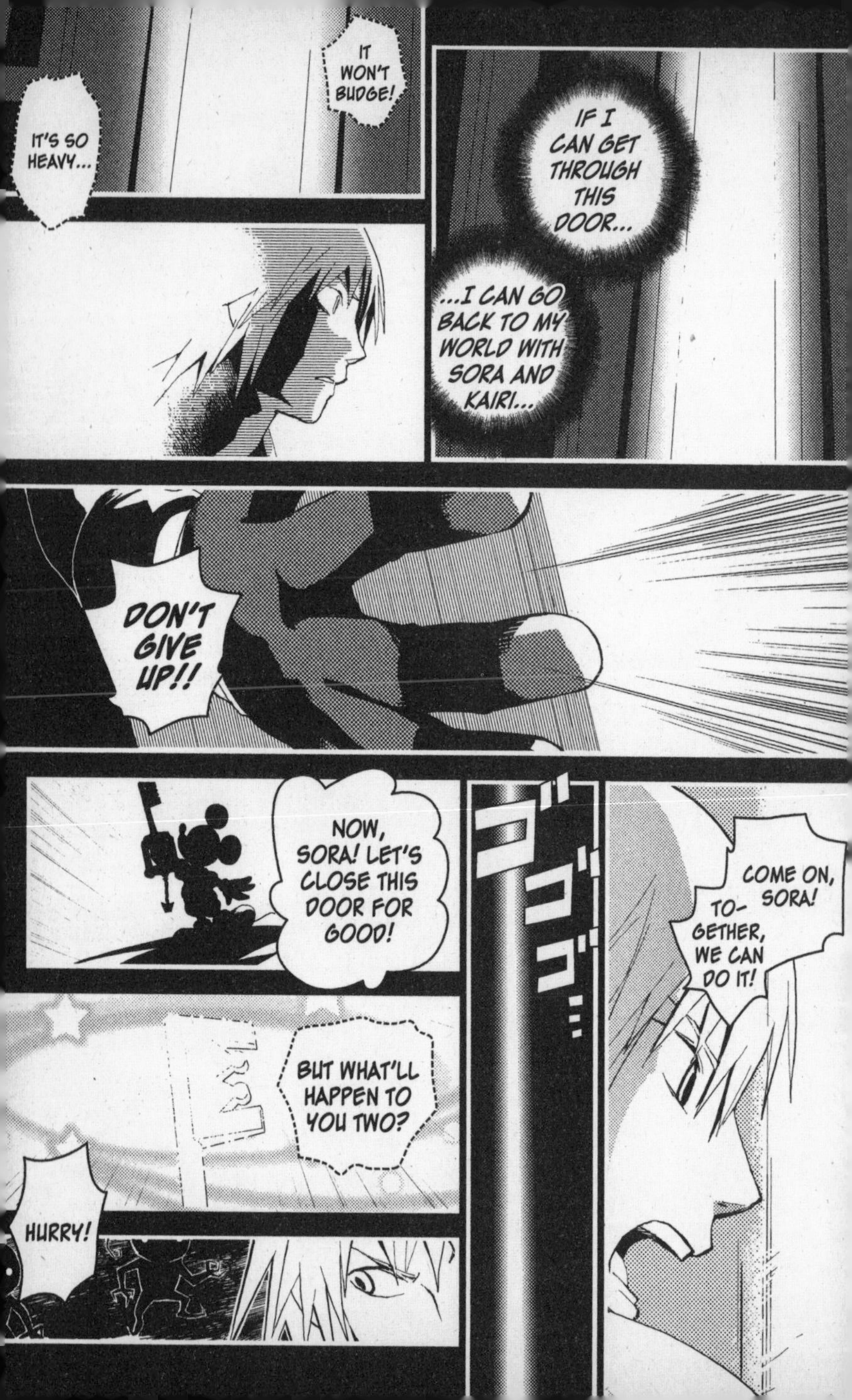
IF I CAN GET THROUGH THIS DOOR...
...I CAN GO BACK TO MY WORLD WITH SORA AND KAIRI...
IT WON'T BUDGE!
IT'S SO HEAVY...
DON'T GIVE UP!!
COME ON, SORA!
TO-GETHER, WE CAN DO IT!
ゴゴゴ…
NOW, SORA! LET'S CLOSE THIS DOOR FOR GOOD!
BUT WHAT'LL HAPPEN TO YOU TWO?
HURRY!

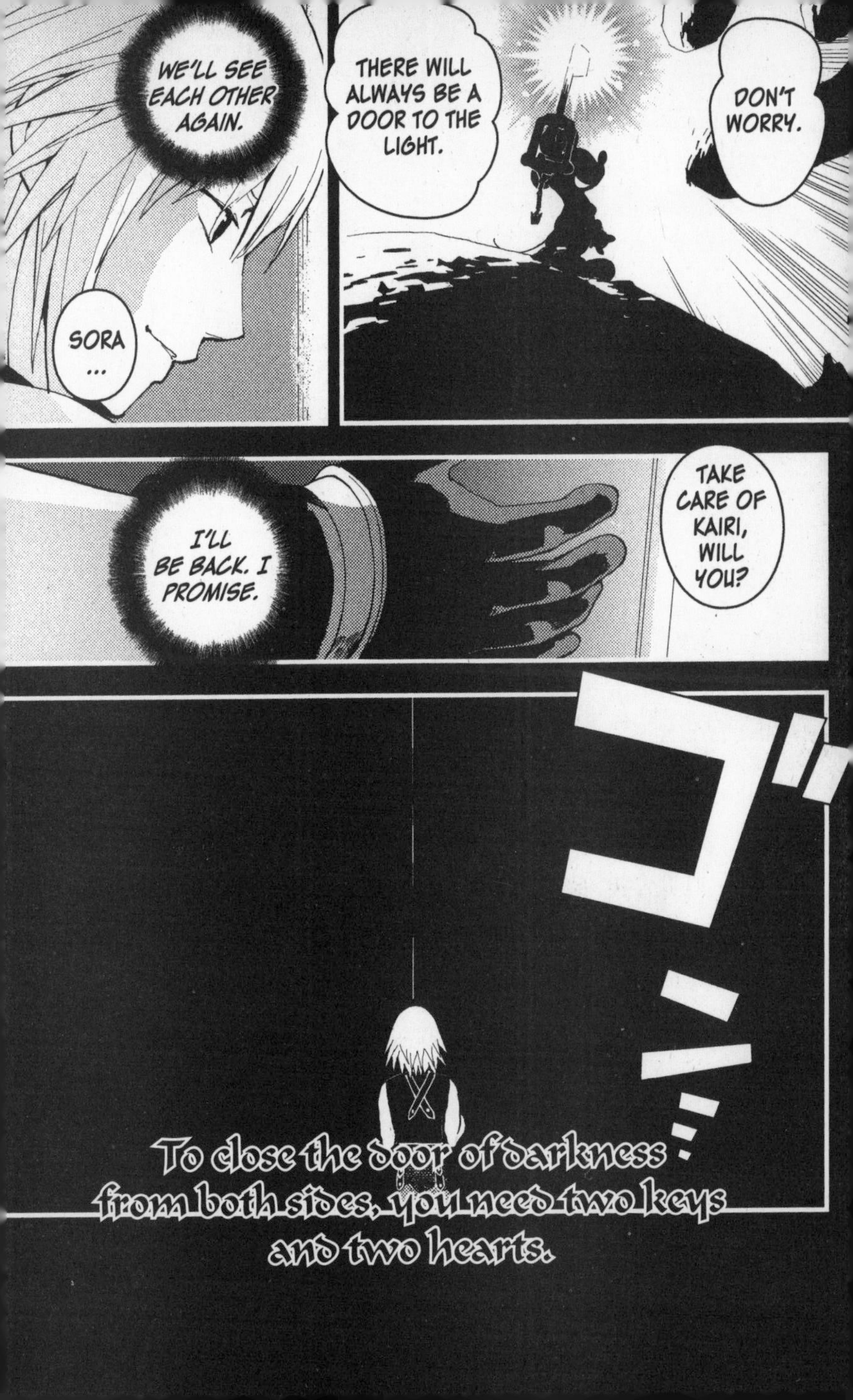
DON'T WORRY.
THERE WILL ALWAYS BE A DOOR TO THE LIGHT.
WE'LL SEE EACH OTHER AGAIN.
SORA ...
TAKE CARE OF KAIRI, WILL YOU?
I'LL BE BACK. I PROMISE.
ゴ
To close the door of darkness from both sides, you need two keys and two hearts.

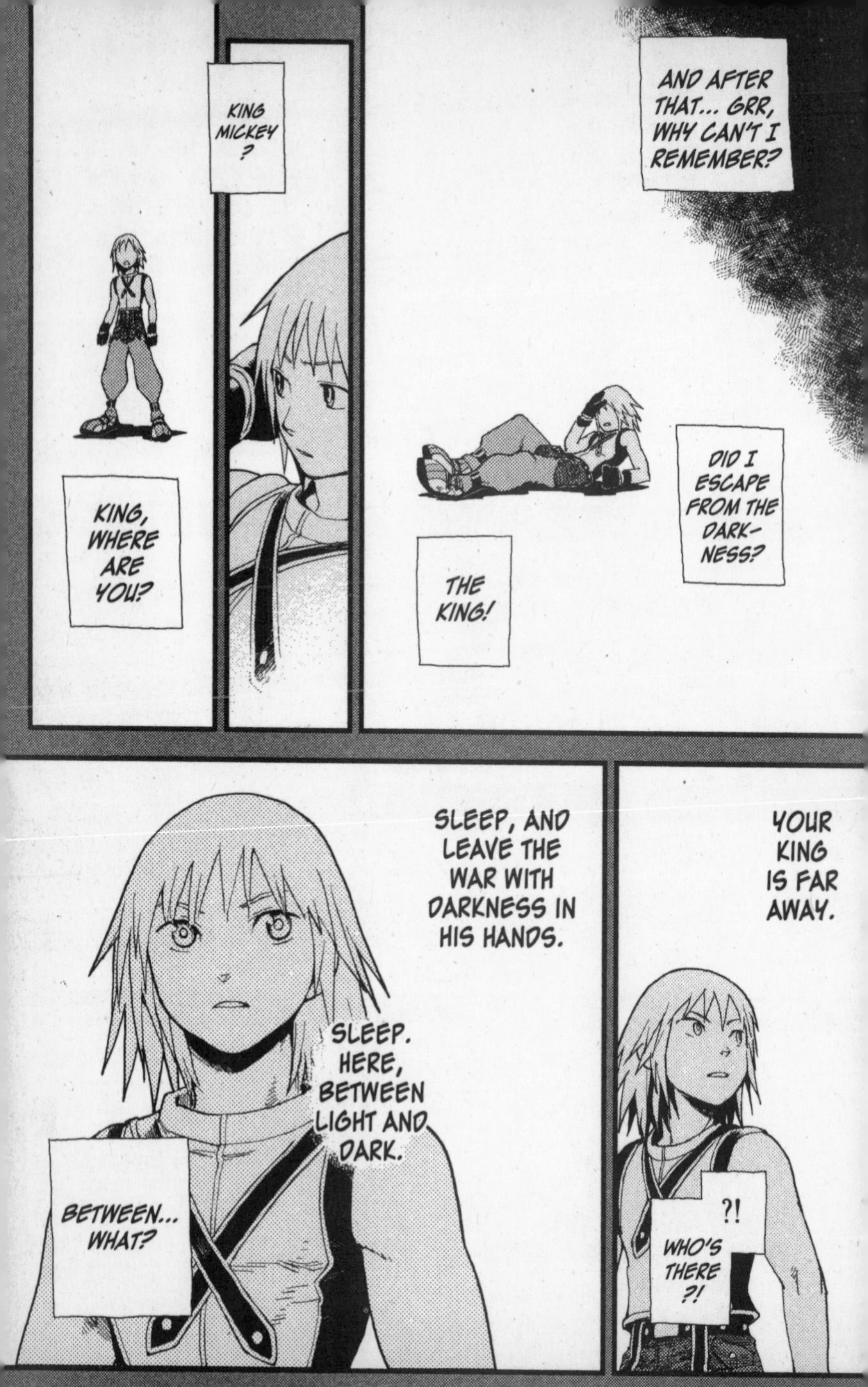
AND AFTER THAT... GRR, WHY CAN'T I REMEMBER?
DID I ESCAPE FROM THE DARK-NESS?
THE KING!
KING MICKEY?
KING, WHERE ARE YOU?
YOUR KING IS FAR AWAY.
?!
WHO'S THERE?!
SLEEP, AND LEAVE THE WAR WITH DARKNESS IN HIS HANDS.
SLEEP. HERE, BETWEEN LIGHT AND DARK.
BETWEEN... WHAT?

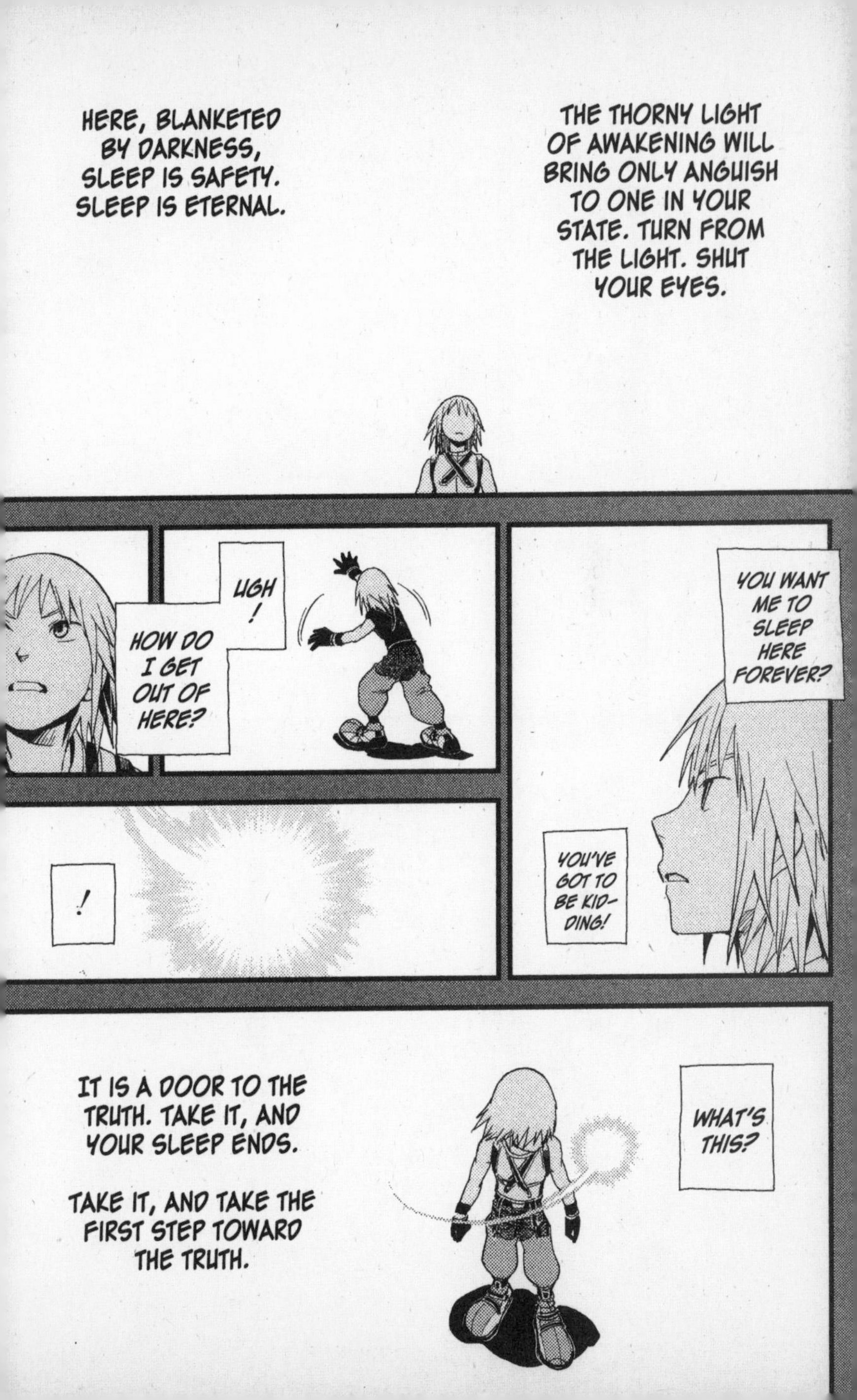
THE THORNY LIGHT OF AWAKENING WILL BRING ONLY ANGUISH TO ONE IN YOUR STATE. TURN FROM THE LIGHT. SHUT YOUR EYES.
HERE, BLANKETED BY DARKNESS, SLEEP IS SAFETY. SLEEP IS ETERNAL.
YOU WANT ME TO SLEEP HERE FOREVER?
YOU'VE GOT TO BE KID-DING!
UGH!
HOW DO I GET OUT OF HERE?
!
WHAT'S THIS?
IT IS A DOOR TO THE TRUTH. TAKE IT, AND YOUR SLEEP ENDS.
TAKE IT, AND TAKE THE FIRST STEP TOWARD THE TRUTH.

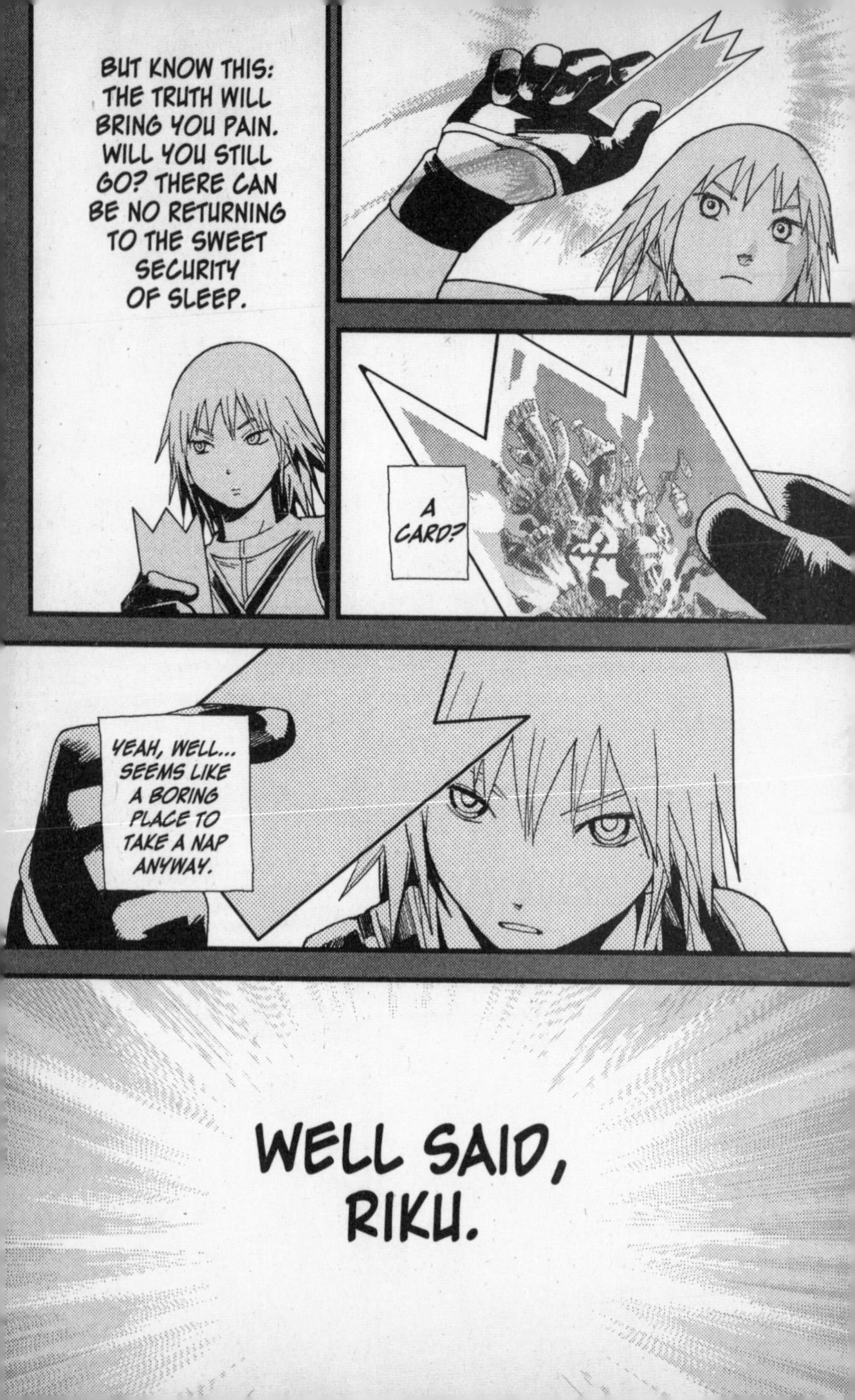
A CARD?
BUT KNOW THIS: THE TRUTH WILL BRING YOU PAIN. WILL YOU STILL GO? THERE CAN BE NO RETURNING TO THE SWEET SECURITY OF SLEEP.
YEAH, WELL... SEEMS LIKE A BORING PLACE TO TAKE A NAP ANYWAY.
WELL SAID, RIKU.

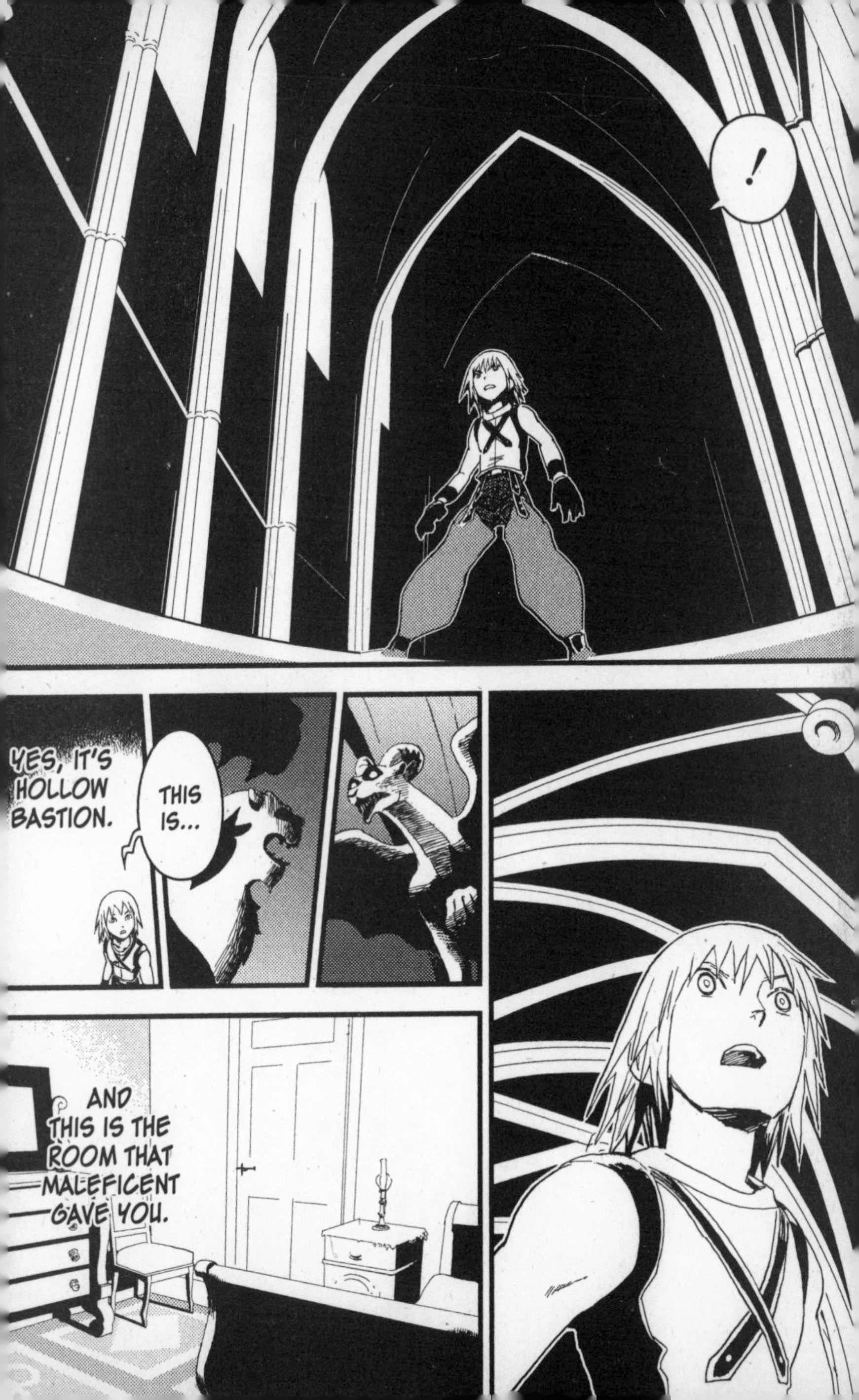
!
THIS IS...
YES, IT'S HOLLOW BASTION.
AND THIS IS THE ROOM THAT MALEFICENT GAVE YOU.

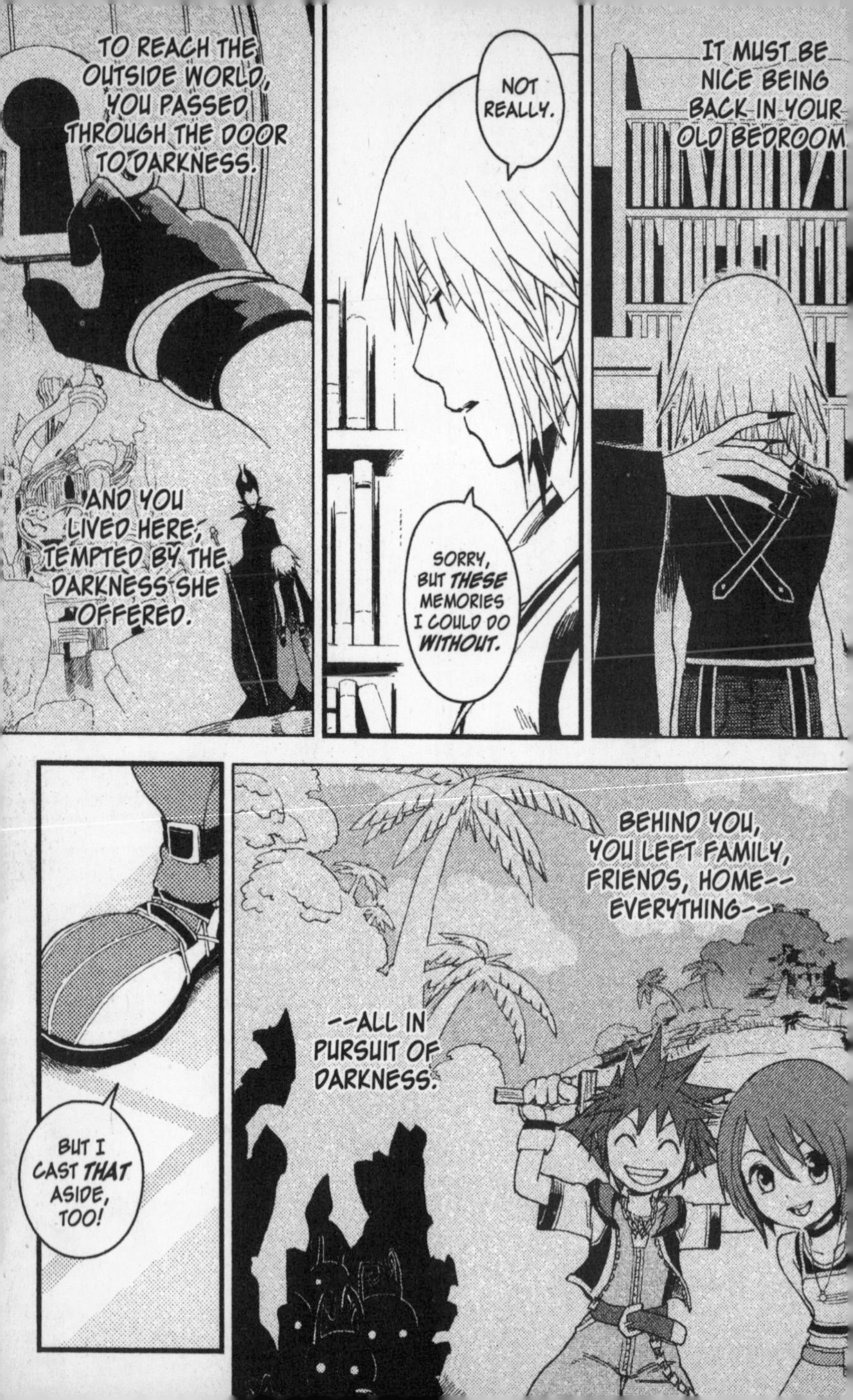
IT MUST BE NICE BEING BACK IN YOUR OLD BEDROOM.
NOT REALLY.
SORRY, BUT *THESE* MEMORIES I COULD DO *WITHOUT*.
TO REACH THE OUTSIDE WORLD, YOU PASSED THROUGH THE DOOR TO DARKNESS.
AND YOU LIVED HERE, TEMPTED BY THE DARKNESS SHE OFFERED.
BEHIND YOU, YOU LEFT FAMILY, FRIENDS, HOME-- EVERYTHING--
--ALL IN PURSUIT OF DARKNESS.
BUT I CAST *THAT* ASIDE, TOO!

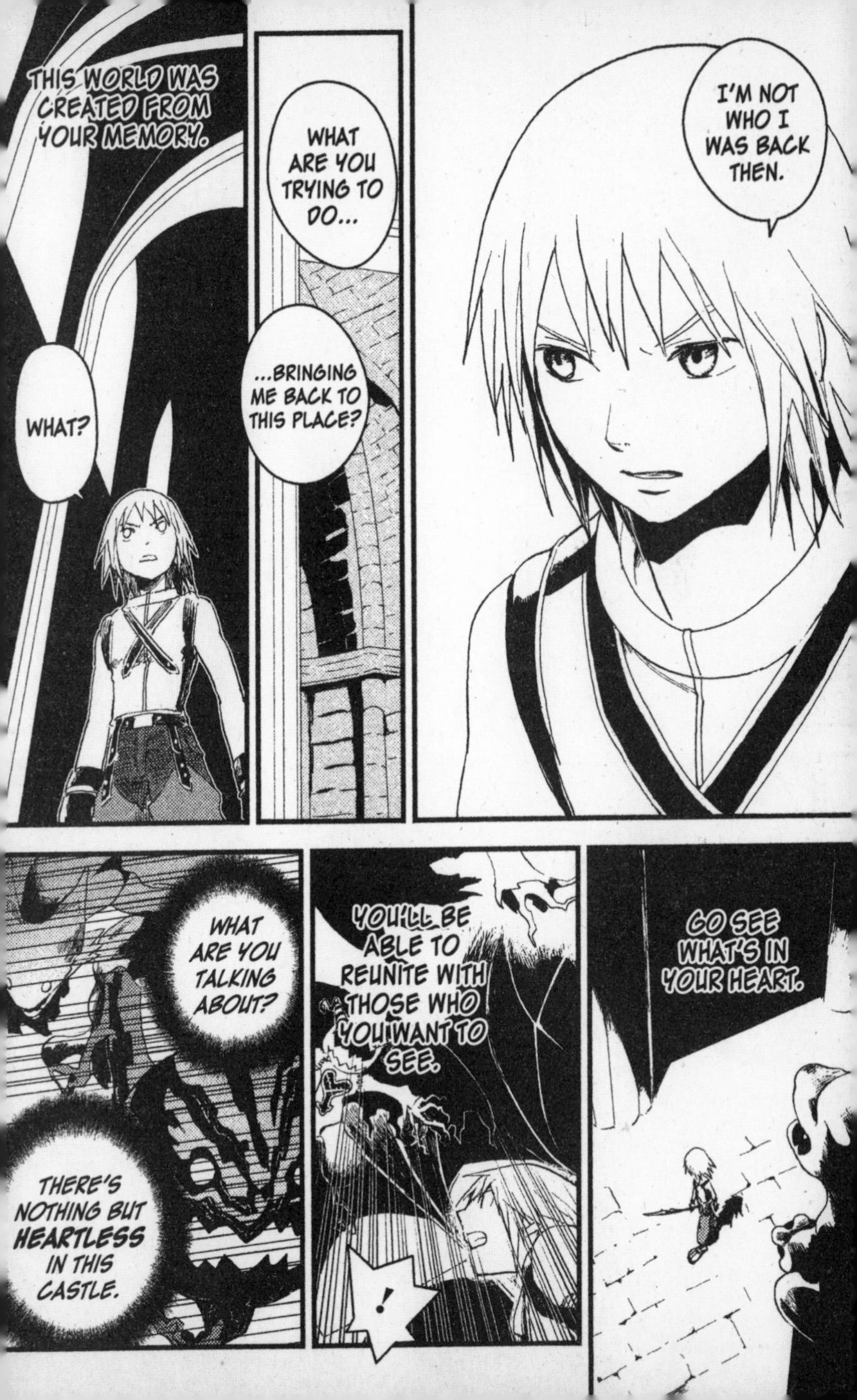
I'M NOT WHO I WAS BACK THEN.
WHAT ARE YOU TRYING TO DO...
...BRINGING ME BACK TO THIS PLACE?
THIS WORLD WAS CREATED FROM YOUR MEMORY.
WHAT?
GO SEE WHAT'S IN YOUR HEART.
YOU'LL BE ABLE TO REUNITE WITH THOSE WHO YOU WANT TO SEE.
!
WHAT ARE YOU TALKING ABOUT?
THERE'S NOTHING BUT **HEARTLESS** IN THIS CASTLE.

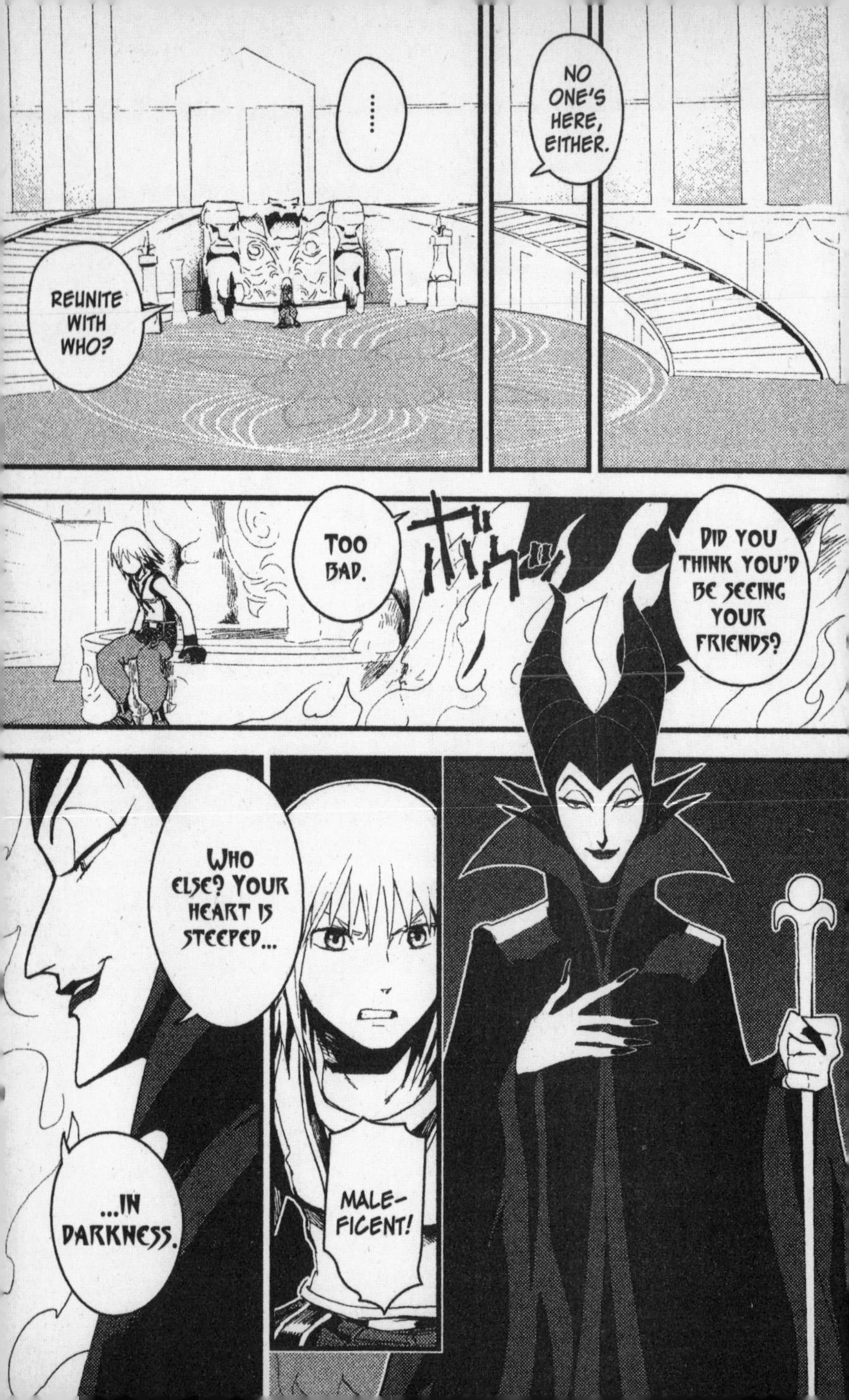
NO ONE'S HERE, EITHER.
......
REUNITE WITH WHO?
DID YOU THINK YOU'D BE SEEING YOUR FRIENDS?
TOO BAD.
MALE-FICENT!
WHO ELSE? YOUR HEART IS STEEPED...
...IN DARKNESS.

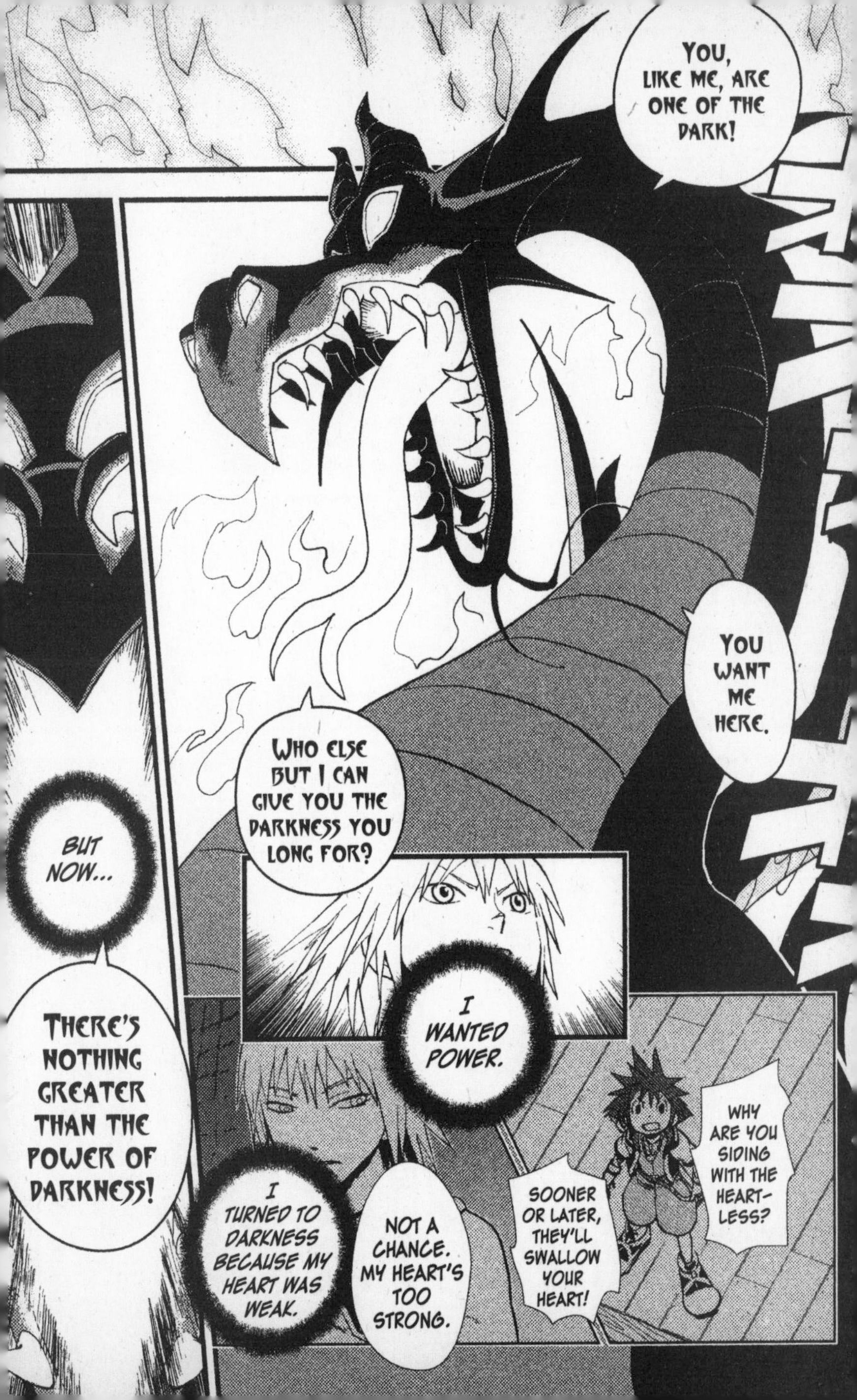
YOU, LIKE ME, ARE ONE OF THE DARK!
YOU WANT ME HERE.
WHO ELSE BUT I CAN GIVE YOU THE DARKNESS YOU LONG FOR?
I WANTED POWER.
WHY ARE YOU SIDING WITH THE HEART-LESS?
SOONER OR LATER, THEY'LL SWALLOW YOUR HEART!
NOT A CHANCE. MY HEART'S TOO STRONG.
I TURNED TO DARKNESS BECAUSE MY HEART WAS WEAK.
BUT NOW...
THERE'S NOTHING GREATER THAN THE POWER OF DARKNESS!

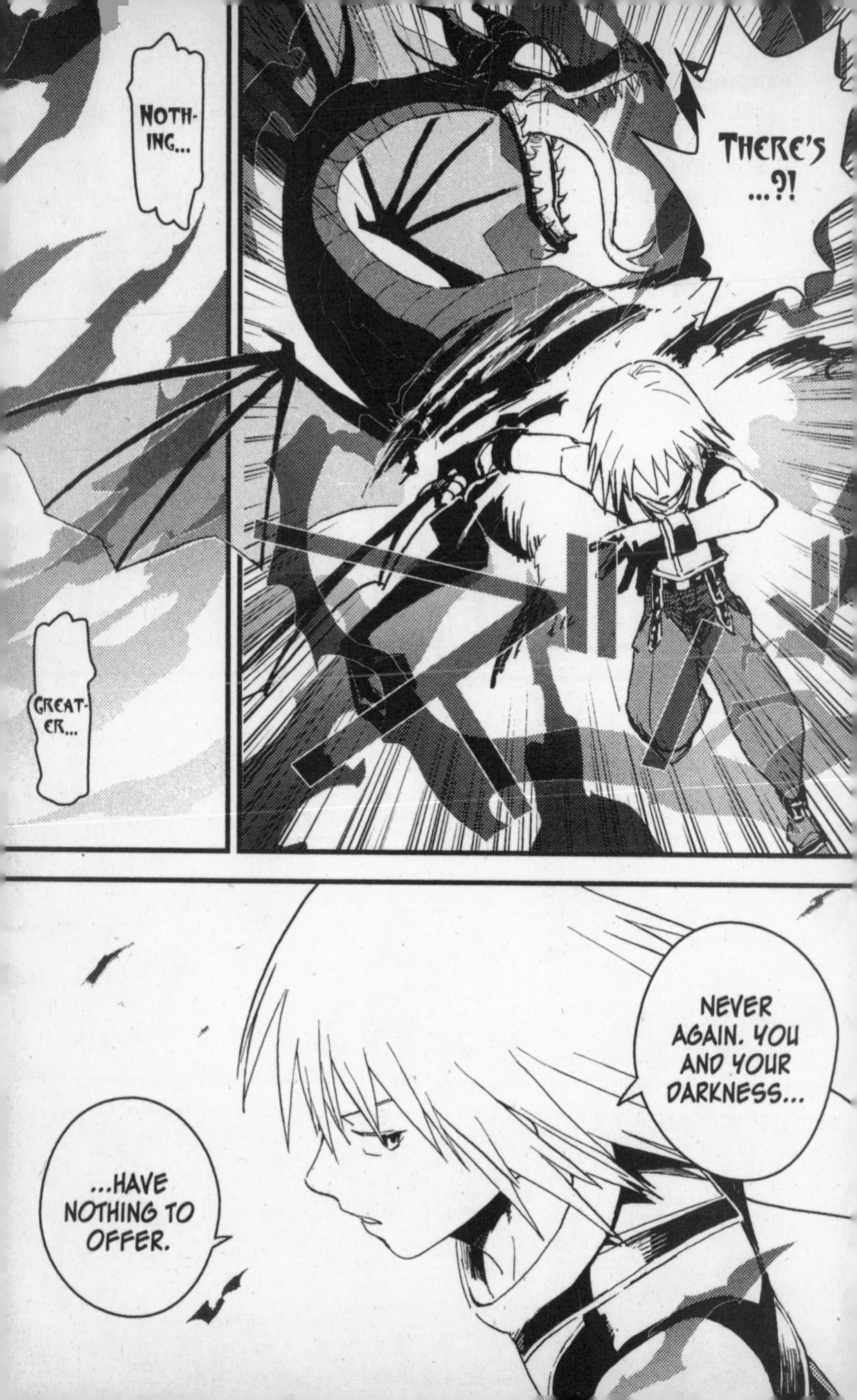
THERE'S ...?!
NOTHING...
GREATER...
NEVER AGAIN. YOU AND YOUR DARKNESS...
...HAVE NOTHING TO OFFER.

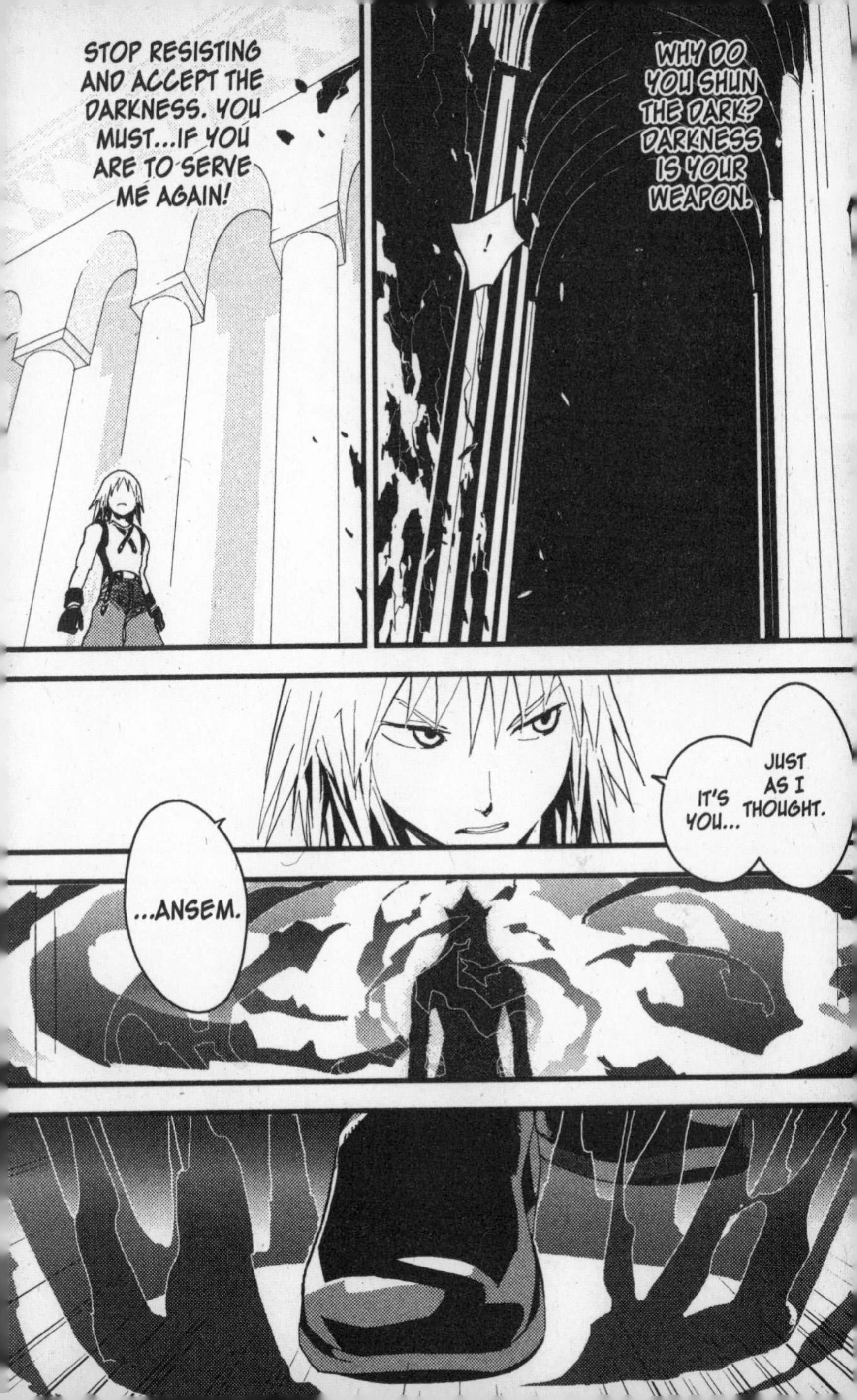
WHY DO YOU SHUN THE DARK? DARKNESS IS YOUR WEAPON.
!
STOP RESISTING AND ACCEPT THE DARKNESS. YOU MUST...IF YOU ARE TO SERVE ME AGAIN!
JUST AS I THOUGHT.
IT'S YOU...
...ANSEM.

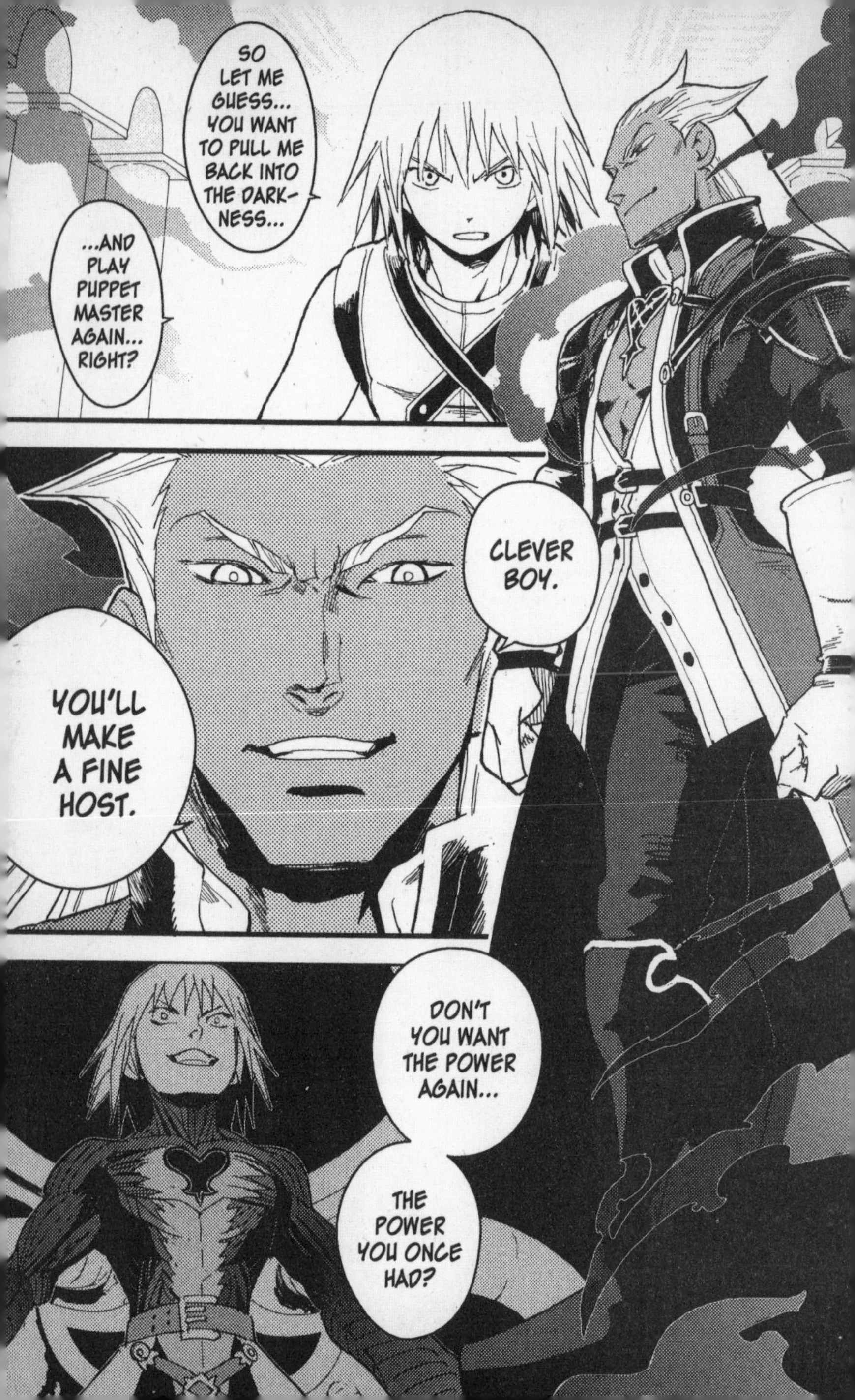
SO LET ME GUESS... YOU WANT TO PULL ME BACK INTO THE DARK-NESS...
...AND PLAY PUPPET MASTER AGAIN... RIGHT?
CLEVER BOY.
YOU'LL MAKE A FINE HOST.
DON'T YOU WANT THE POWER AGAIN...
THE POWER YOU ONCE HAD?

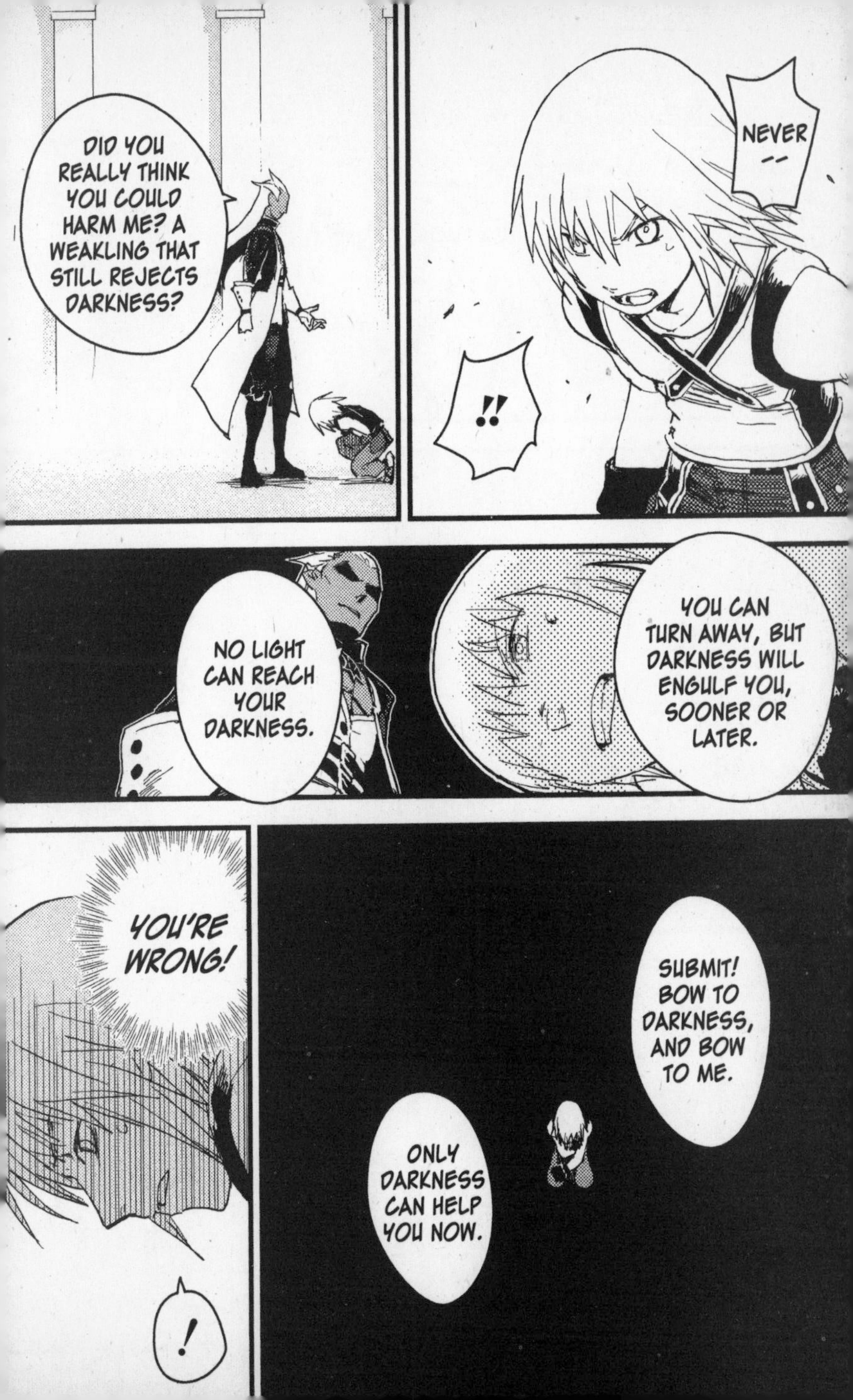
NEVER --
!!
DID YOU REALLY THINK YOU COULD HARM ME? A WEAKLING THAT STILL REJECTS DARKNESS?
YOU CAN TURN AWAY, BUT DARKNESS WILL ENGULF YOU, SOONER OR LATER.
NO LIGHT CAN REACH YOUR DARKNESS.
SUBMIT! BOW TO DARKNESS, AND BOW TO ME.
ONLY DARKNESS CAN HELP YOU NOW.
YOU'RE WRONG!
!

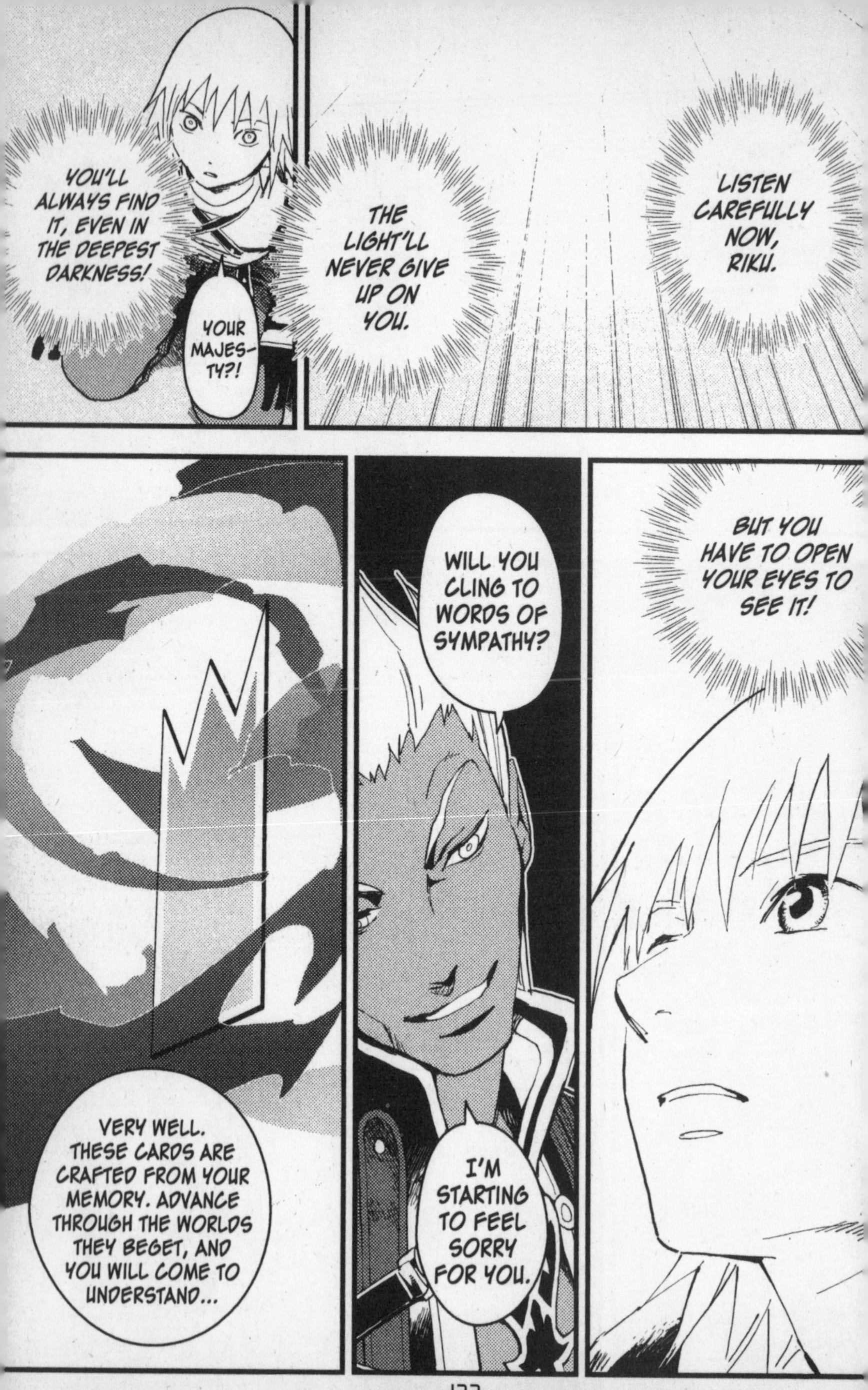
LISTEN CAREFULLY NOW, RIKU.
THE LIGHT'LL NEVER GIVE UP ON YOU.
YOU'LL ALWAYS FIND IT, EVEN IN THE DEEPEST DARKNESS!
YOUR MAJES-TY?!
BUT YOU HAVE TO OPEN YOUR EYES TO SEE IT!
WILL YOU CLING TO WORDS OF SYMPATHY?
I'M STARTING TO FEEL SORRY FOR YOU.
VERY WELL. THESE CARDS ARE CRAFTED FROM YOUR MEMORY. ADVANCE THROUGH THE WORLDS THEY BEGET, AND YOU WILL COME TO UNDERSTAND...

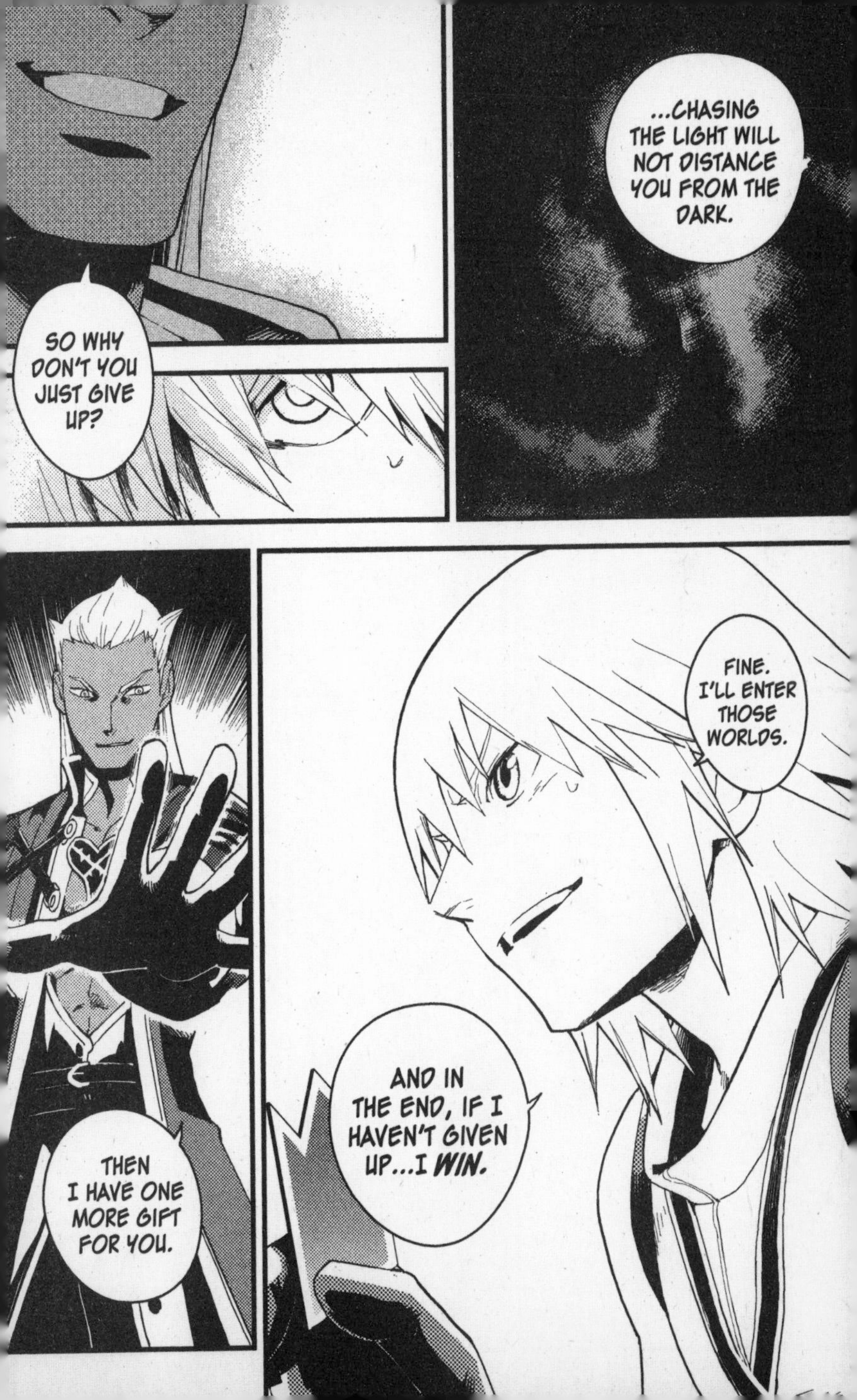
...CHASING THE LIGHT WILL NOT DISTANCE YOU FROM THE DARK.
SO WHY DON'T YOU JUST GIVE UP?
FINE. I'LL ENTER THOSE WORLDS.
AND IN THE END, IF I HAVEN'T GIVEN UP...I WIN.
THEN I HAVE ONE MORE GIFT FOR YOU.

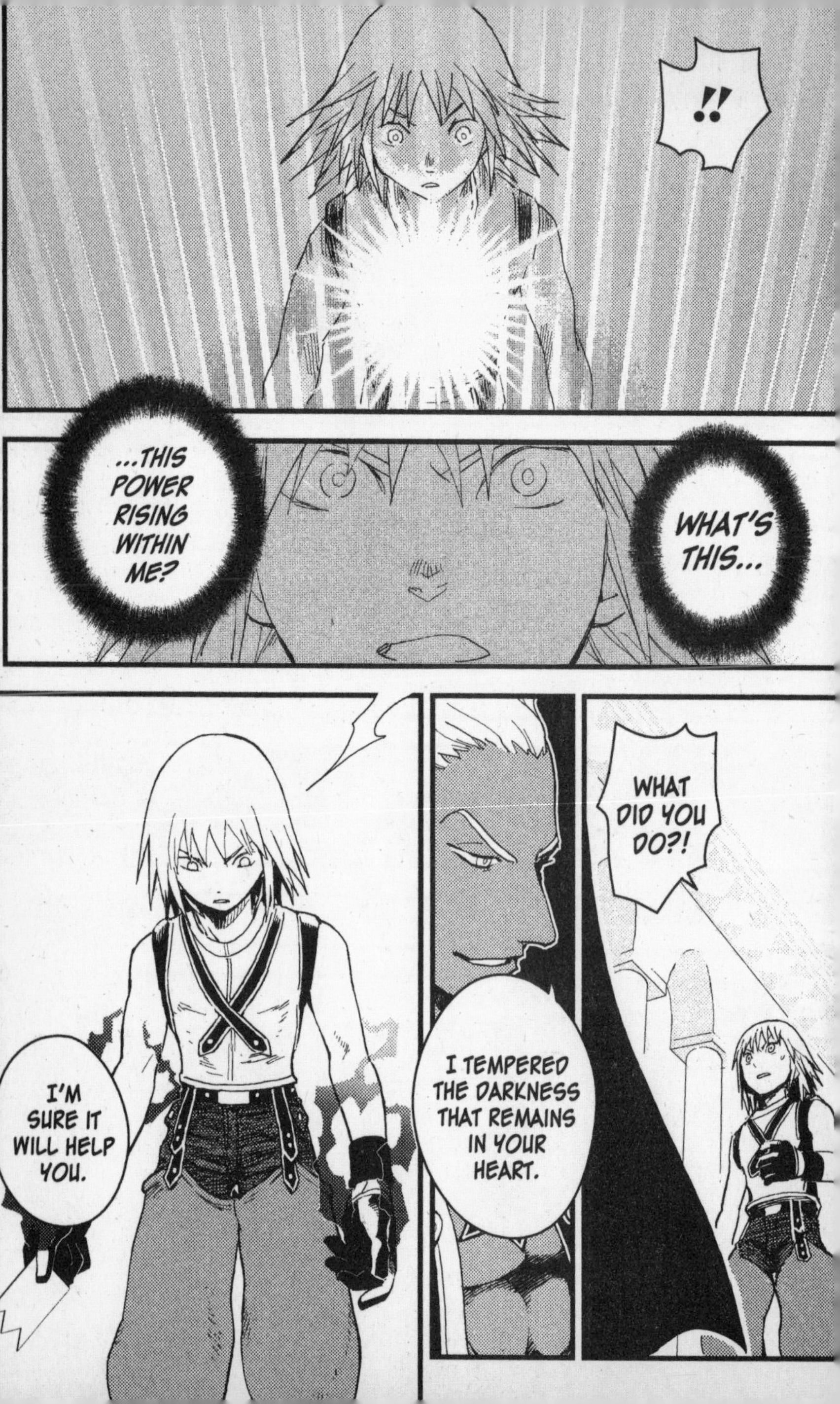
!!
WHAT'S THIS...
...THIS POWER RISING WITHIN ME?
WHAT DID YOU DO?!
I TEMPERED THE DARKNESS THAT REMAINS IN YOUR HEART.
I'M SURE IT WILL HELP YOU.

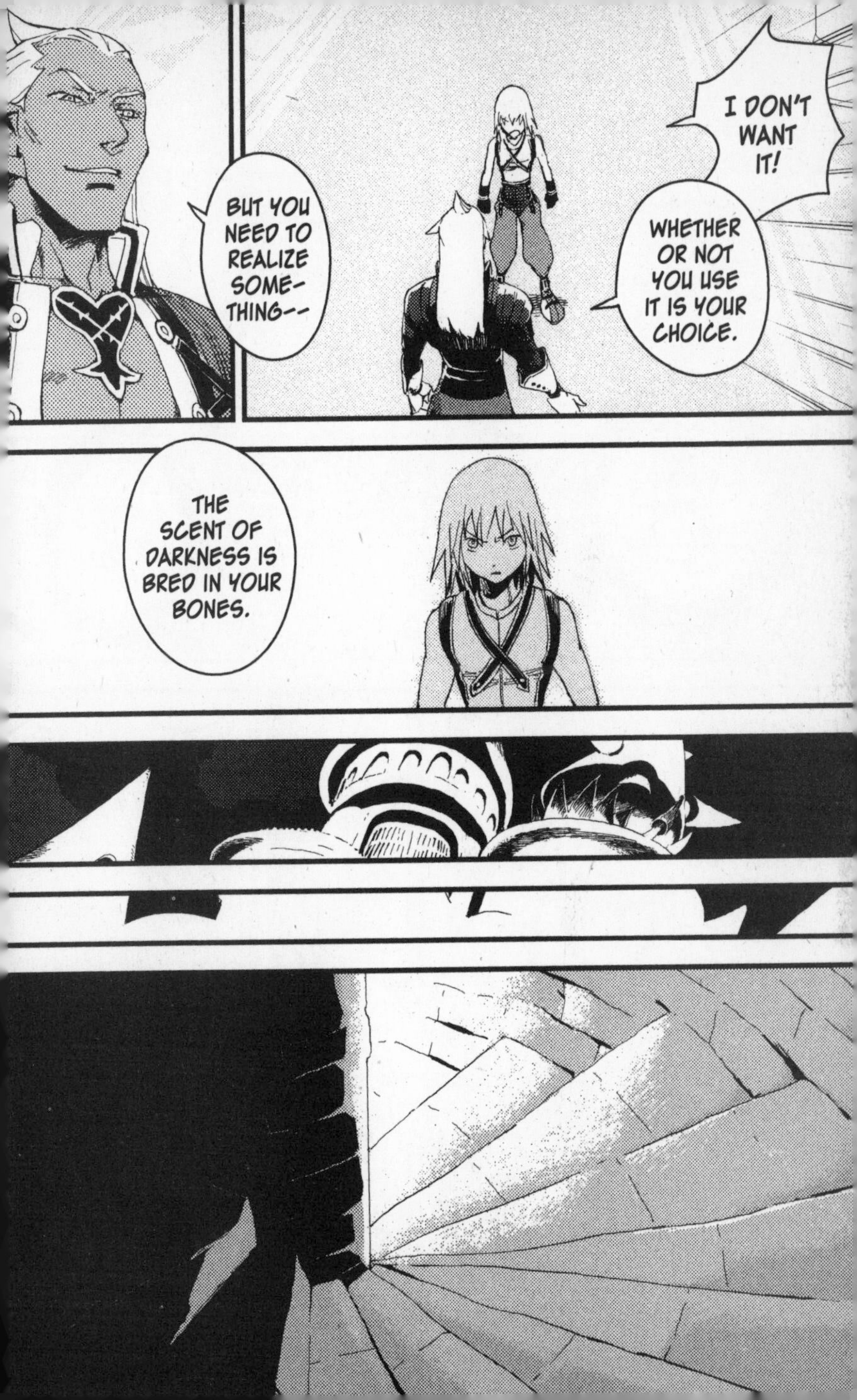
I DON'T WANT IT!
WHETHER OR NOT YOU USE IT IS YOUR CHOICE.
BUT YOU NEED TO REALIZE SOME-THING--
THE SCENT OF DARKNESS IS BRED IN YOUR BONES.

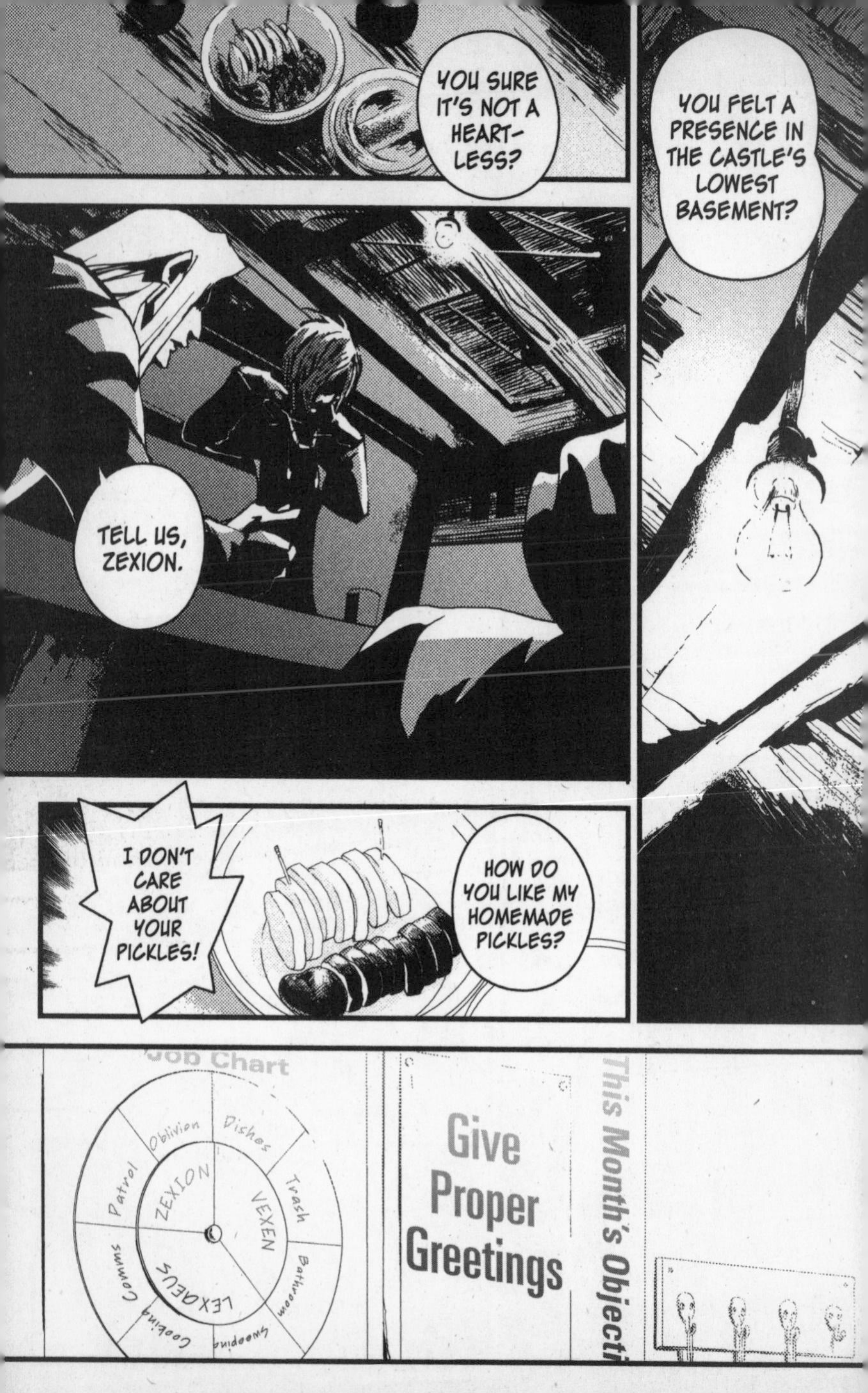
YOU FELT A PRESENCE IN THE CASTLE'S LOWEST BASEMENT?
YOU SURE IT'S NOT A HEART-LESS?
TELL US, ZEXION.
HOW DO YOU LIKE MY HOMEMADE PICKLES?
I DON'T CARE ABOUT YOUR PICKLES!
This Month's Objecti
Give Proper Greetings
Job Chart
Oblivion
Dishes
Trash
Bathroom
Sweeping
Cooking
Comms
Patrol
ZEXION
VEXEN
LEXAEUS

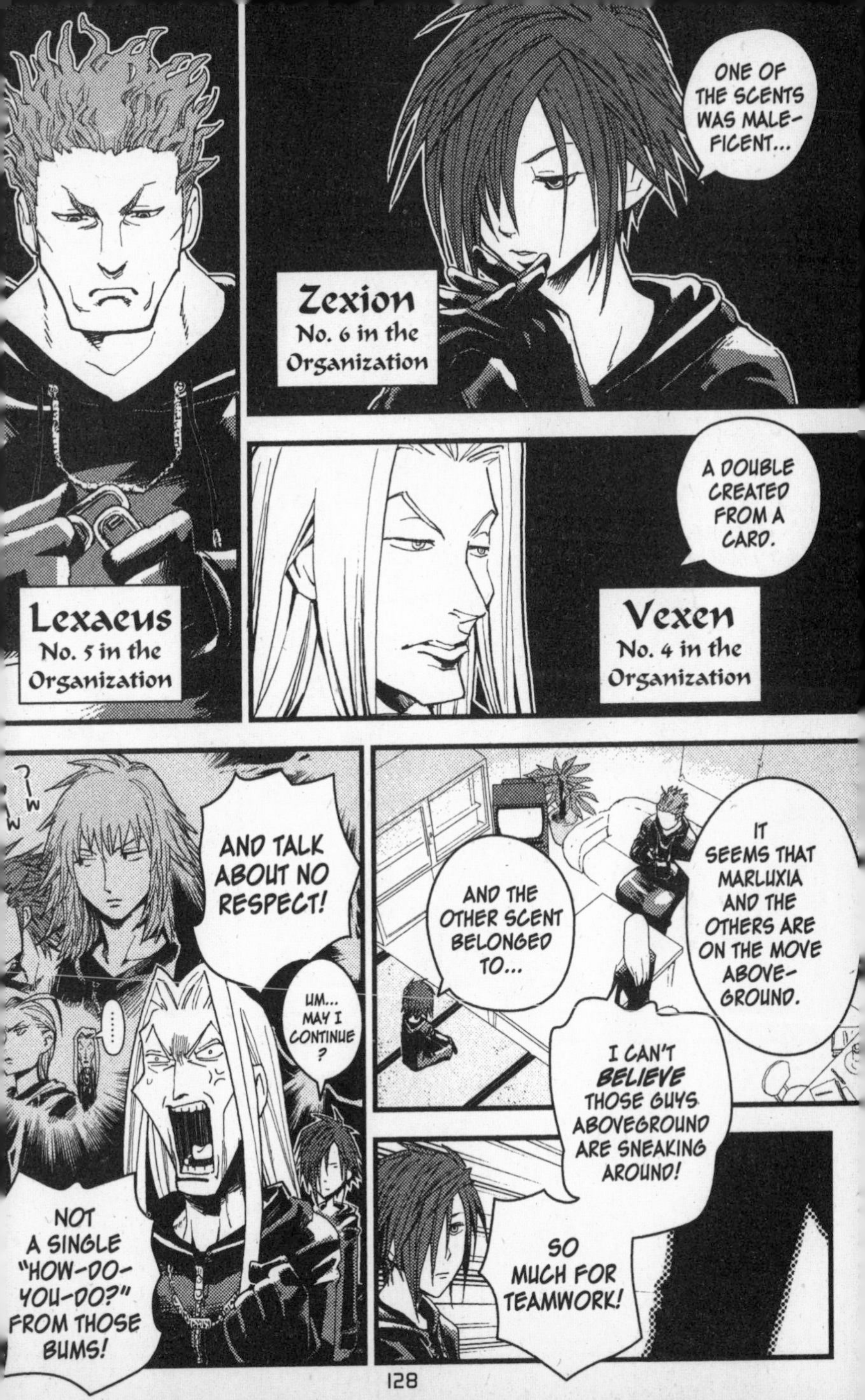
ONE OF THE SCENTS WAS MALE-FICENT...
Zexion
No. 6 in the Organization
A DOUBLE CREATED FROM A CARD.
Vexen
No. 4 in the Organization
Lexaeus
No. 5 in the Organization
IT SEEMS THAT MARLUXIA AND THE OTHERS ARE ON THE MOVE ABOVE-GROUND.
AND THE OTHER SCENT BELONGED TO...
I CAN'T BELIEVE THOSE GUYS ABOVEGROUND ARE SNEAKING AROUND!
SO MUCH FOR TEAMWORK!
AND TALK ABOUT NO RESPECT!
UM... MAY I CONTINUE?
......
NOT A SINGLE "HOW-DO-YOU-DO?" FROM THOSE BUMS!

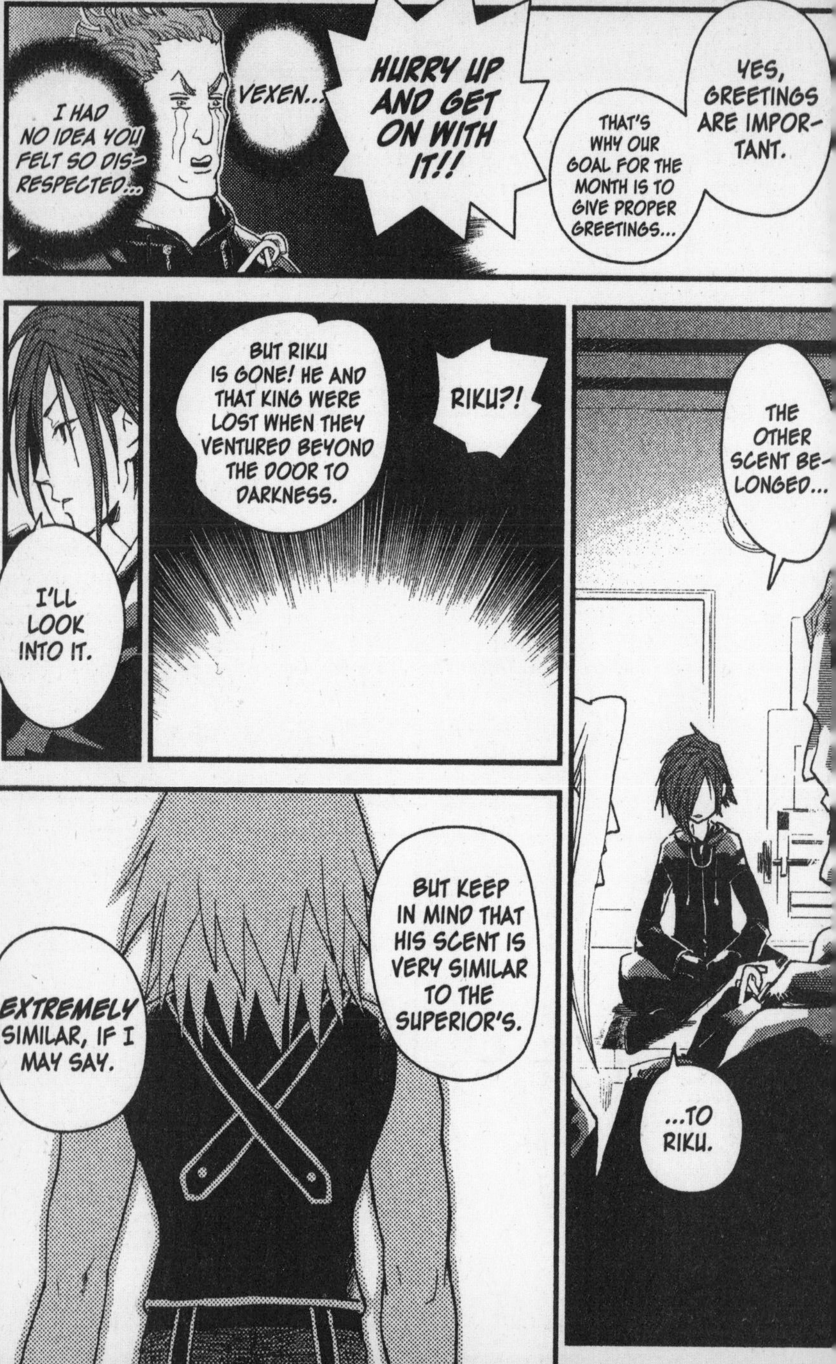
YES, GREETINGS ARE IMPORTANT.
THAT'S WHY OUR GOAL FOR THE MONTH IS TO GIVE PROPER GREETINGS...
HURRY UP AND GET ON WITH IT!!
VEXEN...
I HAD NO IDEA YOU FELT SO DISRESPECTED...
THE OTHER SCENT BELONGED...
...TO RIKU.
RIKU?!
BUT RIKU IS GONE! HE AND THAT KING WERE LOST WHEN THEY VENTURED BEYOND THE DOOR TO DARKNESS.
I'LL LOOK INTO IT.
BUT KEEP IN MIND THAT HIS SCENT IS VERY SIMILAR TO THE SUPERIOR'S.
EXTREMELY SIMILAR, IF I MAY SAY.

MAYBE THEY'RE USING THE SAME COLOGNE?

BUT YOU NEED TO REALIZE SOMETHING--

THE SCENT OF DARKNESS IS BRED IN YOUR BONES.

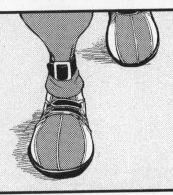

HEH.

HA HA...

sniff

......

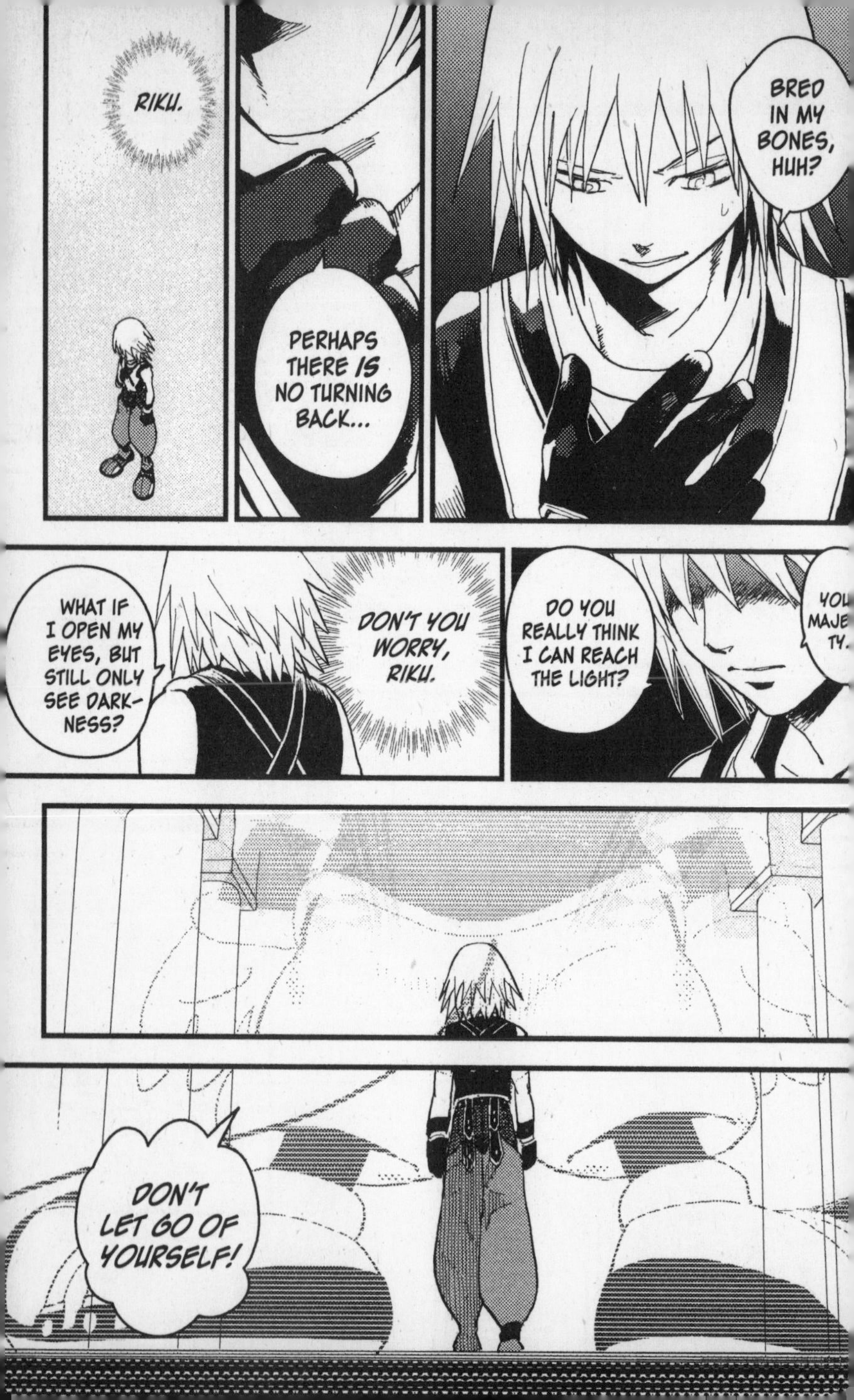
BRED IN MY BONES, HUH?
PERHAPS THERE IS NO TURNING BACK...
RIKU.
YOU MAJE- TY.
DO YOU REALLY THINK I CAN REACH THE LIGHT?
DON'T YOU WORRY, RIKU.
WHAT IF I OPEN MY EYES, BUT STILL ONLY SEE DARK- NESS?
DON'T LET GO OF YOURSELF!

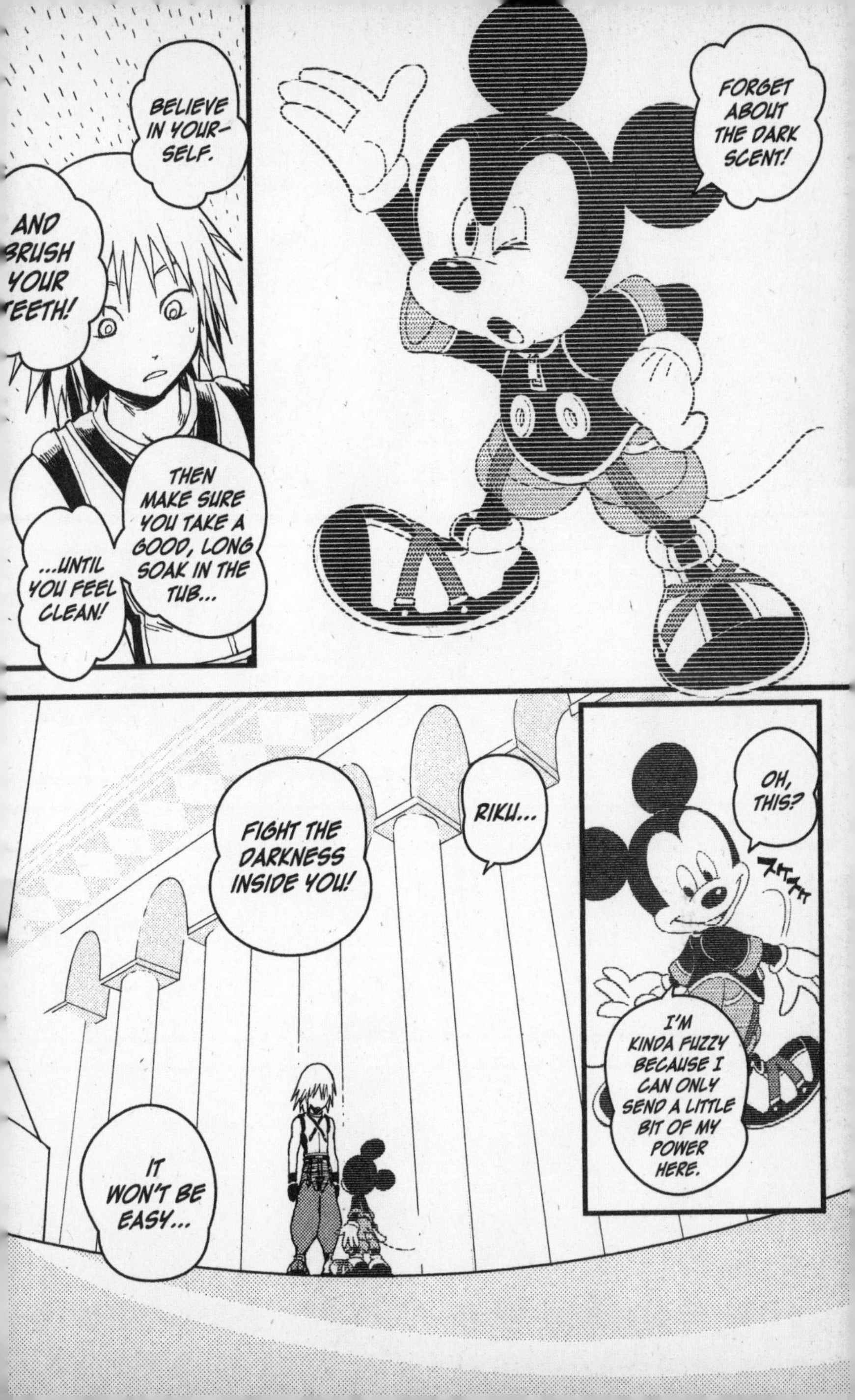
FORGET ABOUT THE DARK SCENT!
BELIEVE IN YOURSELF.
AND BRUSH YOUR TEETH!
THEN MAKE SURE YOU TAKE A GOOD, LONG SOAK IN THE TUB...
...UNTIL YOU FEEL CLEAN!
OH, THIS?
I'M KINDA FUZZY BECAUSE I CAN ONLY SEND A LITTLE BIT OF MY POWER HERE.
RIKU...
FIGHT THE DARKNESS INSIDE YOU!
IT WON'T BE EASY...

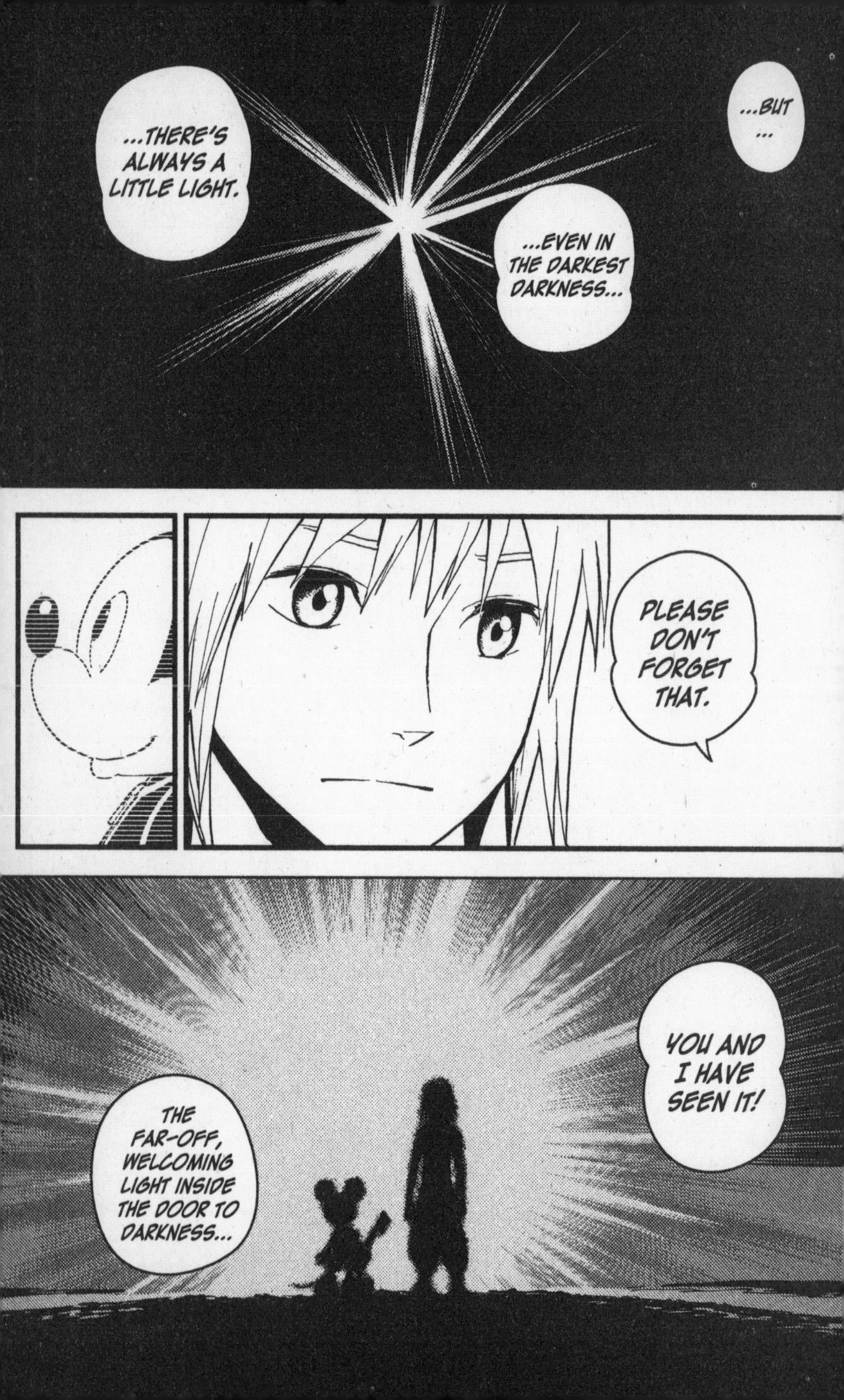
...BUT ...
...THERE'S ALWAYS A LITTLE LIGHT.
...EVEN IN THE DARKEST DARKNESS...
PLEASE DON'T FORGET THAT.
YOU AND I HAVE SEEN IT!
THE FAR-OFF, WELCOMING LIGHT INSIDE THE DOOR TO DARKNESS...

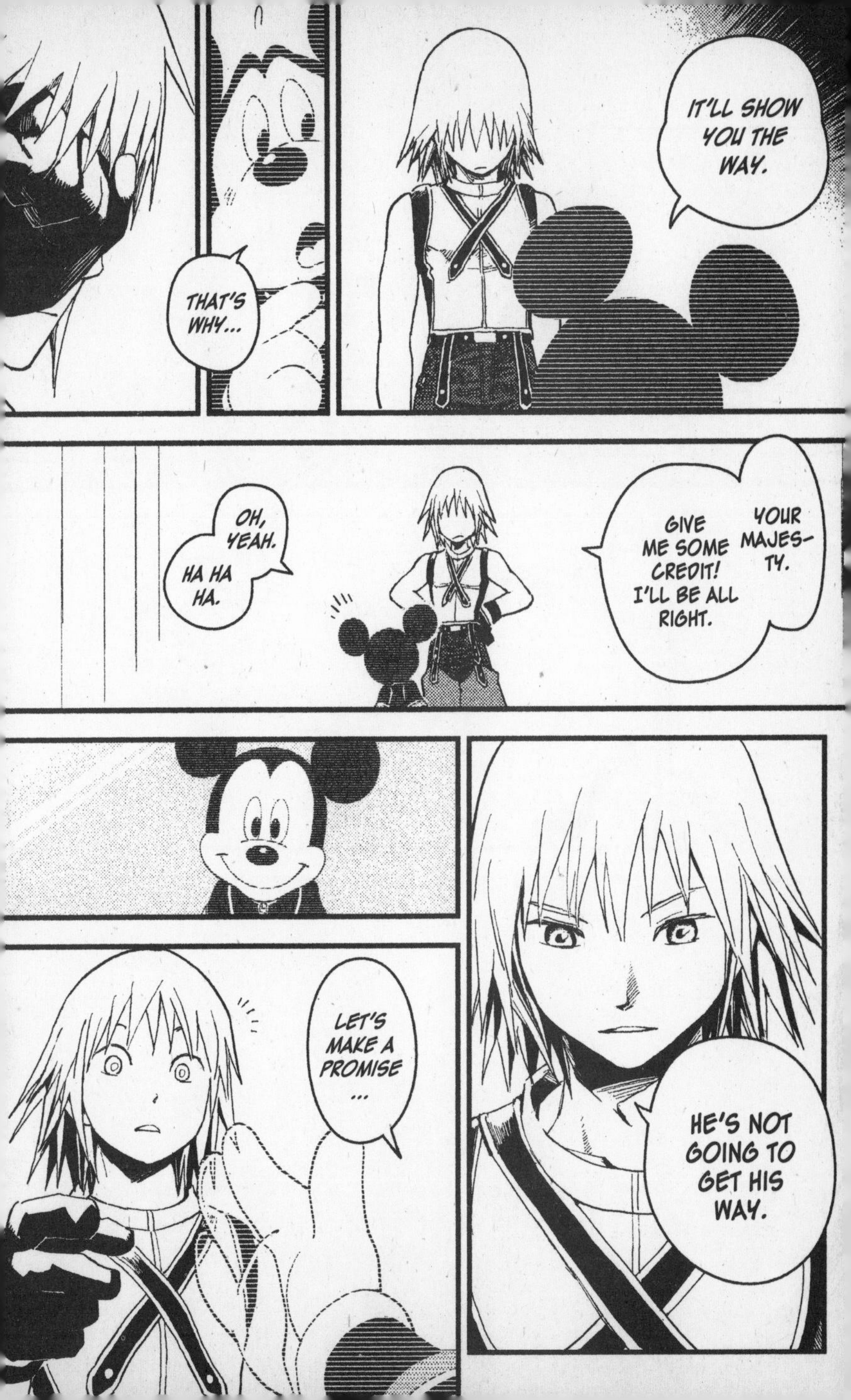
IT'LL SHOW YOU THE WAY.
THAT'S WHY...
YOUR MAJESTY.
GIVE ME SOME CREDIT! I'LL BE ALL RIGHT.
OH, YEAH.
HA HA HA.
HE'S NOT GOING TO GET HIS WAY.
LET'S MAKE A PROMISE ...

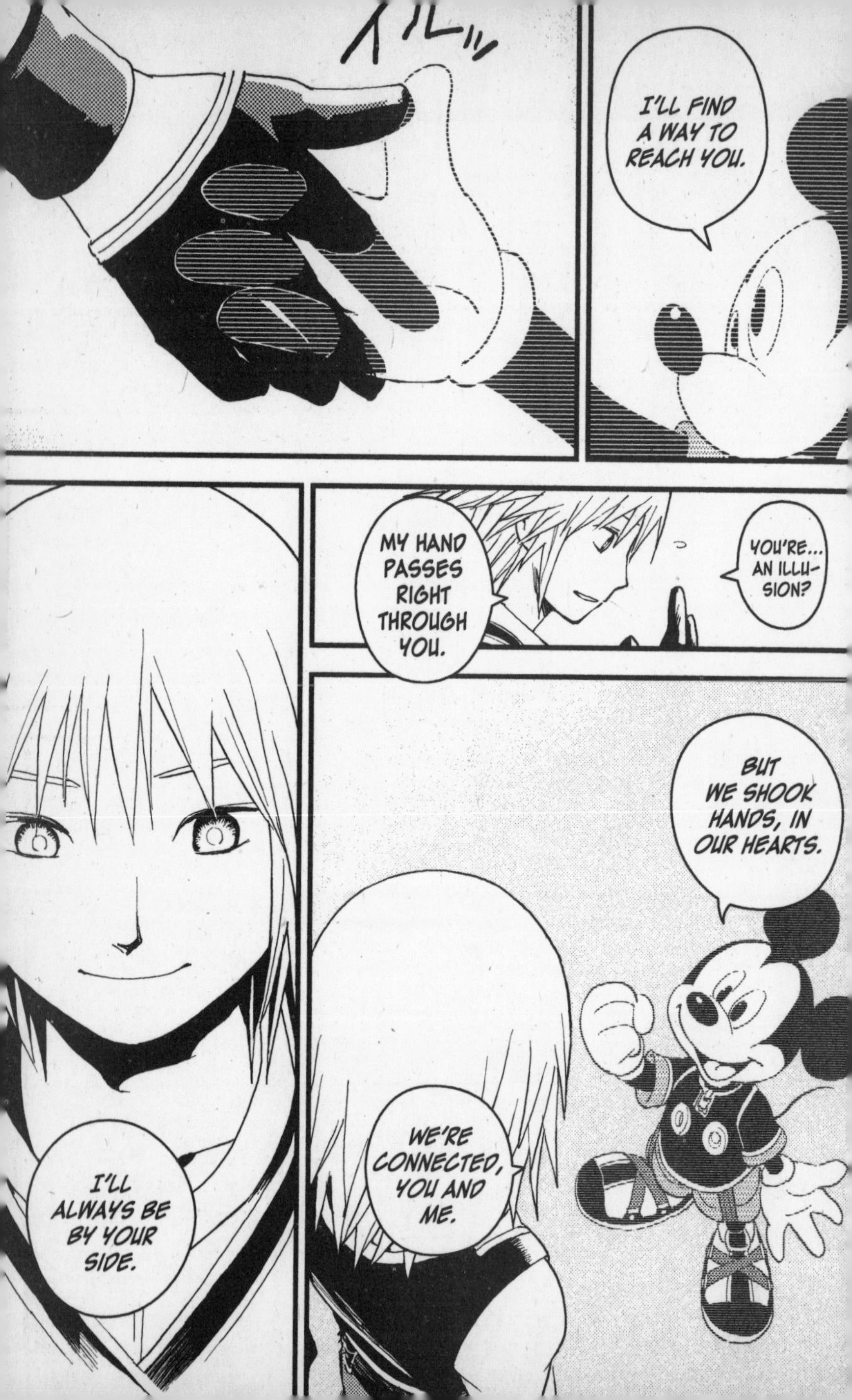
I'LL FIND A WAY TO REACH YOU.
YOU'RE... AN ILLU-SION?
MY HAND PASSES RIGHT THROUGH YOU.
BUT WE SHOOK HANDS, IN OUR HEARTS.
WE'RE CONNECTED, YOU AND ME.
I'LL ALWAYS BE BY YOUR SIDE.

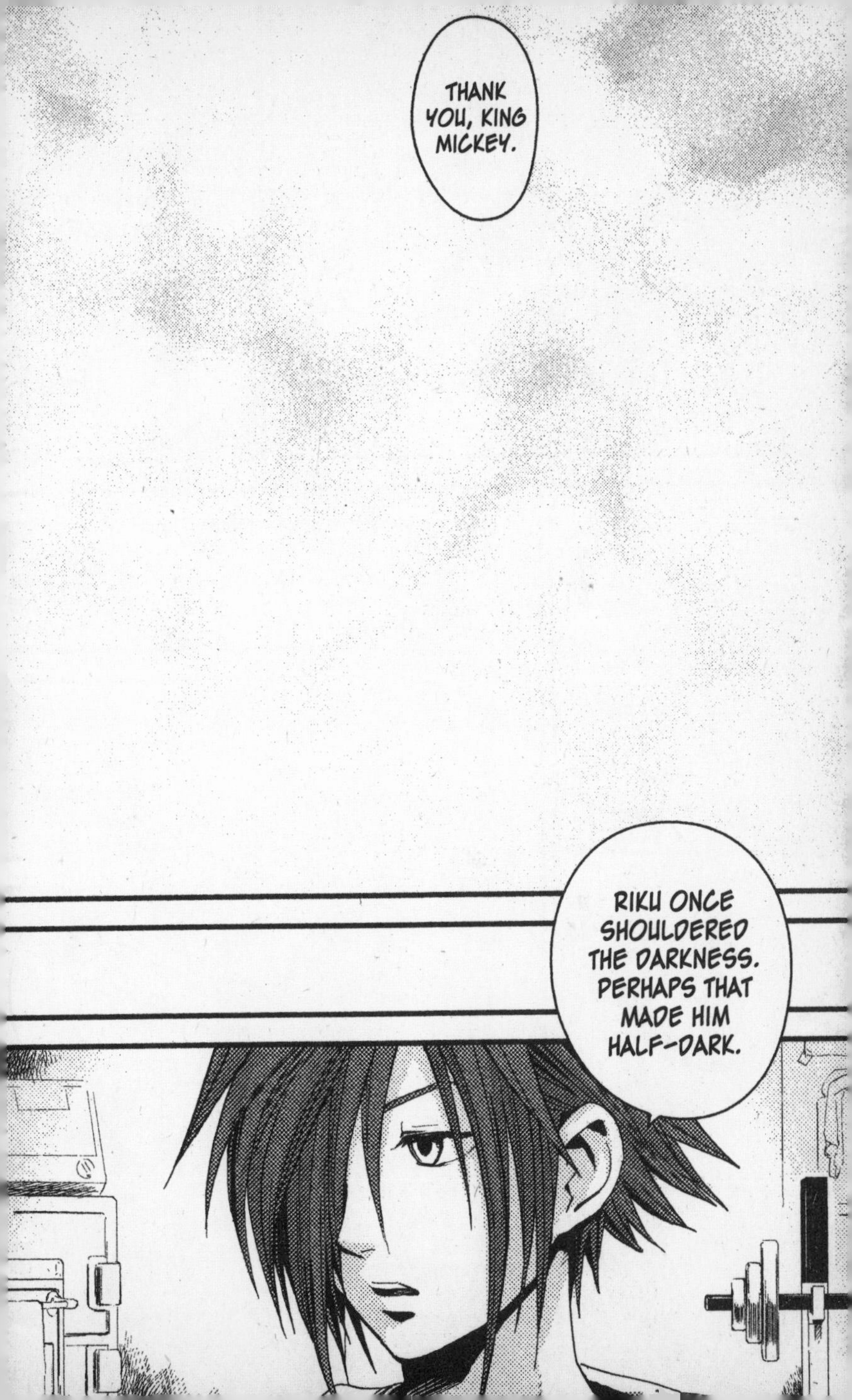
THANK YOU, KING MICKEY.
RIKU ONCE SHOULDERED THE DARKNESS. PERHAPS THAT MADE HIM HALF-DARK.

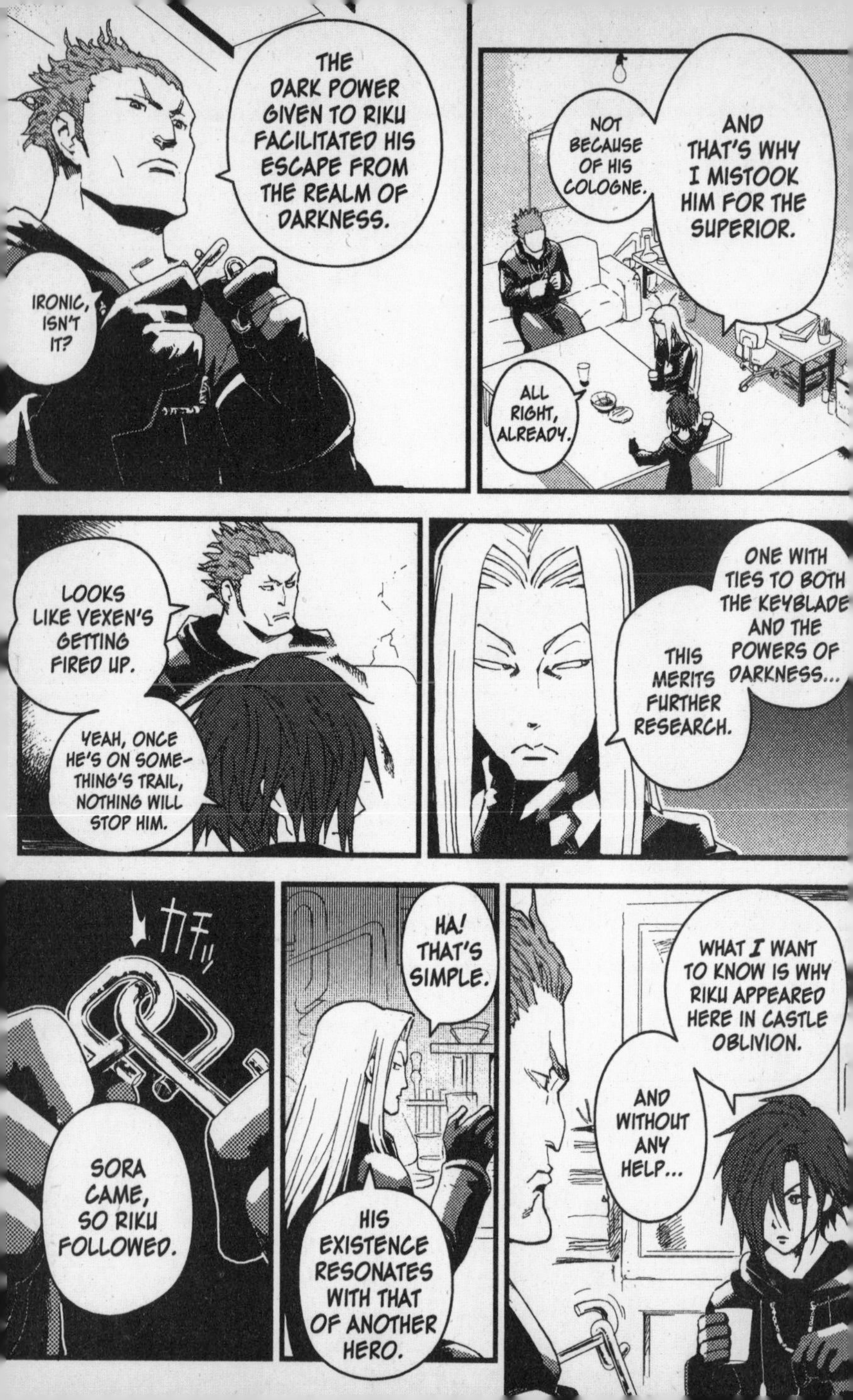
AND THAT'S WHY I MISTOOK HIM FOR THE SUPERIOR.
NOT BECAUSE OF HIS COLOGNE.
ALL RIGHT, ALREADY.
THE DARK POWER GIVEN TO RIKU FACILITATED HIS ESCAPE FROM THE REALM OF DARKNESS.
IRONIC, ISN'T IT?
ONE WITH TIES TO BOTH THE KEYBLADE AND THE POWERS OF DARKNESS...
THIS MERITS FURTHER RESEARCH.
LOOKS LIKE VEXEN'S GETTING FIRED UP.
YEAH, ONCE HE'S ON SOMETHING'S TRAIL, NOTHING WILL STOP HIM.
WHAT *I* WANT TO KNOW IS WHY RIKU APPEARED HERE IN CASTLE OBLIVION.
AND WITHOUT ANY HELP...
HA! THAT'S SIMPLE.
HIS EXISTENCE RESONATES WITH THAT OF ANOTHER HERO.
カチッ
SORA CAME, SO RIKU FOLLOWED.

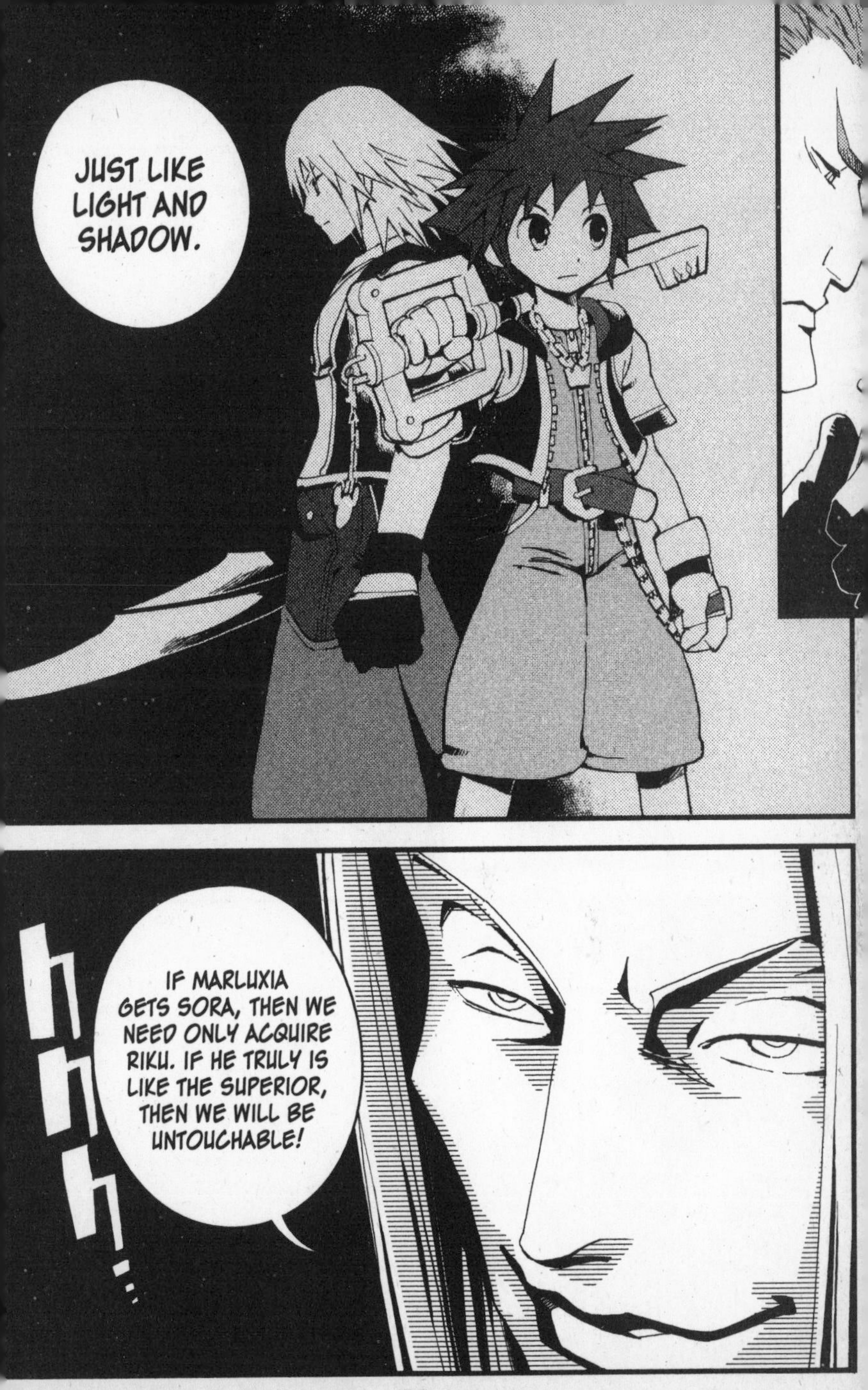
JUST LIKE LIGHT AND SHADOW.
IF MARLUXIA GETS SORA, THEN WE NEED ONLY ACQUIRE RIKU. IF HE TRULY IS LIKE THE SUPERIOR, THEN WE WILL BE UNTOUCHABLE!

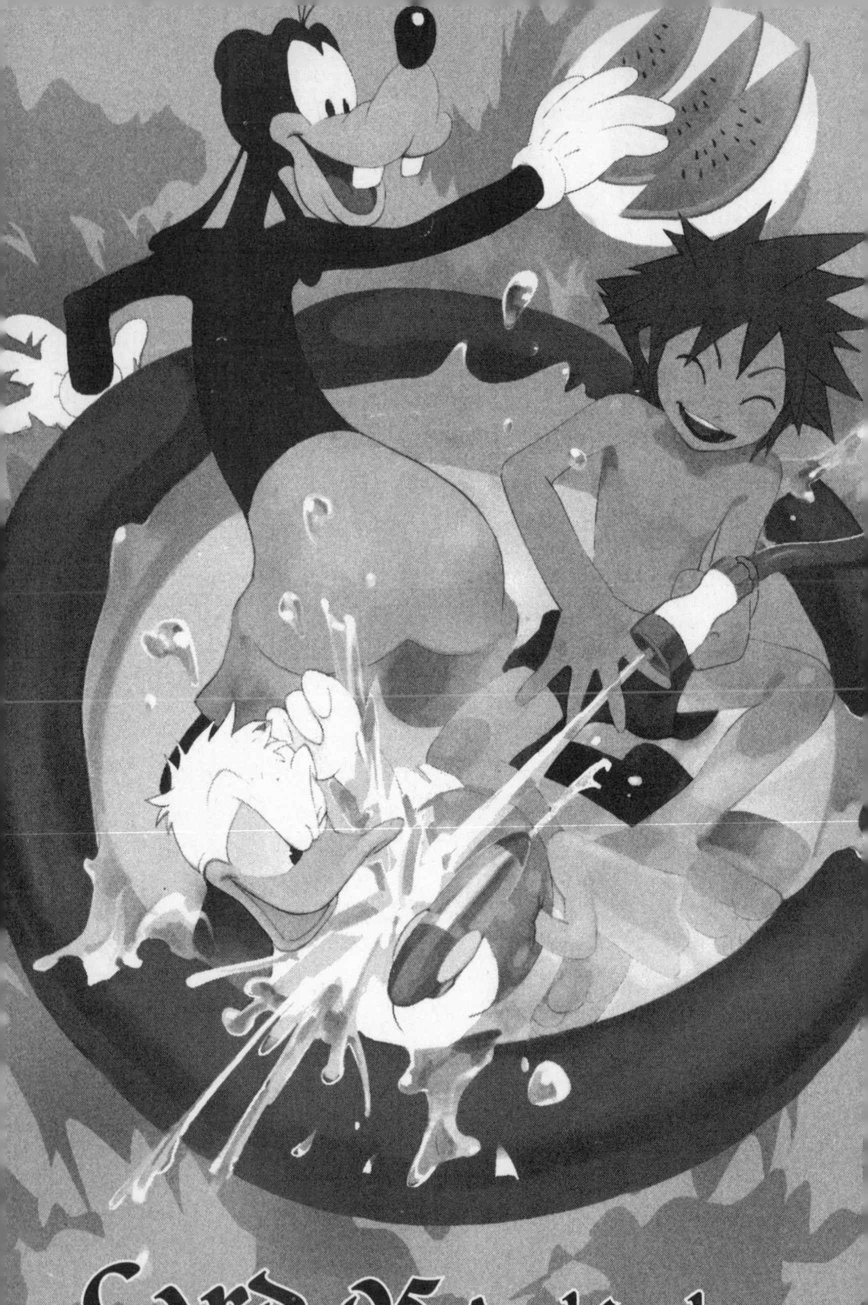

Card 05 Ambivalence

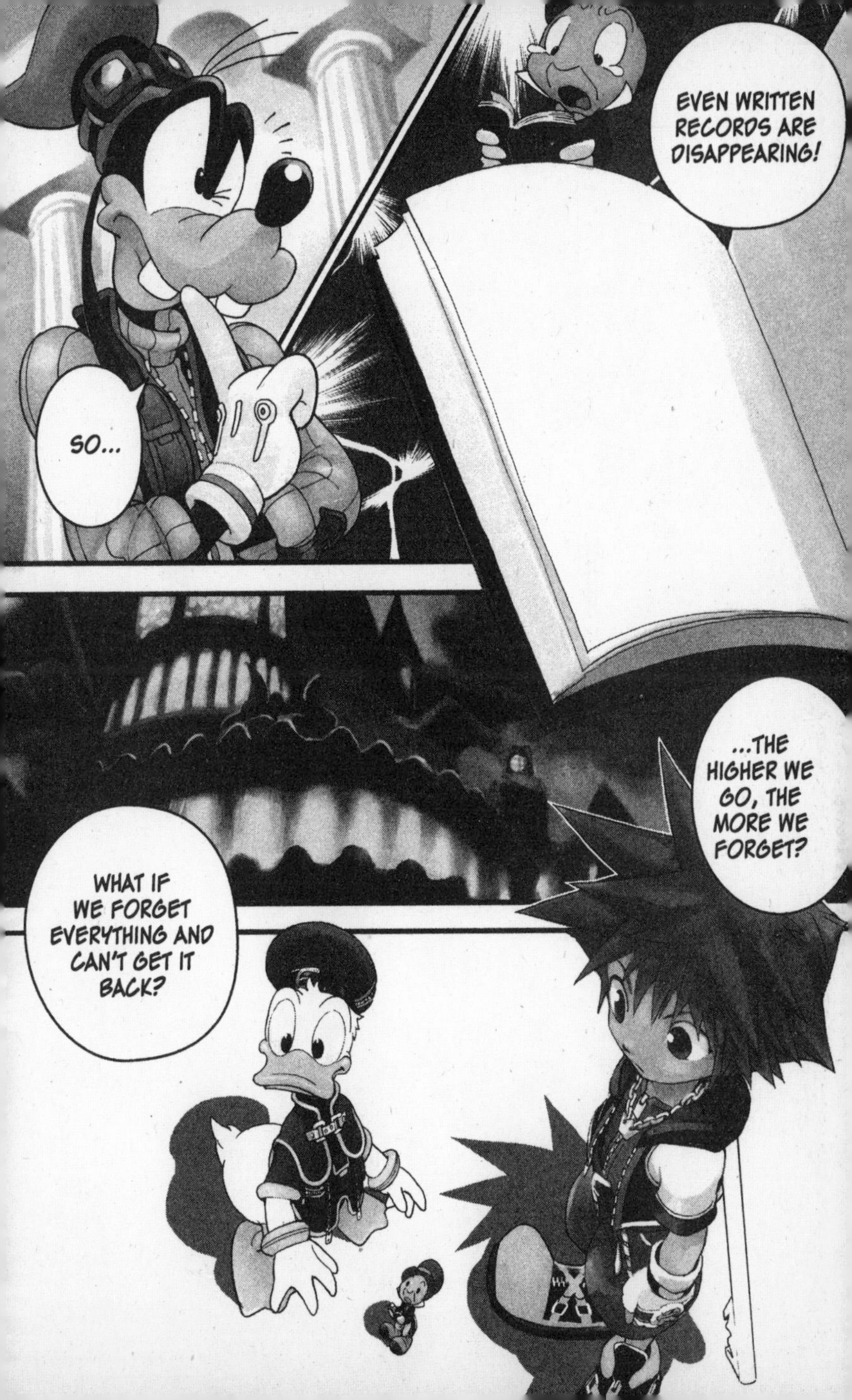
EVEN WRITTEN RECORDS ARE DISAPPEARING!
SO...
...THE HIGHER WE GO, THE MORE WE FORGET?
WHAT IF WE FORGET EVERYTHING AND CAN'T GET IT BACK?

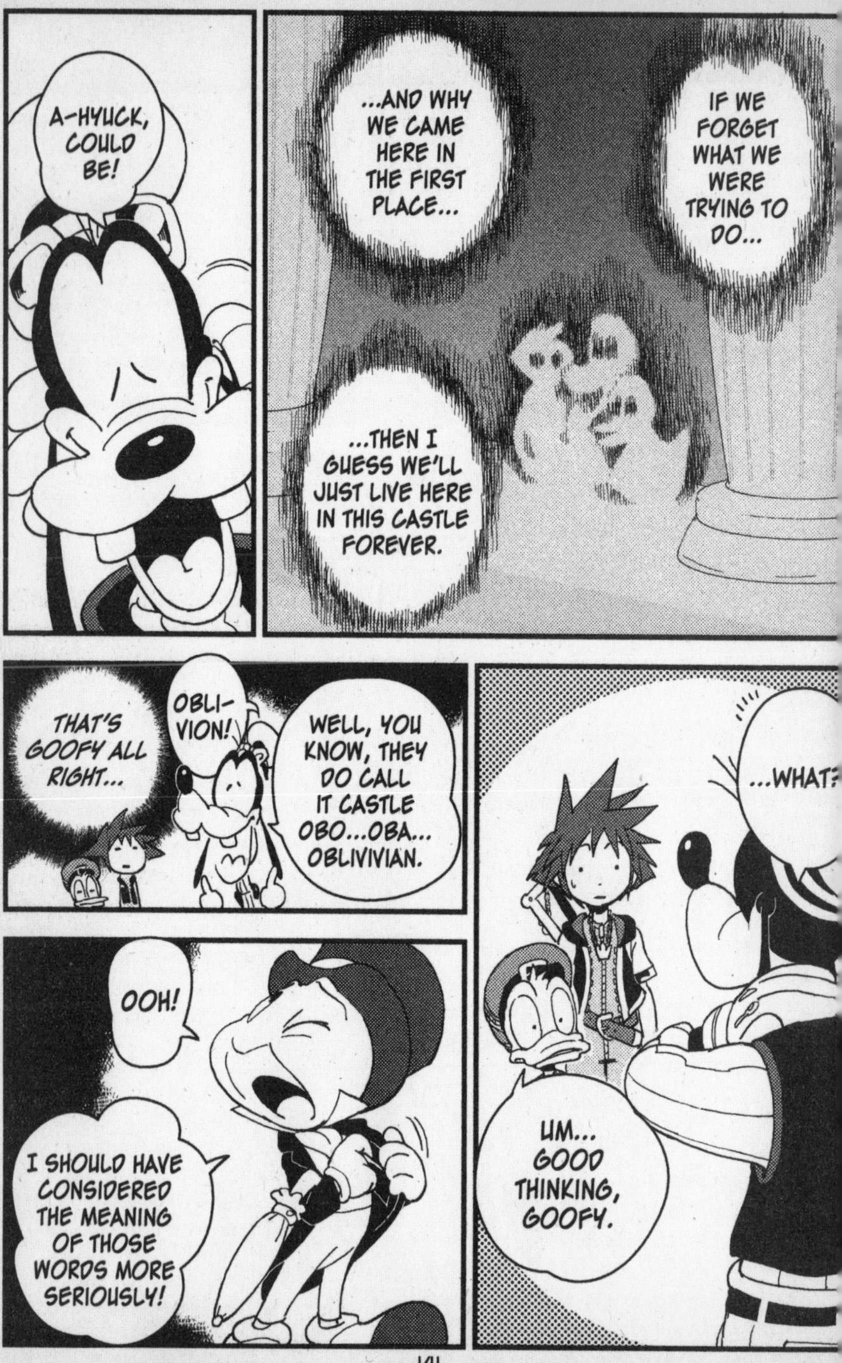
IF WE FORGET WHAT WE WERE TRYING TO DO...
...AND WHY WE CAME HERE IN THE FIRST PLACE...
...THEN I GUESS WE'LL JUST LIVE HERE IN THIS CASTLE FOREVER.
A-HYUCK, COULD BE!
...WHAT?
UM... GOOD THINKING, GOOFY.
WELL, YOU KNOW, THEY DO CALL IT CASTLE OBO...OBA... OBLIVIVIAN.
OBLI-VION!
THAT'S GOOFY ALL RIGHT...
OOH!
I SHOULD HAVE CONSIDERED THE MEANING OF THOSE WORDS MORE SERIOUSLY!

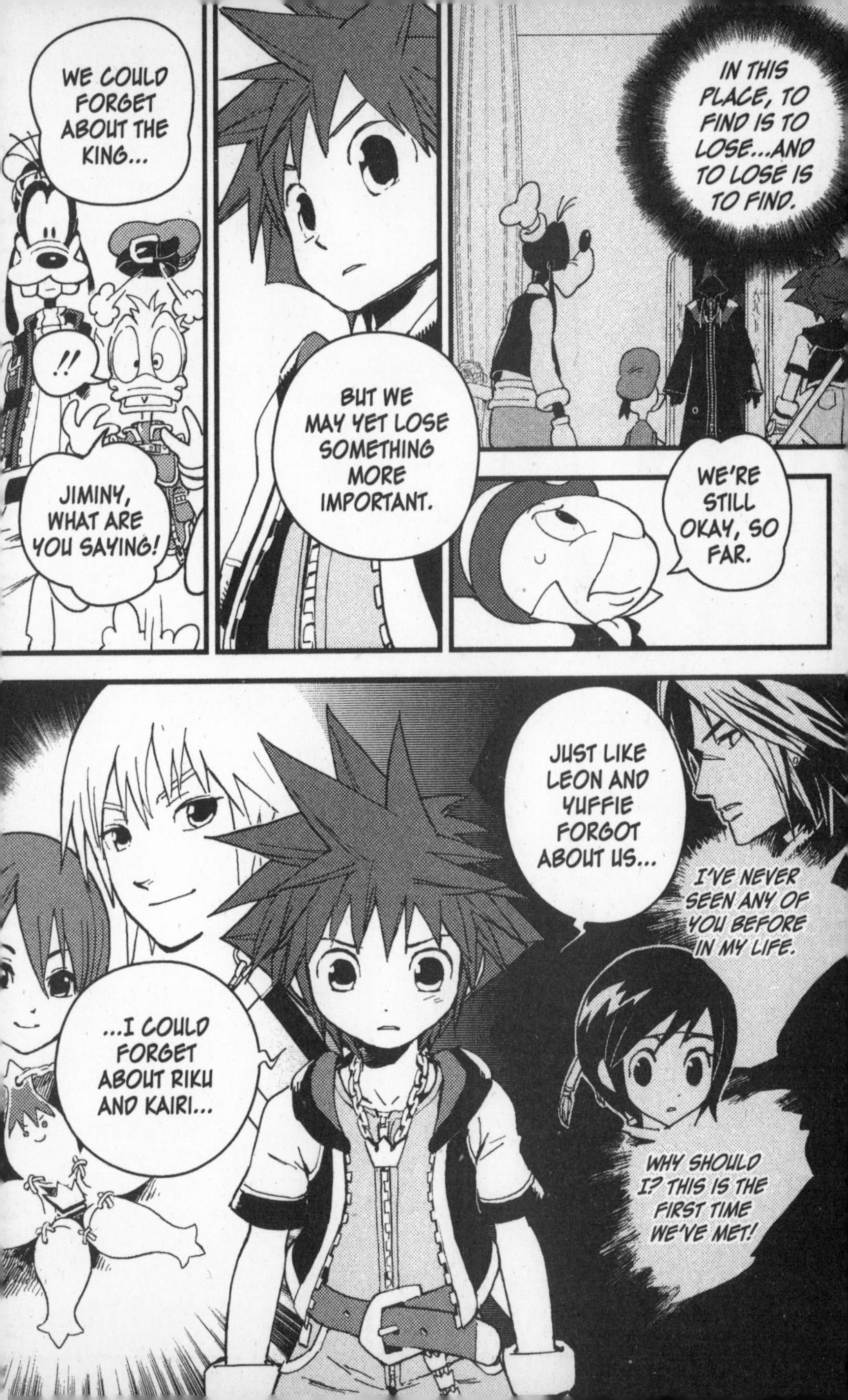
IN THIS PLACE, TO FIND IS TO LOSE...AND TO LOSE IS TO FIND.
WE'RE STILL OKAY, SO FAR.
BUT WE MAY YET LOSE SOMETHING MORE IMPORTANT.
WE COULD FORGET ABOUT THE KING...
!!
JIMINY, WHAT ARE YOU SAYING!
JUST LIKE LEON AND YUFFIE FORGOT ABOUT US...
I'VE NEVER SEEN ANY OF YOU BEFORE IN MY LIFE.
WHY SHOULD I? THIS IS THE FIRST TIME WE'VE MET!
...I COULD FORGET ABOUT RIKU AND KAIRI...

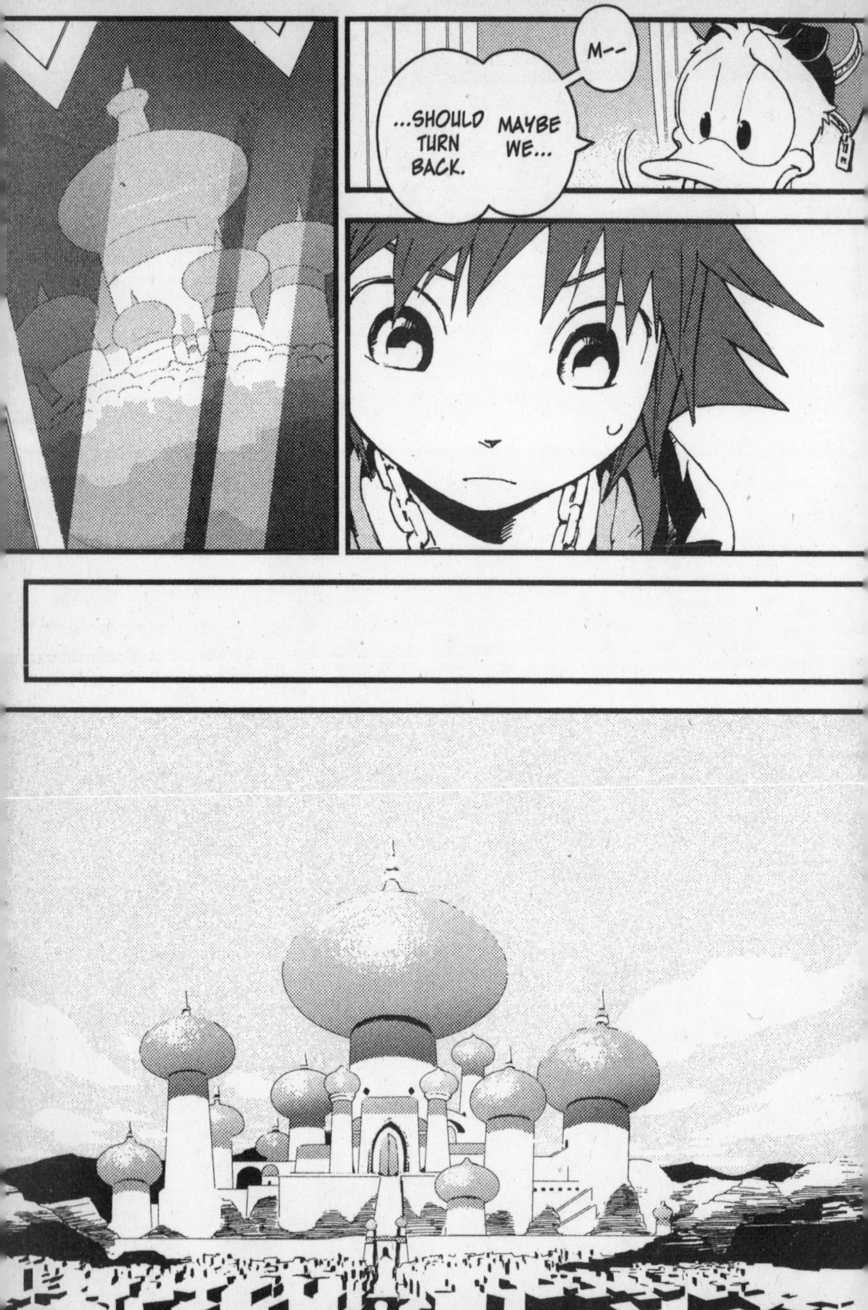
M--
MAYBE WE... ...SHOULD TURN BACK.

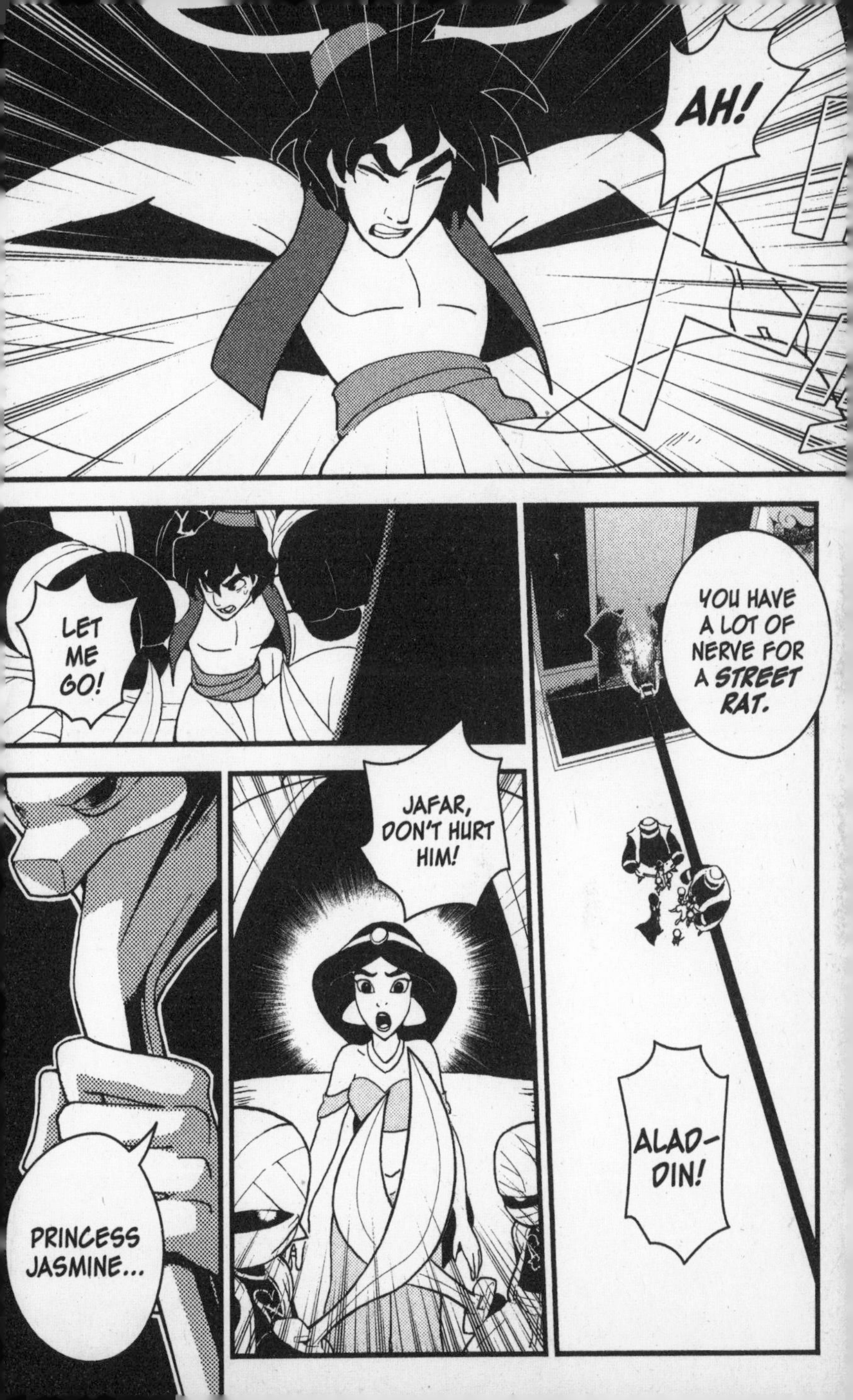
AH!
LET ME GO!
YOU HAVE A LOT OF NERVE FOR A STREET RAT.
ALAD-DIN!
JAFAR, DON'T HURT HIM!
PRINCESS JASMINE...

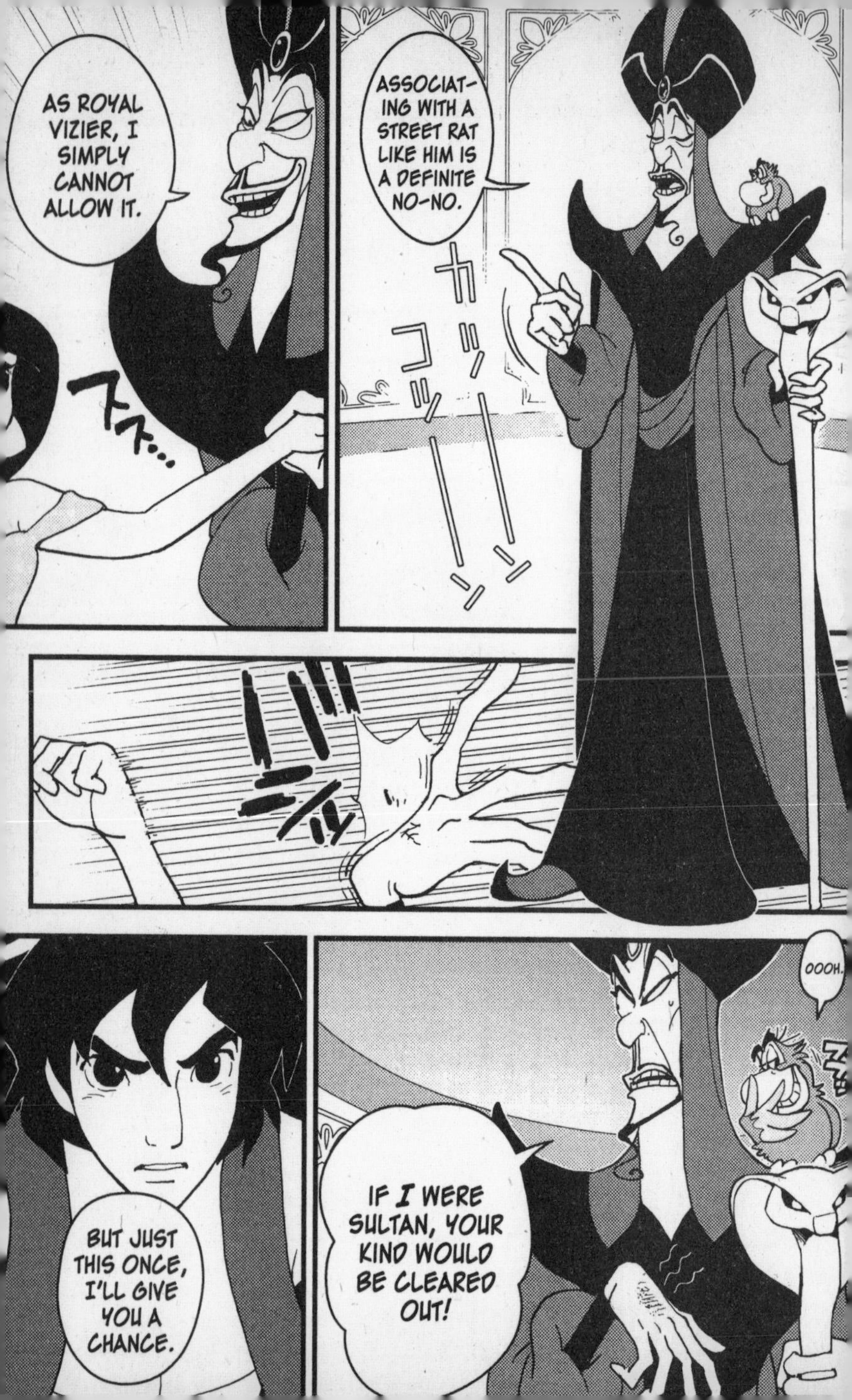
ASSOCIATING WITH A STREET RAT LIKE HIM IS A DEFINITE NO-NO.
AS ROYAL VIZIER, I SIMPLY CANNOT ALLOW IT.
OOOH.
IF I WERE SULTAN, YOUR KIND WOULD BE CLEARED OUT!
BUT JUST THIS ONCE, I'LL GIVE YOU A CHANCE.

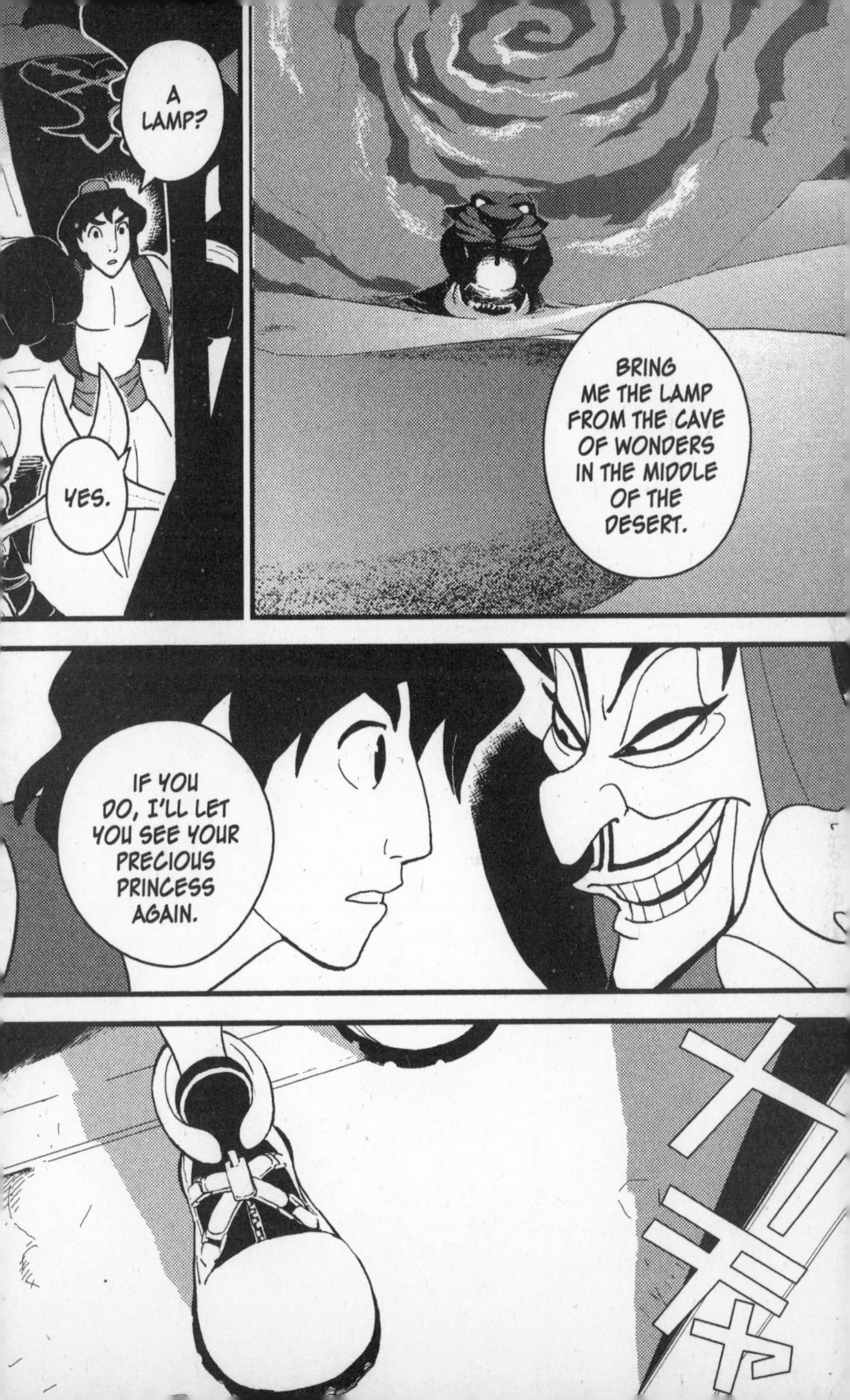
BRING ME THE LAMP FROM THE CAVE OF WONDERS IN THE MIDDLE OF THE DESERT.
A LAMP?
YES.
IF YOU DO, I'LL LET YOU SEE YOUR PRECIOUS PRINCESS AGAIN.

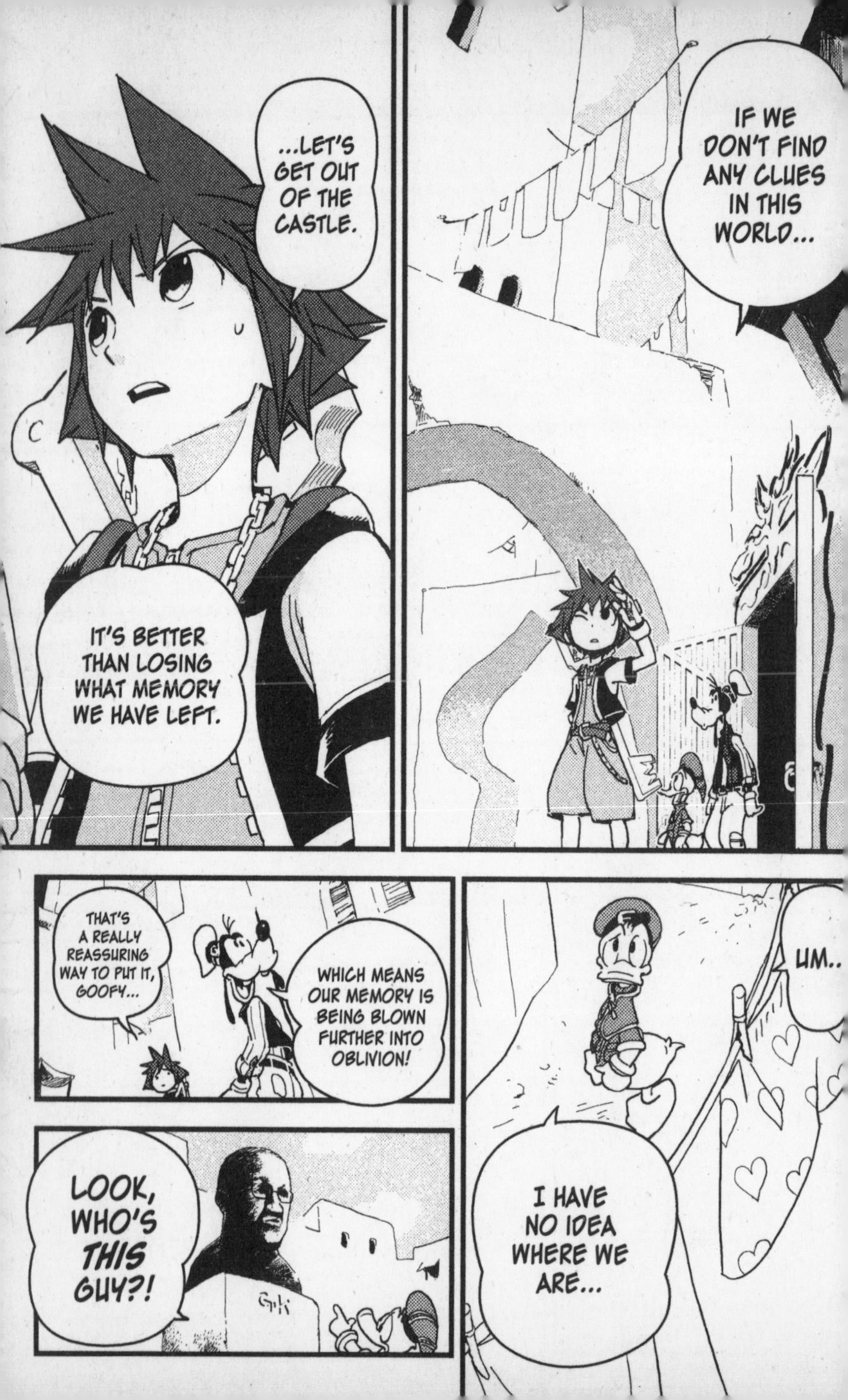
IF WE DON'T FIND ANY CLUES IN THIS WORLD...
...LET'S GET OUT OF THE CASTLE.
IT'S BETTER THAN LOSING WHAT MEMORY WE HAVE LEFT.
UM..
I HAVE NO IDEA WHERE WE ARE...
WHICH MEANS OUR MEMORY IS BEING BLOWN FURTHER INTO OBLIVION!
THAT'S A REALLY REASSURING WAY TO PUT IT, GOOFY...
LOOK, WHO'S *THIS* GUY?!

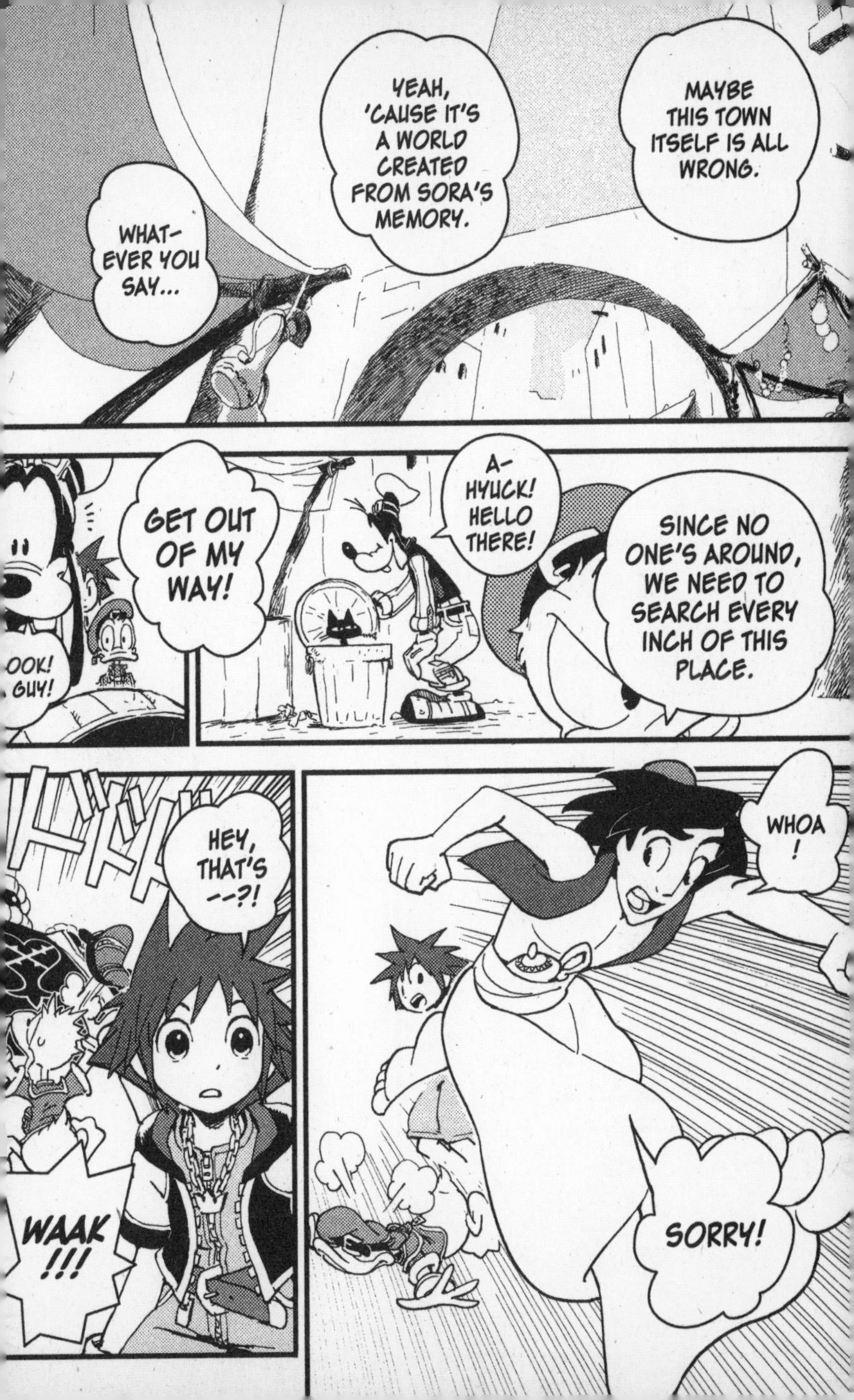

MAYBE THIS TOWN ITSELF IS ALL WRONG.
YEAH, 'CAUSE IT'S A WORLD CREATED FROM SORA'S MEMORY.
WHAT-EVER YOU SAY...
SINCE NO ONE'S AROUND, WE NEED TO SEARCH EVERY INCH OF THIS PLACE.
A-HYUCK! HELLO THERE!
GET OUT OF MY WAY!
OOK! GUY!
WHOA!
SORRY!
HEY, THAT'S --?!
WAAK!!!

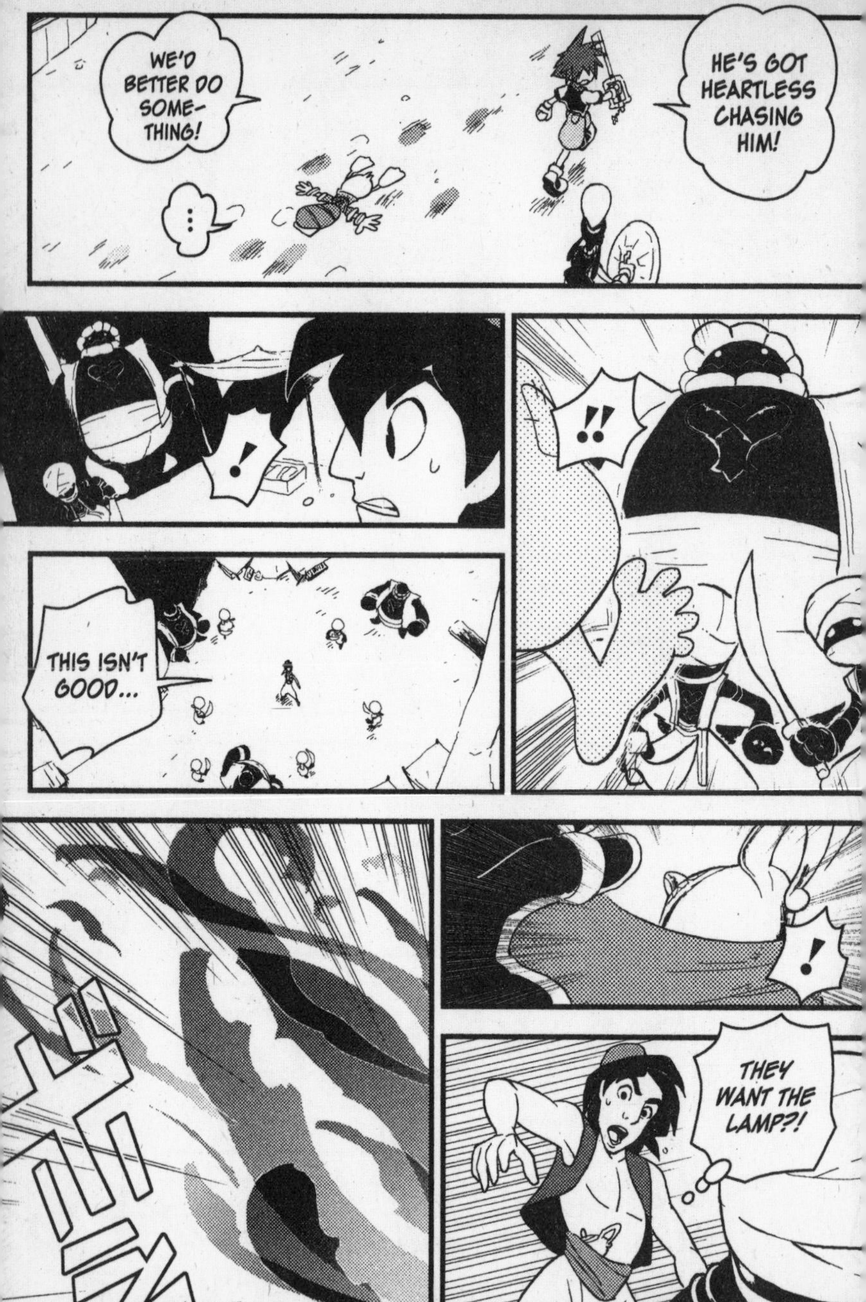
HE'S GOT HEARTLESS CHASING HIM!
WE'D BETTER DO SOME-THING!
...
!!
!
THIS ISN'T GOOD...
!
THEY WANT THE LAMP?!

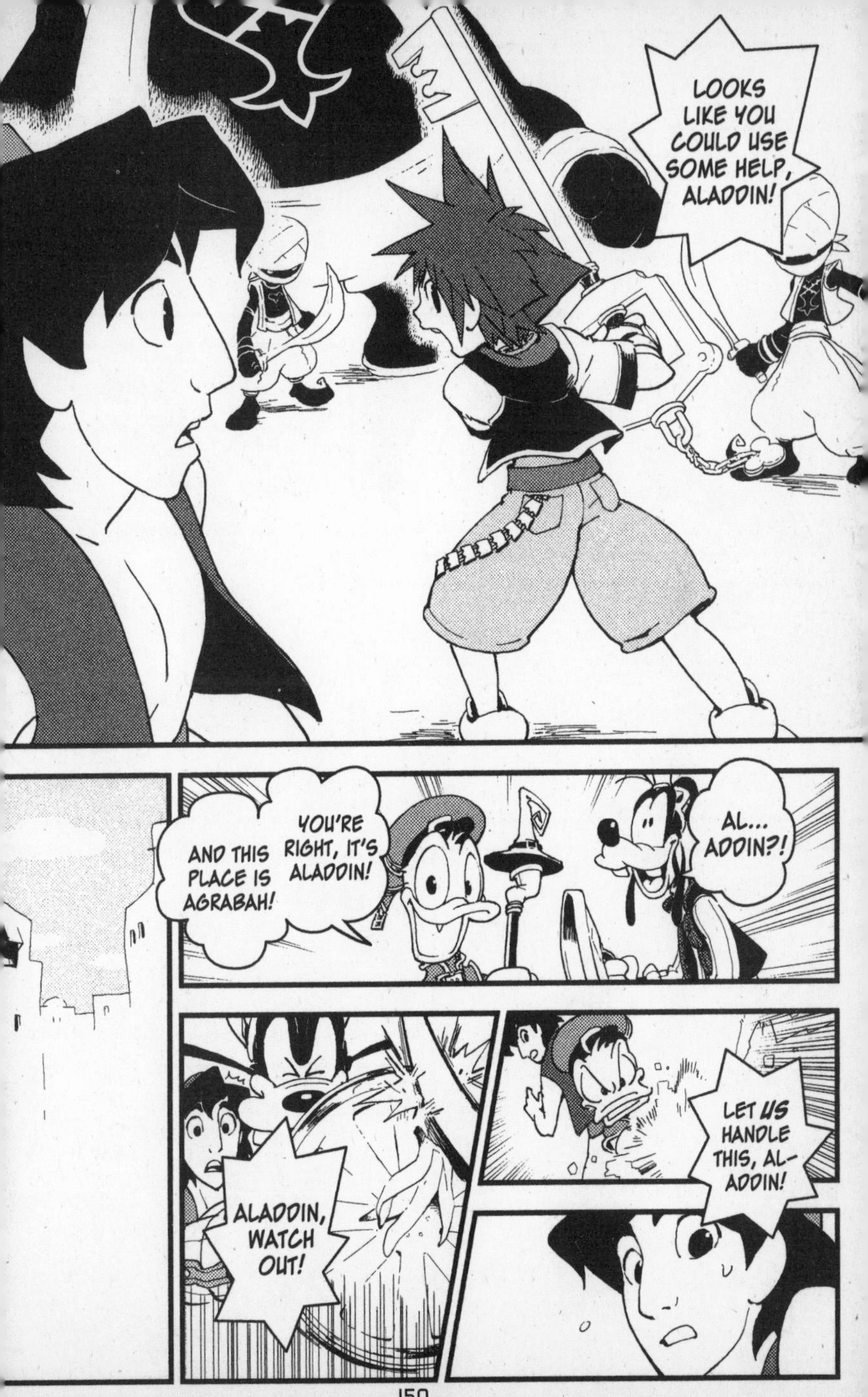
LOOKS LIKE YOU COULD USE SOME HELP, ALADDIN!
AL... ADDIN?!
YOU'RE RIGHT, IT'S ALADDIN!
AND THIS PLACE IS AGRABAH!
LET US HANDLE THIS, AL-ADDIN!
ALADDIN, WATCH OUT!

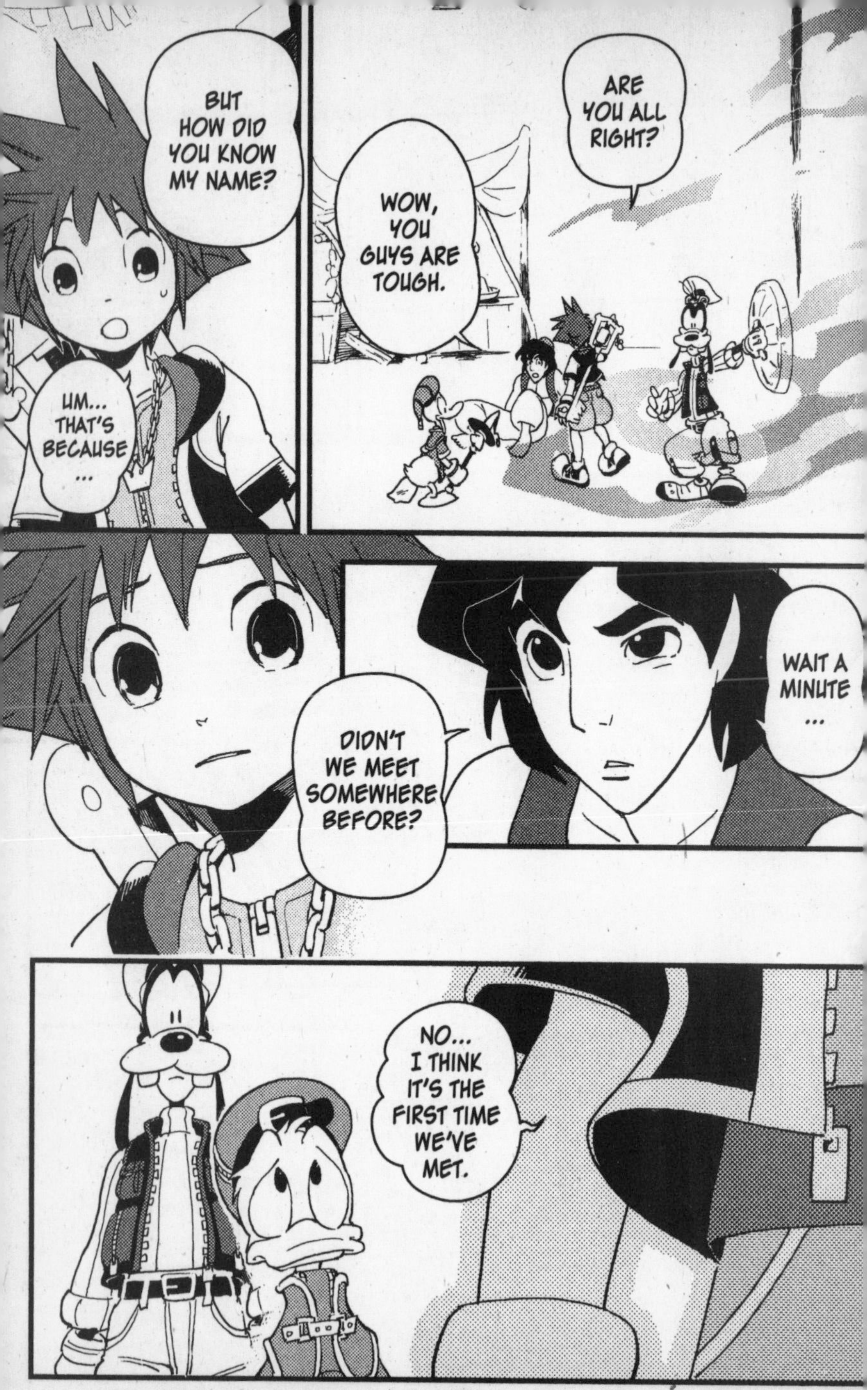
ARE YOU ALL RIGHT?
WOW, YOU GUYS ARE TOUGH.
BUT HOW DID YOU KNOW MY NAME?
UM... THAT'S BECAUSE ...
WAIT A MINUTE ...
DIDN'T WE MEET SOMEWHERE BEFORE?
NO... I THINK IT'S THE FIRST TIME WE'VE MET.

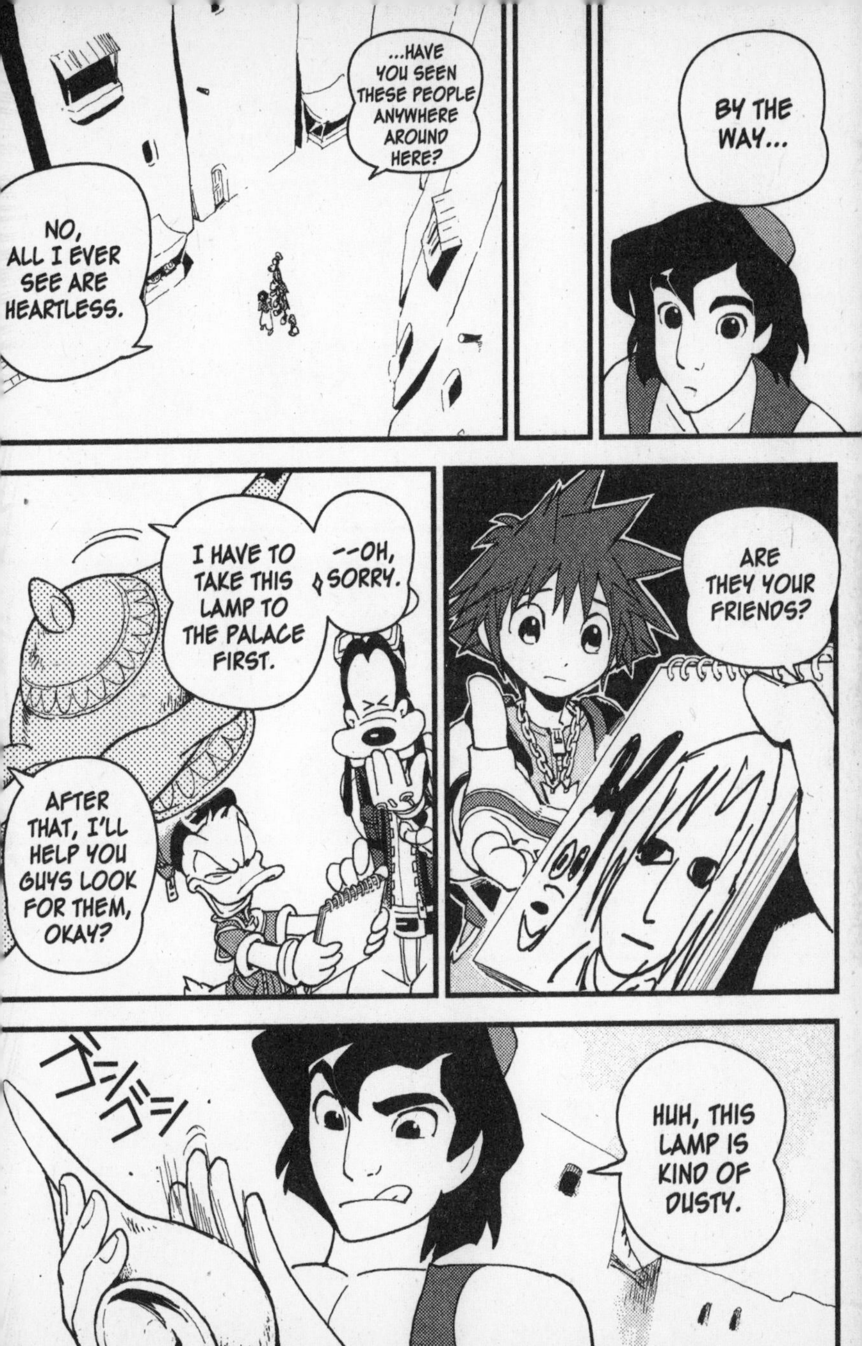

BY THE WAY...
...HAVE YOU SEEN THESE PEOPLE ANYWHERE AROUND HERE?
NO, ALL I EVER SEE ARE HEARTLESS.
ARE THEY YOUR FRIENDS?
--OH, SORRY.
I HAVE TO TAKE THIS LAMP TO THE PALACE FIRST.
AFTER THAT, I'LL HELP YOU GUYS LOOK FOR THEM, OKAY?
HUH, THIS LAMP IS KIND OF DUSTY.

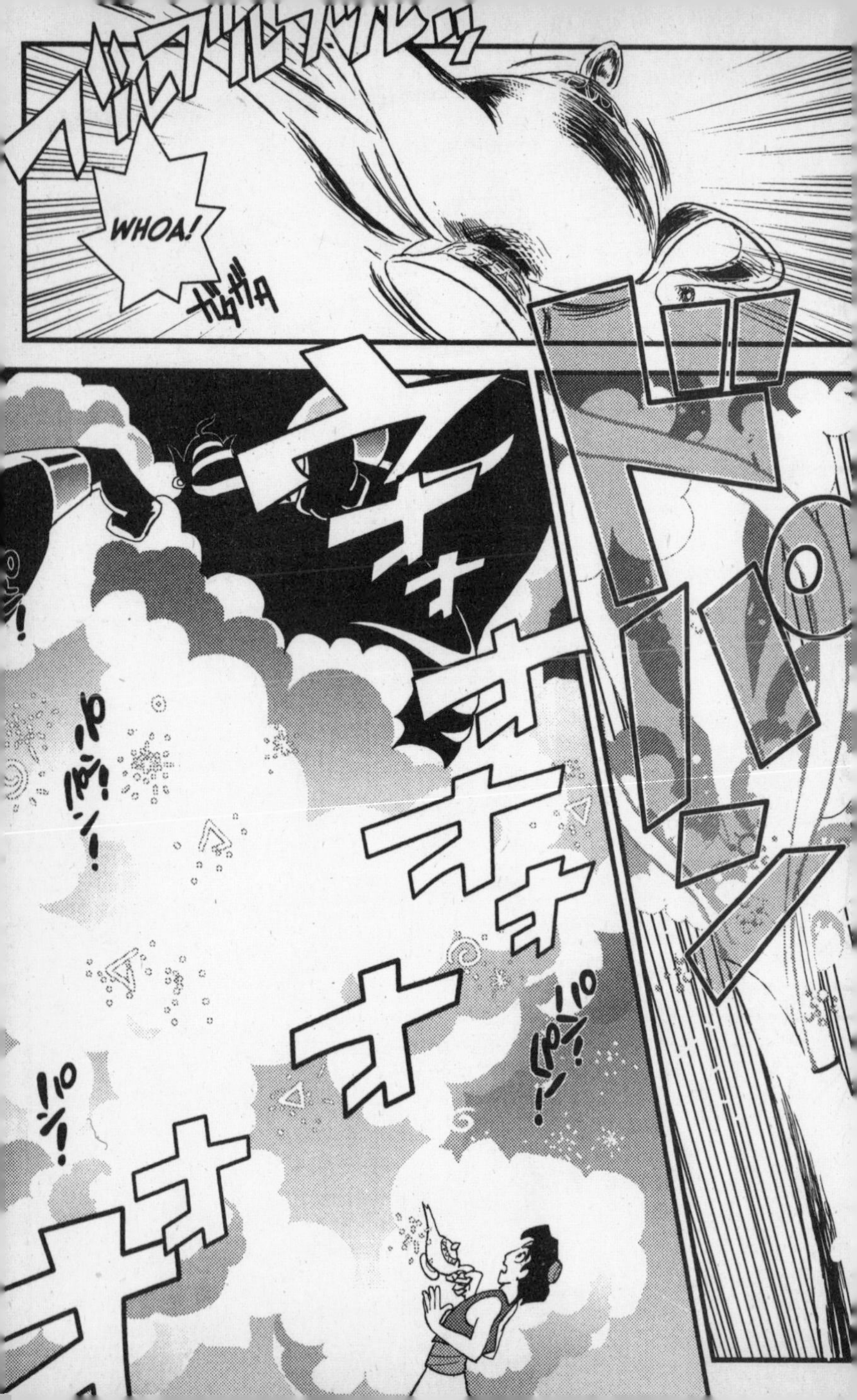
WHOA!

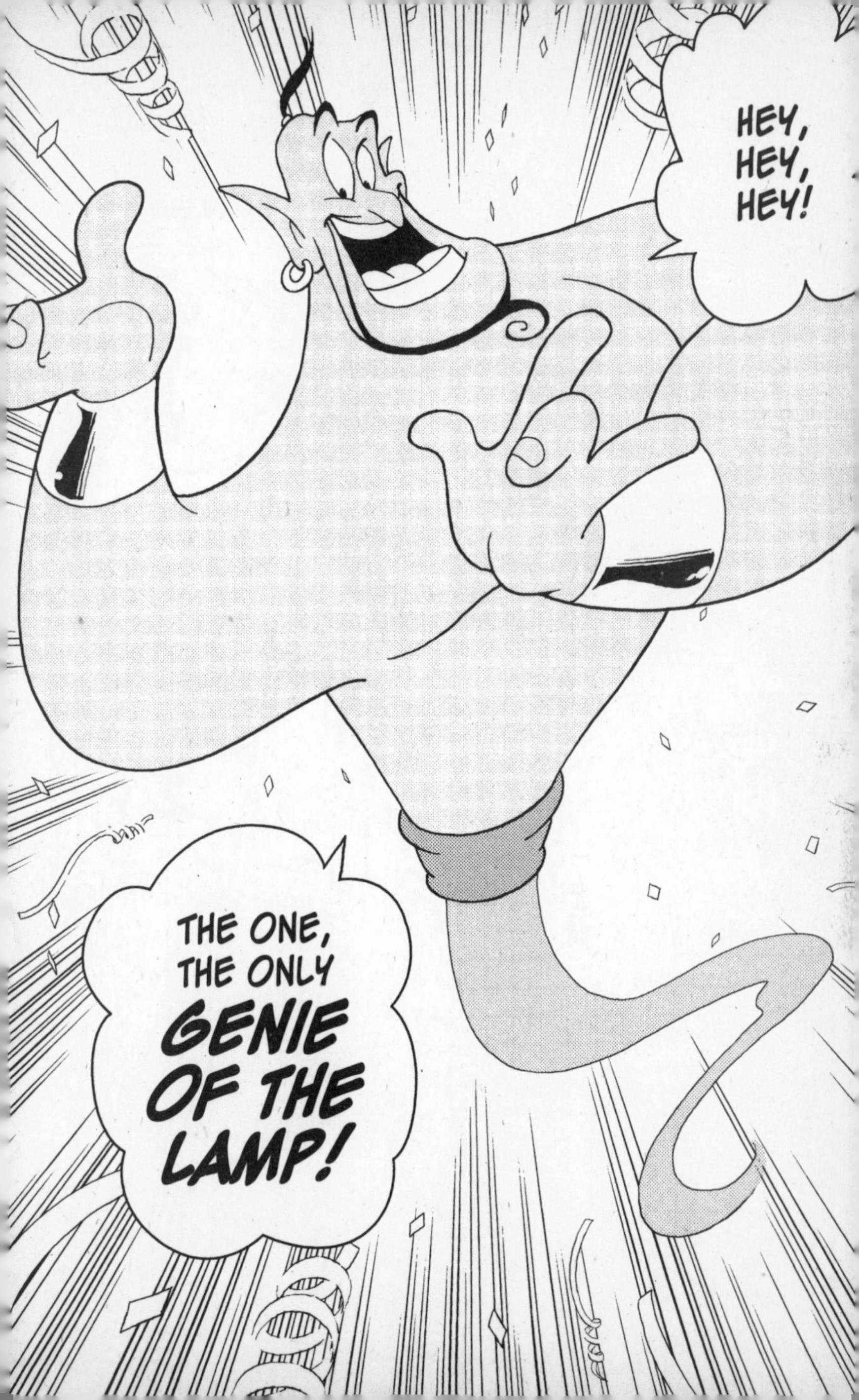
HEY, HEY, HEY!
THE ONE, THE ONLY GENIE OF THE LAMP!

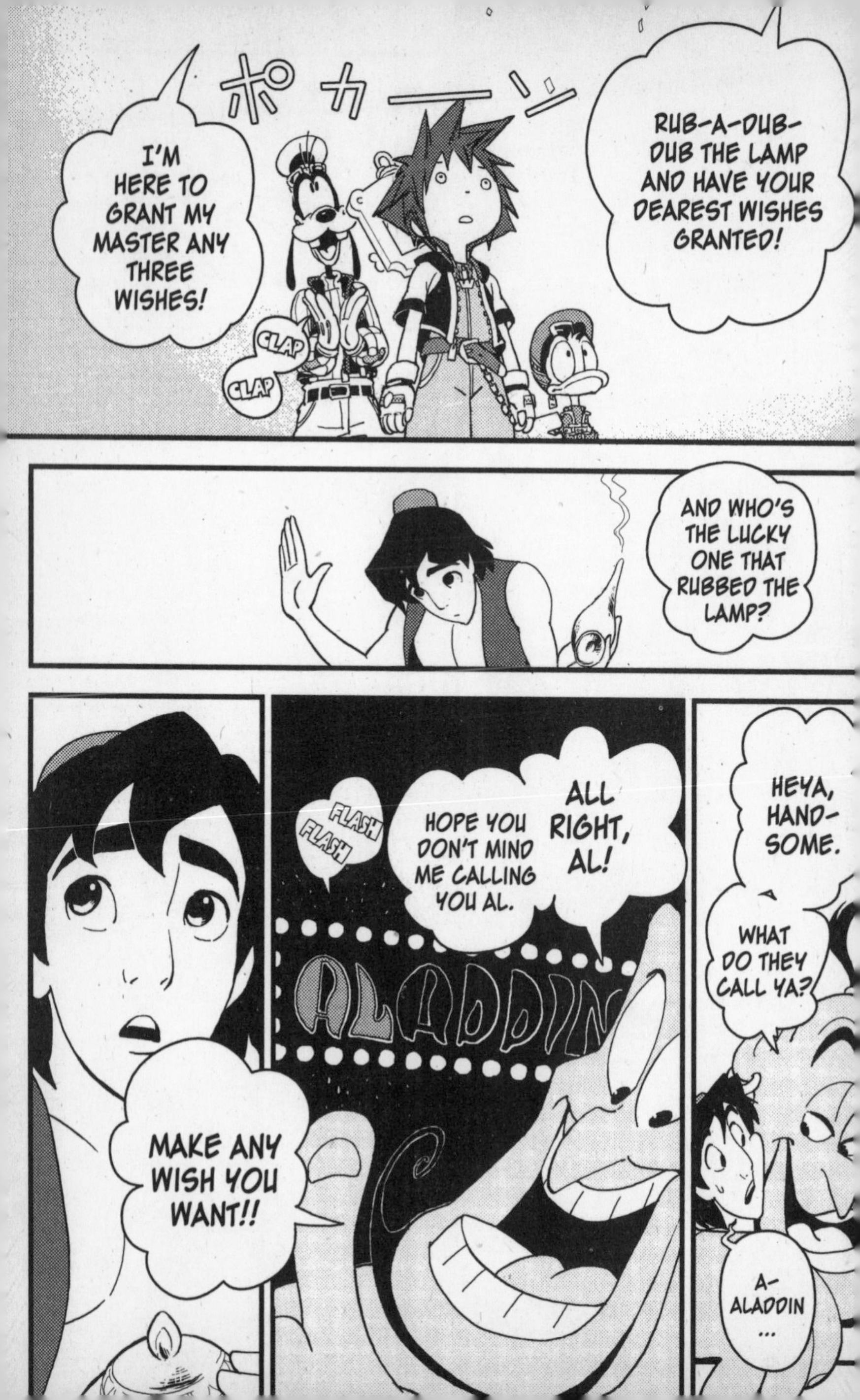
RUB-A-DUB-DUB THE LAMP AND HAVE YOUR DEAREST WISHES GRANTED!
ポカーン
I'M HERE TO GRANT MY MASTER ANY THREE WISHES!
CLAP
CLAP
AND WHO'S THE LUCKY ONE THAT RUBBED THE LAMP?
HEYA, HAND-SOME.
WHAT DO THEY CALL YA?
A-ALADDIN...
ALL RIGHT, AL!
HOPE YOU DON'T MIND ME CALLING YOU AL.
FLASH
FLASH
ALADDIN
MAKE ANY WISH YOU WANT!!

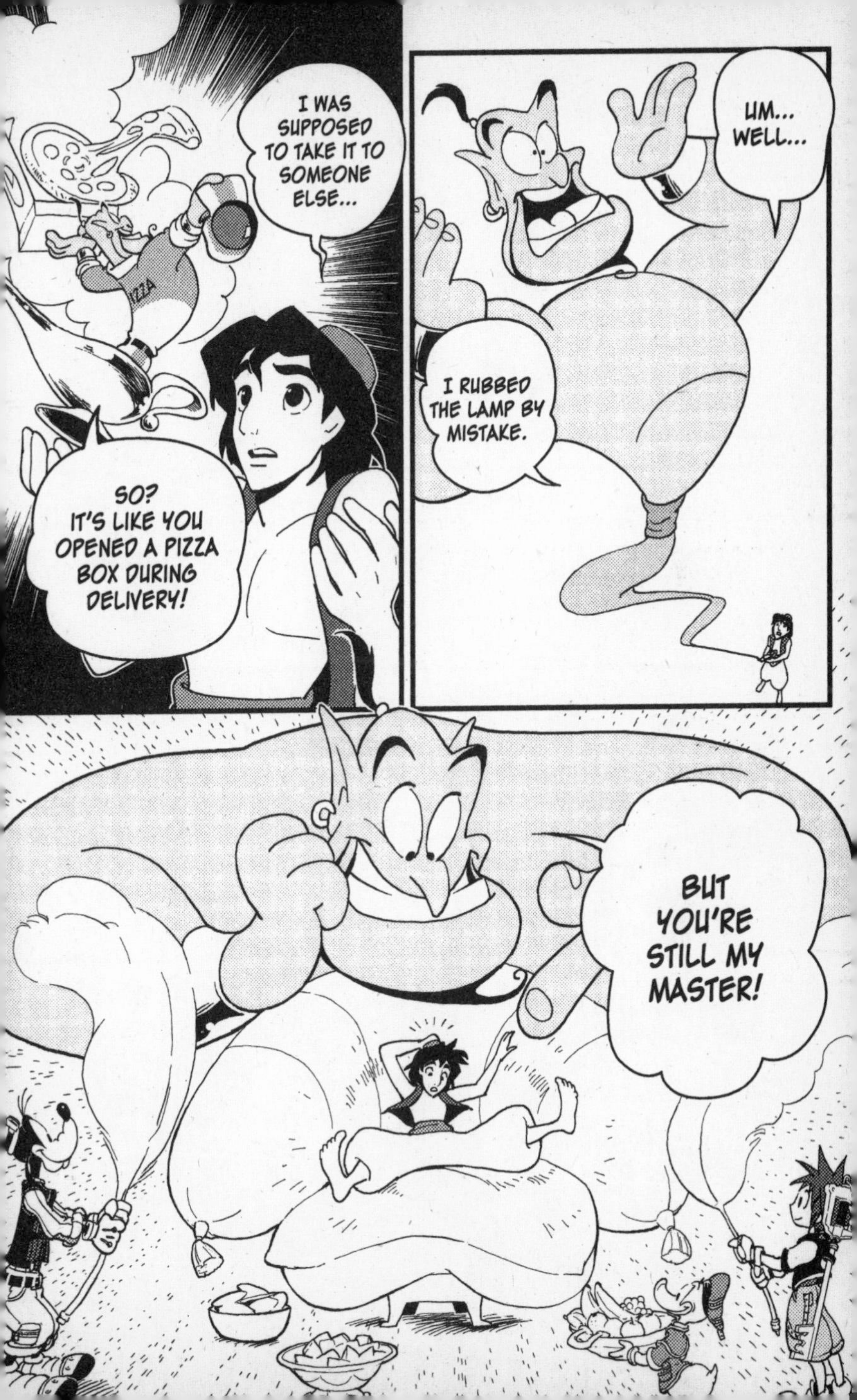
UM... WELL...
I RUBBED THE LAMP BY MISTAKE.
I WAS SUPPOSED TO TAKE IT TO SOMEONE ELSE...
SO? IT'S LIKE YOU OPENED A PIZZA BOX DURING DELIVERY!
PIZZA
BUT YOU'RE STILL MY MASTER!

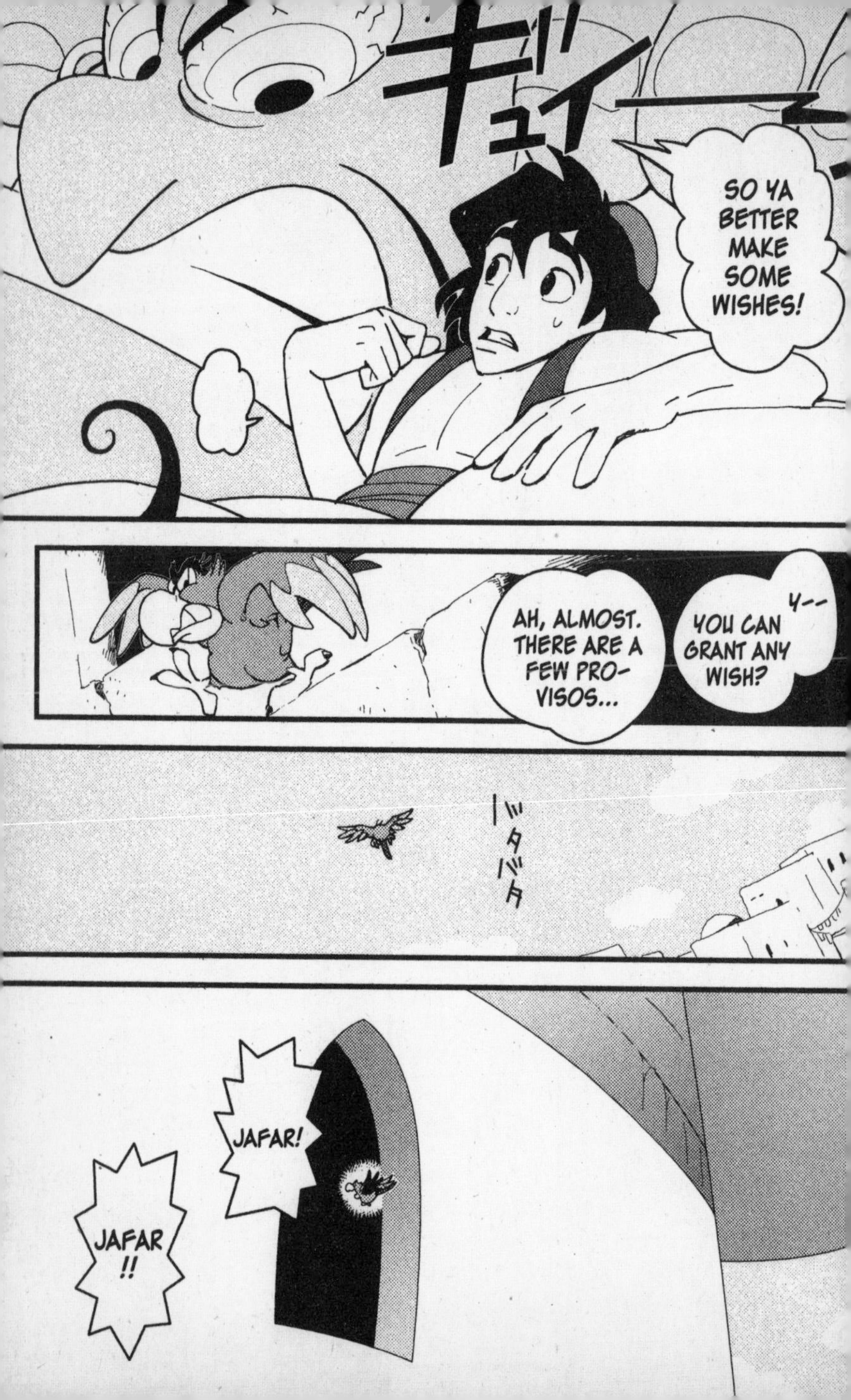
ギュイー
SO YA BETTER MAKE SOME WISHES!
Y-- YOU CAN GRANT ANY WISH?
AH, ALMOST. THERE ARE A FEW PRO-VISOS...
バタバタ
JAFAR!
JAFAR !!

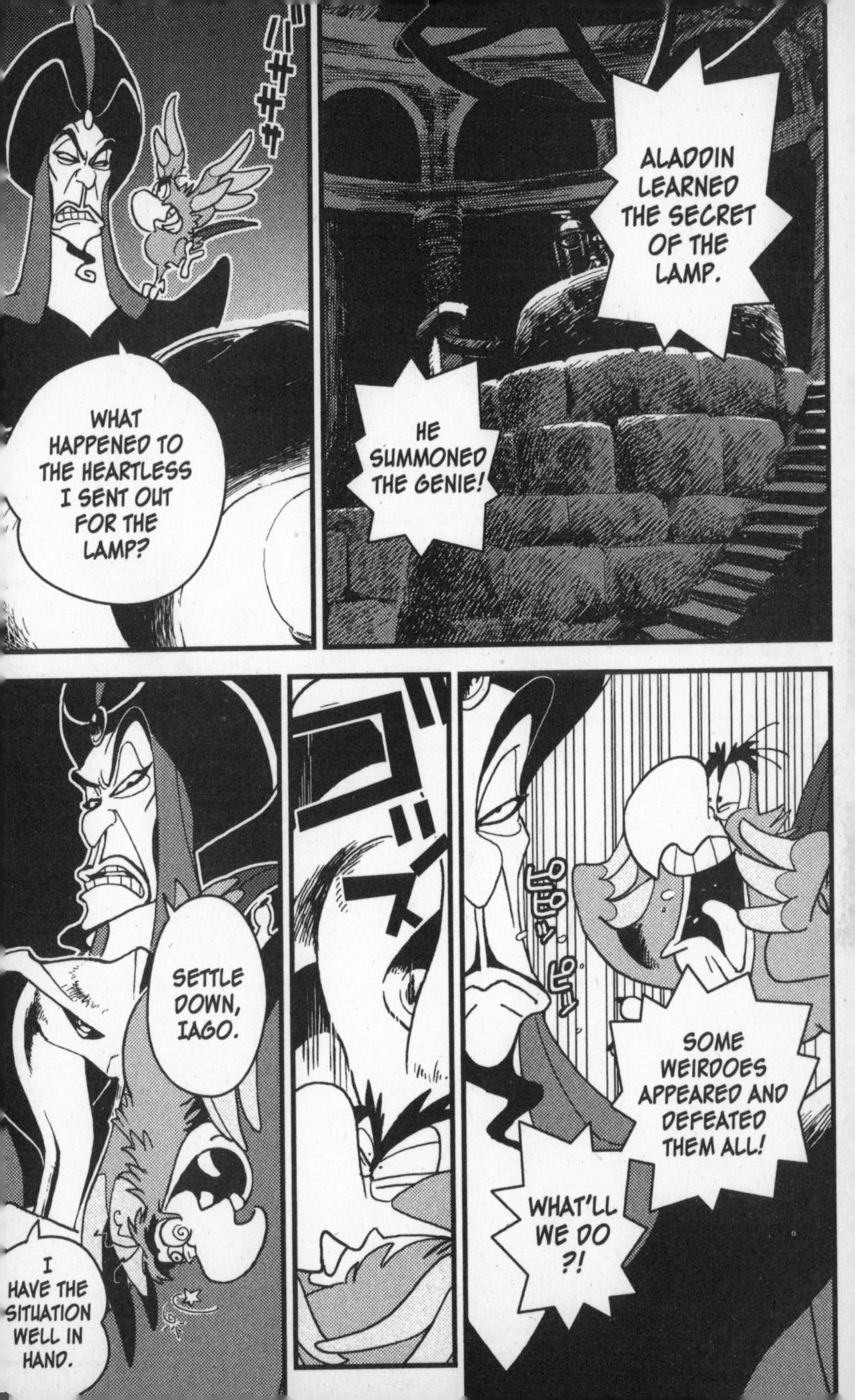
ALADDIN LEARNED THE SECRET OF THE LAMP.
HE SUMMONED THE GENIE!
WHAT HAPPENED TO THE HEARTLESS I SENT OUT FOR THE LAMP?
SOME WEIRDOES APPEARED AND DEFEATED THEM ALL!
WHAT'LL WE DO ?!
SETTLE DOWN, IAGO.
I HAVE THE SITUATION WELL IN HAND.

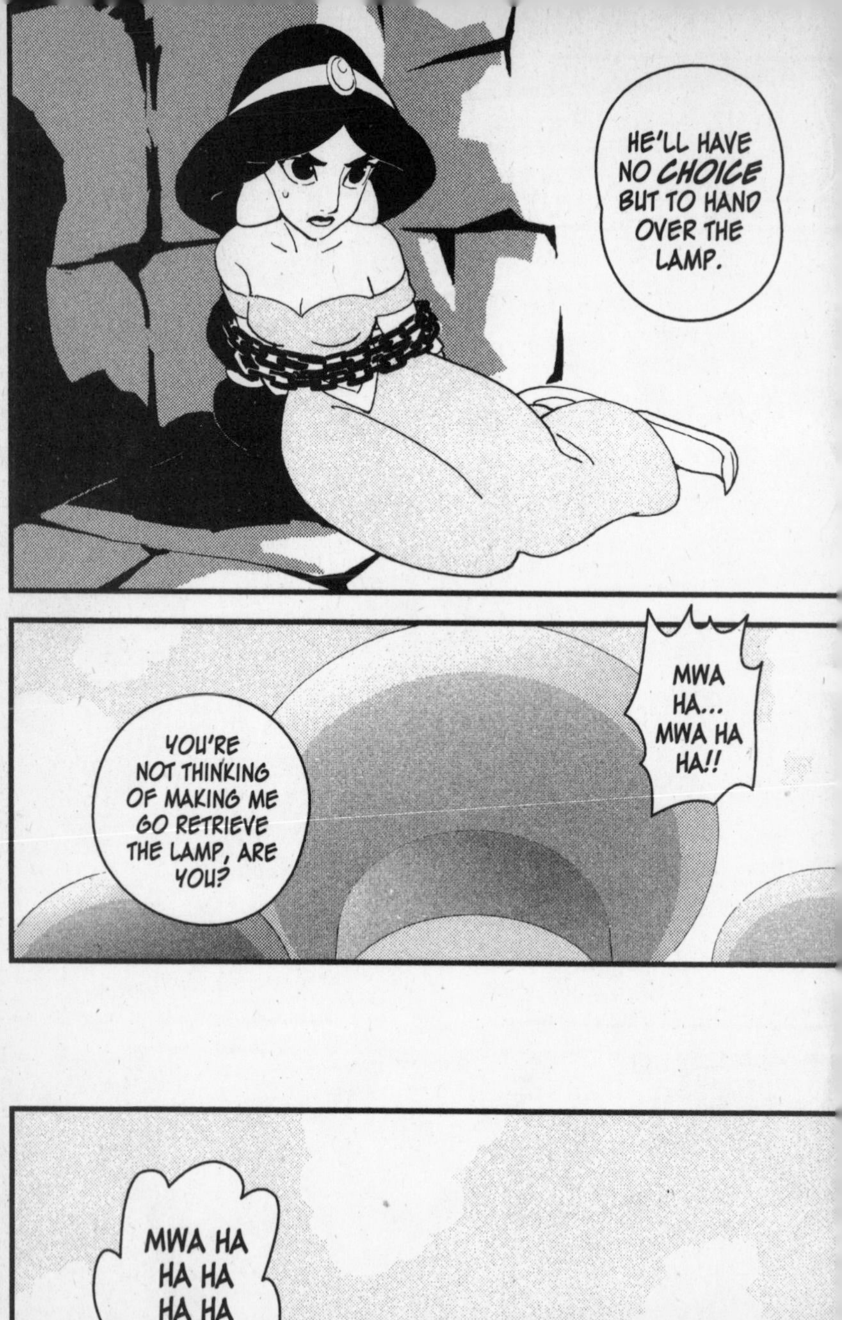
HE'LL HAVE NO CHOICE BUT TO HAND OVER THE LAMP.
MWA HA... MWA HA HA!!
YOU'RE NOT THINKING OF MAKING ME GO RETRIEVE THE LAMP, ARE YOU?
MWA HA HA HA HA HA HA!!

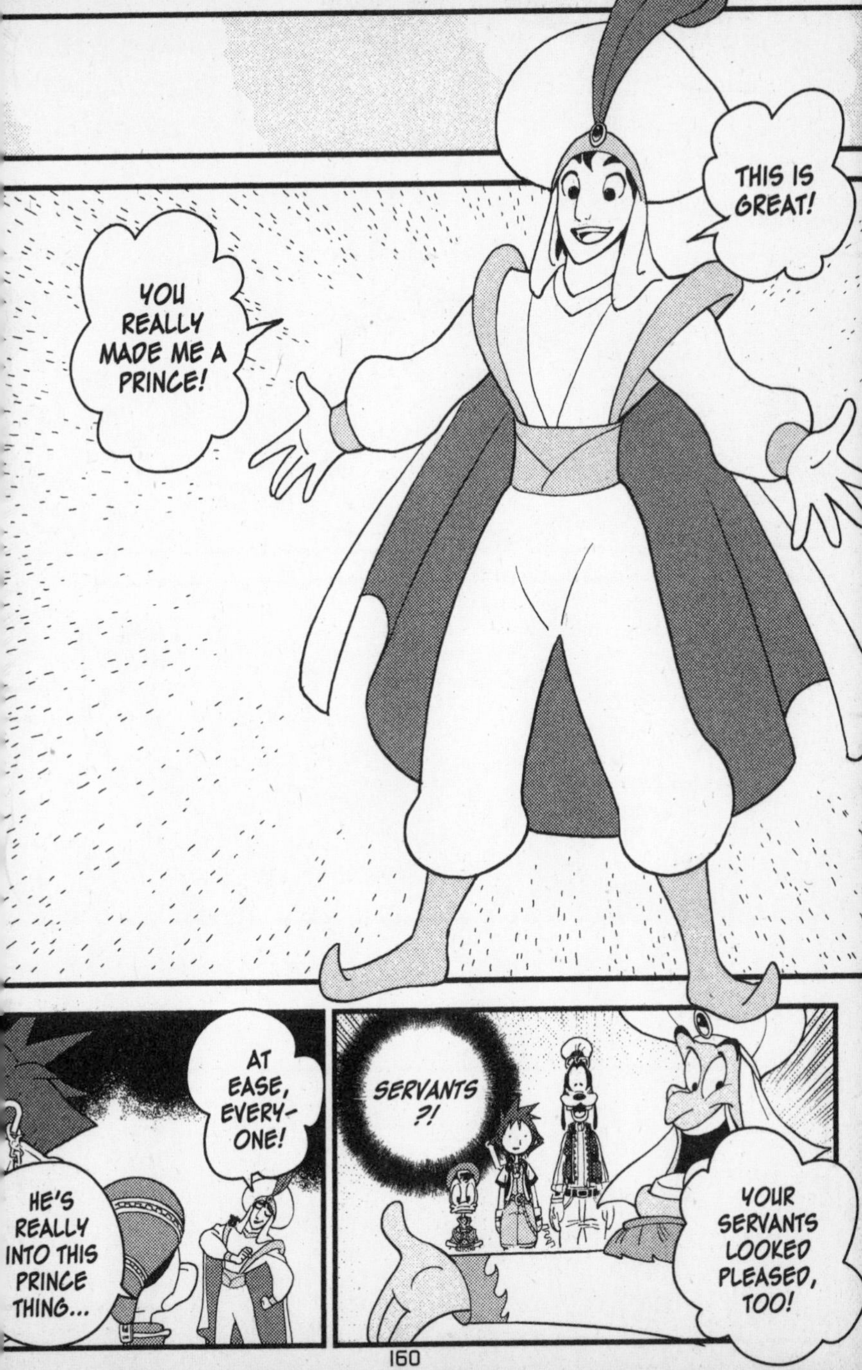
THIS IS GREAT!
YOU REALLY MADE ME A PRINCE!
YOUR SERVANTS LOOKED PLEASED, TOO!
SERVANTS ?!
AT EASE, EVERY-ONE!
HE'S REALLY INTO THIS PRINCE THING...

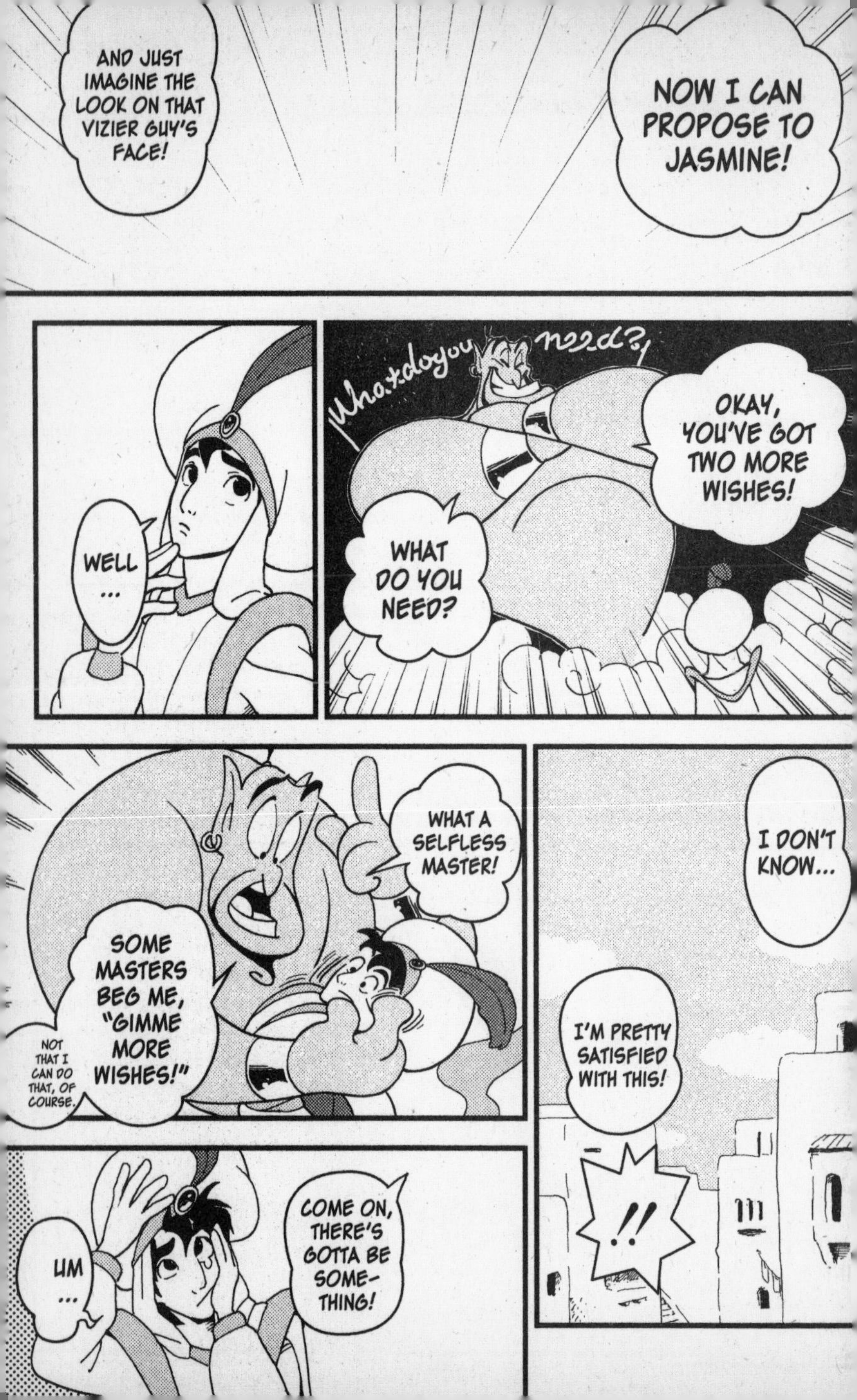
NOW I CAN PROPOSE TO JASMINE!
AND JUST IMAGINE THE LOOK ON THAT VIZIER GUY'S FACE!
What do you need?
OKAY, YOU'VE GOT TWO MORE WISHES!
WHAT DO YOU NEED?
WELL ...
I DON'T KNOW...
I'M PRETTY SATISFIED WITH THIS!
!!
WHAT A SELFLESS MASTER!
SOME MASTERS BEG ME, "GIMME MORE WISHES!"
NOT THAT I CAN DO THAT, OF COURSE.
COME ON, THERE'S GOTTA BE SOME-THING!
UM ...

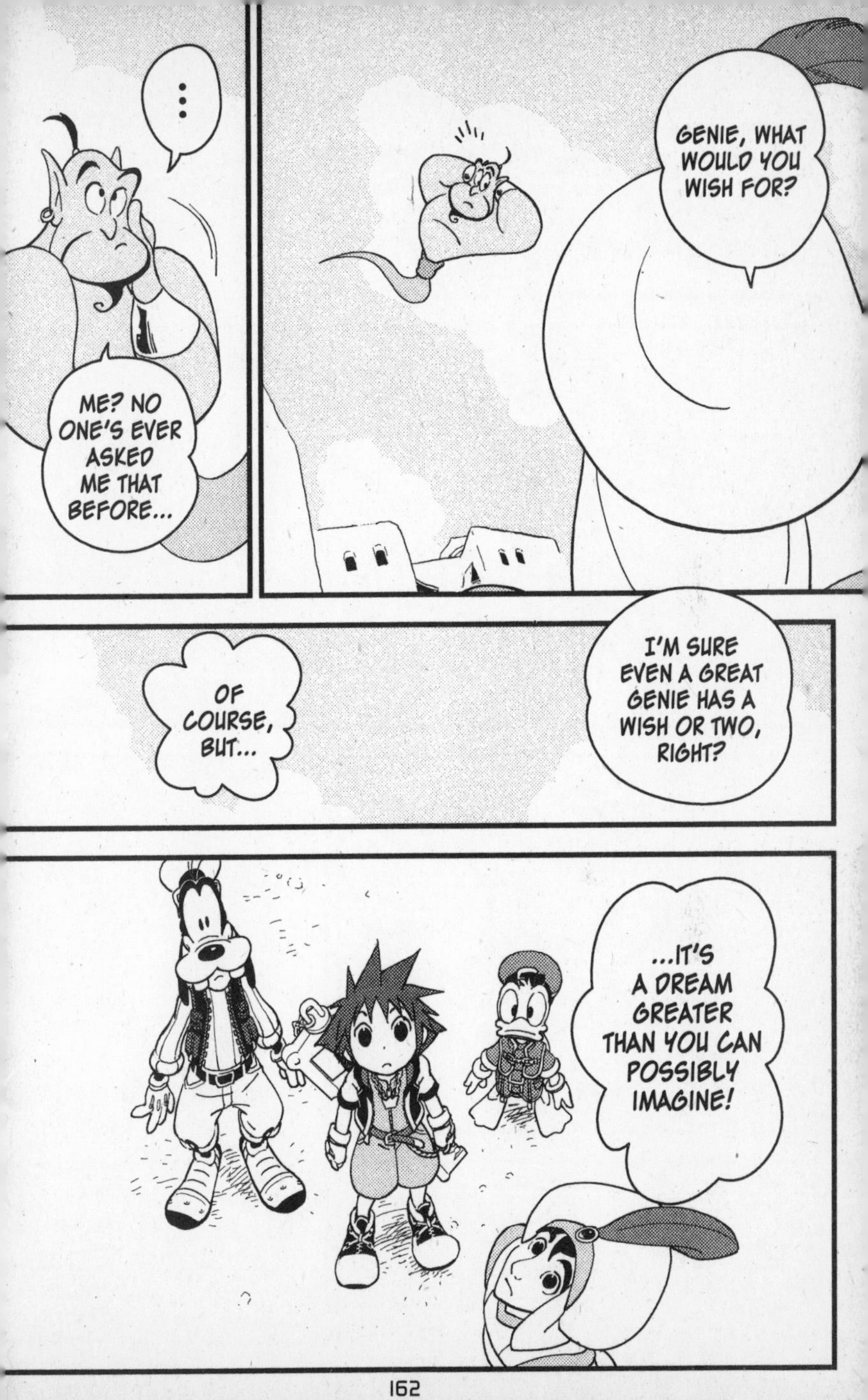
GENIE, WHAT WOULD YOU WISH FOR?
...
ME? NO ONE'S EVER ASKED ME THAT BEFORE...
I'M SURE EVEN A GREAT GENIE HAS A WISH OR TWO, RIGHT?
OF COURSE, BUT...
...IT'S A DREAM GREATER THAN YOU CAN POSSIBLY IMAGINE!

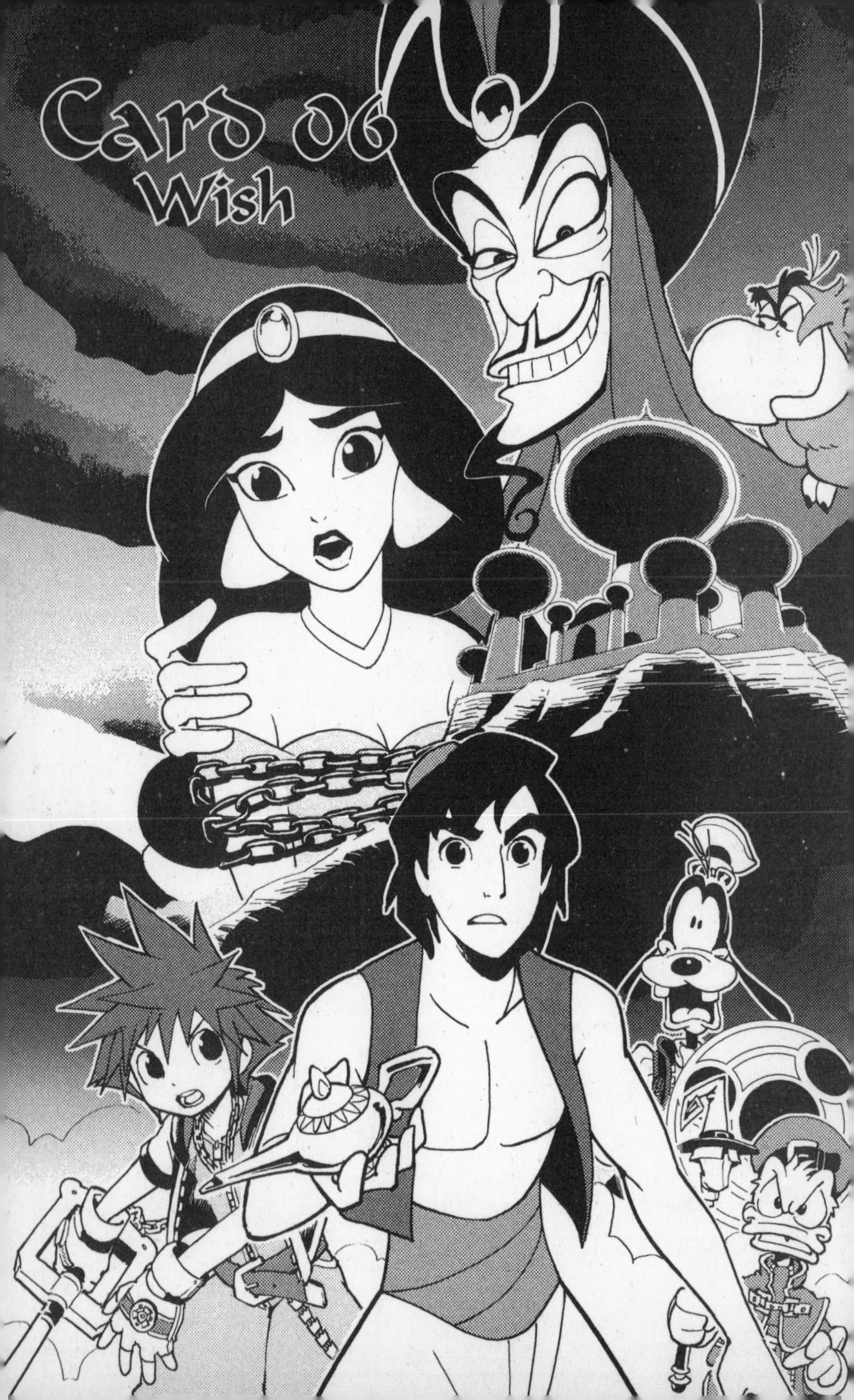
Card 06
Wish

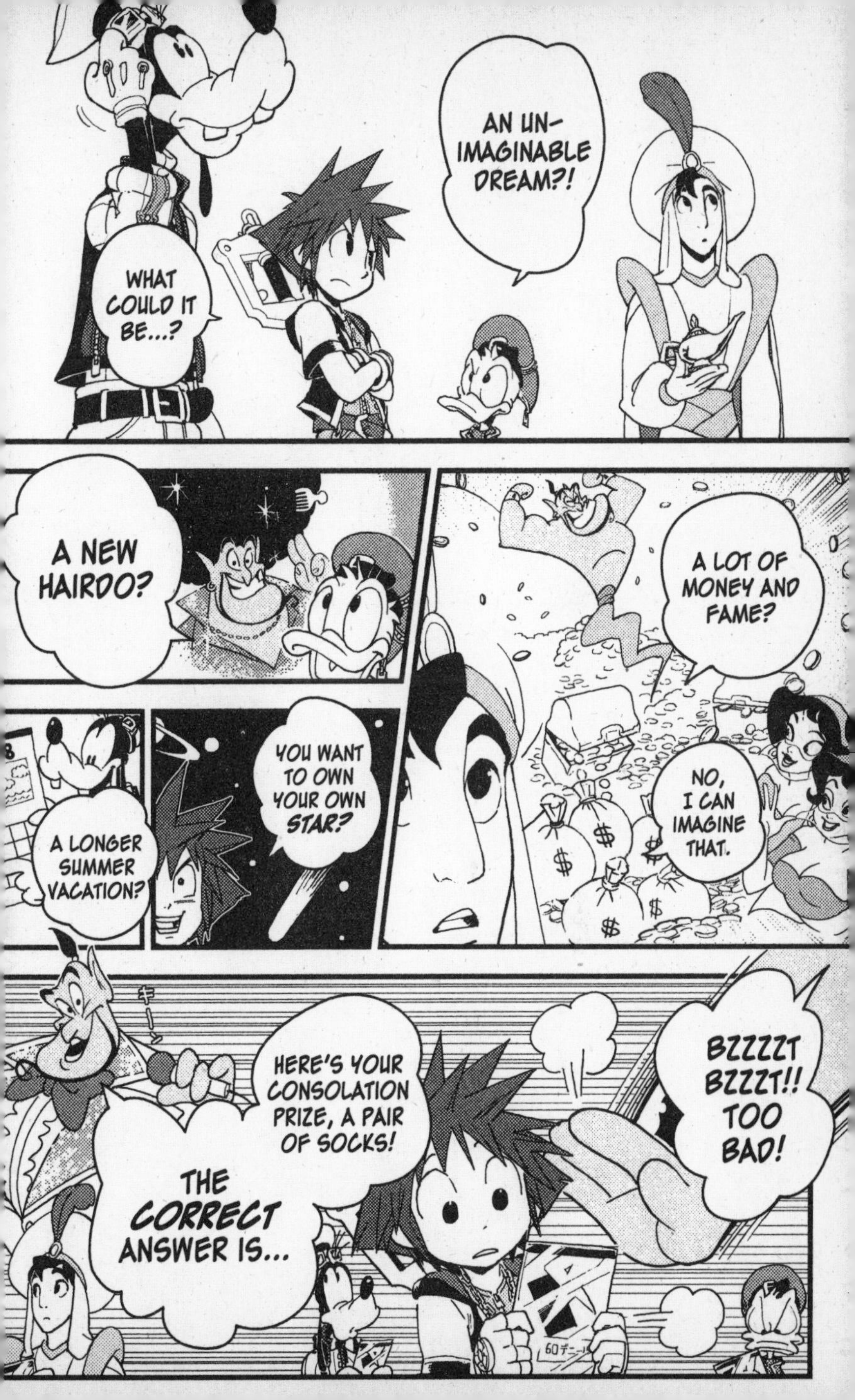
AN UN-IMAGINABLE DREAM?!
WHAT COULD IT BE...?
A LOT OF MONEY AND FAME?
NO, I CAN IMAGINE THAT.
A NEW HAIRDO?
YOU WANT TO OWN YOUR OWN STAR?
A LONGER SUMMER VACATION?
BZZZZT BZZZT!! TOO BAD!
HERE'S YOUR CONSOLATION PRIZE, A PAIR OF SOCKS!
THE CORRECT ANSWER IS...
キーン

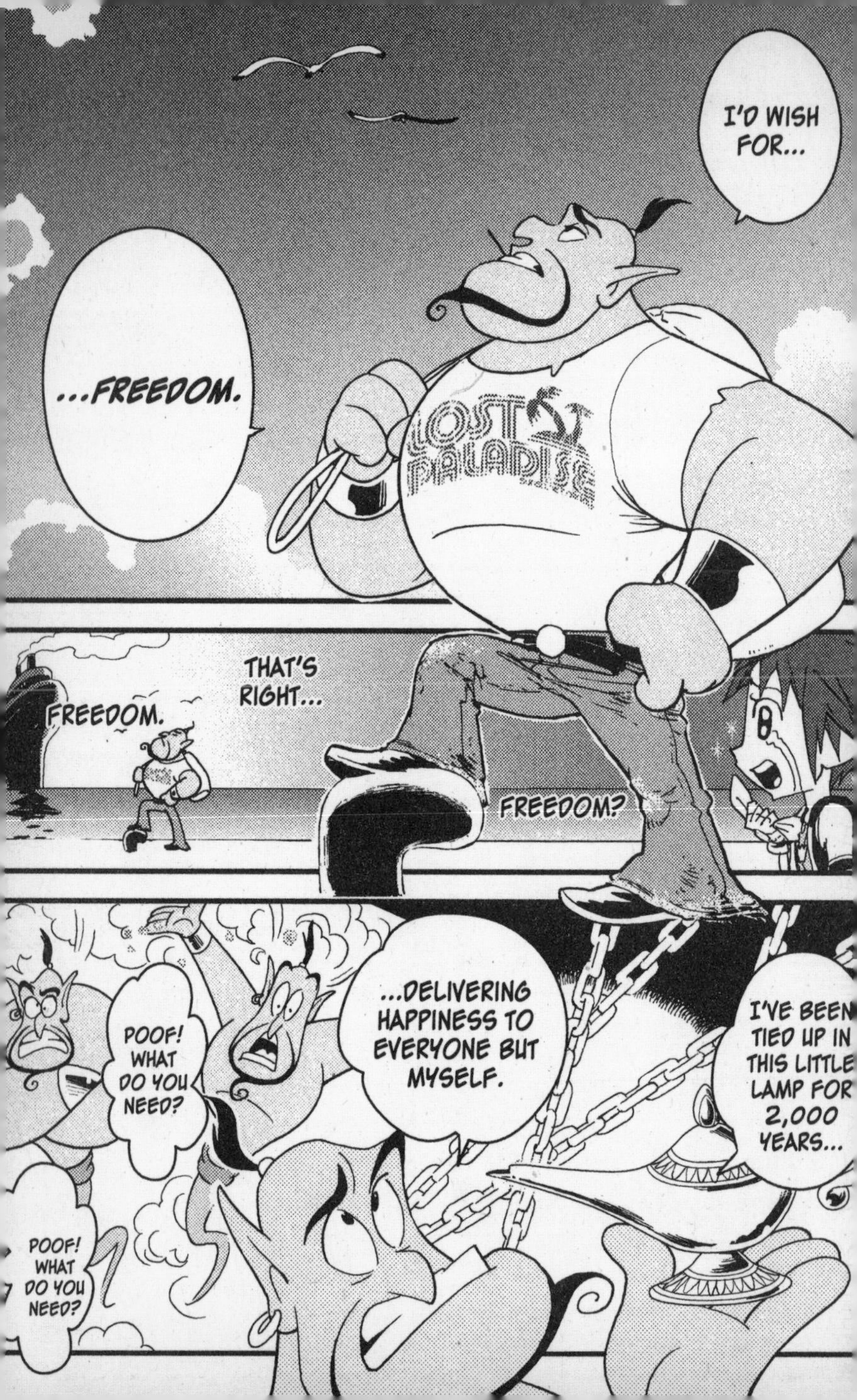
I'D WISH FOR...
...FREEDOM.
FREEDOM?
THAT'S RIGHT...
FREEDOM.
I'VE BEEN TIED UP IN THIS LITTLE LAMP FOR 2,000 YEARS...
...DELIVERING HAPPINESS TO EVERYONE BUT MYSELF.
POOF! WHAT DO YOU NEED?
POOF! WHAT DO YOU NEED?

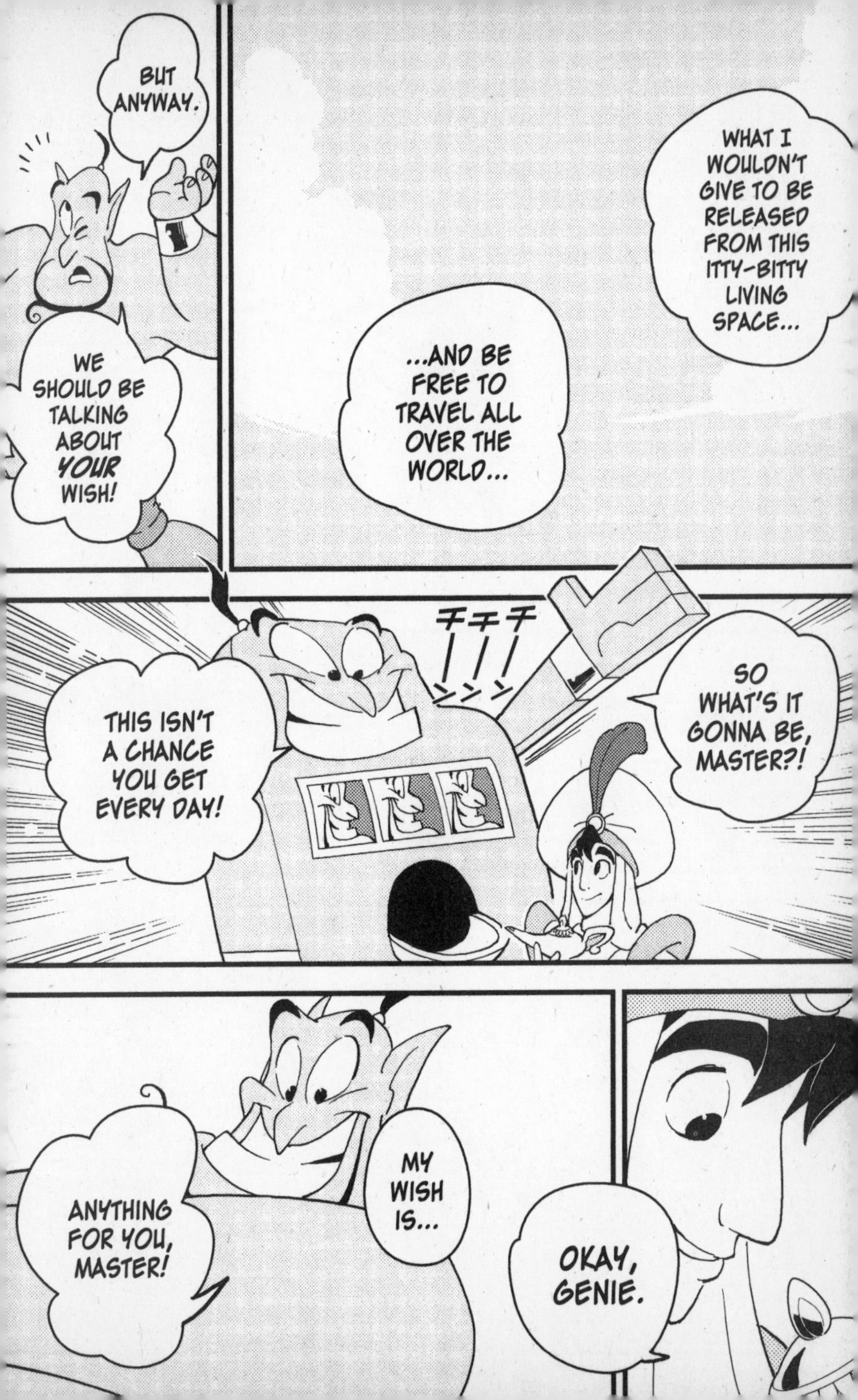
WHAT I WOULDN'T GIVE TO BE RELEASED FROM THIS ITTY-BITTY LIVING SPACE...
...AND BE FREE TO TRAVEL ALL OVER THE WORLD...
BUT ANYWAY.
WE SHOULD BE TALKING ABOUT *YOUR* WISH!
SO WHAT'S IT GONNA BE, MASTER?!
チーン チーン チーン
THIS ISN'T A CHANCE YOU GET EVERY DAY!
OKAY, GENIE.
MY WISH IS...
ANYTHING FOR YOU, MASTER!

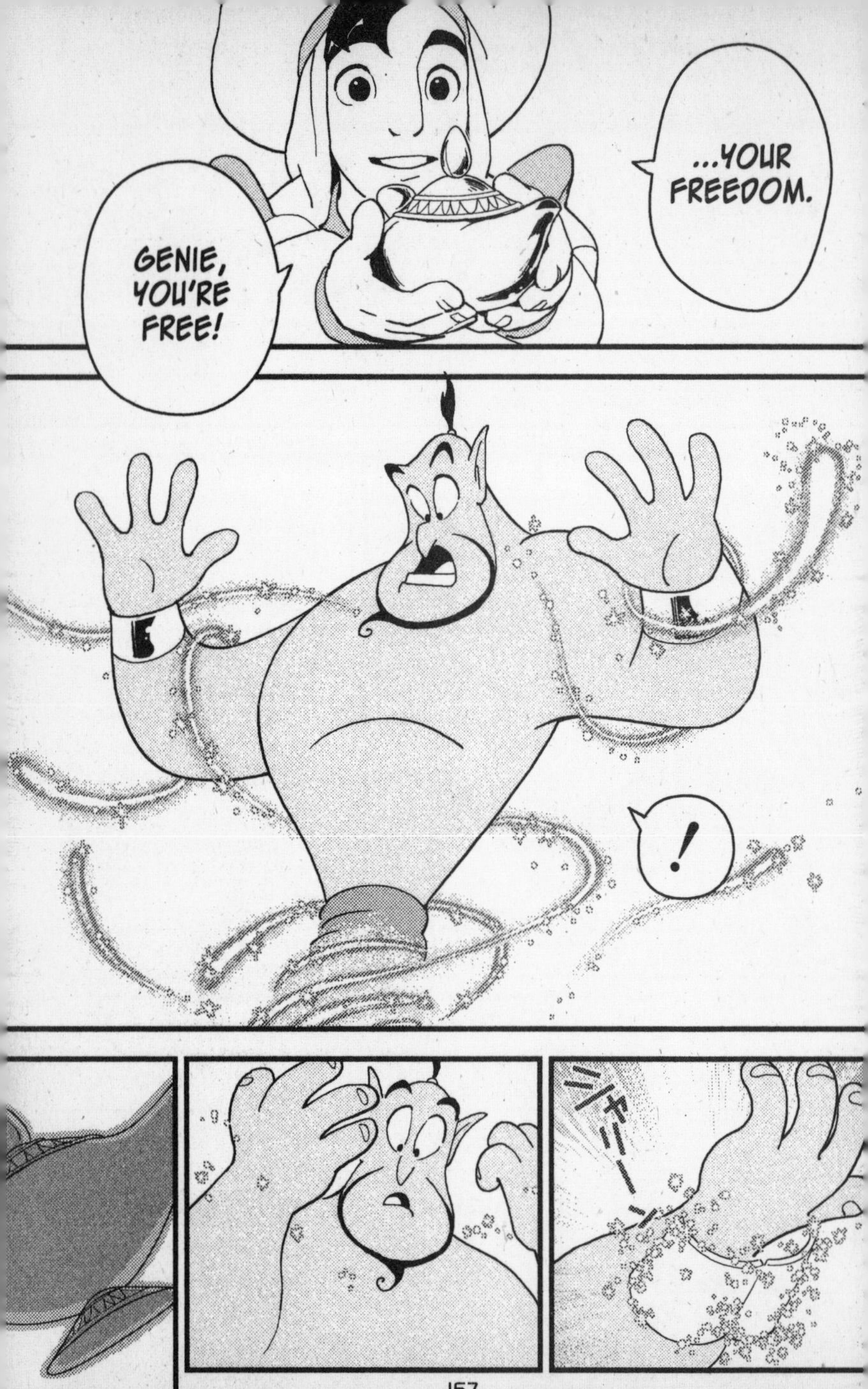
...YOUR FREEDOM.
GENIE, YOU'RE FREE!
!
シャーーン

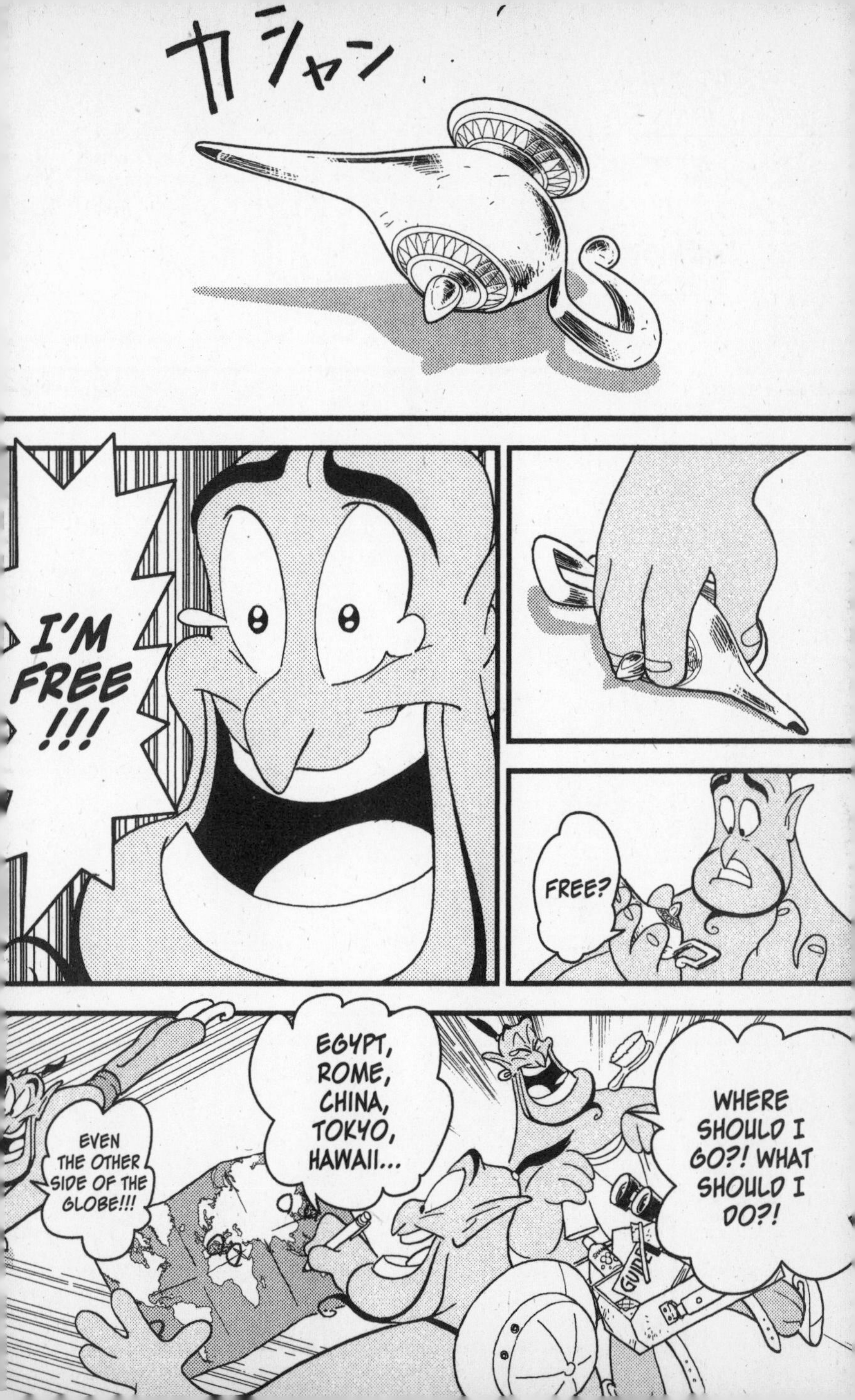
カシャン
FREE?
I'M FREE!!!
WHERE SHOULD I GO?! WHAT SHOULD I DO?!
GUIDE
EGYPT, ROME, CHINA, TOKYO, HAWAII...
EVEN THE OTHER SIDE OF THE GLOBE!!!

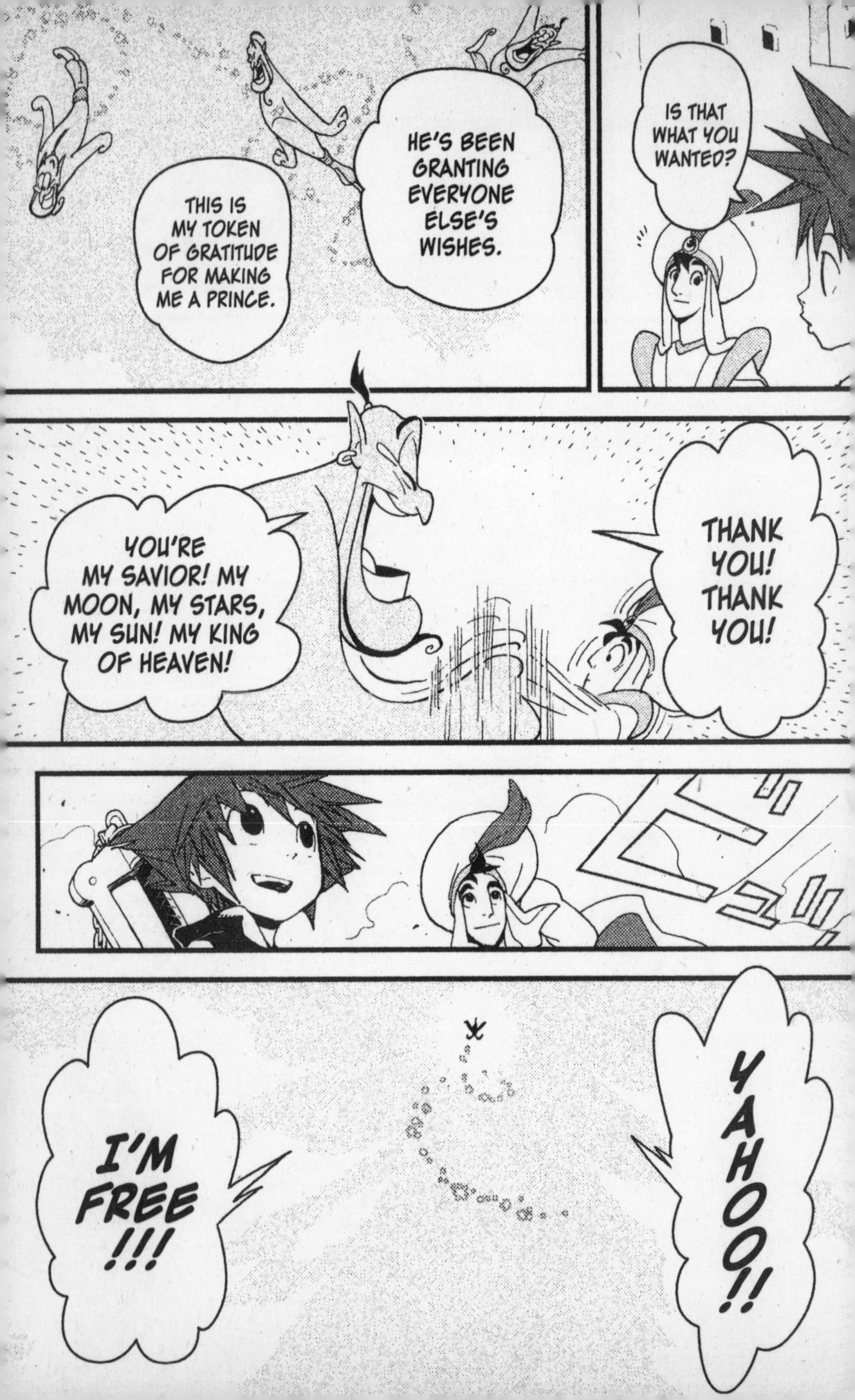
IS THAT WHAT YOU WANTED?
HE'S BEEN GRANTING EVERYONE ELSE'S WISHES.
THIS IS MY TOKEN OF GRATITUDE FOR MAKING ME A PRINCE.
THANK YOU! THANK YOU!
YOU'RE MY SAVIOR! MY MOON, MY STARS, MY SUN! MY KING OF HEAVEN!
YAHOO!!
I'M FREE!!!

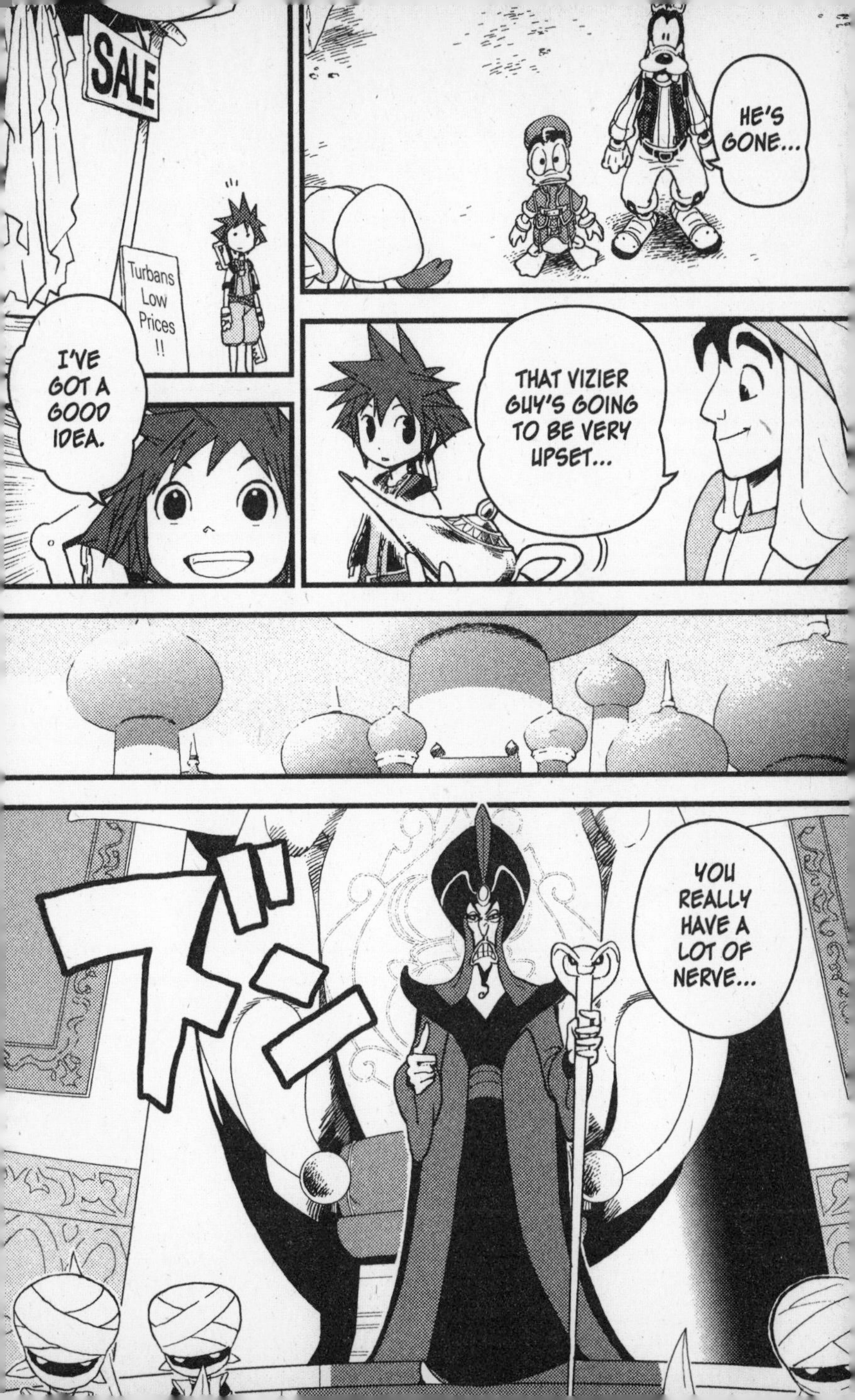
HE'S GONE...
SALE
Turbans Low Prices !!
THAT VIZIER GUY'S GOING TO BE VERY UPSET...
I'VE GOT A GOOD IDEA.
YOU REALLY HAVE A LOT OF NERVE...
ズー

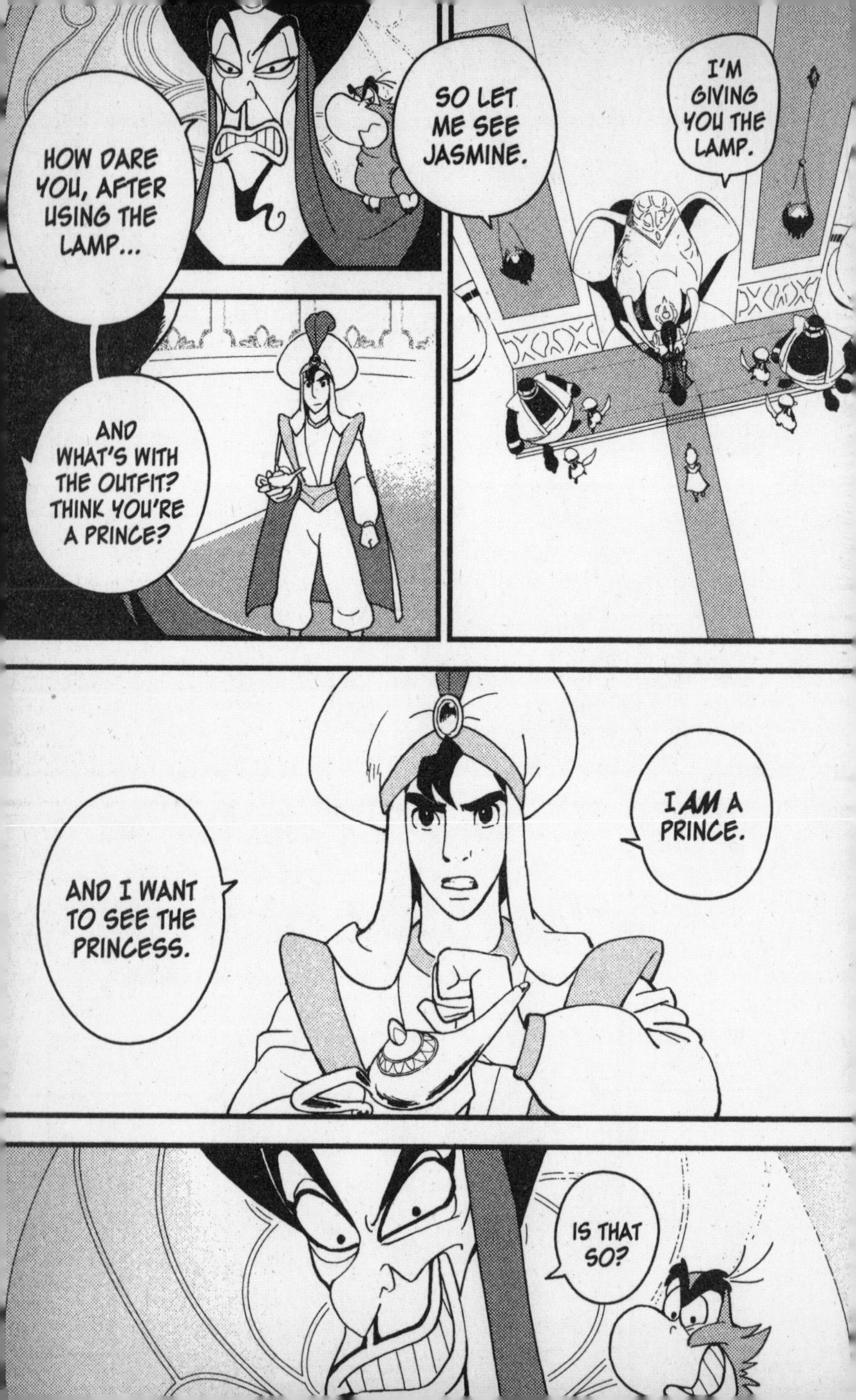
I'M GIVING YOU THE LAMP.
SO LET ME SEE JASMINE.
HOW DARE YOU, AFTER USING THE LAMP...
AND WHAT'S WITH THE OUTFIT? THINK YOU'RE A PRINCE?
I *AM* A PRINCE.
AND I WANT TO SEE THE PRINCESS.
IS THAT SO?

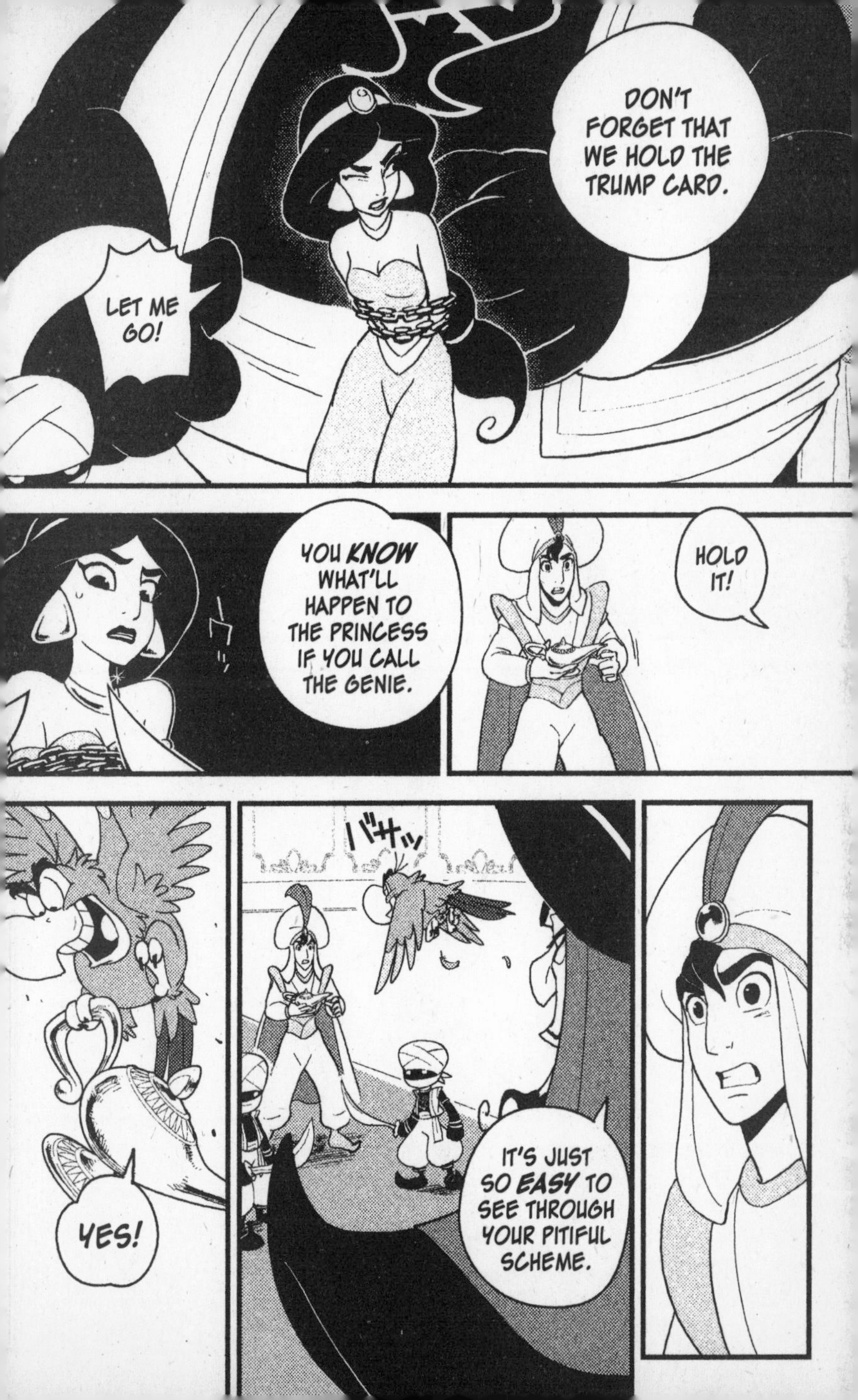
DON'T FORGET THAT WE HOLD THE TRUMP CARD.
LET ME GO!
HOLD IT!
YOU *KNOW* WHAT'LL HAPPEN TO THE PRINCESS IF YOU CALL THE GENIE.
バサッ
IT'S JUST SO *EASY* TO SEE THROUGH YOUR PITIFUL SCHEME.
YES!

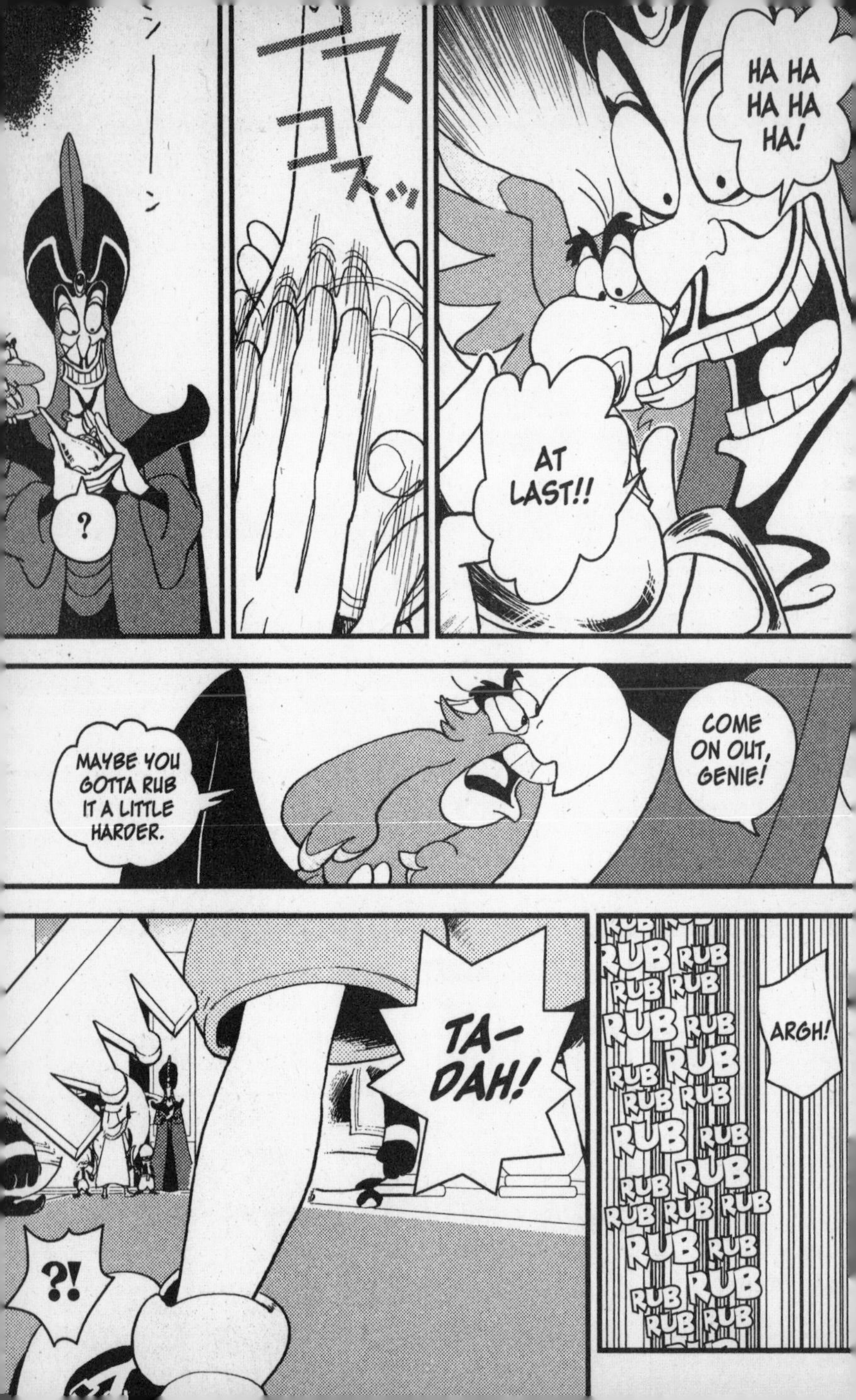
HA HA HA HA HA!
AT LAST!!
コスコスッ
シーーン
?
COME ON OUT, GENIE!
MAYBE YOU GOTTA RUB IT A LITTLE HARDER.
RUB RUB RUB RUB RUB RUB RUB RUB RUB RUB RUB RUB RUB RUB RUB RUB RUB RUB RUB RUB RUB RUB RUB RUB RUB
ARGH!
TA-DAH!
?!

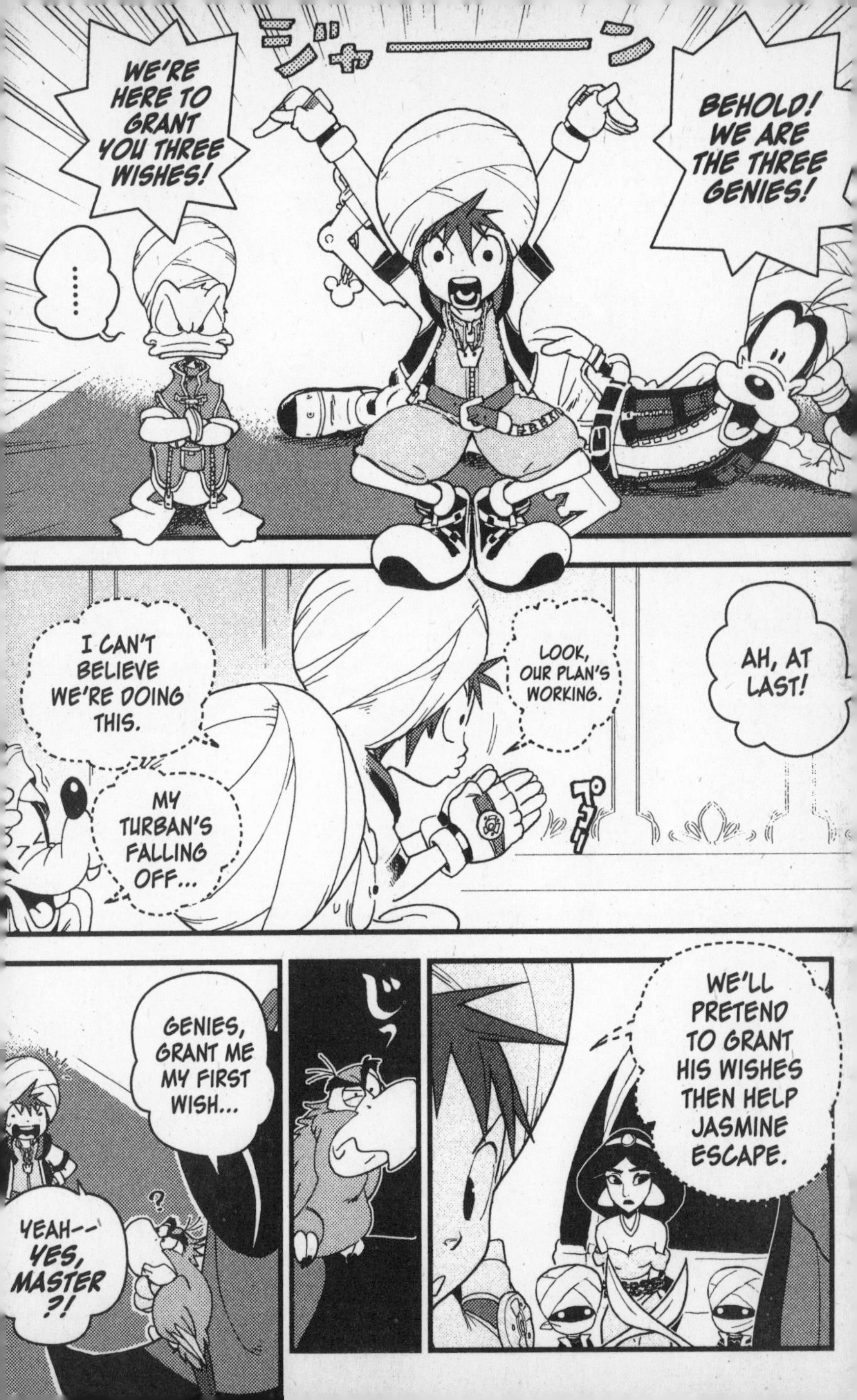
ジャーーーン
BEHOLD! WE ARE THE THREE GENIES!
WE'RE HERE TO GRANT YOU THREE WISHES!
......
AH, AT LAST!
LOOK, OUR PLAN'S WORKING.
I CAN'T BELIEVE WE'RE DOING THIS.
MY TURBAN'S FALLING OFF...
WE'LL PRETEND TO GRANT HIS WISHES THEN HELP JASMINE ESCAPE.
じっ
GENIES, GRANT ME MY FIRST WISH...
?
YEAH-- YES, MASTER?!

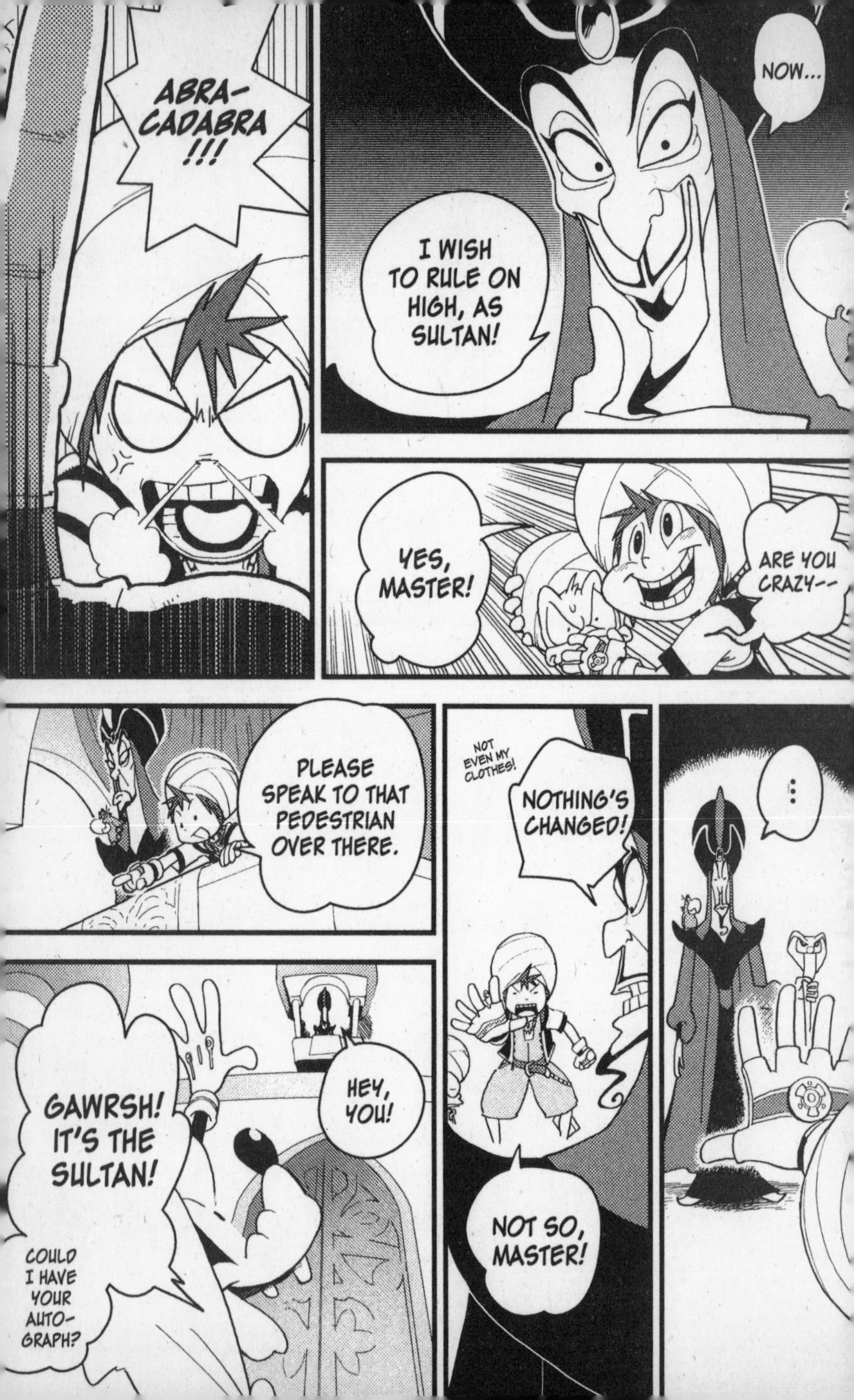
NOW...
I WISH TO RULE ON HIGH, AS SULTAN!
ARE YOU CRAZY--
YES, MASTER!
ABRA-CADABRA!!!
...
NOTHING'S CHANGED!
NOT EVEN MY CLOTHES!
NOT SO, MASTER!
PLEASE SPEAK TO THAT PEDESTRIAN OVER THERE.
HEY, YOU!
GAWRSH! IT'S THE SULTAN!
COULD I HAVE YOUR AUTO-GRAPH?

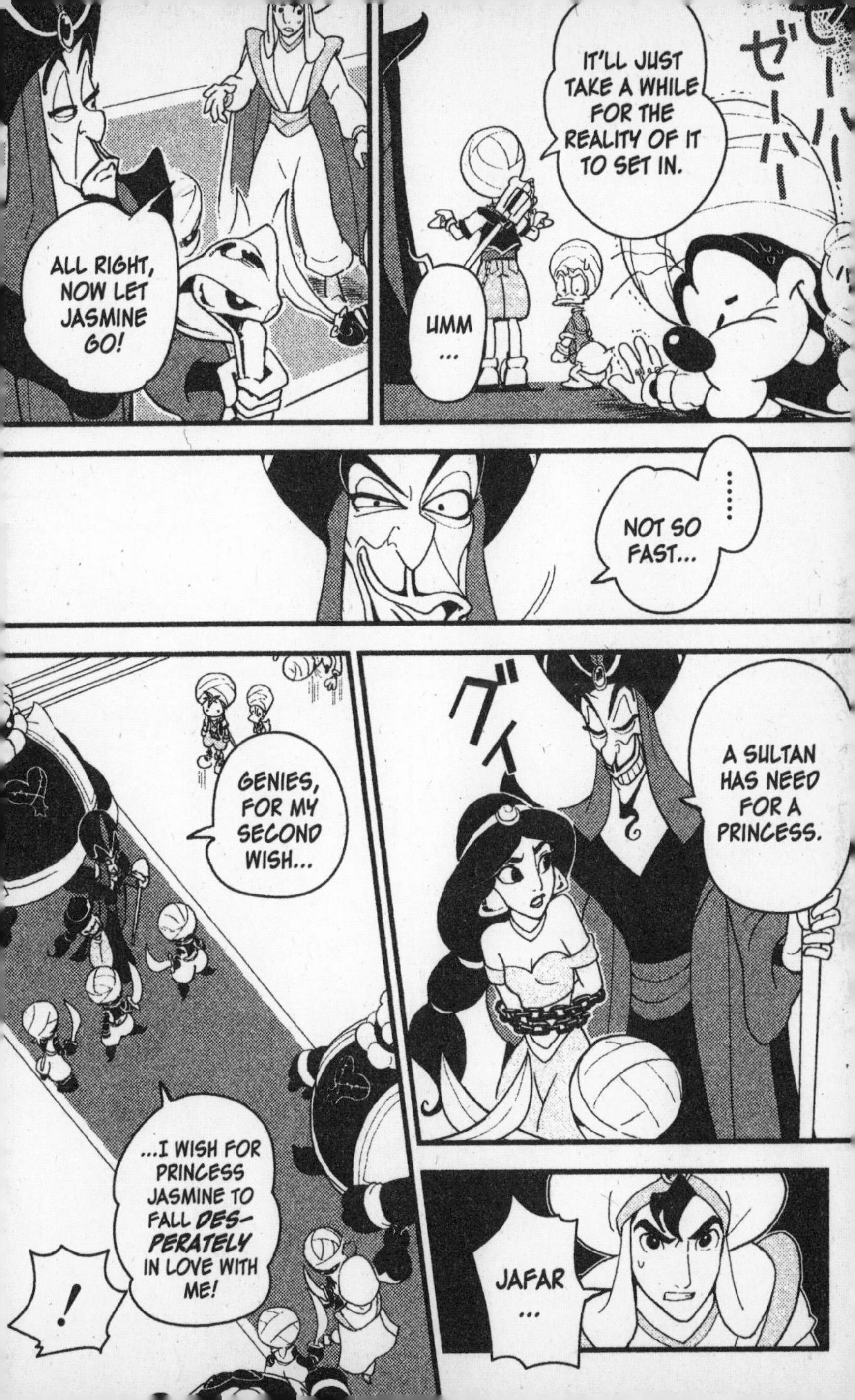
IT'LL JUST TAKE A WHILE FOR THE REALITY OF IT TO SET IN.
ゼーハー
UMM ...
ALL RIGHT, NOW LET JASMINE GO!
...... NOT SO FAST...
グイ
A SULTAN HAS NEED FOR A PRINCESS.
JAFAR ...
GENIES, FOR MY SECOND WISH...
...I WISH FOR PRINCESS JASMINE TO FALL *DESPERATELY* IN LOVE WITH ME!
!

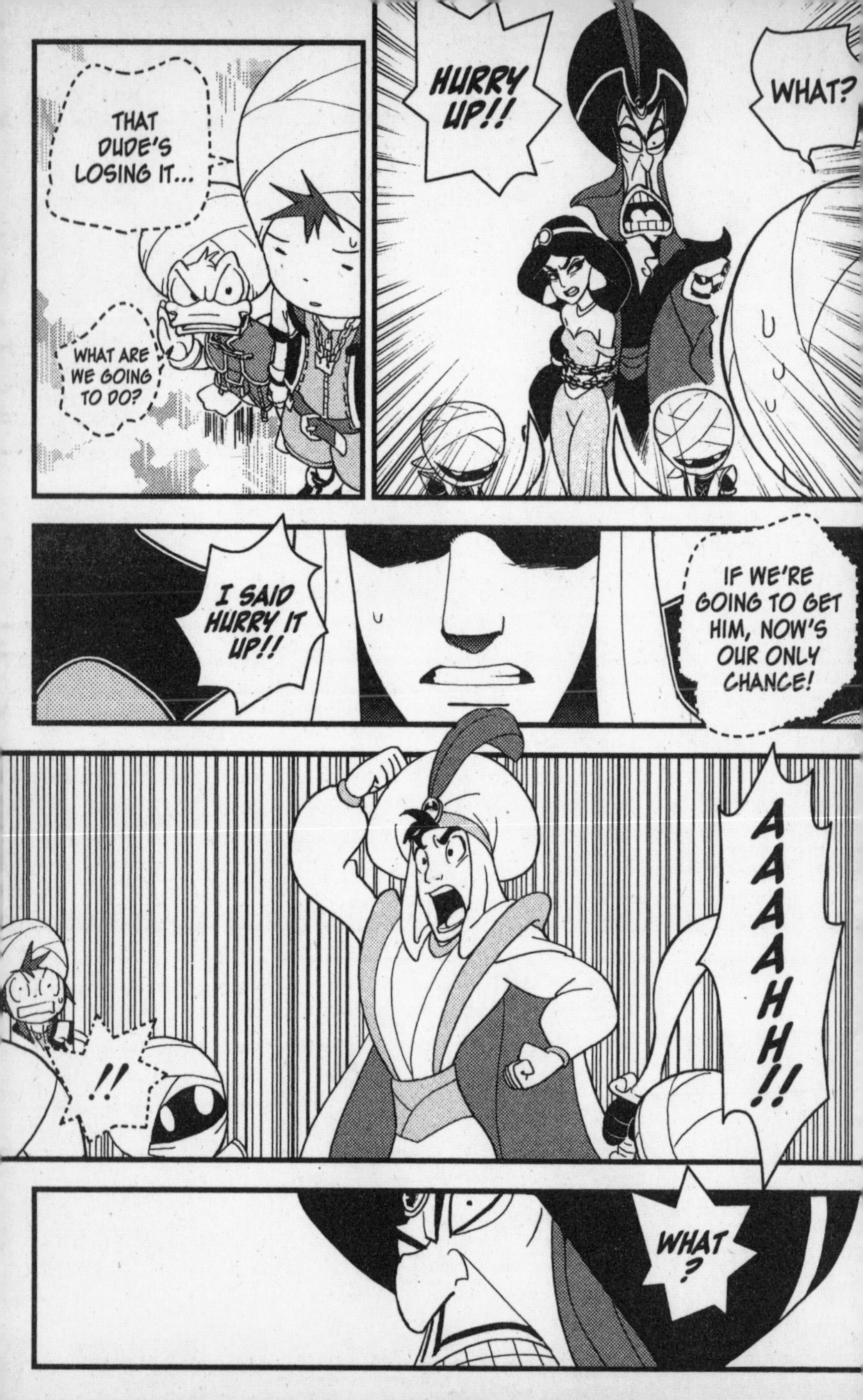
WHAT?
HURRY UP!!
THAT DUDE'S LOSING IT...
WHAT ARE WE GOING TO DO?
IF WE'RE GOING TO GET HIM, NOW'S OUR ONLY CHANCE!
I SAID HURRY IT UP!!
AAAAHH!!
!!
WHAT?

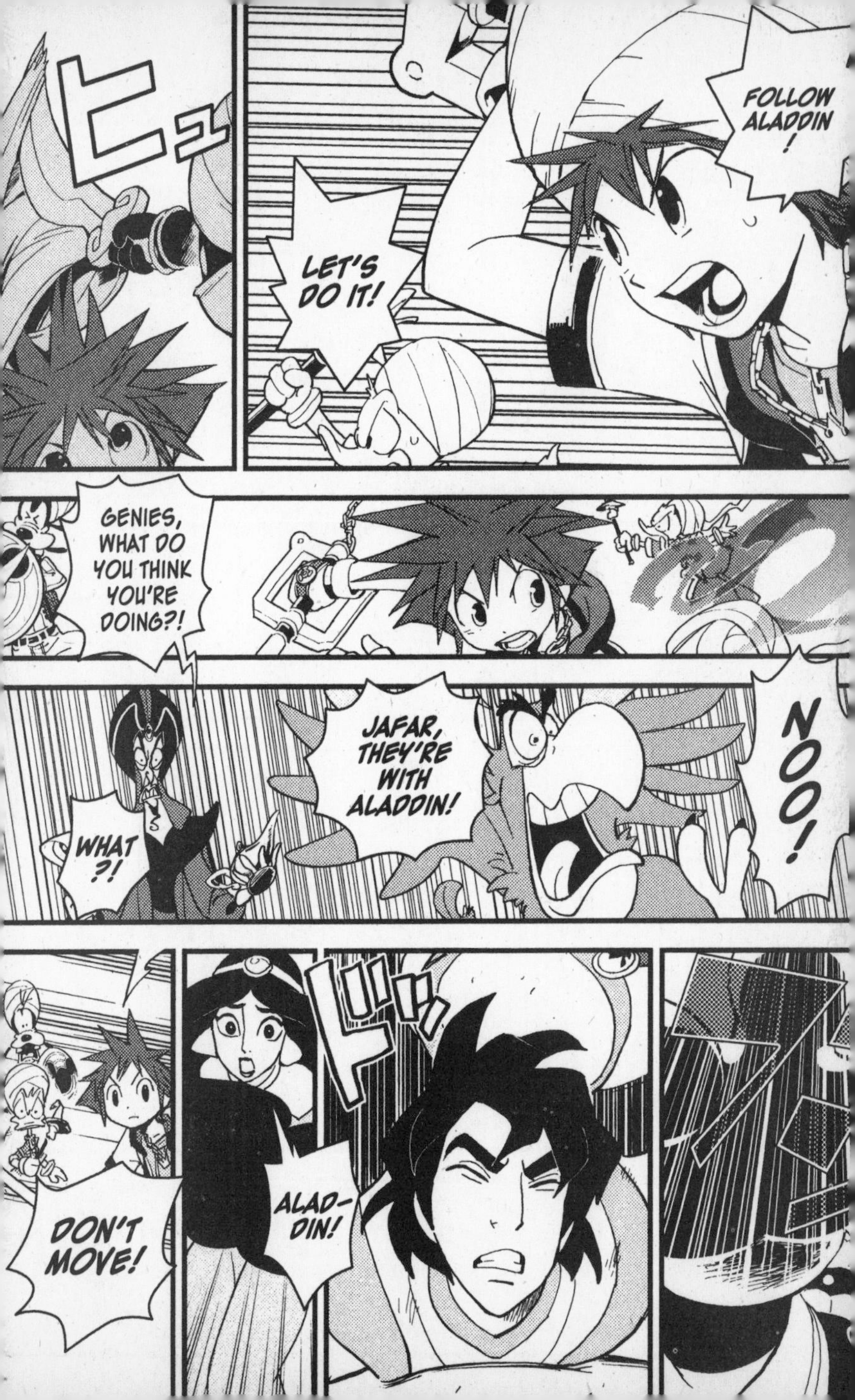
FOLLOW ALADDIN!
LET'S DO IT!
ヒュ
GENIES, WHAT DO YOU THINK YOU'RE DOING?!
NOOO!
JAFAR, THEY'RE WITH ALADDIN!
WHAT?!
ALAD-DIN!
DON'T MOVE!

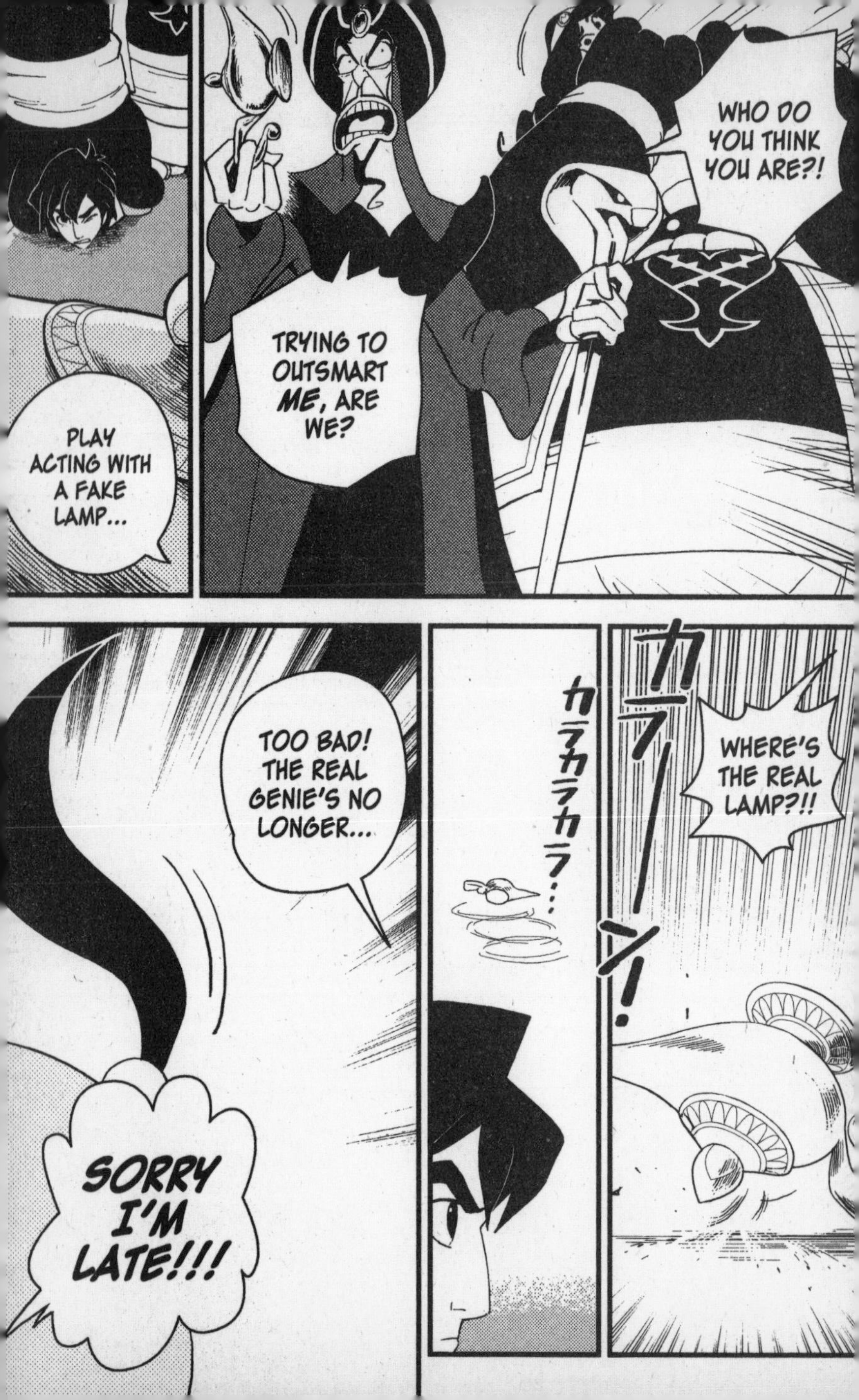
WHO DO YOU THINK YOU ARE?!
TRYING TO OUTSMART ME, ARE WE?
PLAY ACTING WITH A FAKE LAMP...
カラーン!
WHERE'S THE REAL LAMP?!!
カラカラカラ...
TOO BAD! THE REAL GENIE'S NO LONGER...
SORRY I'M LATE!!!

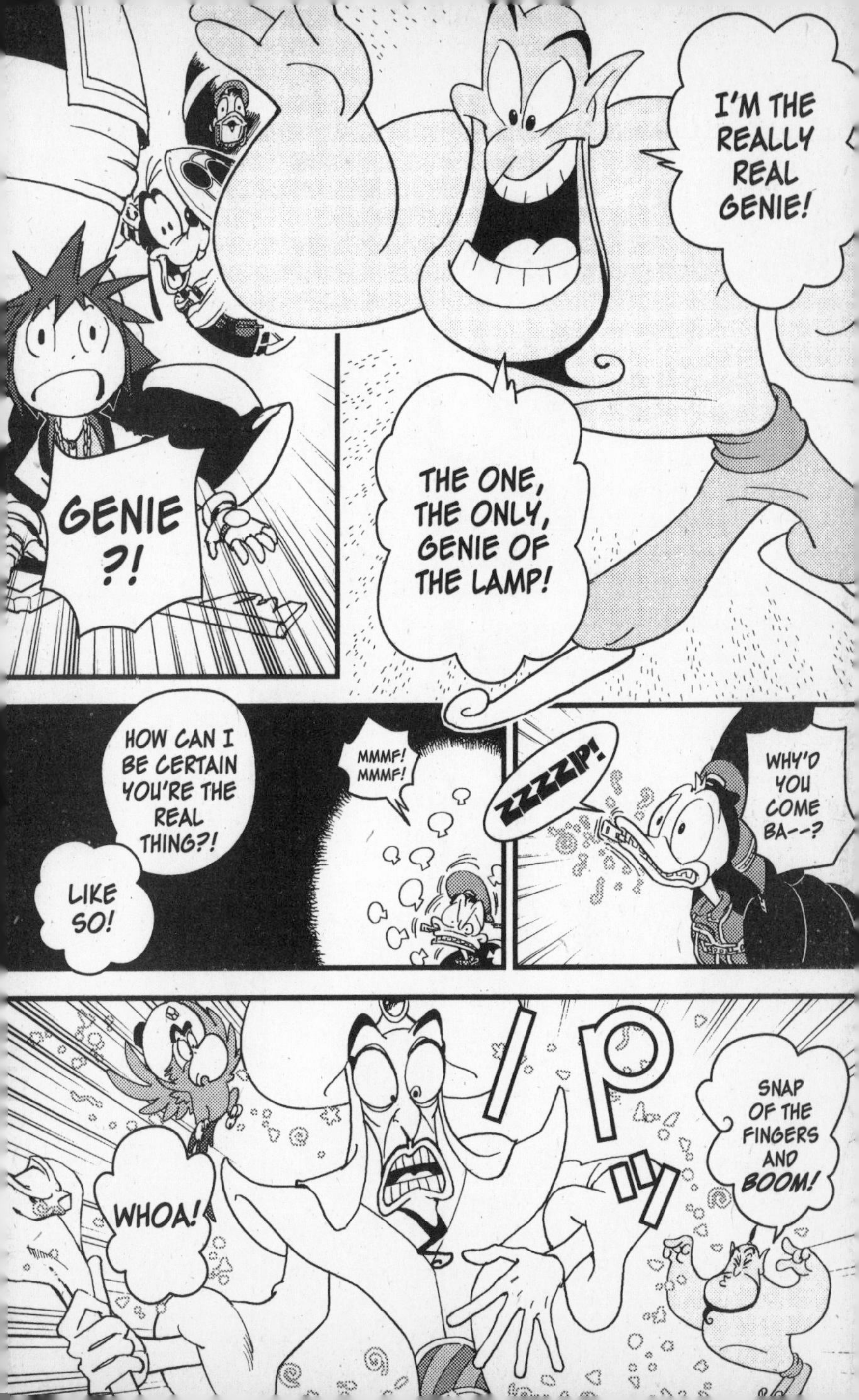
I'M THE REALLY REAL GENIE!
THE ONE, THE ONLY, GENIE OF THE LAMP!
GENIE ?!
WHY'D YOU COME BA--?
ZZZZIP!
MMMF! MMMF!
HOW CAN I BE CERTAIN YOU'RE THE REAL THING?!
LIKE SO!
SNAP OF THE FINGERS AND *BOOM!*
WHOA!

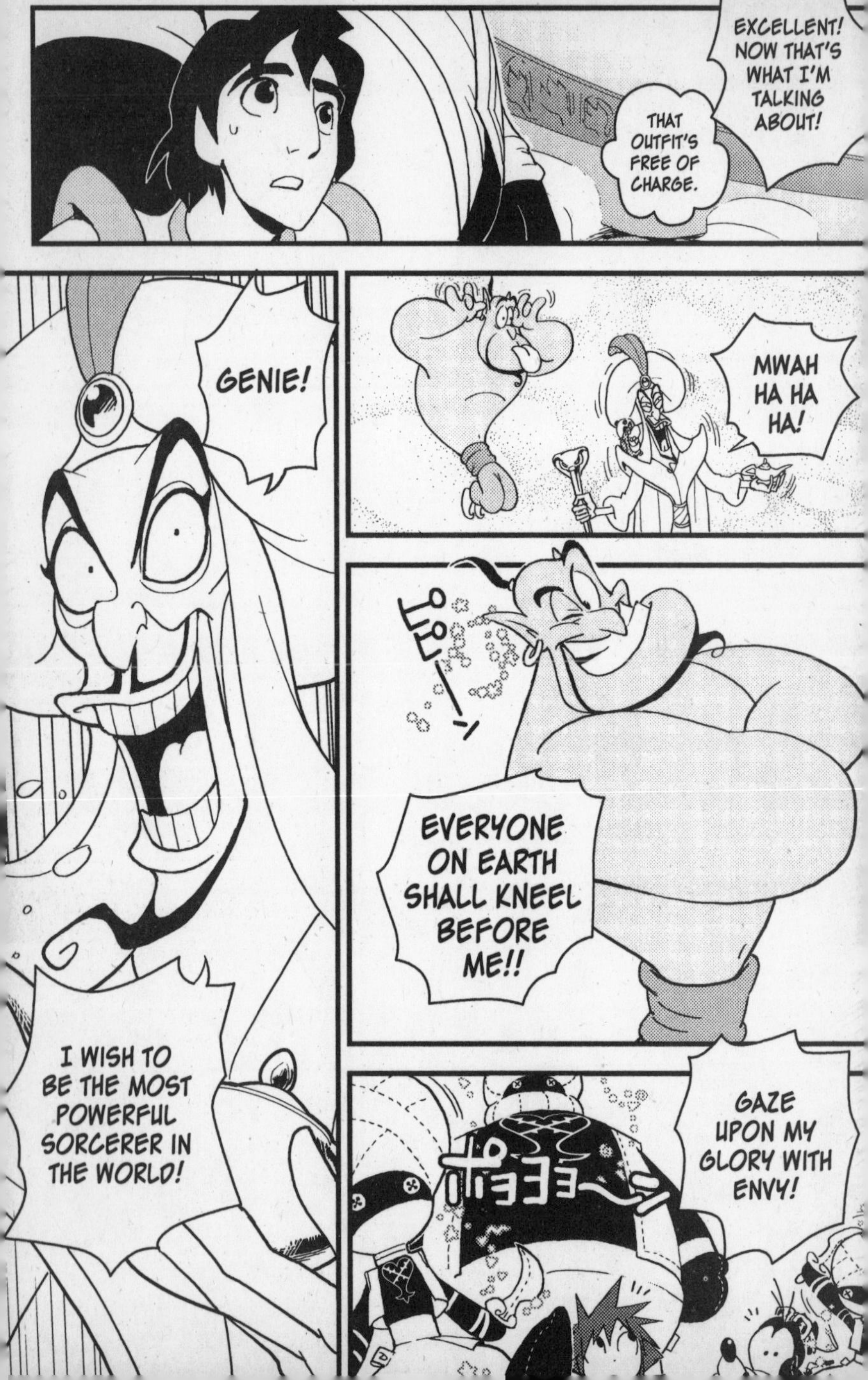
EXCELLENT! NOW THAT'S WHAT I'M TALKING ABOUT!
THAT OUTFIT'S FREE OF CHARGE.
MWAH HA HA HA!
EVERYONE ON EARTH SHALL KNEEL BEFORE ME!!
GAZE UPON MY GLORY WITH ENVY!
GENIE!
I WISH TO BE THE MOST POWERFUL SORCERER IN THE WORLD!

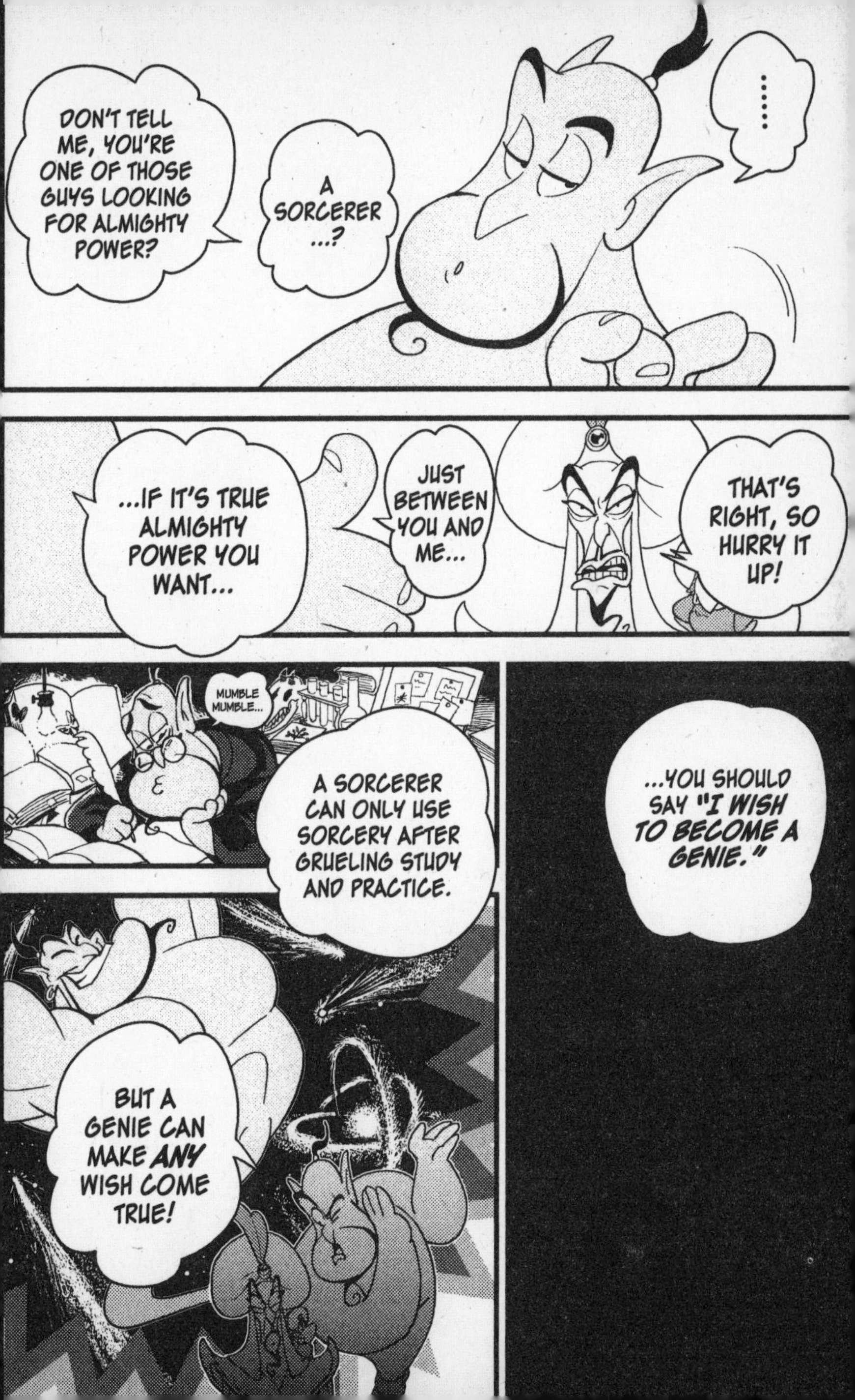

......
A SORCERER ...?
DON'T TELL ME, YOU'RE ONE OF THOSE GUYS LOOKING FOR ALMIGHTY POWER?
THAT'S RIGHT, SO HURRY IT UP!
JUST BETWEEN YOU AND ME...
...IF IT'S TRUE ALMIGHTY POWER YOU WANT...
...YOU SHOULD SAY "I WISH TO BECOME A GENIE."
MUMBLE MUMBLE...
A SORCERER CAN ONLY USE SORCERY AFTER GRUELING STUDY AND PRACTICE.
BUT A GENIE CAN MAKE ANY WISH COME TRUE!

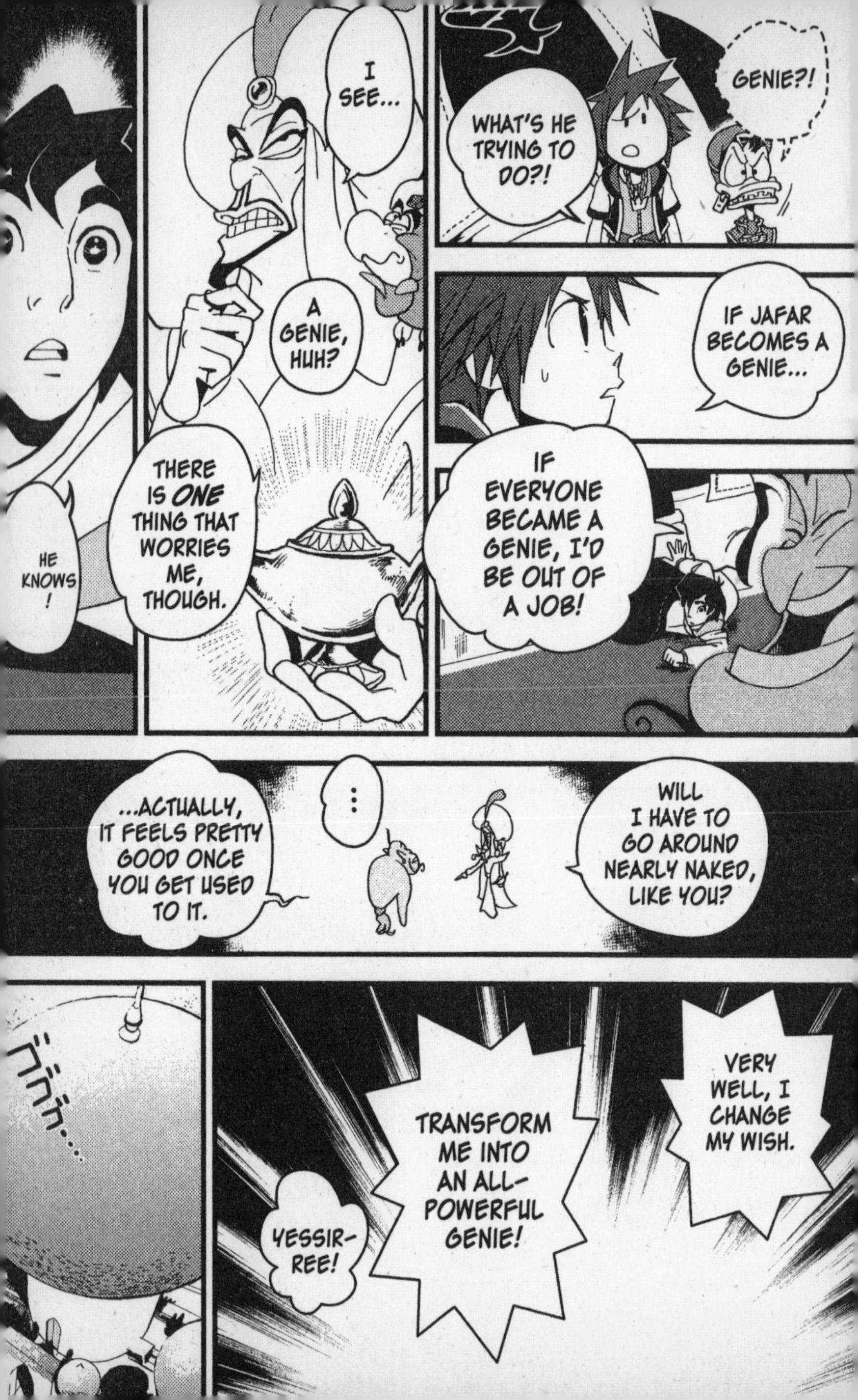
GENIE?!
WHAT'S HE TRYING TO DO?!
IF JAFAR BECOMES A GENIE...
IF EVERYONE BECAME A GENIE, I'D BE OUT OF A JOB!
I SEE...
A GENIE, HUH?
THERE IS *ONE* THING THAT WORRIES ME, THOUGH.
HE KNOWS!
WILL I HAVE TO GO AROUND NEARLY NAKED, LIKE YOU?
...
...ACTUALLY, IT FEELS PRETTY GOOD ONCE YOU GET USED TO IT.
VERY WELL, I CHANGE MY WISH.
TRANSFORM ME INTO AN ALL-POWERFUL GENIE!
YESSIR-REE!
ゴゴゴ…

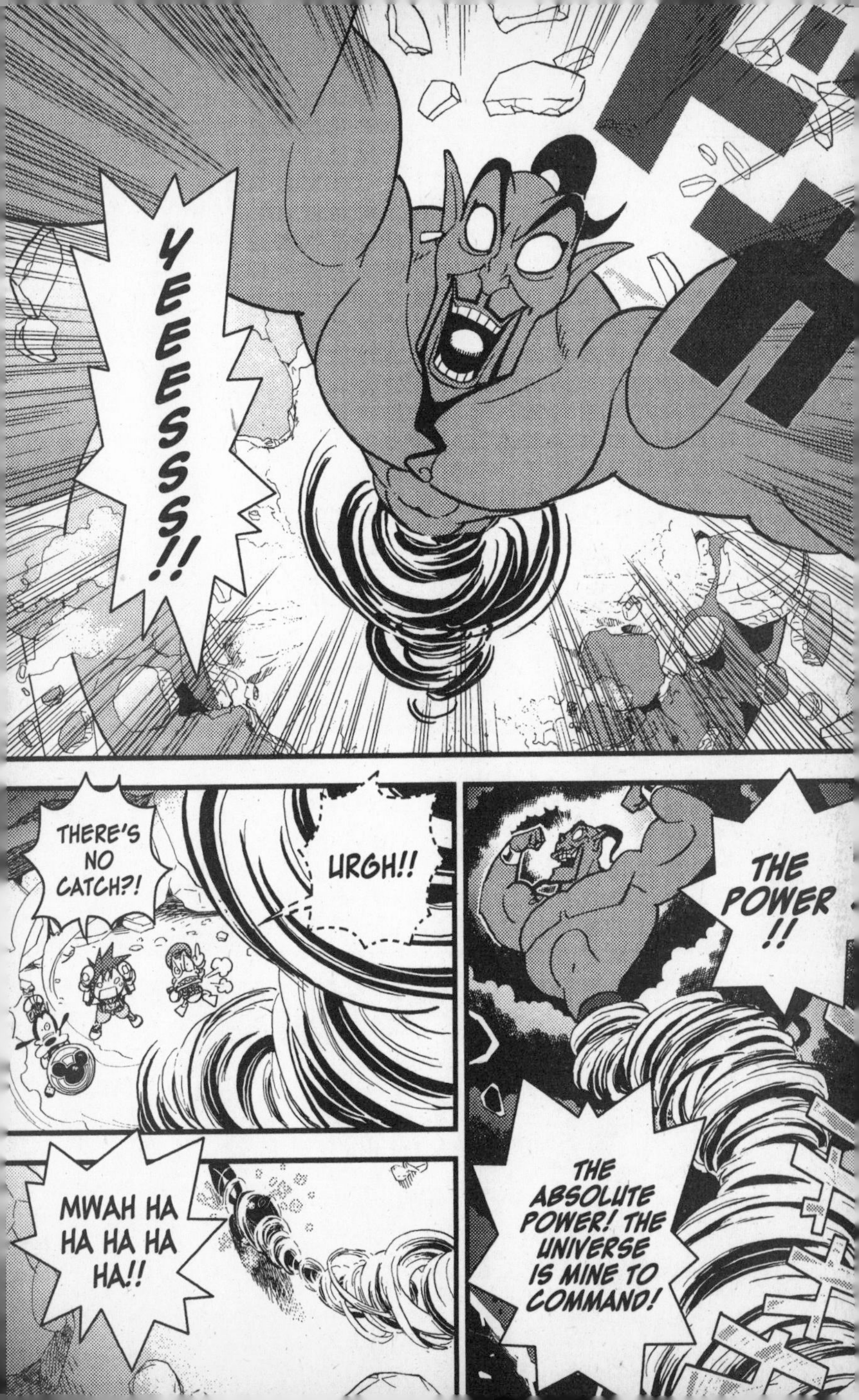
ドカ
YEEEESSSS!!
THE POWER!!
THE ABSOLUTE POWER! THE UNIVERSE IS MINE TO COMMAND!
URGH!!
THERE'S NO CATCH?!
MWAH HA HA HA HA HA!!

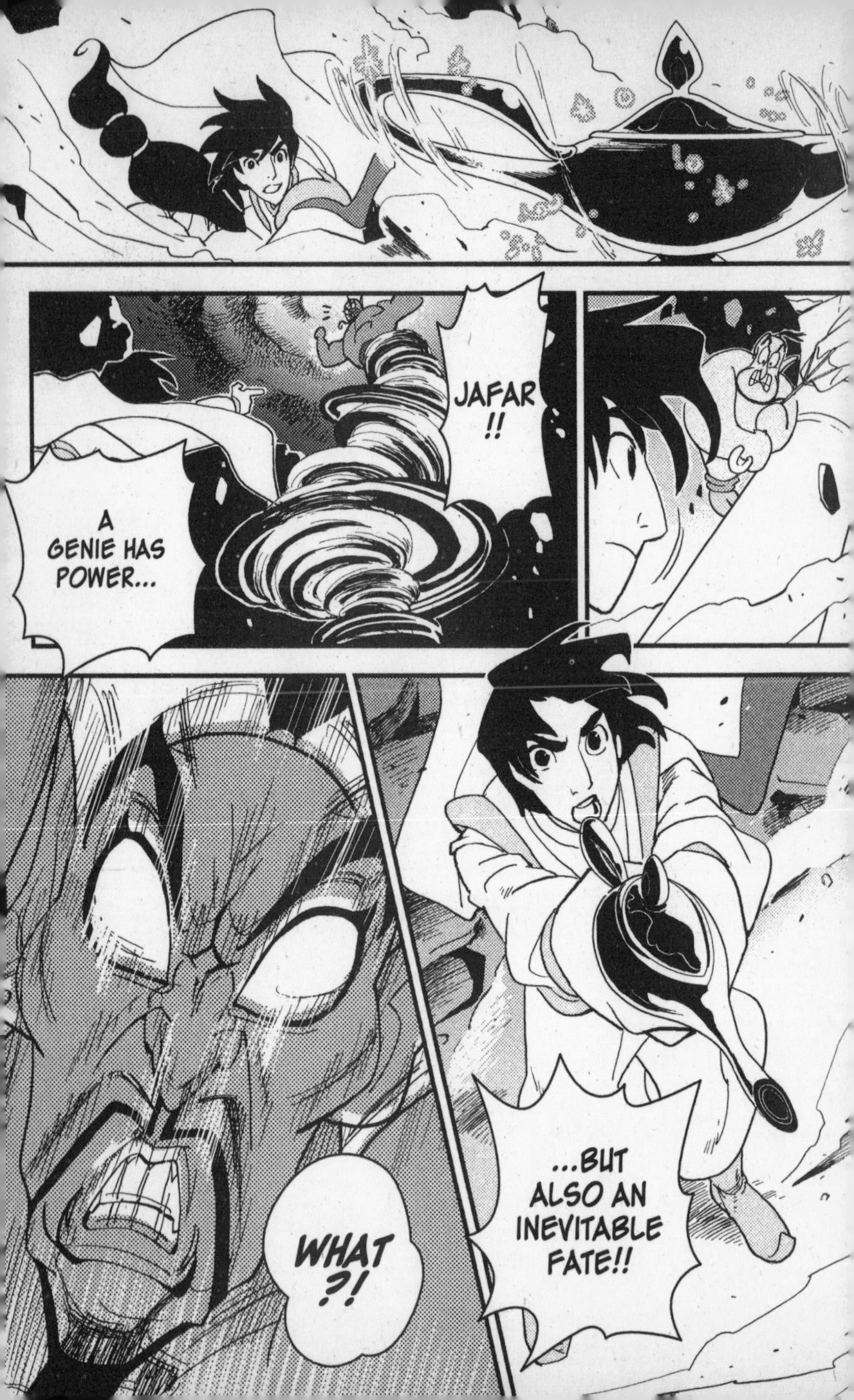
JAFAR !!
A GENIE HAS POWER...
...BUT ALSO AN INEVITABLE FATE!!
WHAT ?!

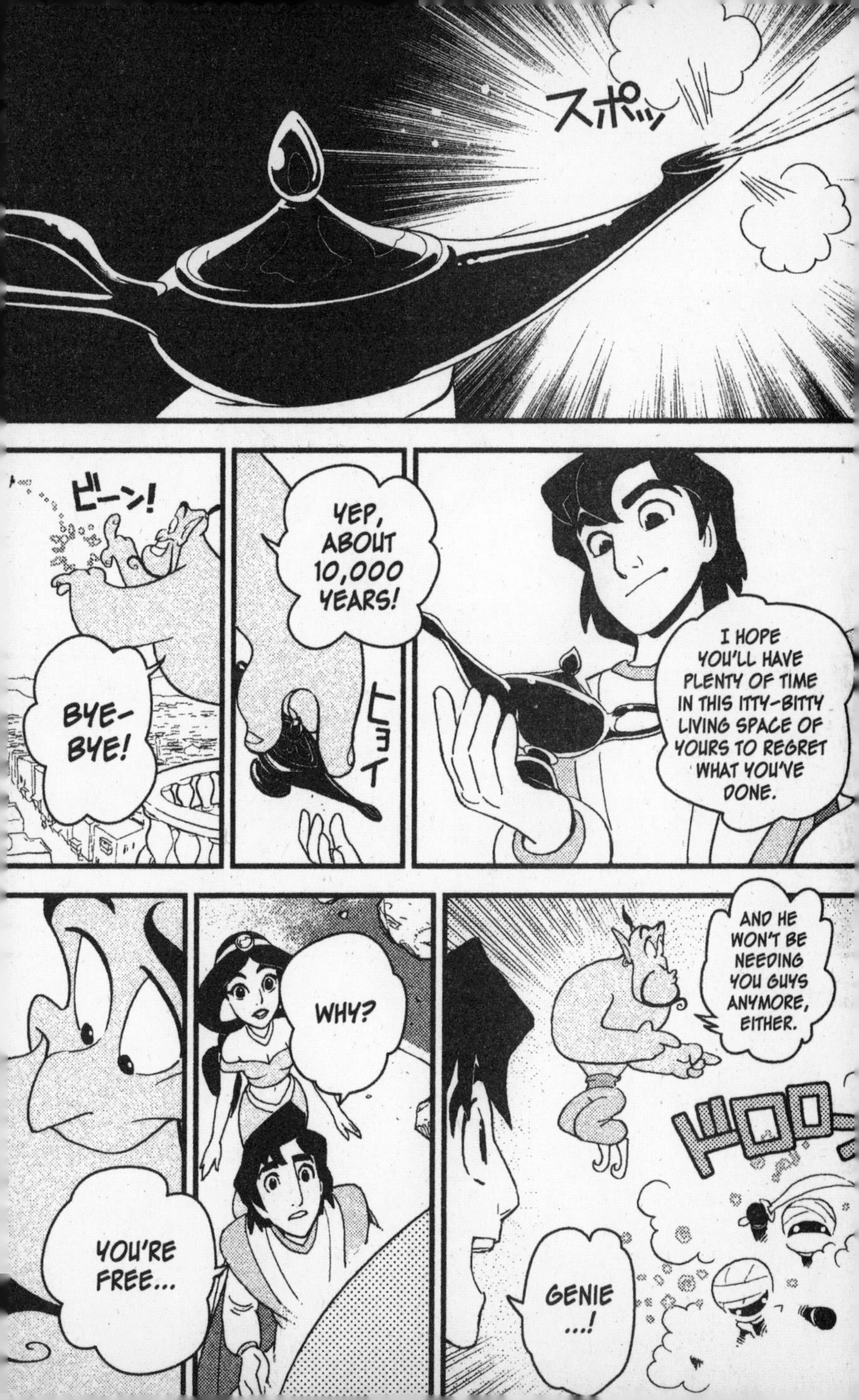
スポッ
I HOPE YOU'LL HAVE PLENTY OF TIME IN THIS ITTY-BITTY LIVING SPACE OF YOURS TO REGRET WHAT YOU'VE DONE.
YEP, ABOUT 10,000 YEARS!
ヒョイ
ビーン!
BYE-BYE!
AND HE WON'T BE NEEDING YOU GUYS ANYMORE, EITHER.
ドロロ
GENIE ...!
WHY?
YOU'RE FREE...

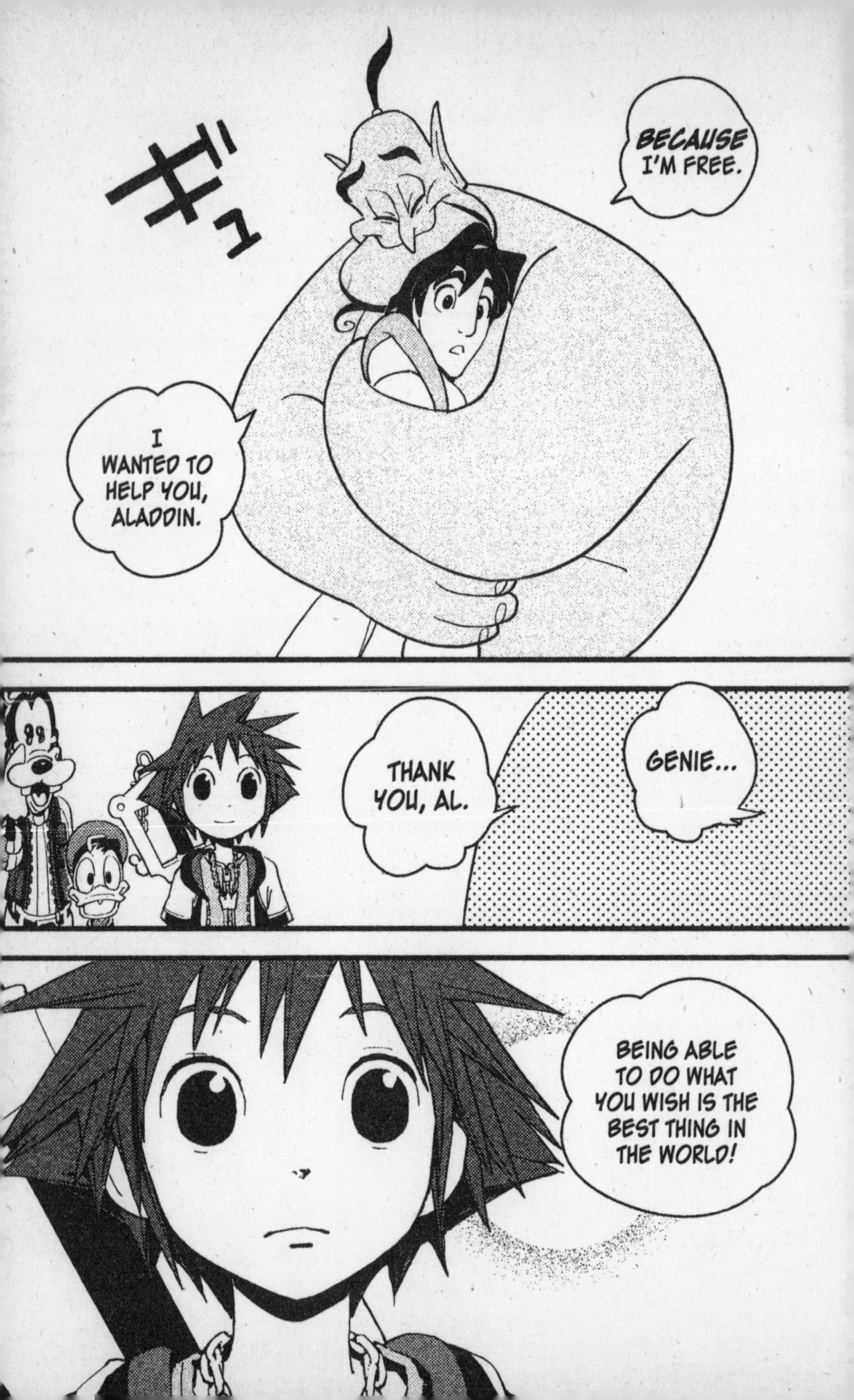
BECAUSE I'M FREE.
ギュ
I WANTED TO HELP YOU, ALADDIN.
GENIE...
THANK YOU, AL.
BEING ABLE TO DO WHAT YOU WISH IS THE BEST THING IN THE WORLD!

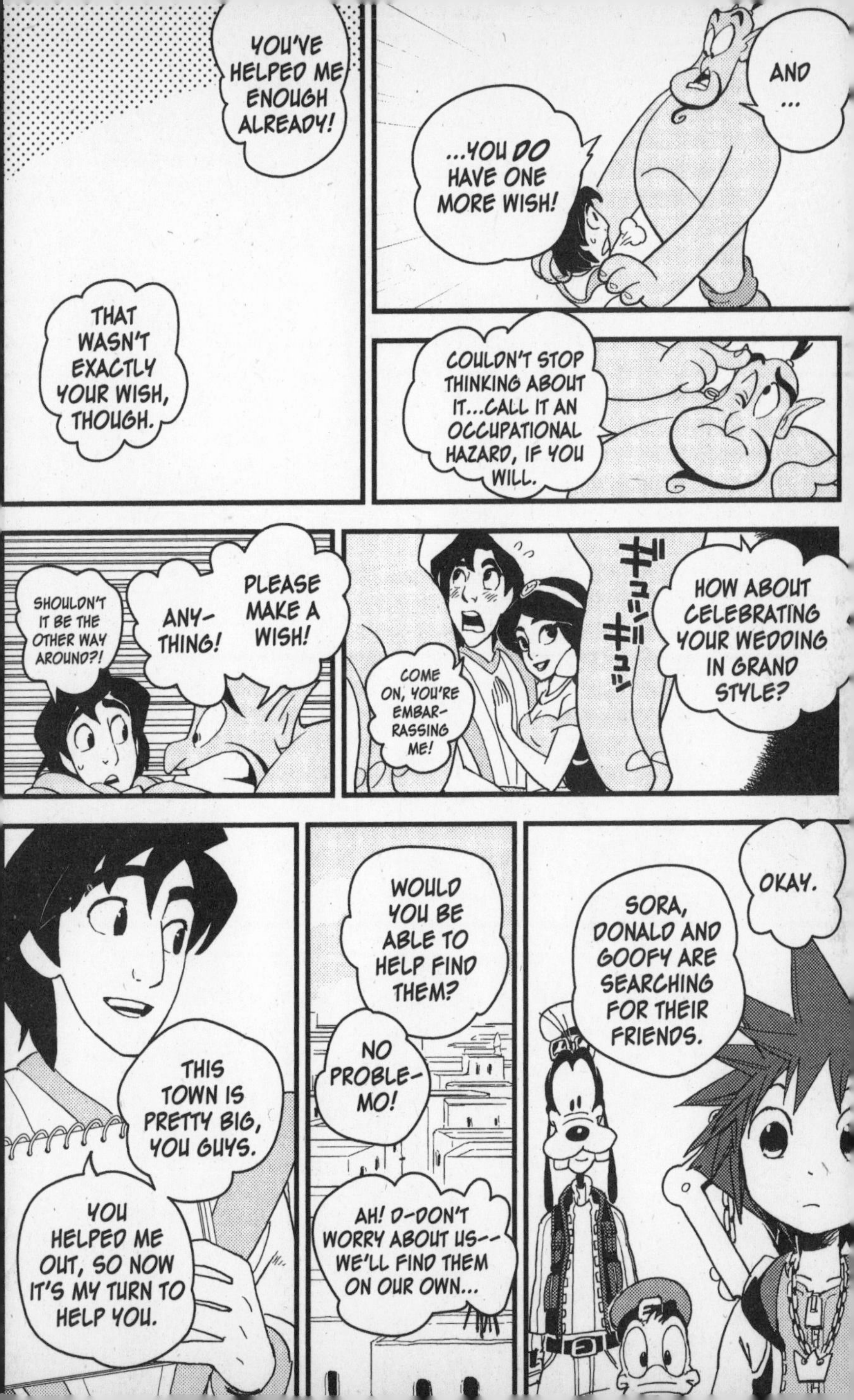
AND ...
...YOU DO HAVE ONE MORE WISH!
COULDN'T STOP THINKING ABOUT IT...CALL IT AN OCCUPATIONAL HAZARD, IF YOU WILL.
YOU'VE HELPED ME ENOUGH ALREADY!
THAT WASN'T EXACTLY YOUR WISH, THOUGH.
HOW ABOUT CELEBRATING YOUR WEDDING IN GRAND STYLE?
ギュッ ギュッ
COME ON, YOU'RE EMBARRASSING ME!
PLEASE MAKE A WISH!
ANY-THING!
SHOULDN'T IT BE THE OTHER WAY AROUND?!
OKAY.
SORA, DONALD AND GOOFY ARE SEARCHING FOR THEIR FRIENDS.
WOULD YOU BE ABLE TO HELP FIND THEM?
NO PROBLE-MO!
AH! D-DON'T WORRY ABOUT US--WE'LL FIND THEM ON OUR OWN...
THIS TOWN IS PRETTY BIG, YOU GUYS.
YOU HELPED ME OUT, SO NOW IT'S MY TURN TO HELP YOU.

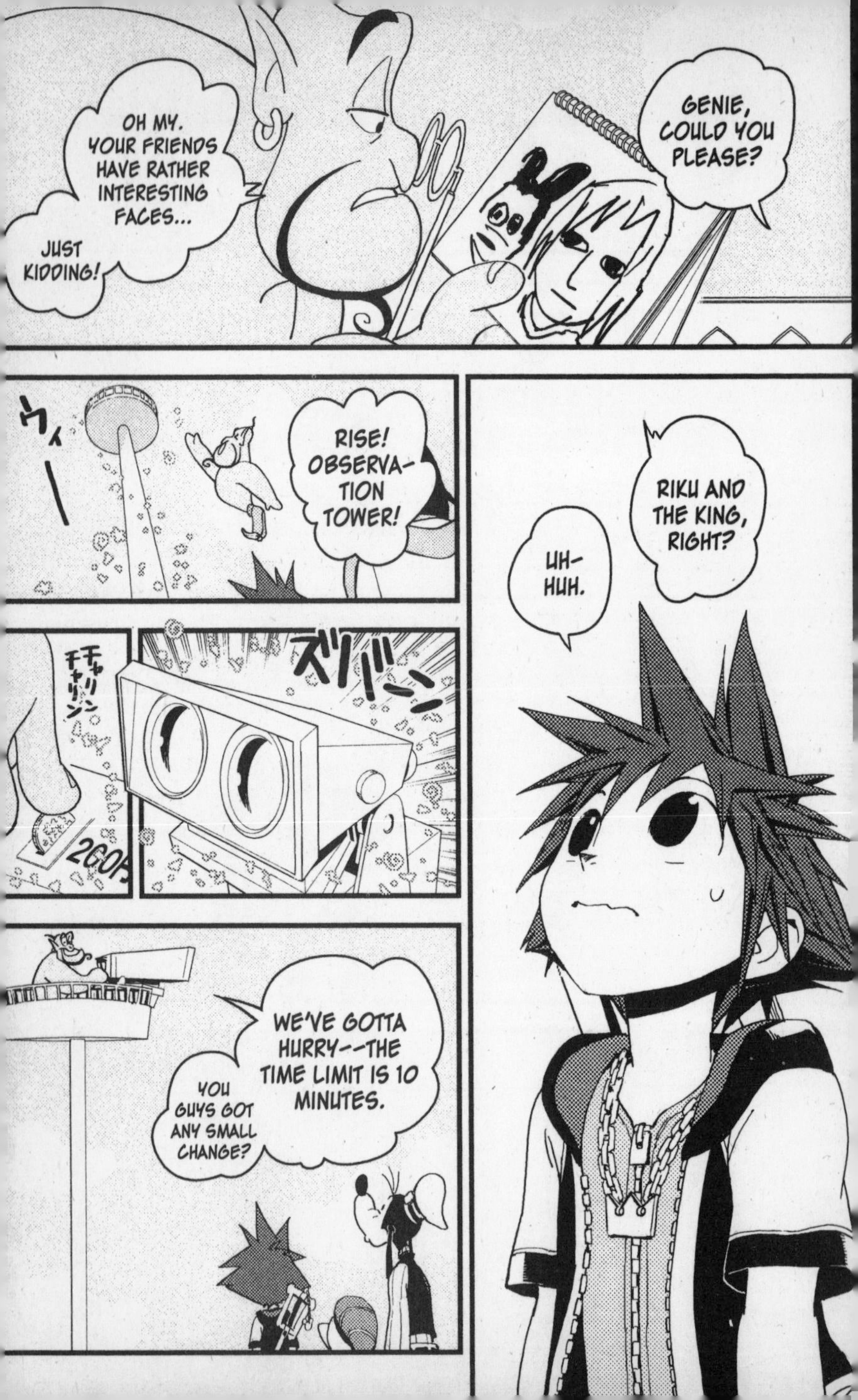
GENIE, COULD YOU PLEASE?
OH MY. YOUR FRIENDS HAVE RATHER INTERESTING FACES...
JUST KIDDING!
RIKU AND THE KING, RIGHT?
UH-HUH.
RISE! OBSERVATION TOWER!
ウィーー
ズドーン
チャリンチャリン
WE'VE GOTTA HURRY--THE TIME LIMIT IS 10 MINUTES.
YOU GUYS GOT ANY SMALL CHANGE?

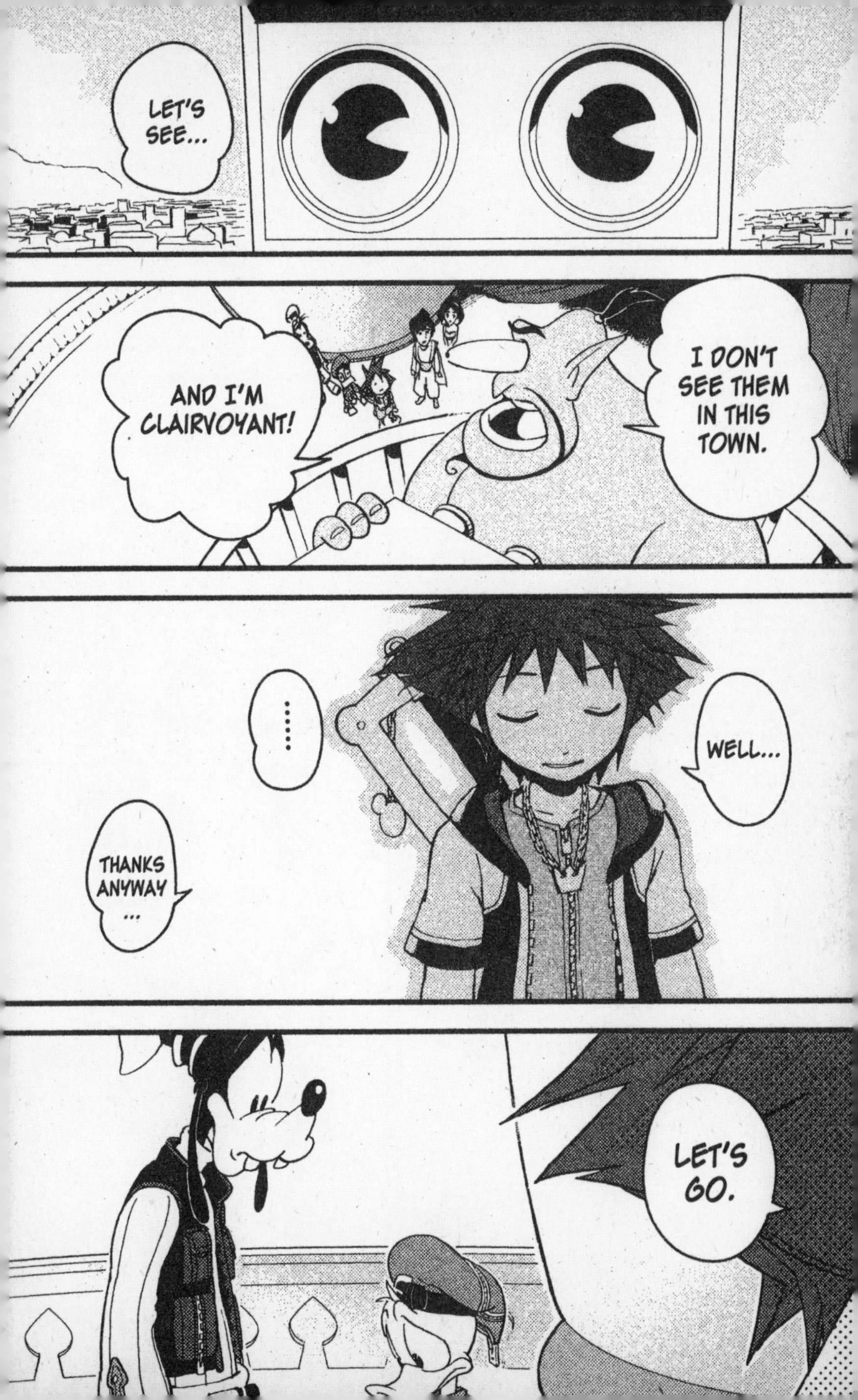
LET'S SEE...
I DON'T SEE THEM IN THIS TOWN.
AND I'M CLAIRVOYANT!
WELL...
......
THANKS ANYWAY ...
LET'S GO.

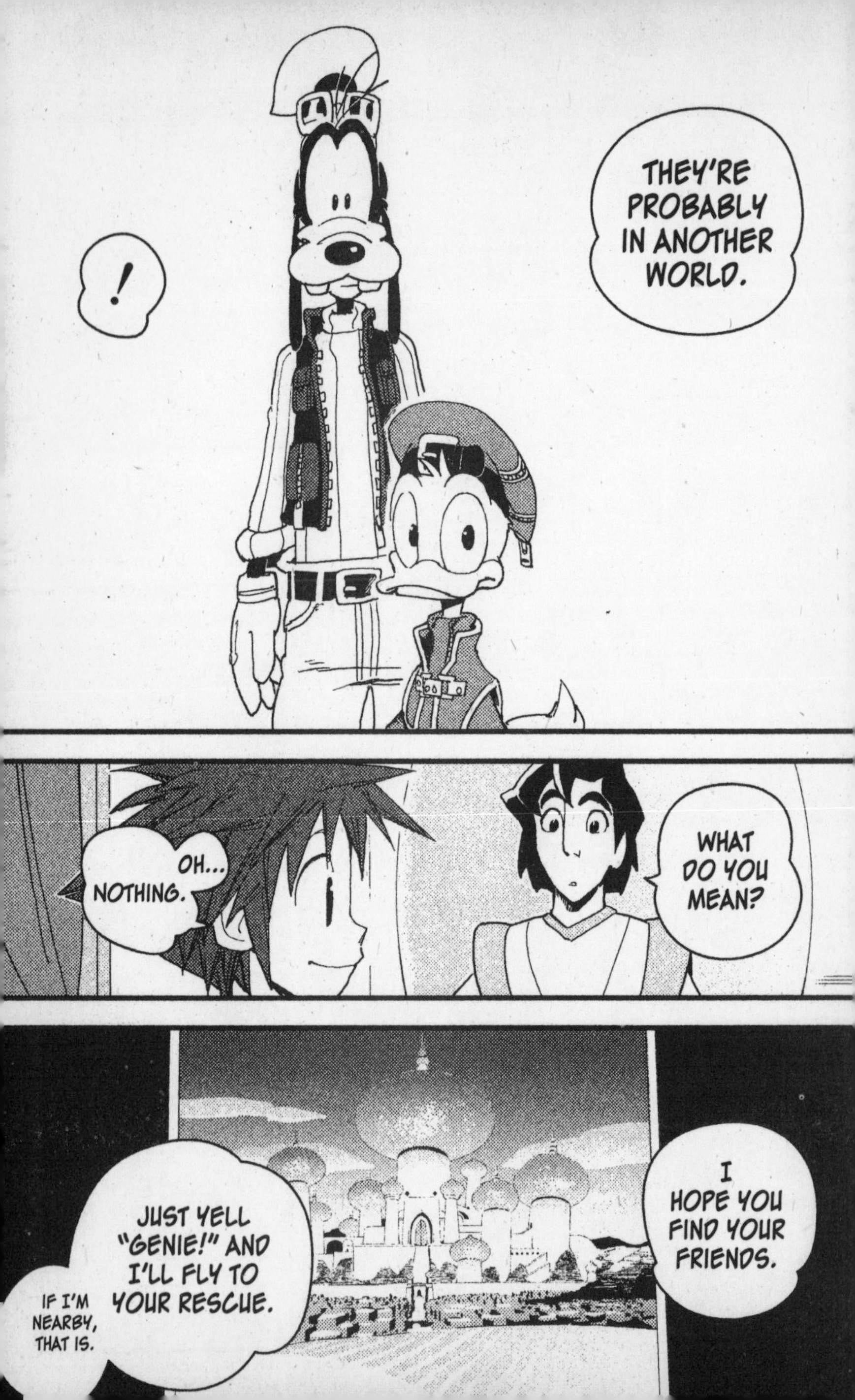
THEY'RE PROBABLY IN ANOTHER WORLD.
!
WHAT DO YOU MEAN?
OH... NOTHING.
I HOPE YOU FIND YOUR FRIENDS.
JUST YELL "GENIE!" AND I'LL FLY TO YOUR RESCUE.
IF I'M NEARBY, THAT IS.

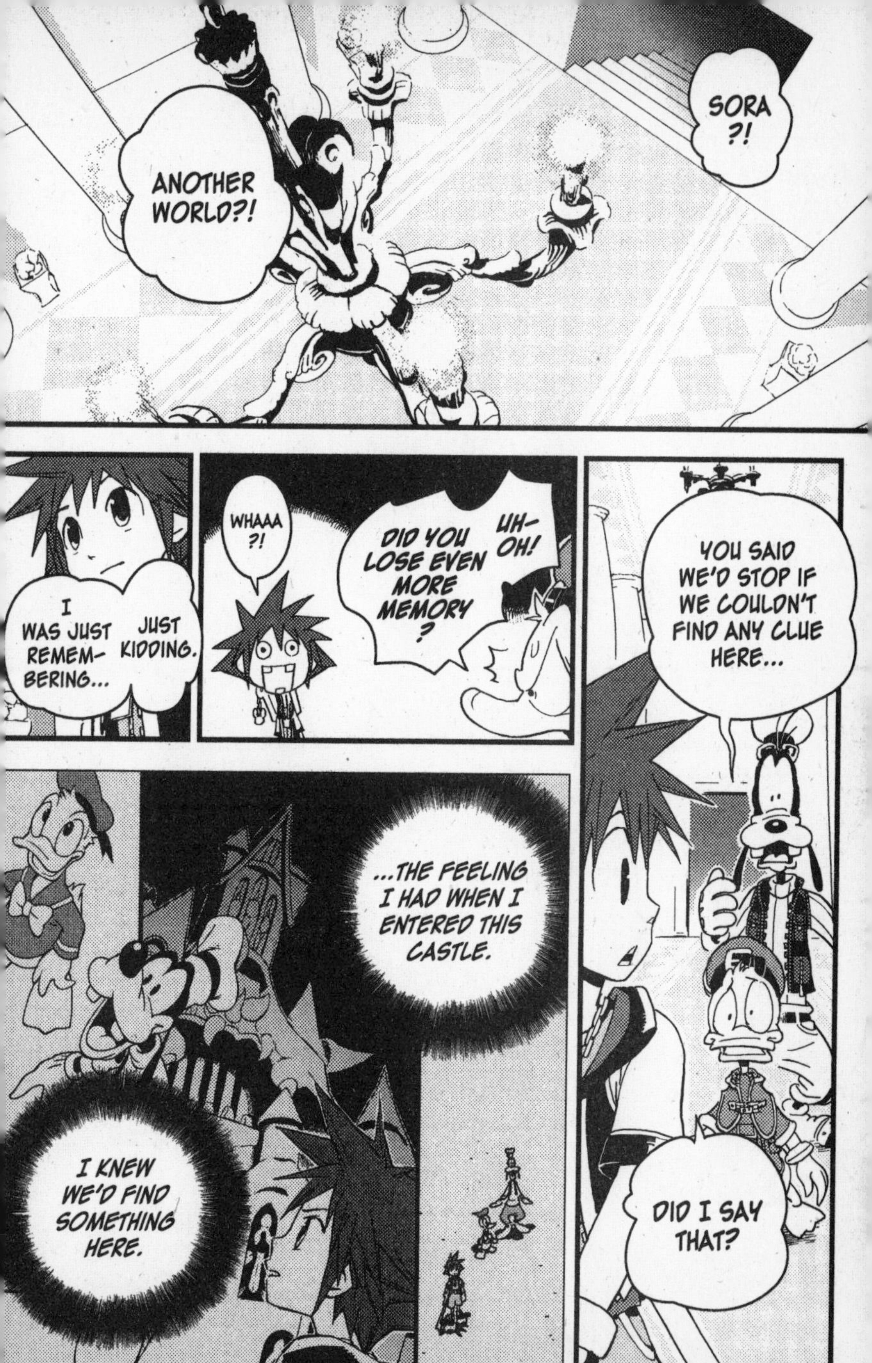
SORA ?!
ANOTHER WORLD?!
YOU SAID WE'D STOP IF WE COULDN'T FIND ANY CLUE HERE...
DID I SAY THAT?
UH-OH!
DID YOU LOSE EVEN MORE MEMORY ?
WHAAA ?!
JUST KIDDING.
I WAS JUST REMEMBERING...
...THE FEELING I HAD WHEN I ENTERED THIS CASTLE.
I KNEW WE'D FIND SOMETHING HERE.

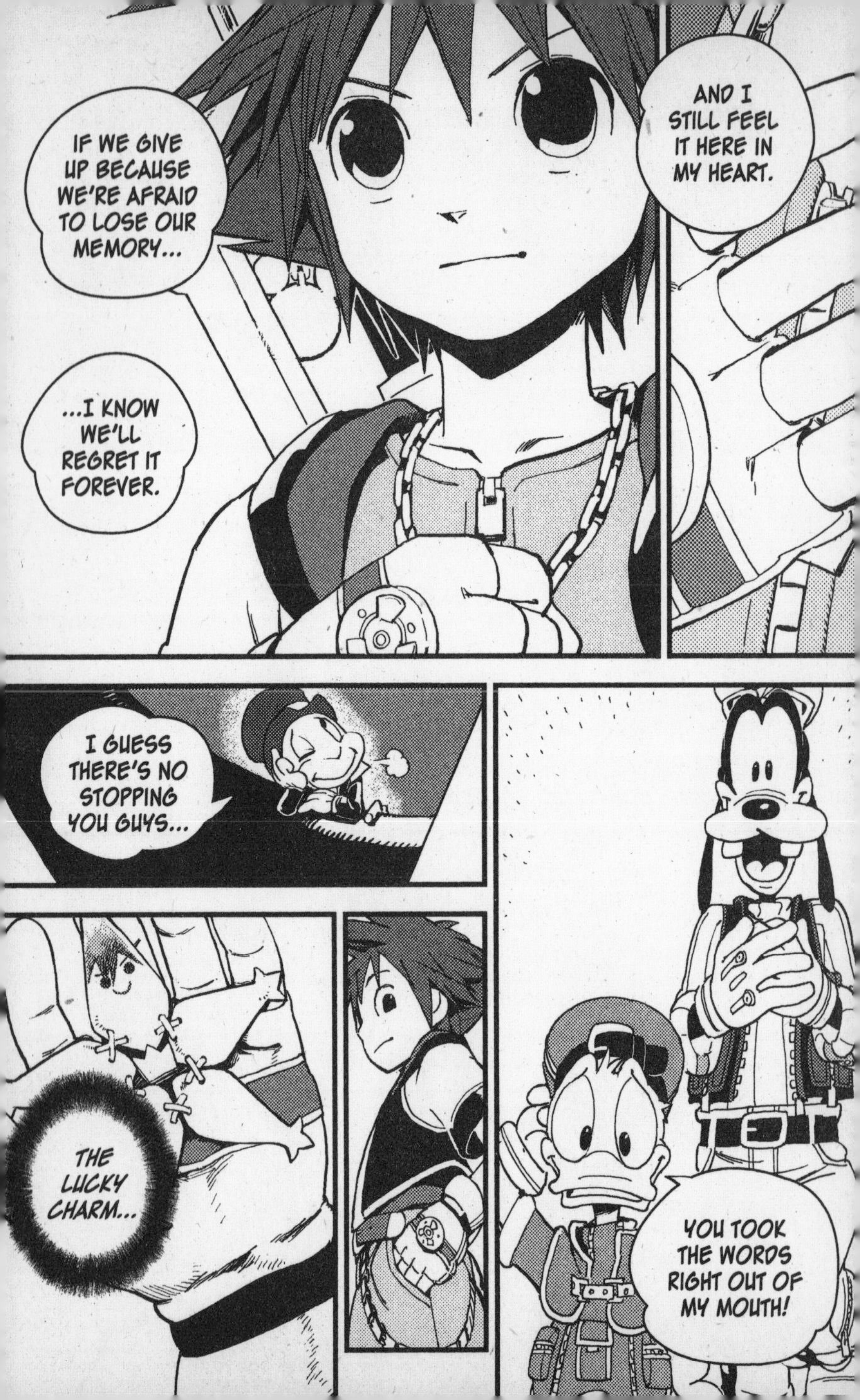
AND I STILL FEEL IT HERE IN MY HEART.
IF WE GIVE UP BECAUSE WE'RE AFRAID TO LOSE OUR MEMORY...
...I KNOW WE'LL REGRET IT FOREVER.
YOU TOOK THE WORDS RIGHT OUT OF MY MOUTH!
I GUESS THERE'S NO STOPPING YOU GUYS...
THE LUCKY CHARM...

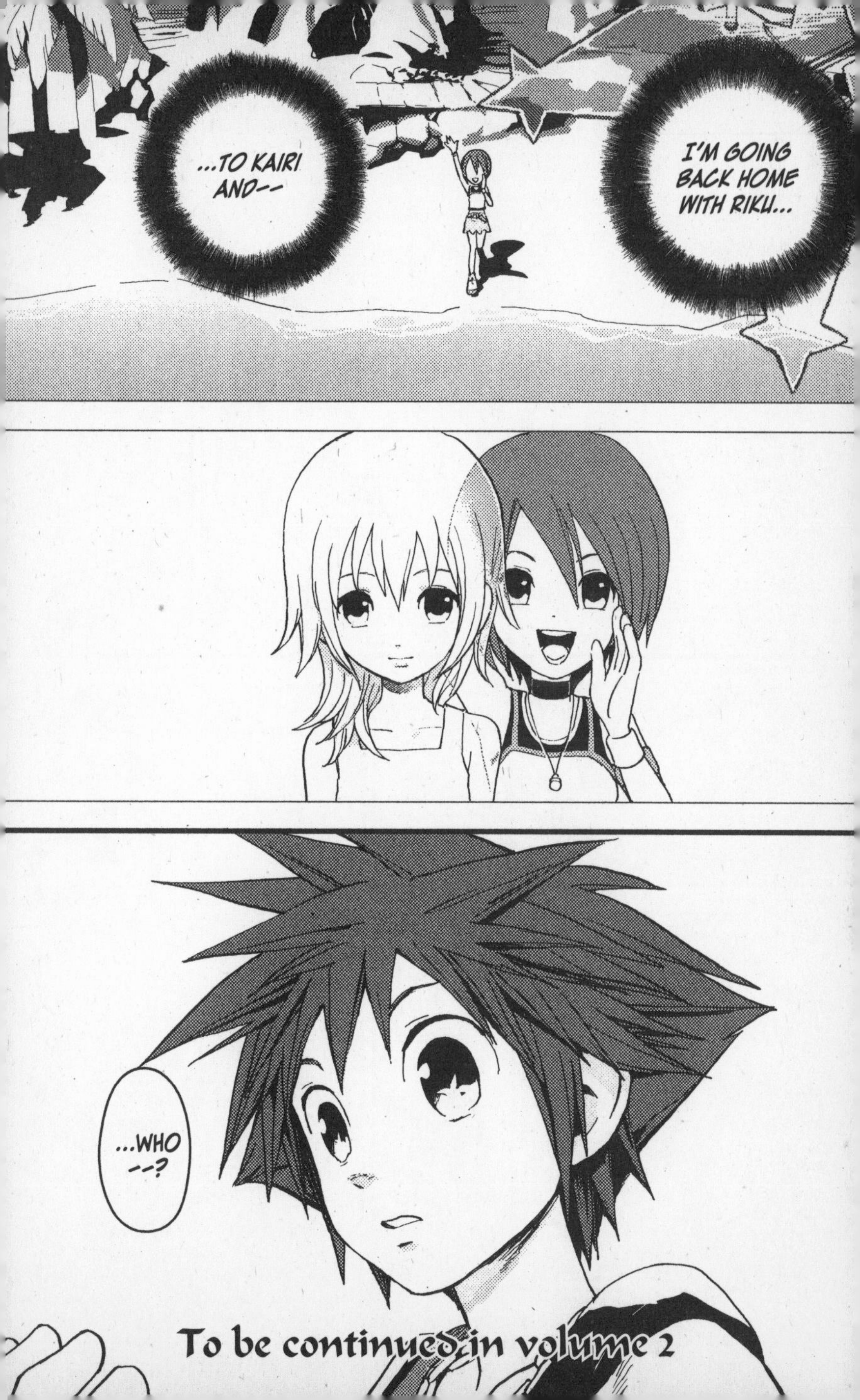
I'M GOING BACK HOME WITH RIKU...
...TO KAIRI AND--
...WHO --?
To be continued in volume 2

Next Issue Preview Illustration

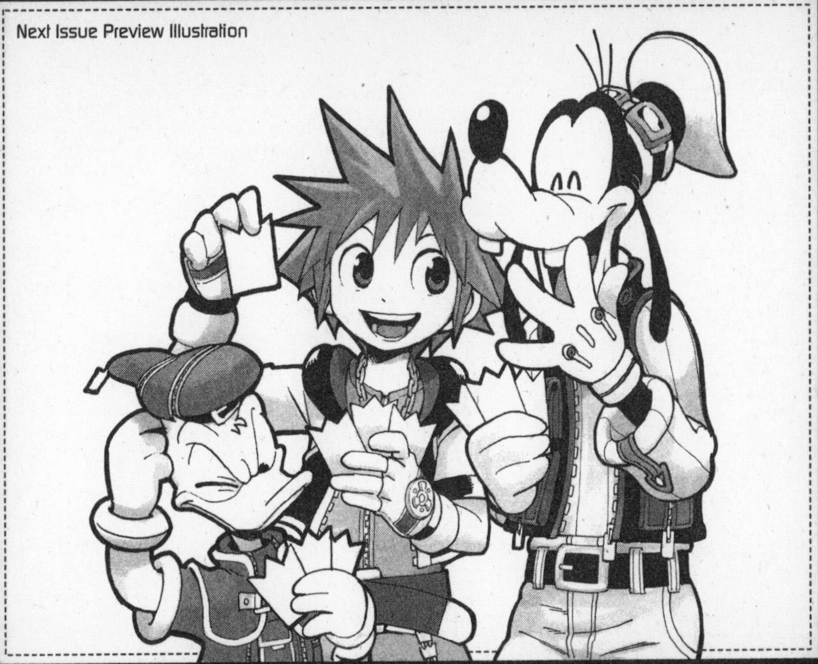

ILLUST COLLECTION

Take a look at the cover and preview illustrations published in Monthly Shonen GanGan!

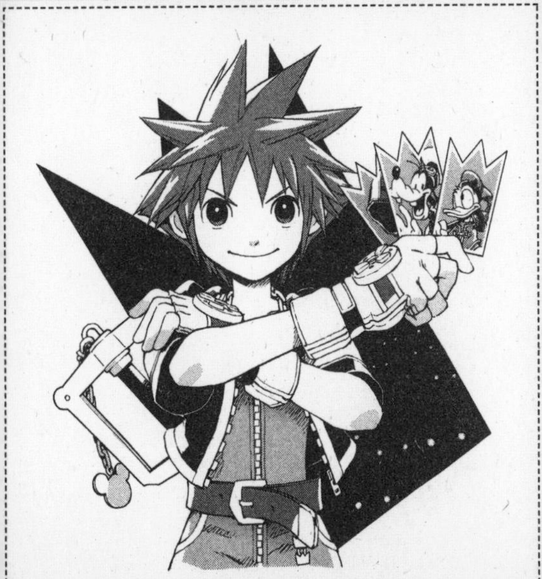

Serialization Preview Illustration

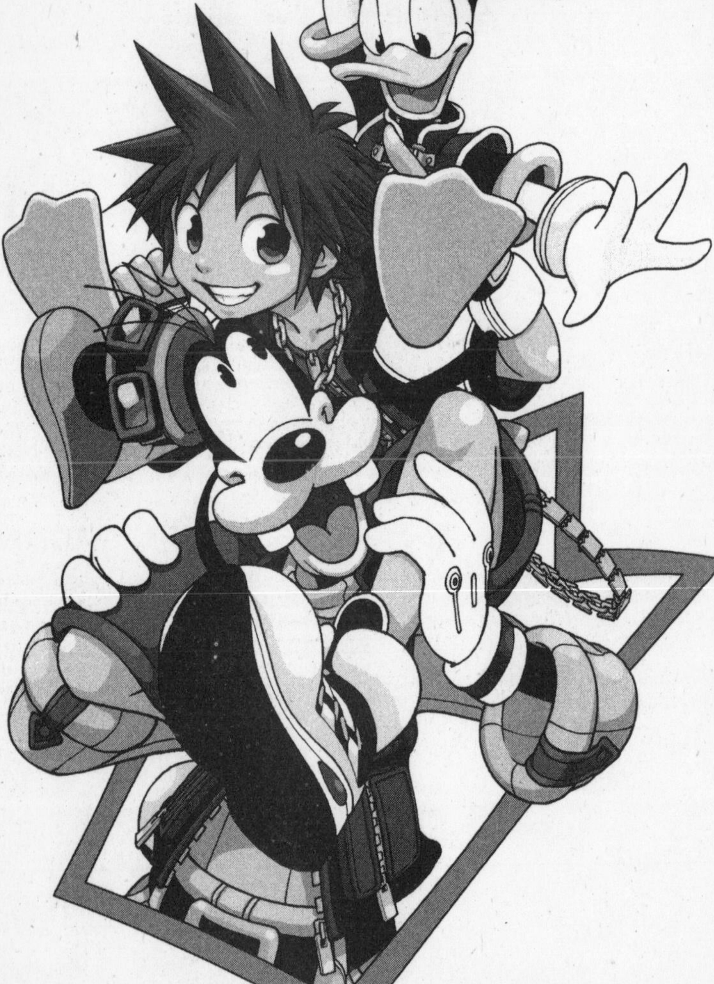

Cover Illustration

Kingdom Hearts
CHAIN of MEMORIES

TRANSFORM SORA

Cut and tape over Sora's face on the cover!

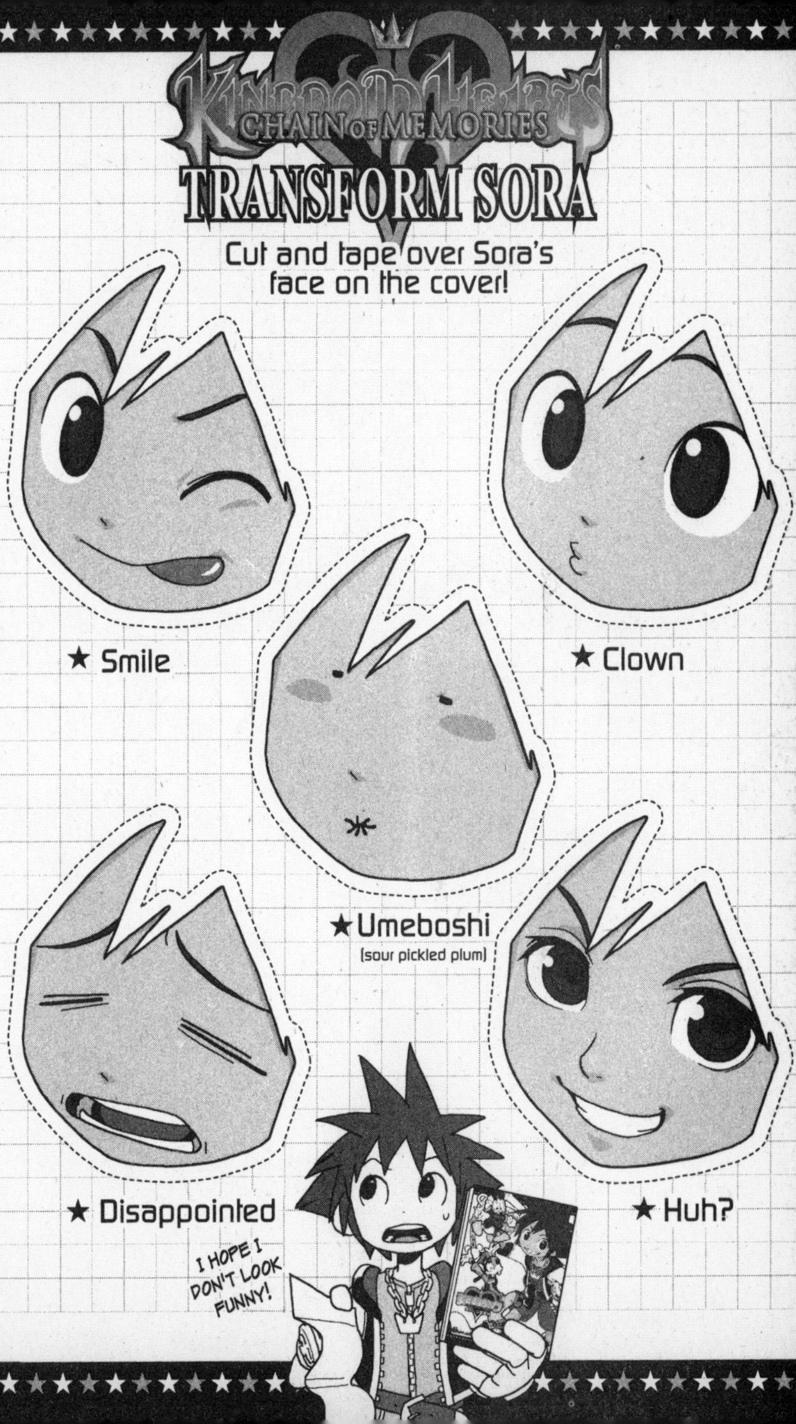
★ Smile
★ Clown
★ Umeboshi
(sour pickled plum)
★ Disappointed
★ Huh?
I HOPE I DON'T LOOK FUNNY!

In Volume 2 of

Disney | SQUARE ENIX

KINGDOM HEARTS
CHAIN of MEMORIES

Sora, Donald and Goofy
continue their quest to rescue
King Mickey and young Riku. But
will they find them in time?

And who is the strange Kairi look-
alike that Sora sees in his vision?

And now we'd like to share
with you a sneak preview
of the upcoming manga
Kilala Princess, vol. I.
Coming soon from
TOKYOPOP!

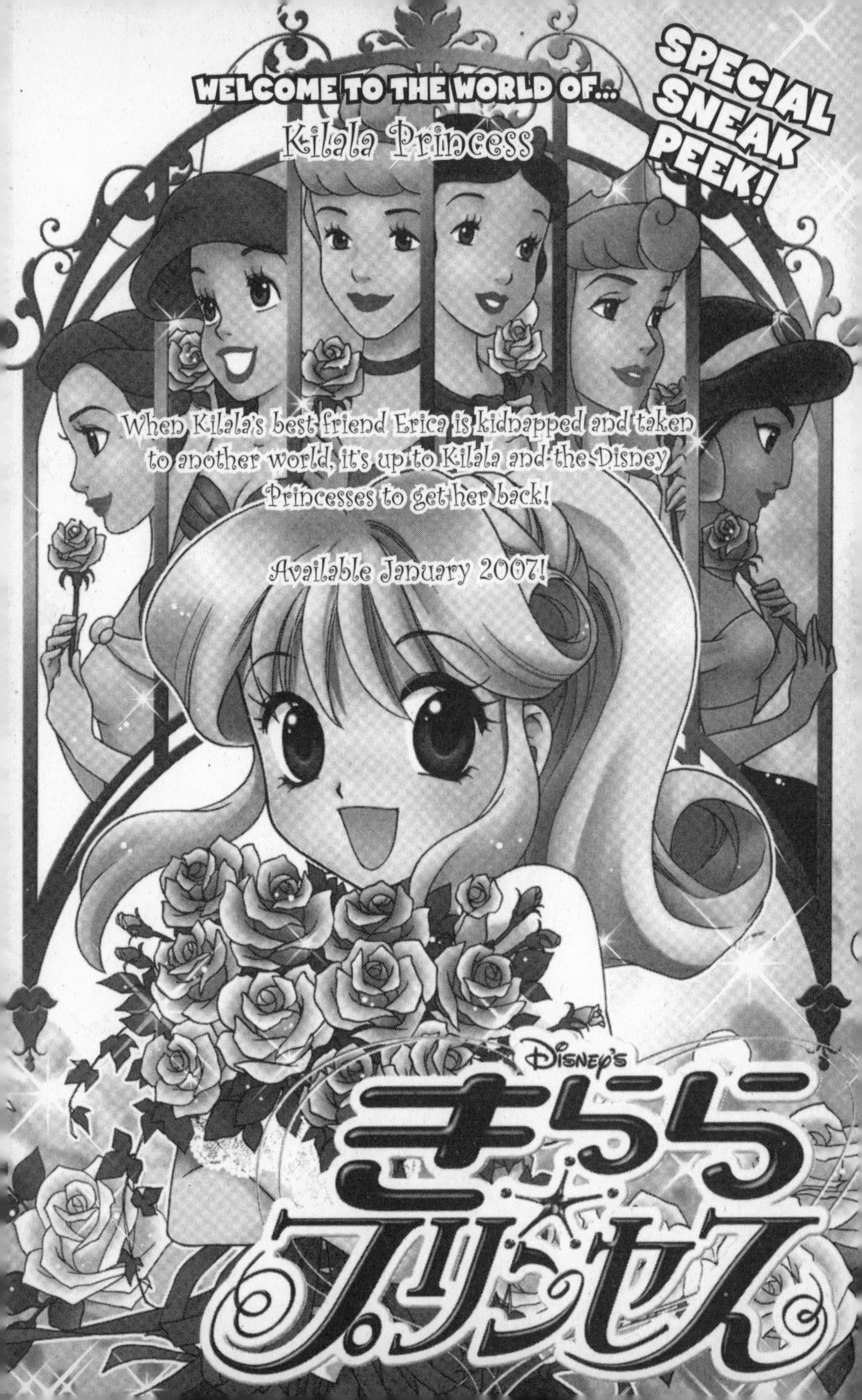
WELCOME TO THE WORLD OF...
Kilala Princess
SPECIAL SNEAK PEEK!
When Kilala's best friend Erica is kidnapped and taken to another world, it's up to Kilala and the Disney Princesses to get her back!
Available January 2007!
DISNEY'S
きらら
プリンセス

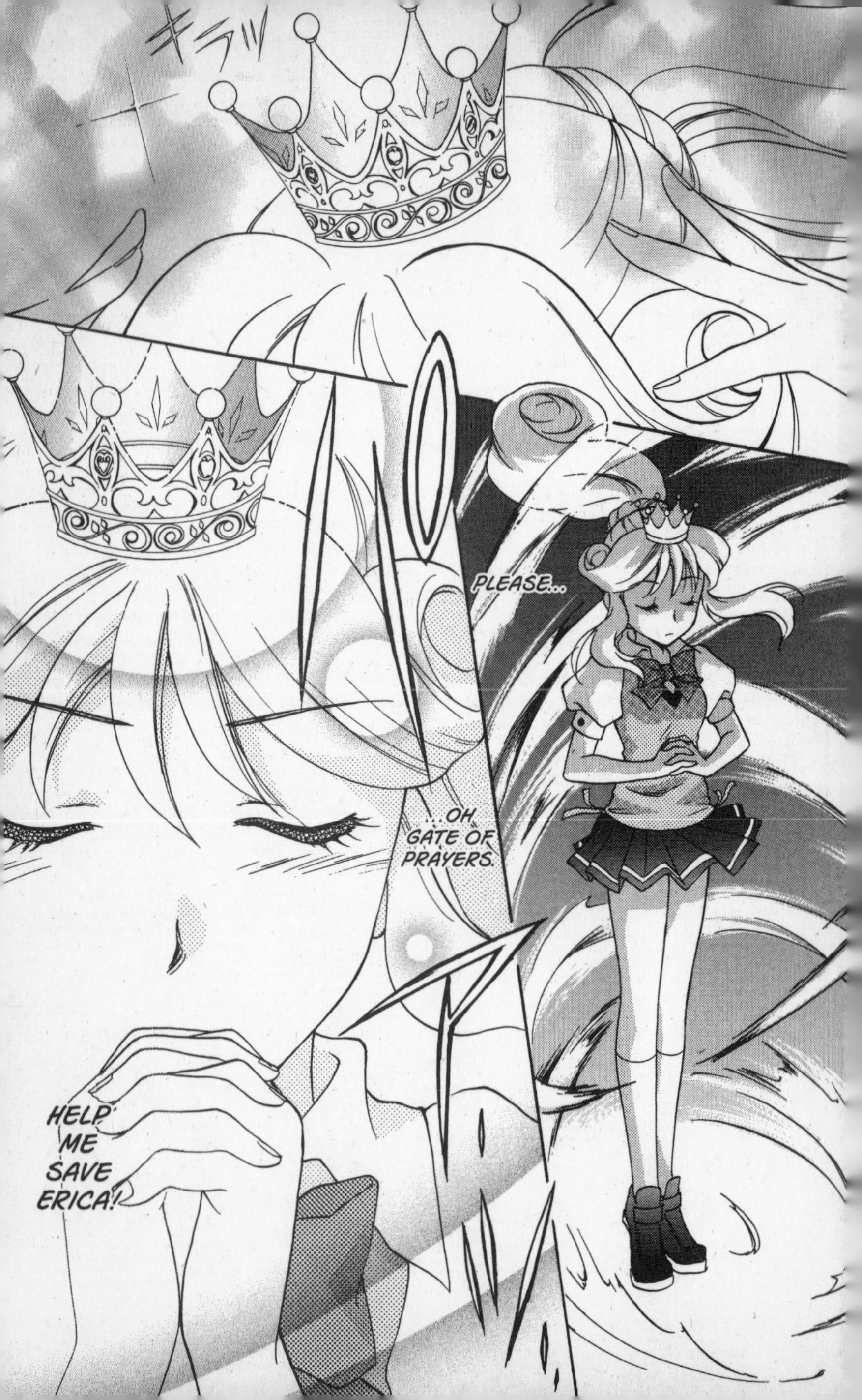
キラッ
PLEASE...
...OH GATE OF PRAYERS.
HELP ME SAVE ERICA!

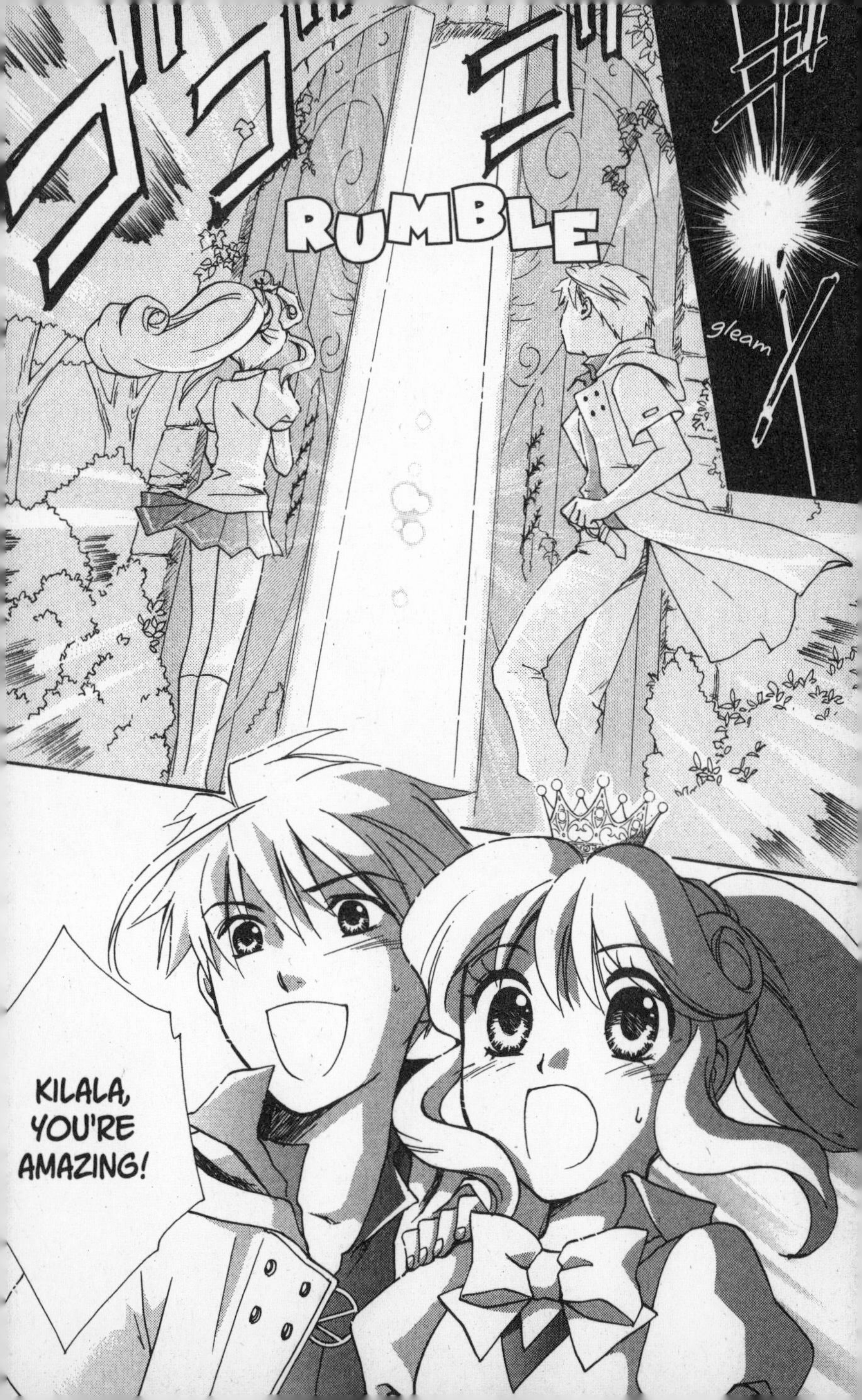
gleam
RUMBLE
KILALA, YOU'RE AMAZING!

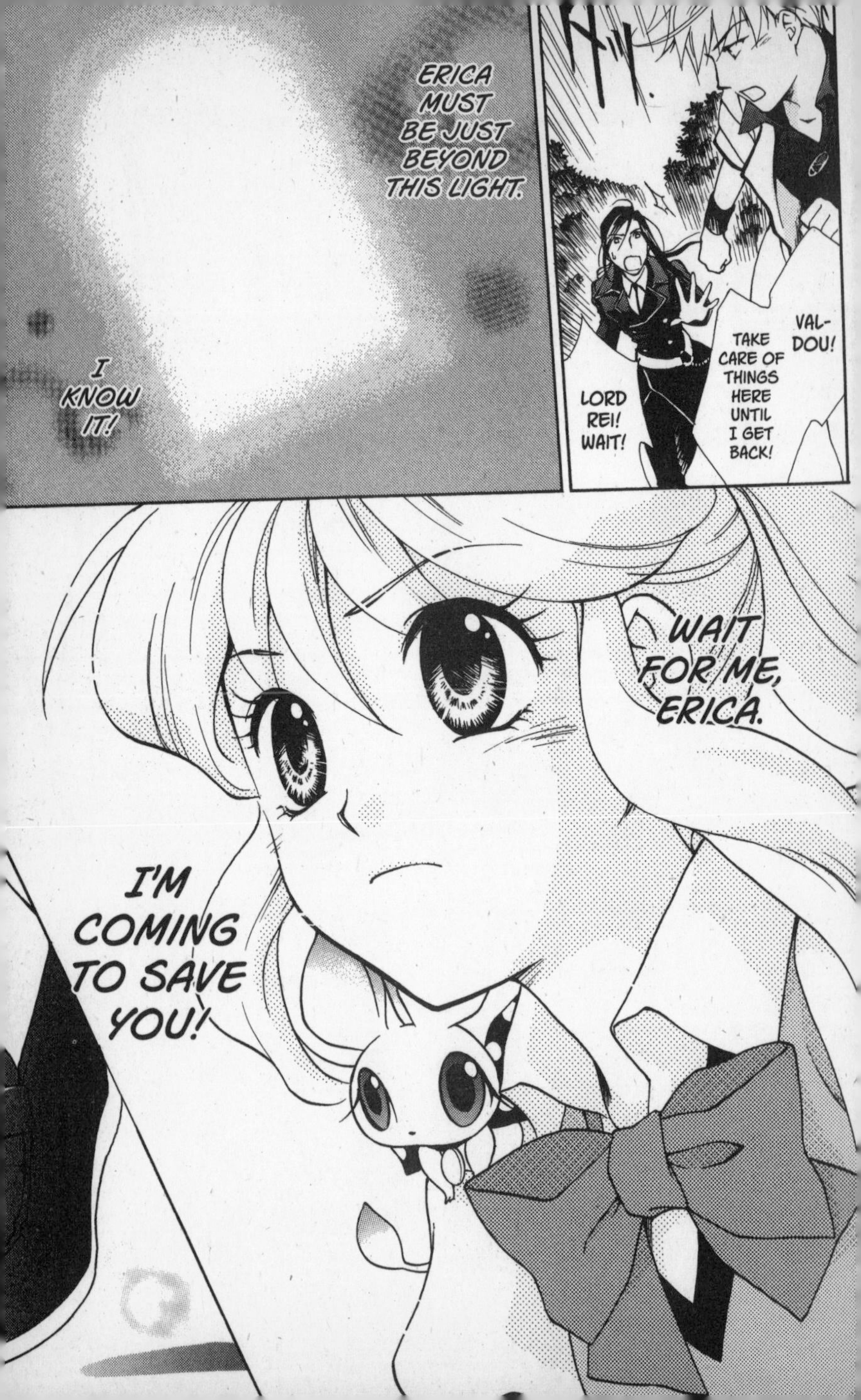
VAL-DOU!
TAKE CARE OF THINGS HERE UNTIL I GET BACK!
LORD REI! WAIT!
ERICA MUST BE JUST BEYOND THIS LIGHT.
I KNOW IT!
WAIT FOR ME, ERICA.
I'M COMING TO SAVE YOU!

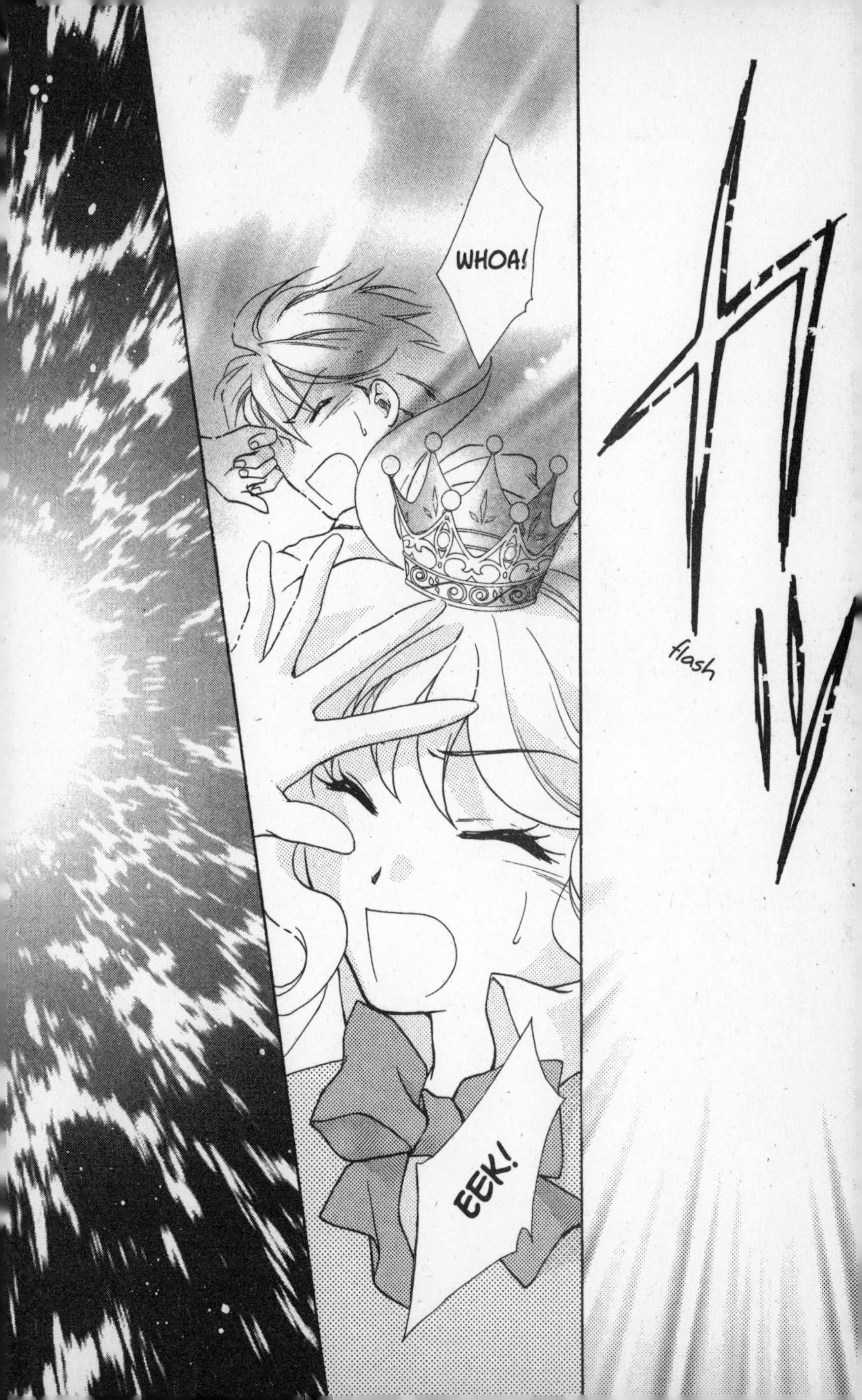
flash
WHOA!
EEK!

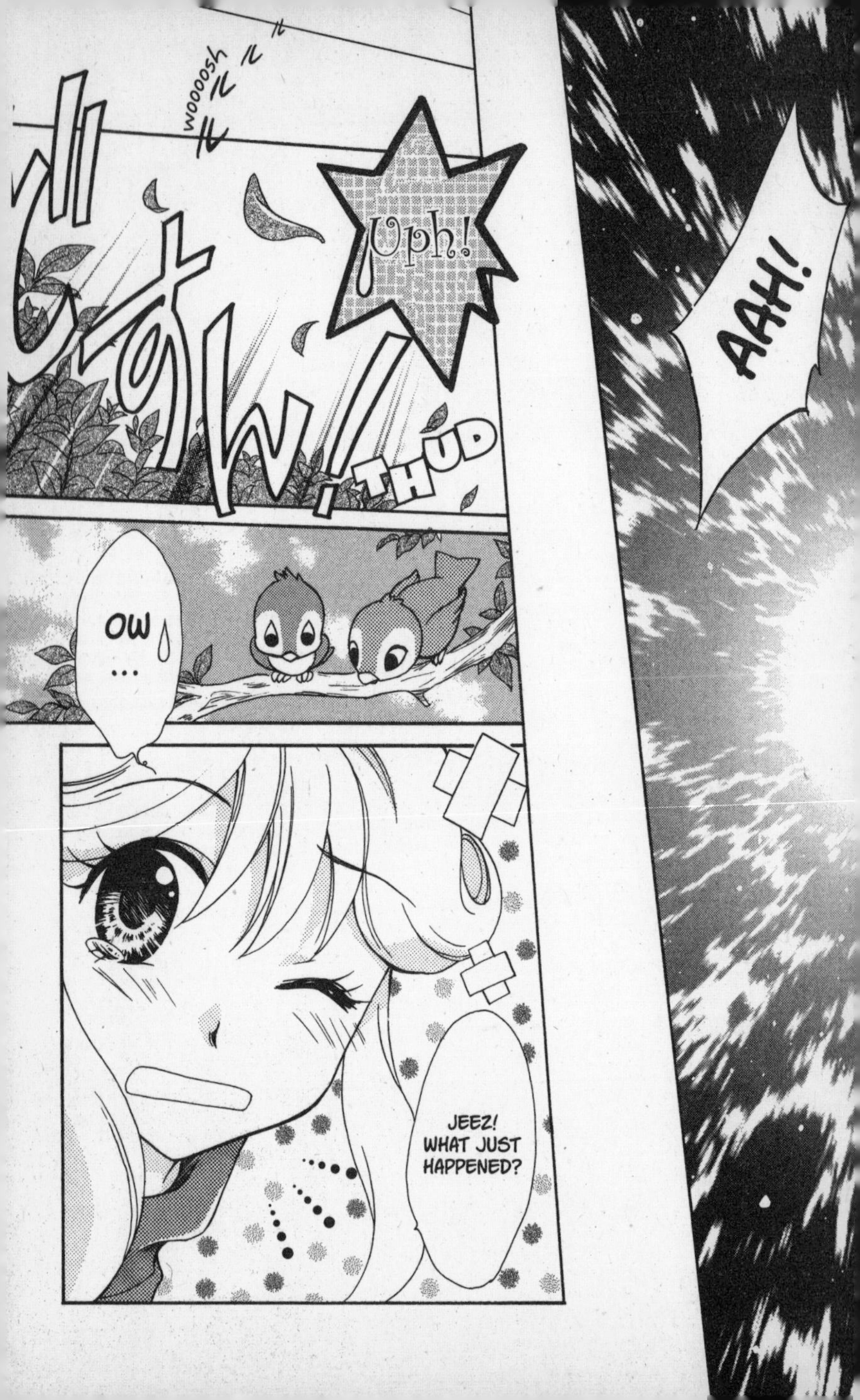
AAH!
woooosh
Uph!
どすん!
THUD
OW ...
JEEZ! WHAT JUST HAPPENED?

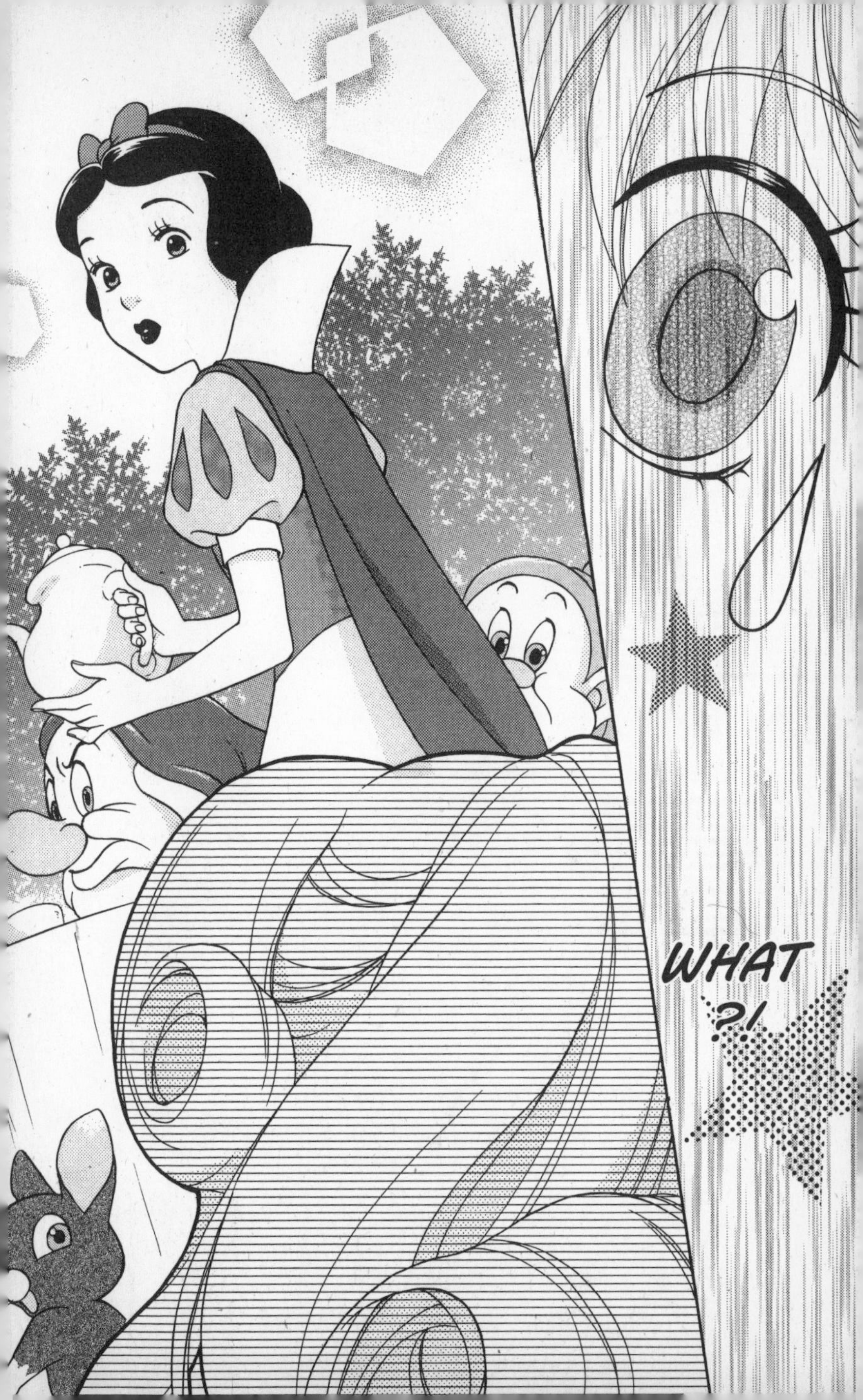
WHAT ?!

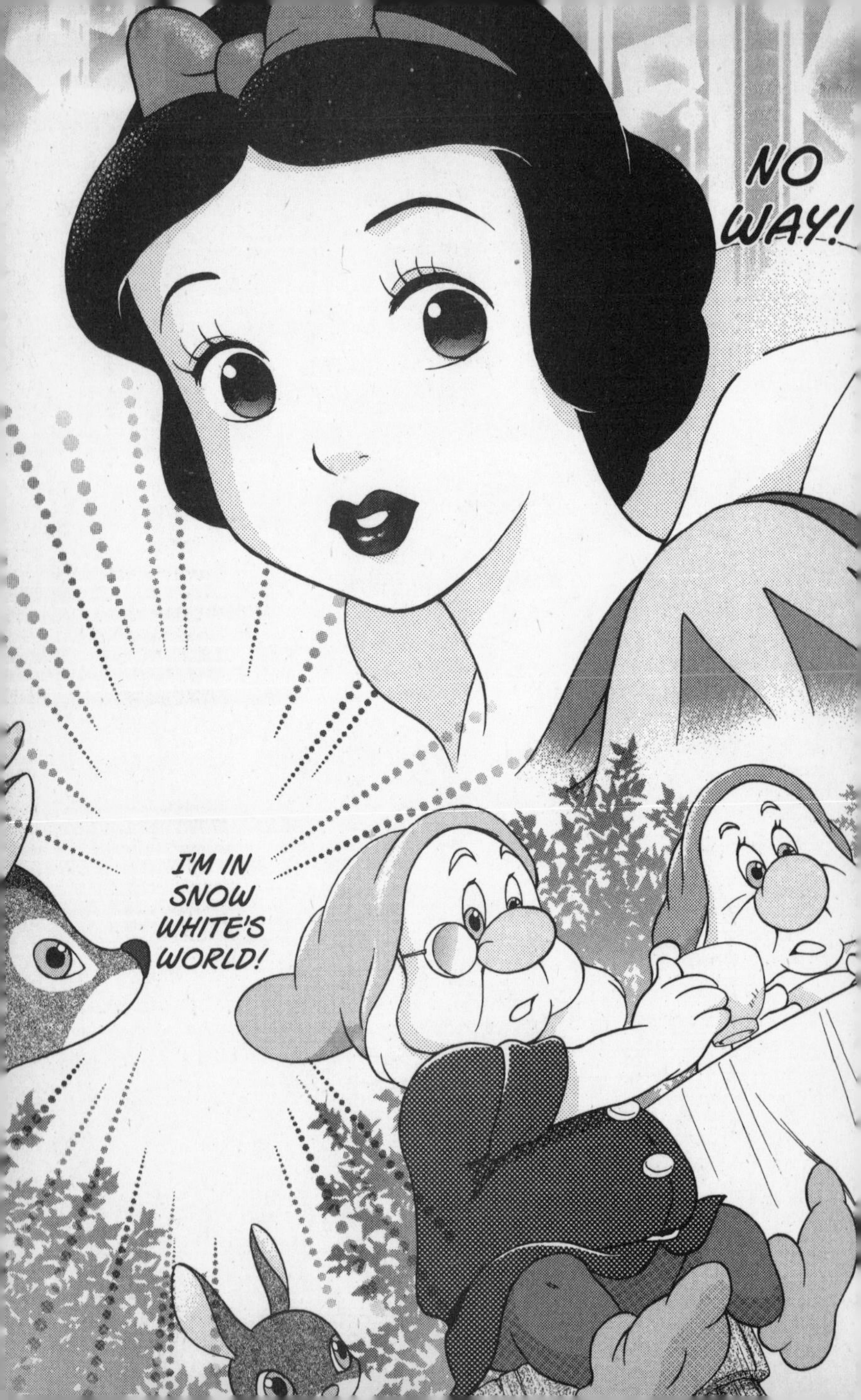
NO WAY!
I'M IN SNOW WHITE'S WORLD!

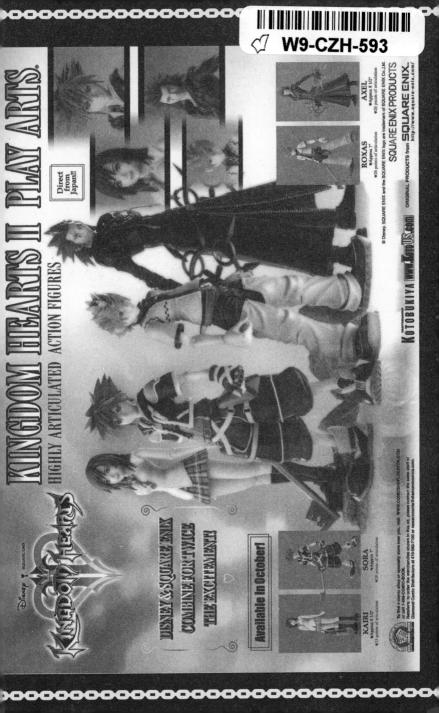